T R A V E L E R ' S
JAPAN
C O M P A N I O N

by Chris Taylor

Photographed by Nik Wheeler

Second Edition

The
Globe
Pequot
Press

GUILFORD
CONNECTICUT

Contents

The 2001–2002 Traveler's Companions
ARGENTINA • AUSTRALIA • BALI • CALIFORNIA • CANADA • CHILE • CHINA •
COSTA RICA • CUBA • EASTERN CANADA • ECUADOR • FLORIDA • HAWAII •
HONG KONG • INDIA • INDONESIA • IRELAND • JAPAN • KENYA •
MALAYSIA & SINGAPORE • MEDITERRANEAN FRANCE • MEXICO • NEPAL •
NEW ENGLAND • NEW ZEALAND • NORTHERN ITALY • PERU • PHILIPPINES •
PORTUGAL • RUSSIA • SOUTH AFRICA • SOUTHERN ENGLAND • SPAIN • THAILAND •
TURKEY • VENEZUELA • VIETNAM, LAOS AND CAMBODIA • WESTERN CANADA

Traveler's JAPAN Companion

First published 1998
Second Edition 2001
The Globe Pequot Press
246 Goose Lane, PO Box 480
Guilford, CT 06437 USA
www.globe-pequot.com

© 2001 by The Globe Pequot Press, Guilford CT, USA

ISBN: 0-7627-0949-9

Distributed in the European Union by
World Leisure Marketing Ltd, Unit 11
Newmarket Court, Newmarket Drive,
Derby, DE24 8NW, United Kingdom
www.map-guides.com
Created, edited and produced by
Allan Amsel Publishing, 53, rue Beaudouin
27700 Les Andelys, France.
E-mail: AAmsel@aol.com
Editor in Chief: Allan Amsel
Editor: Anne Trager
Picture editor and book designer: Roberto Rossi
Original design concept: Hon Bing-wah
Based on an original text by Peter Popham

Printed by Samhwa Printing Co. Ltd., Seoul, South Korea

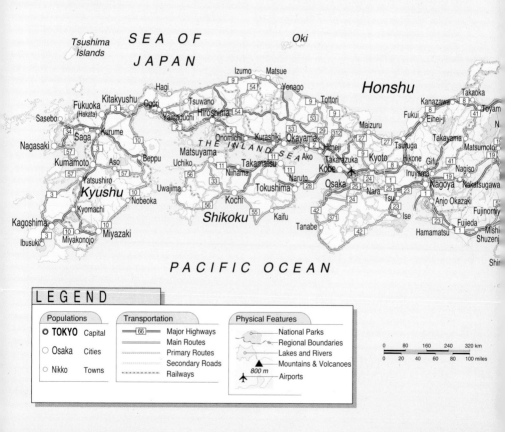

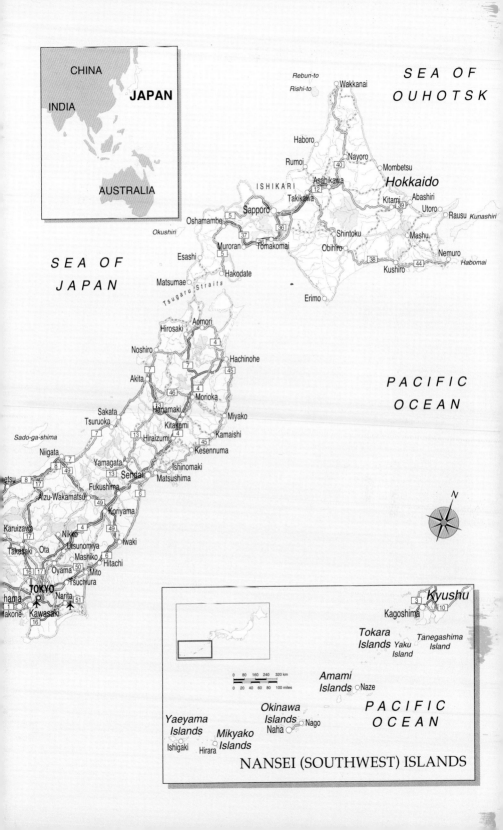

TOP SPOTS

Walk the Path of Philosophy

CAPITAL OF JAPAN FROM AD 794 TO 1868, the only Japanese city spared the ravages of Allied World War II bombing, home to more than 2,000 Buddhist temples and Shinto shrines, Kyoto has such a profusion of sights that seeing it in a tour bus is like seeing Venice on jet ski.

This makes it all the more difficult to tackle for visitors with limited time. The choices are obvious: a whirlwind ticking off of the big attractions, or an atmospheric walk that offers a more intimate view of Kyoto. Either approach has its merits, but the latter will likely leave the best memories.

The Philosopher's Walk, or the *Tetsugaku-no-Michi*, is a one-and-a-half-kilometer (one-mile) paved path that runs alongside a canal that feeds off lake Biwa-ko. The path's name is the legacy of Nishida Kitaro (1870–1945), modern Japan's most important philosopher, a man who spent his life striving for a common ground between Western philosophy and Eastern — mainly Buddhist — philosophy.

A teacher at Kyoto University in his later years, this was his favorite place to walk in contemplation. It's easy to see why: the cherry trees on either side, which blossom in April, almost touch heads to create a tunnel, and two magnificent temples stand at either end. It may not be as ancient as many other parts of Kyoto — the path only came into existence with the canal in 1890 — but it usually offers quiet solitude when the rest of Kyoto is bustling with tour groups.

Ginkaku-ji Temple, at the northern end of the path, is approached by way of a meticulously trimmed but luxuriant hedge, which gives way to a view of the exquisitely crafted temple. Actually that should be "pavilion." The name, Ginkaku-ji, translates literally as "Silver Pavilion," and refers to the original intention of the fifteenth-century shogun who sponsored its building — to have it coated with silver leaf. He died before this could be done, and though the silver never materialized the name stuck. The temple precincts are also famous for a "dry landscape" that features an expanse of raked white sand overlooked by an austere sand cone that is said to represent Mount Fuji. Unfortunately, speakers blast out descriptions and historical details in Japanese for the benefit of sightseers.

Follow the path south from Ginkaku-ji and across Senshin Bridge lies Honen-in, one of Kyoto's less famous and hence quieter temples. In front of the temple entrance is a marker inscribed with a *tanka* (a 31-syllable poem) written by the philosopher who gave the path its name.

From here it is a pleasant stroll southwards alongside the canal and past some charming stone bridges, a few of the usual souvenir shops, and several coffee shops. At the

OPPOSITE: The pavilion at Kinkakuji Temple, Kyoto.
ABOVE: A local woman dresses for the geisha parade in Kyoto.

southern extent of the path is Eikan-do Temple, which is famed for its statue of Amida Buddha looking over his left shoulder. But the chief attraction is Nanzen-ji, which lies immediately south of Eikan-do. Originally an imperial villa, it was converted into a Zen temple in 1291. Its famous main gate, Tenka Ryu-mon, or the "Dragon Gate of the World," which was built in 1628, features drawings of phoenixes and celestial nymphs. The sub-temple Konchi-in, in the Nanzen-ji precincts, is home to one of the city's most famous dry landscapes.

All in all, this modest walk takes an hour or so, longer for those who linger in the temples. But, for the subtlety of its charms, it rates as one of the best introductions to a city that is so crammed with things ancient, hallowed and surprising that the newcomer is too often overwhelmed. It is even worth a return visit by night, especially in the summer, when the chirp of cicadas fills the air.

Get Some Heat Treatment

SWEAT BEADS ON MY BROW. Scalding water laps at my neck. My eyes glaze in fierce concentration, as I repeat to myself the mantra: "I will not bolt from this pool of broth with a yelp of pain." The old hands lounge with meditative poise, occasionally retreating to cool off under a cold shower, before returning again to soak in the sulfurous waters. Suppressing gasps, I follow their lead. Slowly my body undertakes a curious transformation, as if I have been massaged into a state of perfect relaxation. All the tensions of my workaday life melt away. A blissful smile creeps across my face.

Nominations for the definitive Japanese experience? The list is long. But somewhere near the top has to be the *onsen*, or hot spring. In Japan, washing away the grime of the daily grind is far more than a quick shower — it is a total experience, an end in itself.

The Japanese are so particular about hot springs, they even have a Hot Spring Law; it defines the standards by which a hot spring can officially be classed as such. It must be more than 25°C (77°F), "issue from the ground" and contain "a prescribed amount of the specified substances."

Those "specified substances" can even be good for you, a fact that was noted in Japan's first study of the subject of the subject in 1709, though the samurai, who used hot springs to hasten the healing of battle wounds, knew this long before. But for most bathers, a hot spring soak is about steaming away tensions. And

it's an aesthetic experience too, particularly when the spring is a *rotemburo*, or an outdoor hot spring.

In times past, many hot springs featured mixed bathing. It was a puritanical Western influence in the post-War years that put an end to that. A few *konyoku*, or mixed baths, linger on in Tohoku — northern Honshu — but they are generally only found in remote places, and are usually only frequented by the older generation.

But one thing remains unchanged. Hot springs are *hot*. To the novice dipping a tentative toe into the water, it can seem a miracle that anyone can wallow longer than a second in the heat. There can be a frightening sense of blistering skin peeling away from bones before acclimatization to the heat is achieved.

Stick with it. Hot springs may often feel scalding, but they are not. It's simply a matter of the body adjusting to temperatures it is unaccustomed to.

As with so many Japanese rituals, form is to be observed with bathing at a hot spring. There will be a changing room, or perhaps simply a changing corner, where your clothes can be exchanged for a handkerchief-sized "modesty towel." From here, it is time to proceed to the showers, where a good soap-down is in order — the hot spring is for bathing, *not* for washing. The showers will often use piping-hot spring water that can be moderated with cold — the hot water of the shower is a good way to start habituating the body to the shock that is soon to come. Rinse off and proceed to the hot-spring pool. After lowering themselves into the water, most Japanese bathers will place their towel on their heads. Follow suit, by all means, but this is one step in the ritual that is not obligatory. Hot spring bathing is not a competition to see who can linger the longest in the waters. When it becomes uncomfortable, retreat to a cold shower and then return. A series of five-minute soaks is a good way to achieve the maximum effect.

Japan's oldest operating hot spring is at Dogo, near Matsuyama in Shikoku. The imperial family once had their own bath here, though it is no longer in use. It's well worth sampling the common bathing pool here for a look at the brio with which Japanese bathe together — it's a far cry from the formality of usual Japanese interactions. But it's also worth bathing in your own private room.

TOP: The Jungle Baths, Beppu are extremely popular. BOTTOM: Buried under the sands at Ibusuki — one of the favorite Japanese spa towns.

Other famous hot spring areas in Japan include Kyushu's Beppu and Ibusuki, where a variation on the hot spring — hot sand — can be tried. Closer to Tokyo, the Izu-hanto Peninsula is famous for its hot springs: Atami is the best known resort here, but Shimoda, deeper into the peninsula, is far more relaxing place to bathe, and also has some historical attractions of its own.

Hike in the Alpine Country

THE NAME MEANS "ASCEND TO HIGH PLACES," and indeed Kamikochi is where alpine climbing began in Japan. It was an Englishman who awakened the Japanese to the possibility of climbing the mountains that occupy some 85 percent of Japan's land-mass, and today an annual festival honors Walter Weston (1861–1940), the "father of Japanese mountaineering," in Kamikochi every June.

Going to Kamikochi, in other words, is rather like an act of homage to Japan's northern Alps (the Hida Mountain Range). While serious climbs are definitely an option, clamp-ons and pick-irons are unnecessary for the day hikes that take climbers up into the heart of some of Japan's most breathtaking mountain scenery.

Just five hours from Tokyo by a combination of Shinkansen high-speed train (to Matsumoto), local train (to Shin-Shimashima) and bus, the journey itself, from Matsumoto onwards, is almost reason enough to visit, providing fine panoramic views (weather permitting).

And then there is Kamikochi, which is such a splendidly scenic valley that many visitors content themselves with pottering along the riverside and taking photos of each other against the backdrop of glistening, icy peaks rearing skywards and reflected in the Taisho-ike pond. Perfectly acceptable. Kamikochi is one of Japan's hallowed places — pristine waters, fresh air and a scrupulous conservation policy. Not only is there no litter, there aren't even any litter-bins! No private cars are allowed within half an hour's drive.

But if Kamikochi is beautiful, ascend to its high places and it is even more beautiful. A good choice is the Doppyo Ridge, a ridge on the mountain Nishi Hotaka-dake, and a day's hike there and back from Kamikochi. From the cluster of hotels that marks Kamikochi central, walk downstream for 10 minutes to the Tashiro-kyo bridge. Don't cross the bridge, but take the trail that leads off into the woods and is signposted "To Mount Nishihotaka."

The path climbs through giant conifers, with the stream roaring far below in its gorge. After a little over an hour an area of dead trees appears, standing white in the silence. Here the trail turns upwards to the right, and the going begins to get tougher.

The way is clear of snow in summer, but in spring great banks of old snow are likely to obstruct the steep trail. Red ribbons tied to the branches of the trees, however, mark the route up. These ribbons are primarily for the benefit of mountaineers going up in winter when the trail is entirely hidden under snow, and sometimes they follow a slightly different route from the summer path. No matter: they lead to the Nishi Hotaka Mountain Lodge.

It's possible to overnight at the lodge, but most hikers pause for hot coffee and a bowl of noodles before hiking onwards another hour to the ridge itself. It's a gentle, northerly climb. From the top is a glorious view of the highest summits of the Japanese Alps: Okuhotaka-dake (3,190 m/16,340 ft) to the left — second only in Japan to Mount Fuji — and Maehotaka-dake to the right.

The walk back to the mountain lodge is more of an amble after the exertions of the ascent, and follows exactly the same route. But if there is the least bit of snow left, take extra care, and proceed at a snail's pace.

While not overly demanding, the climb meanders upwards from Kamikochi (approximately 1,500 m/4,921 ft) to a height of around 2,500 m (8,334 ft), and at the end of the day, a long hot soak in a bath and a good sleep will be in order. The Nishi-ito-ya Sanso is a recommended mid-range mountain lodge in Kamikochi, but for those who want to go the whole hog and stay in comfort after their exertions on the mountain slopes, the luxury Imperial Hotel, a branch of the famous hotel in Tokyo, is pure indulgence — of the best variety, of course.

June is the first month when this route is clear of snow — and even in June it's wise to confirm conditions before setting out. It's possible to do the hike earlier and navigate the drifts of snow that frequently litter the trail, but it's a tougher proposition and theoretically more dangerous, though the trail is clearly marked and a steady stream of hikers usually means that nobody could remain stranded on the trail for long. Allow eight to nine hours for the round trip.

Beautiful vistas LEFT and RIGHT are easily within reach of hikers setting out from Kamikochi to explore the Japanese Alps.

In Search of Old Edo

IN THE SHITAMACHI PLEBIAN QUARTERS OF OLD EDO EMERGED A TOTALLY NEW JAPANESE SENSIBILITY, one that gave birth to *kabuki* and *sumo*, an age of courtesan-led fashions and the wood-block print. Although mostly swept away by the democratically leveling Meiji restoration, its spirit, if only fleetingly, can still be captured in parts of modern Tokyo.

Shitamachi — literally "downtown" — is actually a generic word for the bustling merchant quarters that sprang up in most of Japan's castle towns (*joka-machi*) during the Edo period (1600–1867). But it is the Edo (now Tokyo) Shitamachi that, in its profusion of worldly delights, brash confidence and brilliant inventiveness, has become definitive of the term, so that Shitamachi today almost invariably refers to the eastern wards of Tokyo or old Edo.

At the entrance to Nakamise Dori, the colorful market alley in Asakusa that leads to Senso-ji Temple, it becomes clear immediately that this is another Tokyo, a Tokyo far removed from the chic districts of Ginza or Shibuya. The shops lining Nakamise once specialized in prayer accessories — incense, Buddhist statuary and the like. Today they are mostly devoted to tourist items and traditional snacks such as *sembei*, soy-flavored crackers. But there is still something of a carnival air to the place that is out of keeping with what most visitors expect of a Buddhist temple. The raucous atmosphere continues in the temple precincts, where a constant stream of the faithful gather at a huge incense cauldron to rub the holy smoke against their bodies, before proceeding to the entrance of the temple's main building to bow and clap.

It was in the shadow of Asakusa's Senso-ji, a temple that commemorates the founding of Edo, that a host of bawdy entertainments sprang up, catering to a class who did not give a fig for the austere samurai code espoused by the governing Tokugawa clan. *Kabuki*, with its elaborate costumes, stylized entrances and noisy musical accompaniment, is a quintessentially Shitamachi entertainment, as are the woodblock prints of the era, with their depictions of courtesans and bustling street scenes. The *kabuki* performed here was a front for prostitution, forcing the government in 1629 to decree it only be performed by men; the public baths were a front for prostitution, forcing the government to put an end to mixed bathing in 1791. But it did little to curtail the area's sensual atmosphere.

Little remains of this today, but stroll out of the temple into the streets immediately to the east, and some tawdry echoes of the past can be found: strip parlors and cinemas showing soft-core pornography. East again, on the far side of Kokusai Dori, the past reasserts itself again in a couple of blocks thick with tiny temples, some of them very old. They lead, continuing east, to Kappabashi Dori, Tokyo's traditional restaurant supplies area, which is packed with shops selling plastic bowls of noodles, plastic steaks, and everything a restaurateur could possibly need to go into business.

The atmosphere continues back in Ueno, which is on the Yamanote line. Ameyoko Arcade has an air of Shitamachi's bustle, but for a fascinating glimpse into the Shitamachi world, go to the Shitamachi History Museum, next to Ueno station. Here it is possible to poke around inside recreations of a merchant's house, an ordinary city dweller's house and a sweet shop.

But the ultimate Edo experience is in the Edo-Tokyo Museum in Ryogoku. This massive,

ABOVE: Mixing *togarashi* (seven-flavored spice) at Senso-ji Temple, Tokyo. RIGHT: Lake Ashinoko, in Hakone, with the ever-present Mount Fuji, is Japan's favorite retreat for relaxation and leisure activities.

futuristic museum takes the visitor on a six-floor journey through a world that has mostly disappeared — the so-called "flowers of Edo" — through fires, earthquakes and aerial bombings.

Thrills Without Spills

TRUST THE JAPANESE TO TAKE A VAST SCENIC AMPHITHEATER AND TURN IT INTO A SERIES OF "RIDES." The urge to domesticate, or at least tidy-up, runs deep in Japan, and as such Hakone is more than just a splendid natural retreat from the hubbub of downtown Tokyo, it's an introduction to Japanese tourism in full flight. Don't be put off. Only the most jaded traveler could fail to be charmed by a day trip that packs in fabulous views of Japan's iconic mountain, a winsome switch-back railway journey, a bouncing "ropeway" (that's "cable car" to the rest of the world) jaunt past bubbling volcanic springs, and a pirate ship cruise across a crystal-clear lake. Even if at times it all feels just a little processed, nature — grand and elemental — is never far away.

A former barrier station on the old Tokaido road that linked Edo with Kyoto, Hakone is now the center of the Fuji-Hakone-Izu

National Park. As national parks go, even Japanese national parks, this is quite a mouthful. But the operative word is Fuji. Weather permitting, Hakone provides magnificent views of the famous mountain that are worth the price of admission alone.

Although the private Odakyu line runs a special "Romance Car" train service (highly recommended) from Shinjuku station, the fun really begins at Odawara, where it's time to change to what looks like a toy train. The Hakone–Tozan line takes over here, running through the hot spring town of Hakone-Yumoto, before undertaking a nine-kilometer (five-and-a-half-mile) switch-back ascent of the mountains to the tiny village of Gora. It's a wonderful, creaky, jerking journey that has passengers holding their breaths on the train's behalf as it follows a ravine up and ever up. Just before Gora, the train stops at Chokoku-no-Mori, where a vast open-air museum features sculpture by Auguste Rodin and Henry Moore (among many others), and a Picasso Pavilion houses more than 200 of the Spanish artist's work.

There is no need to linger in Gora. It's merely the gateway to Mount Soun-zan, which is ascended by a funicular. Rather like the Peak Tram in Hong Kong, the funicular rattles up the steep gradient of the mountain

face to the summit in just 10 minutes. At the top awaits the next installment of Hakone's transportation-fest: the cable car. For 30 minutes it glides through the air over the mountain top and down to the Ashino-ko Lake. Don't make the journey uninterrupted, however. Stop at least at Owakudani, a volcanic valley complete with bubbling springs and sulfurous waftings. A natural history museum documents the valley's tumultuous beginnings 3,000 years ago. Afterwards follow the crowds to a collection of simmering mud pools in which eggs are boiled until they are black — allegedly good for the health, it's probably not a good idea to follow the example of Japanese tourists and eat any if you are expecting intimate company later in the day. This area is one of the best places in the whole Hakone region for views of Fuji, and it's worth wandering away from the crowds — who are usually busy with the

eggs — to contemplate the view and perhaps take some pictures.

From here, jump on one of the cable-car gondolas and continue the journey to Ashino-ko. The lake has the most famous views of Fuji, and justly so in the right weather. It's possible to hike around the western edge of the lake to the former barrier town of Hakone-machi, but nearly everyone elects to take a kitsch but fun jaunt across the lake on a pirate ship. Whoever thought of this and apropos of what, it's impossible to say but it's certainly a hit with Japanese tourists, who spend most of the 30-minute journey photographing each other.

But trains, funiculars, cable cars and pirate ships aside, the best conclusion to a Hakone day trip is to go for a hike. A section of the old Tokaido road runs for around a kilometer (half a mile) north of Hakone-machi to the village of Moto-Hakone and is shaded by towering

The traditional inn, or *ryokan*, is one of those Japanese experiences that allows the traveler to become one with Japan, and as such it is not to be missed. There are some 80,000 of them scattered the length and breadth of the Japanese isles, ranging from tatami-mat flop houses to samurai-era paragons of service and style that would put some of the world's more famous hotels to shame. But they have one thing in common — they are always small and intimate, creating a cocoon-like ambiance that echoes the Japanese ideal of hearth and home.

Everything is in its proper place; guests are treated like royalty; for those who speak some Japanese, there will be a little small-talk before the maid retires, leaving the guests to their privacy, their dinner, perhaps eaten with a fine view of a miniature garden complete with a carp-filled pond.

The rituals can be confusing at first, but it doesn't take long to settle into their rhythms. Once mastered they hold good for every *ryokan* in the country. After all, the only surprises of a Japanese inn should be of the pleasurable kind — a particularly fine meal, a hot-spring bath with a view.

The rules are not so formidable. Shoes are removed immediately inside the entrance, where a rack, usually with numbered pigeon-holes, can be found. Change into a pair of slippers (invariably too small). After registering, a maid or the mistress leads the way to the room. Here the slippers are removed before entering. The maid will disappear for a few moments, only to return with a delicate pot of green tea.

In the most classic of *ryokan* — and usually the most expensive — the fittings will be all traditional. Decor in such places is minimal — a tatami woven straw floor, a knee-high table (for serving dinner) with *zabuton* (seating pads) around it, *fusuma* (sliding paper doors), and the futon and bedding, rolled up, until it is time for sleep, in a closet that is distinguished from the walls only by a catch to open it. In the room's *tokonoma* (alcove) will be displayed a painting or a piece of calligraphy and an arrangement of freshly cut flowers. In winter the table will be replaced with a *kotatsu*, a table with an electric heat-ring element underneath, covered with a quilt under which guests toast their feet — odd at first, but wonderful cozy after a while.

Look out for the *yukata*, or cotton dressing-gown, and maybe *geta* (wooden clogs). These can be worn anywhere inside the *ryokan* —

cryptomeria trees (Japanese cedar). They date from the early seventeenth century and have been designated as "National Treasures." It's a beautiful walk, and at the end of it awaits yet another mode of transportation: buses run from here to Hakone-Yumoto, where it's back on the Hakone–Tozan line, back to Odawara for the Romance Car, and eventually back to Tokyo.

Savor a Japanese Inn

IT CAN BE DISCOMFORTING AT FIRST TO HAVE A BOWING AND SCRAPING WOMAN SHUFFLE INTO THE ROOM, perhaps with a pot of green tea, or perhaps to lay out the bedding. But settle onto a futon for an evening, the cicadas chirping outside, the faint smell of tatami in the air like last year's summer, and it is hard not to fall in love with Japan's most traditional of accommodations.

The lady of the house welcomes guests to her mellow, elegant, 100-year-old *ryokan* in Narai.

indeed, it's usual to do so, less usual — but not impolite — not to.

The hour or so before dinner is bathing time. In expensive *ryokan* rooms may have their own hot tub. This is not the norm. Usually the bath is a deep, huge affair to be lounged in, and shared (though not at the same time) by all the guests; if the *ryokan* is in a hot spring area, all the better — the mineral-rich, piping hot water will be piped in from deep underground.

At inexpensive *ryokan*, such as those recommended by the Japanese Inn Group, rates will be simply for an overnight stay. Move up a notch in comfort, however, and it is expected that guests go whole hog and savor the inn experience to the full — in other words, take dinner and breakfast at the inn, though never lunch. Meal times usually have a degree of flexibility built into them, but remain fairly rigid — say, 6:30 PM to 8:30 PM for dinner, and 7 AM to 9 AM for breakfast. Dinners are usually served *kaiseki* style, or in a series of morsels that only slowly amount to a meal, often served with sake or beer. Breakfasts are usually Japanese style — pickles and rice — though at many inns Western breakfasts of eggs and toast are also offered nowadays.

After supper the maid will clear away the table and spread out the futon, quilt and pillow. The pillow may be filled with rice husks, which can feel odd at first but turns out to be quite comfortable. Such pillows are believed to keep the head cool. A cool head and warm feet is the healthy way to sleep in the Japanese scheme of things.

In the morning the bed-making procedure is reversed and breakfast is served. Check-out, as in almost all Japanese accommodations, is relatively early; at 10 AM or 11 AM. It is time to leave … or perhaps stay another night.

Explore a Medieval Castle

IT IS NOT WITHOUT REASON THAT JAPAN'S FINEST SURVIVING CASTLE GOES BY THE NAME OF THE "WHITE EGRET." Himeji-jo's graceful curves hover over its surrounding town with a deceptively fragile appearance, as if it could very well take to flight at any moment.

Deceptive is, however, the key word. As beautiful a castle as Himeji appears to be from a distance, up close it is a fortified labyrinth built with two reasons: to awe the local populace and to annihilate all unwanted infiltrators.

Take the meandering approach to Himeji and it soon becomes apparent that every detail conspires to the single principle of defense.

The Hishi-no-Mon Gate by which visitors enter, for example, leads into an enclosure that is surrounded on all sides by imposing walls with "loophole" openings that allowed defenders to shoot down onto anyone trapped within. Beyond lies yet another enclosure, equally well defended. Beyond is yet another. And so it goes. Attackers would have to negotiate a total of five heavily defended enclosures, one incorporating a narrow walled passage from the top of which arrows and rocks could be rained down on anyone passing below, before even approaching the castle proper.

Castle building in Japan began in earnest in the turbulent medieval period, which ran roughly from the twelfth to the sixteenth century. The earliest castles were usually constructed of wood and occupied a vantage point that commanded views of the surrounding countryside. By the sixteenth century, feudal lords began building more permanent structures, some of them featuring massive earthworks on the plains. By the time of the Tokugawa shogunate (1600–1867) the plain castle had become the most prevalent kind of Japanese castle, and each of the land's many (between 200 and 250) feudal domains featured one as its last line of defense and center of power.

At the heart of the castle complex — Himeji easily provides the finest surviving example of this — is the donjon, or the keep. Actually, in the case of Himeji, there are four linked donjons, each of them as heavily defended as the approach. But it is the main donjon, which soars above the rest of the complex, that automatically catches the eye. Five stories on outside, and seven on the inside, this was the administrative heart of the feudal domain, and at its apex was the operations center of the lord in the event of war, a surprisingly small area, but compensated by all-encompassing views of the surrounding countryside, as far as the Inland Sea in good weather. Massive wooden pillars, said to have been carved from a cypress tree nearly eight centuries old, support the donjon.

In its time, Himeji-jo, which was never attacked — hence its superb condition — was second in stature only to nearby Osaka-jo Castle. Like many of Japan's castles today, Osaka-jo is a recent reconstruction, though a particularly good one. Only 12 of Japan's

Rising majestically above Himeji, "White Egret" Castle is the finest castle in Japan. It dates back to the sixteenth century and was carefully restored in the late 1950s and early 1960s.

original castles survive. Many have been reconstructed with varying degrees of success, and some, such as the great Edo-jo Castle, now the site of Tokyo's Imperial Palace, are only remembered in history books.

The English guided tours ((792) 85-1146 that are available at Himeji are highly recommended. It's a good idea to book well in advance.

Spellbound by Puppeteers

BY ALL MEANS SEE KABUKI. Try and catch a performance of *no*. But don't forget Japan's least known theatrical tradition: *bunraku*, the professional puppet theater. Be prepared to be surprised.

For a start Japanese puppets are not controlled by strings. Three "operators," each with distinct responsibilities — one is responsible solely for the puppet's left arm — manipulate the puppet, together simulating the slightest gesture or body movement, down to the rolling of an eyeball or a fluttering caress. Two of them are all in black and hooded so as to be invisible to the audience. The third, the *omozukai*, or "chief operator," wears no hood — invisibility is not required of him because he is a star.

Not that he — and here is another surprise — is responsible for anything more than the puppet's facial expressions and right arm. The puppet's voice comes from the side of the stage, where the *tayu*, or chanter, accompanied by a three-stringed samisen player provides the voices for all the puppets in a performance, whether they are children, women or men, young or old.

It is 4 PM at the Tokyo National Theater, and a four-and-a-half-hour *bunraku* performance is about to get under way. The title is *The Love Suicides at Sonezaki*, a play dating from 1703 and based on a true story. The scene is a rural idyll, with a shrine in the foreground and a lake behind it, pale hills in the distance. The main character, in love with a courtesan, has been thrown from his uncle's home for refusing to marry his uncle's choice of a bride and has been swindled of all his money. He demands return of his money, and instead is accused of fraud and beaten while his courtesan lover looks on.

After the first act, the floor on which the narrator and samisen player are sitting swings backstage and two new performers are whirled into view. When the narrator and instrumentalist are replaced once again by a third pair, the scene also changes. Now it's a beautiful Japanese interior, where Ohatsu, the

courtesan, has Tokubei, the main character, hidden under her kimono. The two hard-done-by souls resolve to commit suicide together, and the rest of the play depicts their journey to the eventual tragic end when Tokubei stabs his lover in the throat and turns the blade on himself. As they walk to their death they compare themselves "to the frost by the road that leads to the graveyard/ vanishing with each step we take."

Bunraku emerged as a popular art form around the same time as *kabuki*, and its themes are similar: often dealing with tragedies that have befallen the merchant class — Tokubei, for example, is the nephew of a soy sauce merchant. But it is a far more sedate art than *kabuki*. Where *kabuki* is spectacle, full of shrill sounds and grand entrances, the stories of *bunraku* unfold in a measured way accompanied by the deep thrumming of the three-stringed samisen. The effect is often very profound.

The *Love Suicides at Sonezaki* is the most famous *bunraku* play for a host of reasons. Firstly it reinvigorated the theater with an enormous commercial success in Osaka when it was first performed in 1703 (the same year as the actual suicides it is based on); and secondly it was the occasion for a bold experiment in which the leading puppeteer operated his puppet unmasked.

A fascinating art, it is unfortunately the most tenuously surviving of the Japanese theatrical traditions. This is partly because of the long years of training the puppeteers must endure. A chief puppet operator has usually undergone 10 years of training operating just the puppet's legs, graduating to another 10 years operating the left arm, before finally achieving the pinnacle of his (they are always men) career. Performances today are only held in Tokyo in May, September and December, for three weeks each time. But at other times

of the year you can see the company, Japan's finest, at their home theater, the Osaka National Bunraku Theater.

Be sure to spend a little extra on the simultaneous English commentary device. It works like a radio and is keyed to the action as it is performed.

Over the Top

FEW VISITORS TO JAPAN HAVE TIME TO HIKE IN HONSHU'S GLORIOUS CENTRAL ALPS. But it is possible at least to cross them. The only walking involved — or at least the bare minimum — lasts a brief 10 minutes from one vehicle to another.

Okuhotaka-dake, the summit of the Japanese Alps. In clear weather the climb is not too strenuous and is certainly very rewarding.

Opened in 1971, the Tateyama–Kurobe Alpine Route is now one of those touchstones of Japanese tourism that provide a unique insight into the Japanese at play. With its designated viewing points and its regulated succession of stops, it can, as at Hakone, all end up feeling a little like conveyor-belt tourism. But the views more than compensate, and for those with the energy for a short walk, the crowds are easily escaped.

The 90-km (56-mile) traverse across the Omachi district of the Japan Alps is an often breathtaking journey over the 3,015-m (10,005-ft) Tate-yama mountain range. Detours on foot are possible en-route, though it's a good idea to set off as early as possible if this is the plan.

The journey begins at Toyama, which is accessible by JR (Japan Rail) from Tokyo (more than five hours), Nagano (four hours) and Takayama (one and a half hours). From here the private Chiho Tetsudo line trundles up to the village of Tateyama at the base of the mountain (actually a group of three mountains) of the same name — one of Japan's holy big three, along with Fuji and Haku-san.

In Tateyama, a cable car whisks travelers up to Bijodaira (977 m/3,257 ft) in seven minutes. It's mostly a tourist town, a cluster of hotels and restaurants. But it sits amid fine upland scenery. Buses head from here to Murodo (2,450 m/8,017 ft), where the popularity of this route is underscored by a big and extremely ugly bus terminal complete with quick-service noodle restaurants and their ilk. Leave the terminal behind and set off on foot for Mikuriga-ike Pond, which fills a volcanic crater 15 m (50 ft) deep and 600 m (2,000 ft) in circumference. Farther on from the pond, and around 20 minutes walk, is Jigoku-dani Valley, or Hell Valley, a place of bubbling, sulfurous super-hot springs, that sees relatively few tourists, who are mostly back at the terminal slurping down noodles.

Murodo's most challenging hike is to the summit of Mount O-yama (2,992 m/9,816 ft), which is marked by a small shrine. It takes two hours, and should only be undertaken in good weather conditions. Inquire at the Murodo Bus Terminal about the viability of making the hike. The panoramic views at the top are, it goes without saying, nothing short of superb.

From Murodo buses embark on what can only be described as the least scenic section of the entire journey — a 10-minute drive via a tunnel cut through Mount Tate-yama — to Daikanbo. This, presumably due to the expense of creating the tunnel, is a stunningly expensive 10-minute trip, at ¥2,060.

Daikanbo has perhaps the best views of the entire route, with flowery slopes and aquamarine lakes, and these can be enjoyed even further on the cable car that descends from here to Kurobe-daira, staging post for another cable car down to the huge Kurobe Dam. Those with an interest in dams will note that this is an "arch-type dome dam" and the biggest of its kind in Japan reaching a height of 186 m (610 ft). Those without will be content to walk 800 m (875 yards) across the top of it, admiring the lake beneath (created by the dam) and the mountain scenery, to connect with the trolley bus that descends from here to the village of Ogisawa (1,433 m/4,800 ft). Buses connect Ogisawa with Shinano Omachi, a nondescript town with direct rail connections (Japan Rail) with Matsumoto and beyond.

In a hurry the entire trip can be done in a few hours or less — at least the scenic part of it — but it's worth taking some time to appreciate the views. It goes without saying that it is pointless to do the trip in inclement weather. The route shut downs in winter, when heavy snowfalls close the roads. It is normally operative between April 25 and November 30, though late winter conditions in any particular year might delay the opening of some sections by a few days. The last section to open is usually the one on the west-facing flank of the range, linking Murodo and Tateyama — the opening of this section is on occasion delayed until early May.

Take the High Road

NEARLY EVERYONE WHO VISITS JAPAN ENDS UP TRAVELING ON THE TOKAIDO RAILWAY LINE THAT CONNECTS TOKYO WITH OSAKA AND KYOTO. Not everyone realizes it takes its name from an ancient highway. The Tokaido — literally the Eastern Sea Road — is old indeed, perhaps coming into existence as early as the fourth century, and emerging as the most important route linking the Japanese heartland of Kansai (Nara–Kyoto–Osaka) with the east and north of Honshu. By the Tokugawa period (1600–1867) it was the main route between Kyoto and Edo (now Tokyo), with a total of 53 post stations along its 488-km (303-mile) route.

It is difficult to imagine this road now, though it is memorialized in many wood-block prints. By the Tokugawa period it was made of crushed gravel lined with sand, with paving stones for the mountainous stretches. Horses had to be shod with straw to prevent damage to the road, and the main form of transport was by palanquin. Government barriers, or sekisho, were erected along the route to demand proof of identification from travelers, with the most

carefully guarded of them at Hakone. All along the road were the post-towns, most of them home to as many as 200 inns.

Given that it roughly parallels the Shinkansen (bullet train) route between Tokyo and Osaka, travelers can let their minds wander back to these long-gone days as their bullet-train chews up miles by the minute that once took days to traverse. Better yet, take a day or two out to savor the highway of times past.

In actual fact, Japan's best surviving stretch of ancient highway is not on the Tokaido, but an alternative inland route between Edo and Kyoto, the Nakasendo. One of the Gokaido, or Five Great Roads, it traveled 500 km (310 miles) past a total of 67 post towns. Three of these — Narai, Tsumago and Magome — survive, almost unaltered from their early days, providing an opportunity not only to hike the old road as travelers long ago did but also to stay at an Edo-era inn at the end of the day's journey.

The highlight of this journey is the hike between the historic post towns of Magome and Tsumago. Both are delights to explore, with almost all reminders of the twentieth (and twenty-first) century banished from sight. The streets are lined with charming wood and plaster buildings, the inns are

maintained as they were in days long gone, and it takes very little imagination — particularly on setting out early morning for the three-hour hilly walk between the two villages — to feel transported back in time to when a journey between Japan's two major cities was a major undertaking.

It's a beautiful hike, particularly on a fine day. There is an ancient tea house at around the halfway point, where a short break is recommended. Beyond the tea house is an ascent past waterfalls and wooded hills. It is difficult not to reflect along the way on all the contemporary traveler has lost in having the world made so much smaller by bullet trains and planes.

The small town of Tsumago is the perfect place to overnight, as most of the tourists who hike between the two towns tend to move on by nightfall, leaving the old post-town in peace. There is little to do here except visit the local folk museum, housed in what was once the town's best lodging (reserved for lords on the move) and choose one of the town's many old *ryokan* for dinner and bed. But Tsumago is one of those places that is more about ambiance than about doing

The famous Shinkansen (bullet train) speeds passengers through the country in comfort.

work, to school, to the park. Both cities are important stops on the Japan circuit, but Hiroshima, as the site of the first explosion, is virtually emblematic of atomic destruction.

In Japan, August 6, 1945 is a date every schoolchild knows. On that day an American bomber called the *Enola Gay* set out from the United States Air Force Base on Tinian Island in the Pacific and, at 8:15 AM, released what the military called "a new kind of bomb," curiously named "Little Boy." It exploded moments later 580 m (1,934 ft) above the city.

The mayors of Hiroshima have sent telegrams protesting against every nuclear test ever since, and their protests line the walls of the main exhibition hall of the Peace Memorial Museum. Hiroshima has become a world peace site, and the museum (entrance a mere ¥50) is not so much a memorial to that 1945 blast as an active protest against modern nuclear weapon stockpiles.

The museum exhibits a roll-call of tragedy. Somehow the existence of a special word for the victims, *hibakusha*, and their characteristic understated self-description "I met with the A-bomb" is terribly harrowing. Photographs of eminent figures being shown the museum are on display. They all look grim — Gorbachev, Pope John-Paul II, Mother Theresa — as does every member of the big crowd always to be found there.

The exhibits hit home with their specificity — a twisted bicycle that one wonders survived at all; a watch, its hands frozen at 8:15 AM; the ruin of the Hiroshima Prefecture Industrial Promotion Hall, which stands unrepaired as a reminder.

The Atomic Bomb Museum in Nagasaki is no less moving, and achieves a chilling symbolic effect with its spiraling rampway that takes the visitor ever-deeper into the destruction caused by the bomb, before terminating in a dark place of shattered masonry and warped girders. Close by is the Urakami Cathedral, a legacy of Nagasaki's Christian heritage. It's a postwar reconstruction, but the statuary at the door is original and the scorch marks that can be seen on it were left by the bomb. The cathedral hammers home the terrible irony of the fact that the home of Japan's earliest settlement of foreigners and one of Japan's important gateways for the import of "Western learning" should have become the second atomic bomb target.

anything — the perfect place, of an evening, to putter about the streets in a *yukata* (light kimono) and *geta* (wooden sandels) after an evening bath at the inn.

Give Peace a Chance

IT IS DIFFICULT TO APPROACH EITHER OF JAPAN'S PEACE MEMORIALS, IN HIROSHIMA AND NAGASAKI, WITHOUT CONFLICTING FEELINGS. Both cities have become Meccas for the "give peace a chance" contingent, and a visit to either of them is a sobering experience. And yet …

Any visit to the memorials to the detonation of nuclear devices over Hiroshima and Nagasaki has to be put in the context of Japan's World War II adventurism. It is a thorny issue in Japan, and pressure to expand Hiroshima's Peace Memorial Museum to include exhibits that depicted Japan's war atrocities was opposed by local elements for years until a more balanced approach was finally taken in 1994. It's still, however, difficult not to be reminded, both in Nagasaki and Hiroshima, of a peculiarly Japanese tendency to see these two exclamation points on Japan's World War II defeat as proof of Japan's victimization.

But, even in light of such caveats, the memorials remain profoundly moving. They are moving in terms of their local tragedy, a sense heightened by the fact that Hiroshima and Nagasaki are perfectly normal cities today, inhabited by normal people riding buses to

Japan's earliest Christians suffered persecution at the hands of the Edo government. Here (ABOVE) a Nagasaki memorial remembers 26 martyrs crucified in 1596. RIGHT: Preserved as it survived the atomic explosion, the former Industry Promotion Hall, now named the Atomic Bomb Dome, is Hiroshima's memorial to the catastrophe.

YOUR CHOICE

CAMPING

Camping can be enjoyed virtually everywhere, and it's almost always the case that you can rent tents, sleeping bags and other equipment at the *kampu-jo*, or campsite. Rates are very low, usually between ¥200 and ¥400, though occasionally they can be surprisingly high. The downside: camping is basically not an option if you do not have your own transportation. It's ideal for cyclists and those who rent cars, but otherwise getting to campsites, which are invariably in out-of-the-way locations, is too much trouble.

The other problem with camping in Japan is finding reliable information on the location of campsites. First stop should be a branch of the TIC (Tourist Information Center), which publishes a brochure that lists some of Japan's campsites, with phone numbers, addresses and rates. The information, however, is sketchy and incomplete. If you read Japanese, or can have a Japanese speaker help you, a very good web site is **www.travel.mimo.com/camp/map.html**. It has information on campsites around the country broken down by region. You will need Japanese-language software to read it.

Local information offices also provide information about campsites. These are listed in this book under the individual destinations.

Some travelers, cyclists mostly, put up their tents wherever they can find an unoccupied space. This is frowned upon in Japan, but it's possible all the same, providing you are discrete (choose an inconspicuous spot), and put up your tent after sunset, preferably moving on as early as possible. It is not recommended to travel this way.

The Great Outdoors

The Japanese work hard, but they play hard too. Outdoor pursuits, even if their object is fun, are carried out with the same by-the-book earnestness that almost everything is carried out with in Japan. "Organized" is the operative word, and there are times when the results are somewhat sanitizing — it is inevitably disappointing to hike up a hill only to find sightseeing crowds at the top who arrived by way of a cable car on the other side. Don't let it get you down. Bear in mind that Japan is far bigger country than most Japanese care to admit — "we live in a small country" is a common complaint — and it's always possible to escape the crowds, the neatly trimmed hedges, manicured lawns and paving-stone paths.

For a superb overview of Japan's outdoor activities and attractions, visit **Outdoor Japan** WEB SITE www.outdoorjapan.com, which is devoted to the Japanese great outdoors.

OPPOSITE: An artist captures the mountain landscapes of Kamikochi on canvas. ABOVE: A brilliant burst of flowers in the Japanese Alps.

NATIONAL PARKS

National parks in Japan divide into national parks and quasi national parks. The distinction is administrative more than anything else, with national parks overseen by the central government Environment Agency and quasi national parks managed by local prefectural governments. There are 28 of the former and 55 of the latter.

The majority of the big parks are in Japan's sparsely populated north: in Tohoku (northern Honshu) and Hokkaido. They tend to be much easier to access if you have your own transportation, and many, such as **Kamikochi** in central Honshu, are completely shut off from the outside world during the winter months.

Some, on the other hand, are popular destinations for foreign travelers, who might not even realize they are in a national park. Examples are **Nikko National Park** and **Fuji-Hakone-Izu National Park**, both of which are popular excursions from Tokyo. As is the case in all national parks, they offer the opportunity for hiking, as well as sporting some famous tourist attractions. Other popular national parks include **Ise-shima National Park**, home to the famous shrine of Ise-jingu, and **Tottori National Park**, with its celebrated sand dunes. **Aso National Park** in Kyushu has superb hiking in one of the world's largest volcanic craters, while in Okinawa the subtropical **Iriomote National Park** even sports jungle walks.

HOT SPRINGS

Water is the one natural resource with which Japan is blessed in really ample quantities. Due to the countrywide volcanic activity, hot water, rich in health-giving salts and minerals, putters and bubbles out of the earth in innumerable places, and has long provided the Japanese with one of their cheapest, yet richest, delights: hot-spring bathing.

Soak away the day's strains in the startlingly hot water of the large bath in your *ryokan* and you are already tasting that pleasure. But to get the full effect, travel to the resort towns that cluster around almost all of Japan's hot springs, or *onsen*. For a comprehensive guide to the *onsen* of Japan, go to the **Japan Outdoors** web site (see above), which has information on hot springs across the length and breadth of the land.

Some of Japan's more famous hot springs include **Hakone-Yumoto**, a charming old spa town on the old Tokaido road to Kyoto, just one and a half hours from Shinjuku, Tokyo; **Atami**, just 55 minutes by Shinkansen from Tokyo, and one of the biggest spa resorts in Japan; **Beppu** and **Ibusuki**, in Kyushu, two resorts that see Japanese hot-spring mania in full flight; and **Noboribetsu** in Hokkaido, one of the few mixed-bathing (men and women together, which means hopeful men and very few women) baths remaining in Japan.

Before entering a public hot-spring bath, wash yourself with soap and hot water and rinse off thoroughly, sitting on one of the small

stools provided and using hot and cold water from the taps. At this point you are ready to lower yourself into the usually scalding water. Don't let your hair get in the water. After soaking for about five minutes, most Japanese cool off under a cold shower — there are sometimes cold plunge pools provided, which once you've tried you will be going back for more of.

The average cost of staying overnight at a hot-spring hotel, which will have both private and communal spring baths, is ¥13,000 including dinner and breakfast. Reservations, particularly on weekends and during holiday seasons, are essential.

BEACHES

Japan is not a destination for beaches, though guidebooks and tourist brochures will often waffle on about the glories of Kyushu and Okinawa beach culture. The truth is, while it is possible to swim at various beach destinations around Japan, unless you are resident in Japan, there are far more attractive and less expensive beach destinations in Asia. **Okinawa** provides the best opportunities for swimming and other water sports, particularly the southern islands of **Miyako** and **Ishigaki**.

MOUNTAINS

With some 85 percent of Japan's landmass occupied by mountains, taking to the hills is an obvious activity. From early times the Japanese regarded the mountains with awe,

seeing them as the domain of *kami*, or gods, and for most of Japan's history the ascent of mountains was associated with pilgrimage to holy places. That changed in the early twentieth century, when Englishman Walter Weston founded the Japan Alpine Club, a club whose later exploits in the Himalayas sparked nationwide interest in mountaineering.

Clearly mountaineering is a specialized sport. This is not the place to enumerate Japan's popular climbing peaks, but many less vertiginous ascents are viable at numerous mountains around Japan. Japan's most famous mountain, 3,776-m (12,587-ft) **Mount Fuji** is the obvious first choice. During the open season of July and August, it literally swarms with climbers looking to accomplish that once-in-a-lifetime (only a fool climbs it more than once, goes a Japanese saying) ascent to the summit. Destinations in the Japananese Alps such as **Kamikochi** are also extremely popular places for high-altitude hiking in season.

Next in popularity are probably **Mounts Haguro**, **Yudono** and **Gas-san** in Tohoku, followed by the often frozen volcanic heights of Hokkaido. But there are 1,000 to 2,000-m (3,334 to 6,668-ft) peaks the length of the country, excepting Okinawa.

OPPOSITE: Cherry blossoms, a symbol of Japan, at Lake Okutama, west of Tokyo. Their evanescence is part of their appeal. ABOVE: With sweeping curves, the wood and stone Kintai Bridge spans the river at Irakuni.

Sporting Spree

Far more so than any of their Asian neighbors, the Japanese are a nation who relish sport in all its varieties. Western-style sports such as tennis and winter sports were first introduced during the Meiji period (1868–1912) by foreigners and by Japanese returning from abroad. There were setbacks during the pre-war years, when traditional Japanese sports were emphasized, but with the conclusion of World War II, Western-style sports once again became popular.

Visitors to Japan, however, are more likely to experience sport as a spectator than as a participant. Of course, certain luxury hotels provide facilities for tennis and swimming, and some winter travelers in Japan head to the slopes for skiing, but in general, competition for use of sporting facilities is intense, making sports like golf — to take a famous example — prohibitively expensive for most travelers.

GOLF

Golf was introduced to Japan by an Englishman, Arthur H. Groom, in the early twentieth century. The sport took off in a way he probably could never have imagined, becoming a prestige sport for which club memberships commanded vast sums of money. Japan's economic slump has taken some of the wind out of golf's elitist sails, and golf club memberships in early 2001 were at their lowest in 19 years. Despite this, it remains an extremely expensive habit to indulge while in Japan, with around at any of the top clubs costing as much as US$500.

SKIING

If golf is for the snobs, skiing in Japan is truly democratic. It's easy to get the impression on winter weekends — when the stations of Tokyo are crammed with skiers in designer gear — that half of urban Japan has decamped for the slopes.

Skiing is a huge industry in Japan, and a sure indication of the high quality of skiing facilities was the selection of Nagano Prefecture in the Japanese Alps as the location for the 1998 Winter Olympics. For visitors, a jaunt up to the slopes is not as expensive as you might think. Providing you are prepared to spend around ¥4,000 per day for lift passes and about the same for equipment rental (it's usually possible to get accommodation, if you need it, at a pension for around ¥7,000 to ¥8,000 with meals), spending some time on Japan's mountain slopes is perfectly feasible.

For detailed information about skiing destinations in Japan, check with any of the TICs (Tourist Information Centers), or take a look at the extremely informative **Ski Japan** web site at www.skijapanguide.com. With the latest on more than 400 ski resorts around Japan, it is the best one-stop on-line destination for information. It even includes snowfall reports, and daily reports on the state of the slopes at the biggest resorts.

Nomugitoge, **Norikura Kogen** (one of Japan's premier skiing sites) and **Sun Alpina Kashimayari** are all resorts in easy reach of Matsumoto, under three hours by Japan Rail from Tokyo's Shinjuku Station. There's even helicopter access to a 14-km (eight-mile) downhill course at **Tsugaike Kogen** ski resort in the north of Japan's Alps (at Otari).

You can ski in innumerable places in Hokkaido at any time during the winter — at **Niseko Kokusai Hirafu** with its 21 ski-lifts; at **Niseko Annupuri Kokusai**, two and a half hours from Sapporo; or at **Alpha Resort Tomamu** or **Ski Resort Furano**, each two hours from Sapporo by JR (Japan Rail) and bus respectively.

The Christmas and New Year period tends to be very busy at ski resorts, as major public holidays occur at this time. Fine weekends, too, can see long queues and fully-booked accommodation. It's best to avoid these peak periods.

WATER SPORTS

Japan, as noted above, is most definitely not a beach destination. There are far better — and much cheaper — places to head to in Asia if it's fun in the sun you are after. Throughout much of Japan, such beaches as have become tourist attractions are almost invariably disappointing. But for those who make it to the far south of Japan, particularly to the islands of Okinawa, diving and other water sports are an option.

The chief Okinawan islands for diving and snorkeling are **Miyako** and **Ishigaki**. Sea Friends ((09808) 20863 is one of several diving centers on Ishigaki. On Miyako you could try Twenty-four North ((09807) 23107.

BICYCLE TOURING

While you can rent bicycles at most Japanese tourist destinations, and it's possible to buy a bike reasonably inexpensively if you are planning on living in Japan and want something to get to your nearest station on, for a road trip you should bring your own bike. Before you set out, take a look at the **Japan Cycling Navigator** WEB SITE www.t3.rim.or.jp/~sayori/, which is edited by the Japan Adventure Cyclist Club and has information about some of Japan's most picturesque and challenging cycling routes; it also has contact details that will put you in touch with other cycling enthusiasts.

It goes without saying that parts of the country are far more suited to two wheels than others. Cycling the vast conurbation that unfolds between Tokyo and Osaka, for example, is likely to be nobody's idea of fun. Remote destinations such as Hokkaido and Kyushu, on the other hand, are altogether another proposition. The best thing to do is to get your bike onto a train and get outside the big cities before launching out into the traffic. A small bicycle transport supplement fee of ¥270 is levied on bikes taken on trains. Strictly speaking the bike should be carried in a bike bag.

BASEBALL

Known in Japanese as *yakyu*, literally "wild ball," Japan's first professional baseball team, the Yomiuri Giants, was organized in 1934, and by 1936 there were five more, forming the first professional league. By 1950 there were two leagues: the Central League and the Pacific League. Each team plays the other teams in its league 36 times a season, and highest scorers from each league face each other off once a year in the Japan Series. During the season, from April through October, expect blanket coverage on television, and if you like you might join the approximately 20 million fans who will attend a live match.

ABOVE: In overcrowded Japan, the chance to take to the hills is very tempting. RIGHT: For golf lovers, limited space means that a driving range has to be shared with many other enthusiasts.

The WEB SITE **www.inter.co.jp/Baseballindex.html** is an excellent source of news and details on up-coming matches.

SOCCER

The fast-growing popularity of soccer in Japan is evidenced by the fact that it will be co-hosting the World Cup with South Korea in 2002. It's very much a newcomer to the Japanese sports scene, making a heavily financed entry in 1993 with inception of the "J League." Some predicted at the time that this was nothing more than another Japanese fad, but with 19 teams competing and probably more to come, the game has gone from strength to strength, and has been spurred by big-name Western players joining local teams. For more information, including upcoming matches and the latest scores, check out their WEB SITE **www.j-league.or.jp/ sitemap_english/index.html**.

AIKIDO

An interesting offshoot of jujitsu, with religious overtones (it means the "way of spiritual harmony"), aikido is a purely self-defensive martial art that blends elements of other Japanese martial arts. It is overseen by the **International Aikido Federation** ((03) 3203-9236 in Shinjuku, Tokyo, where it is possible to watch practice sessions if you ring ahead — you will need the help of a Japanese speaker to do so.

JUDO

Japan's most famous martial art, literally the "way of softness," evolved from jujitsu at the end of the nineteenth century, making it a quite recent development. Under the **All Japan Judo Federation** ((03) 3818-4172, however, it has become a major martial art, and in 1964 was formally entered into the Olympics. The federation has a spectator gallery for its training sessions, though you will need to call in advance.

KARATE

The **Japan Karate Association International Headquarters** ((03) 3440-1415 in central Tokyo has morning and evening classes that visitors can view for free. The sport, like judo, is relatively new, originating in China and making its way to Japan in the 1920s via Okinawa. No English is spoken, so if you don't speak Japanese, you will need the help of a speaker to contact the association.

KENDO

The "way of the sword" is a fascinating sport to watch, and with genuine samurai antecedents it's the oldest of Japan's martial arts, originating in the Muromachi period from 1392 to 1573. The **All Japan Kendo Federation** ((03) 3211-5804 presides over the sport and can be contacted for information about studying it. Practice sessions are not open to the public, though it is worth contacting the Tokyo TIC (Tourist Information Center) about occasional tournaments in Tokyo's Budokan.

SUMO

Make no mistake: sumo, a sport with a 2,000-year history, bears no resemblance to Western-style wrestling. To be sure, out in the ring, it's a clash of titans. With an average height of 185 cm (six feet) and an average of weight of 148 kg (326 lbs), these guys lurch ponderously at each other as they seek to win by forcing their opponent out of the ring. But with its ceremony, rituals and intense training, the sumo tournament is not a slap-stick clash of good and evil but a dramatic test of skills. Many foreigners become addicted, and spend their days glued to the television during the big annual tournaments.

Professionals live out their careers in *heya*, or stables, where a morning of hard training is followed by a hot bath and a huge lunch of meat, fish, tofu, vegetables and mountains of rice. The wrestler then happily snoozes away the afternoon while his meal converts itself into fat.

Modern sumo is a brilliant marriage of feudalistic ritual and highly telegenic drama. The elaborate Shinto ceremonies preceding and following the brief bouts have been simplified for the sake of modern audiences without sacrificing the sport's highly exotic flavor.

After several minutes of preparation, during which the combatants stamp, squat, gargle "power water" and scatter purifying salt on the clay ring, the bout begins — and is often over within seonds, with the loser either pushed out of the ring (sometimes somersaulting spectacularly into the arms of those in the front row) or forced to touch the ground with some part of his body other than the soles of his feet.

Six major tournaments are held each year, every other month, alternating between Tokyo, Nagoya and Osaka. Each tournament lasts for 15 days. For information about getting seats, contact the Tokyo or Kyoto TIC (Tourist Information Center).

The baroque mysteries of sumo are involved enough to sustain a lifetime's curiosity. Here, wrestlers train at Yasukuni Shrine.

The Open Road

If driving is an adventure, to say the least, in most of Asia, Japan is one Asian destination where drivers play the rules, and renting a car isn't a leap of faith. Sign-posting is ubiquitous, and for the most part is romanized as well as in Japanese. Unexpectedly, America-obsessed Japan drives on the left.

Driving allows you to see a side of Japan that is denied to the JR (Japan Rail) pack. You can take detours wherever you like, and chances are you will find yourself from time to time in destinations where the arrival of a foreigner is something of an event — listen for cries of "*gaijin da!*" ("it's a foreigner!").

Hokkaido is ideal for driving because the roads are comparatively empty. That many of them will be closed off by snowfalls for much of the winter is the only downside on an island that is almost definitive of the open road. A week would be more than enough to circle the island, take in a couple of the superb national parks, and experience a side of Japan's "deep north" that few other foreign travelers get to see.

Honshu's roads are more crowded than Hokkaido's though; for relief look to **Tohoku**. Here conditions approach Hokkaido's and driving is a pleasure, though many of the rural roads are narrow and winding.

While driving north from Tokyo to Sapporo or Hakodate — the main staging posts for a Hokkaido excursion — is not recommended due to the capital's never-ending sprawl, starting a road-trip north from Sendai is perfectly feasible. As in Hokkaido, a car allows you to get off the beaten track in Tohoku, though it is not reasonable to expect much English to be spoken there. The north coast of **western Honshu** offers a pleasant and uncongested road trip that can be made via Toyama, Masuda and Hagi, rather than the southern route through the major cities (Kyoto, Osaka, Kobe, Hiroshima and farther west).

Aside from peak holiday periods, the roads in **Kyushu** compare to the north coast of western Honshu, to which it is connected by bridge. With the exception of the ugly sprawl of Kitakyushu in the far north of the island, Kyushu is easy to navigate, and the south of the island, in particular, offers unspoiled scenery and light traffic conditions.

Driving in **Okinawa** will require renting a vehicle all over again. The traffic, on the other hand, is at least comparatively light, though driving is only a possibility on Okinawa island, where open road vistas are limited by the relatively small landmass.

Backpacking

It's not impossible to see Japan on a budget, but there is no point pretending it's easy. The good news: the yen has taken something of a battering in recent years, and prices have remained steady, so Japan is not as expensive as it was. The bad news: it remains the most expensive destination in Asia. While it's easy enough to get by on US$15 a day or less as a backpacker in many Asian destinations, in Japan that basic daily budget is more likely to be around US$50. You may be able to shave a few yen off here or there, but the reality is by the end of your trip you will be lucky to have got away with spending much less unless you cycle, stay at campsites and make instant noodles the staple of your diet — don't laugh, people do it.

The two big expenses in Japan are transport and accommodation. Fortunately it's possible to economize on both. If you really want to save money, take a tent (see the GREAT OUTDOORS, above) and a bicycle (see GETTING AROUND, page 225 in TRAVELERS' TIPS). Most budget travelers, however, opt to stay in youth hostels and travel via a combination of hitchhiking and cheaper modes of transportation such as *futsu* (ordinary) trains and overnight buses, which save on the cost of a night's accommodation.

Japan's youth hostel network runs to an impressive 400-plus operations across the country. They are invariably clean, well organized and friendly, and the best of them offer the bonus of being housed in atmospheric traditional farm houses and the like. The average rate is around ¥2,800 per person, and meals are optional, usually at around ¥600 for breakfast and ¥1,000 for dinner. Some have cooking facilities. Not all youth hostels require membership, but it's wise to organize it before arriving in Japan for those that do. Don't forget to pick up a copy of the *Youth Hostels Map of Japan* at one of the TICs, and if you plan to be traveling extensively in Japan using the youth hostel network, buy a copy of the *Youth Hostel Handbook*, which has vague but nevertheless useful locator maps for each of the hostels in the country.

If your budget extends to the occasional night of relative luxury, pick up the *Japanese Inn Group* brochure at a branch of the TIC also. This group is an organization representing usually small and always reasonably priced *ryokan*. Overnight rates are around ¥4,000 a night per person.

Enormous savings can be made by buying a **Japan Rail Pass** before you get to Japan, especially if you are covering a lot of ground fast. If you aren't intending to travel enough to justify getting a Rail Pass, then long-distance buses are the next-best option. Once you arrive at your destination, bicycles are available for rent just about everywhere.

Hitchhiking isn't common in Japan, but it's possible. As is the case anywhere, it is not recommended for single women, and even if you are male it's safest to travel with a friend. A bold sign with the name of your destination (in *kanji*) is a great aid. Tales abound of Western hitchhikers in Japan overwhelmed with kindness and drivers going miles out of their way to deliver hitchhikers to their destinations.

On the dining front, it's possible to eat out quite economically in Japan once you get the hang of things. The vicinity of train stations is the best place to seek out cheap eats. Look for the ubiquitous *ramen* noodle restaurants, where you can usually get a big bowl of filling noodles for around ¥500. *Kare raisu* — curry rice — restaurants are another common and inexpensive place to fill up. A plate of Japanese-style curry (nothing like the Indian variety) with rice (sometimes with a cup of coffee thrown in) will usually cost around ¥650. Also worth looking for are branches of the coffee shop chain **Doutor** and its look-alikes, where good coffee costs around ¥110 per cup, and inexpensive hot dogs and sandwiches are also available — they're good places for breakfast.

Living it Up

Few Asian destinations lend to themselves to the high life like Japan does. It has fine hotels, luxurious traditional inns, feasts whose historical roots lay in the imperial past, not to mention branches of world-famous restaurants.

EXCEPTIONAL HOTELS

As to be expected, Tokyo and Kyoto, Japan's two most important destinations, have the lion's share of luxury accommodation. There may be luxurious treats scattered the length and breadth of the land, but it is in the capital and the one-time imperial capital that visitors find themselves spoiled for choice.

There's no point attempting to award the number-one spot on Tokyo's long accommodation list, but one hotel that consistently appears in the context of such commendations is the **Park Hyatt Tokyo**, a fabulous sky-scraping luxury number located on the upper floors of the Shinjuku Tower which culminates on the fifty-second floor in one of the city's best restaurants (see below), overlooking the city from a height of 233 m (765 ft). If the idea of earthquakes makes you nervous, west Shinjuku is the most geologically stable part of Tokyo, hence the high proportion of high-rises in the area.

The familiar silhouette of the Great Torii at Miyajima, a feature on longer trips from the capital.

Another opulent treat can be found in the heart of Ginza, the most elite of Tokyo addresses, at the **Hotel Seiyo Ginza**. It is almost a Japanese inn in concept — personal, small, fastidious in its attention to detail — and yet the rooms are individually furnished and designed in Western style. Among its many luxury touches is the provision of a personal secretary for each of the hotel's guests.

Kyoto has some superb Western-style hotels, of course, but it is its high-class *ryokan* that take the prize in the luxury stakes, as befitting the most traditional of Japan's cities. The **Hiiragiya Ryokan** is a journey back into the samurai days of yore. It's the perfect place to indulge a private fantasy of having been transported back in time, as kimono-clad waiting staff shuffle, bowing as they go, in and out of your room with trays of delicious *kaiseki* treats that were once the private pleasures of Japan's ruling elite. Almost next door is the **Tawaraya Ryokan**, which with 300 years worth of satisfied guests behind it, is even more traditional than the Hiiragiya. Reservations for either should be made as far in advance as possible.

EXCEPTIONAL RESTAURANTS

Again, as with accommodation, the best places to sample Japanese (and international) cuisine at its finest is Tokyo and Kyoto, though Osaka has some fine dining as well.

Already mentioned above was the Park Hyatt Tokyo, where you will find the **New York Grill**, which has been voted one of the world's best hotel restaurants. Exploiting the superlative views from up here, it's glass on all sides, nevertheless managing to incorporate four massive paintings by Italian artist Valerio Adami (you'll have to go there to see just how they do it). Serving Asian-Western fusion cuisine, the restaurant features live jazz by night, though you can have a taste of its fabulous food at more affordable prices without the jazz by visiting at lunch time.

But, of course, it's the best in Japanese dining that is the true allure of Japan. **Kisso** is a long-running Tokyo institution that never fails to impress newcomers. It takes Japan's famous *kaiseki* imperial cuisine and gives it a modern twist that is thoroughly complemented by the artistically designed interior. **Tatsumiya**, on the other hand, takes a traditionalist approach to Japan's most highly esteemed cuisine, serving its banquets in an appropriately old-Edo setting.

Anyone who loves Japanese food is going to want to have the ultimate sushi experience, and once again Tokyo is the place to do it. **Fukuzushi**, in fashionable Roppongi, comes complete with a babbling stream, a cocktail bar, and some of the city's most lauded sushi. Another highly recommended Tokyo experience is **Inakaya**, a down-at-the-farm grill restaurant in which the chefs put on a winning show with the ingredients you pick out at the bar before it is served at the end of huge wooden paddles. Not the place for an intimate dinner, but certainly the place for an entertaining evening that will stay in your memory for years to come.

Kyoto, as you might expect, is the place to experience traditional cuisine in traditional surroundings. Make a point, while you are there, of at least once dining in the grounds of one of the city's countless temples, where Zen vegetarian cuisine is the specialty. **Izusen**, at Daitoku-ji Temple is one of the best places to do so, and in the warm summer months tables are set in the temple grounds, a unique experience that shouldn't be missed.

With three centuries of business behind it, **Hyotei** is one of Kyoto's most famous restaurants. Kyoto *kaiseki* (*kyoryori*) is served to diners in their own traditional cottages with service standards that Japan is justly famous for.

TRAVEL IN STYLE

Japan is famed for its rail network, but mostly for its Shinkansen, which glide at breathtaking speed from one end of the country to the other (or very nearly). If you want to experience the Shinkansen at its best, the so-called Green Cars, a euphemism for the otherwise elitist term "first class," offer high standards of comfort in compartments containing only four seats, arranged round a table. You can racket the luxury up a notch by taking one of the Nozomi super-expresses, the fastest trains in the world. All seats in these are reserved, and they are not available on a Japan Rail Pass, even if you have bought your pass in the superior Green Car category.

Family Fun

Japan is easily the best place in Asia to take children. There is almost a theme park — or so it seems at times — on every corner; there are fantastic museums, many with hands-on, high-tech displays; great aquariums; and even some of the cultural sights, especially the castles, won't leave the kids bored. Many of the ideas featured in THE GREAT OUTDOORS (above) are a kids' paradise. Hiking up or around a volcano, for example, is an experience they'll never forget.

But overwhelmingly the main attraction — indeed families all over Asia fly to Tokyo just for the pleasure of visiting it — is **Tokyo Disneyland**. With more than 10 million visitors every year, one thing is certain: you will spend a lot of times in lines. Nevertheless, if you are traveling with children, it is unlikely you will be able avoid a visit. An almost exact replica of the original, it is easy to spend a day or more exploring the place and taking the rides. See WHAT TO SEE AND DO, page 86 under TOKYO, for details about tickets, prices and getting there, or alternatively check the WEB SITE www .tokyodisneyland.co.jp/.

Another major children's attraction in the Tokyo area (and a lot less expensive) is **Children's Land** ((0436) 74-3174 (9 AM to 4 PM, closed Monday and the first and third Tuesday of every month). It has a farm, zoo, playgrounds, cycling, all set in woods and fields. All kinds of activities are organized, involving such things as milking cows, a magic rope tournament, baton twirling, a Ninja Haunted House maze, drum concerts, hikes, and much more. Children's Land can be reached by bus from Tsurukawa Station on the Odakyu line — ask for *"kodomo no kuni."*

The **National Children's Castle** ((03) 3797-5666, 5-53-1 Jingumae Shibuya-ku, Tokyo (10 AM to 5:30 PM weekdays, 12:30 PM to 5:30 PM weekends, closed Mondays), has play rooms, an "exploratorium," crafts classes and an indoor swimming-pool. It's even possible to stay here, which isn't such a bad idea if you are with children, as its location not far from Shibuya is central for Tokyo sightseeing. It's close to Omotesando subway station (Exit B2) on the Ginza line.

OPPOSITE: The architecture of a *ryokan* is all that one imagines a Japanese inn should be — clean lines and a tranquil interior fashioned out of wood and paper. LEFT: Kids, young and old, are seduced by Disneyland.

There are countless other Tokyo attractions that will fascinate children, all of them listed in the Tokyo section. Try the fantastic **Edo-Tokyo Museum**, with its recreation of old Edo, or the high-tech display's in Ginza's **Sony Showroom**. Meanwhile, in Ueno, **Tokyo Zoo** is recommended if you have children with you.

At Yokohama, **Wild Blue Yokohama** ((045) 511-2323 WEB SITE www.wildblue.co.jp/english.htm is a massive indoor water-sports theme park. Also in Yokohama, the **Minato Mirai** complex has a host of attractions, including a ship museum, that are sure to get children's attention.

At Hakone, Tokyo's back garden, there's a **Children's Village**. To get here, alight from the Hakone Tozan line train (see page 117 in AROUND TOKYO) at Kowakudani station.

Farther afield, near Niigata, **Shirone Odako Museum** ((025) 372-0314 has the world's largest collection of kites. You can make your own kite there, with advice from an expert, and then test it in an "Aerodynamics Tunnel." Exhibits include not only the many varieties of regional Japanese kites, but kites from all over the world.

In Kyoto, **Toei Movieland** (Toei Uzumasa Eigamura) is a film studio where scenes for samurai movies are shot, and at the same time a tourist attraction. It's a haven for kids as much as for adults, with remote-controlled boats, sense-around movie screenings, and numerous other attractions certain to appeal to youngsters.

In Osaka, the **Osaka Aquarium** is easily one of Japan's best.

Cultural Kicks

A journey to Japan is a journey into one of the world's richest and most unique cultures. The twentieth century for Japan, like China and much of the rest of Asia, was a century of massive dislocations and ruptures with tradition, but unlike China, Japan has managed to preserve an enormous amount of its past. For the visitor this means a feast of architecture and traditions.

TEMPLES

It doesn't take long in Japan to realize that there are two kinds of religious architecture — Buddhist temples (*ji* or *tera*/*dera*) and Shinto shrines (*jinja* or *jingu* or *gu*). While the architectural influences of the latter are native Japanese, the latter are usually Chinese, occasionally Korean, and ultimately, in forms like the pagoda, Indian.

There are so many temples in Japan — around 77,000 — that seeing even a fraction of them is enough to temple-out the average traveler. Certain temples, however, are must-sees. A prime example is **Senso-ji Temple** in Tokyo. No architectural triumph, this uninspired reconstruction is a compelling attraction because of its atmosphere. With its bustling push-and-shove crowds and fair-ground stalls selling everything from *sembei* crackers to geisha wigs, this is very much a lived-in temple.

Of course, some temples attract the crowds because of their longevity, or simply because they awe. Kamakura's Kotuku-in Temple, for example, is home to the **Daibutsu**, or the Great Buddha, a giant 11.4-m (37.4-ft) bronze image of Amida who sits as serene as ever, despite surviving tidal waves and earthquakes in the centuries since 1495.

An even greater Great Buddha can be seen at Nara's **Todai-ji Temple**, built in AD 752 and housed in the biggest wooden building in the world.

Both Nara and Kyoto are rich in temple sights. Todai-ji, for example, is considered by experts to represent the apogee of Japan's imperial-sponsored Buddhist architecture and should not be missed. Meanwhile, in Kyoto, temple highlights include the spectacular **Kiyomizu-dera** and **Ginkaku-ji** temples — you could restrict your visit to just these two and still feel that it was worth visiting Kyoto.

Not that all of Japan's most splendid temples are in the cultural heartland of Kansai. In Nagano, **Zenko-ji Temple**, a multi-denominational Buddhist temple whose founding dates back to the seventh century, has an eerie atmosphere that is compounded if you summon up the courage to plunge into darkness in quest of its "key to salvation."

Lastly, **Mount Koya-san** in Kansai is a Buddhist mountain retreat where all you will find are temples — indeed if you spend the night here, you will be staying in one.

SHRINES

While Japan's temples are for Buddhists; its shrines are the provenance of the country's indigenous religion, Shinto. They are not exclusive. Most Japanese pay their respects at both, despite — or perhaps because of — the fact that they are worlds apart. Shinto shrines range from simple and austere, as at one of Japan's most famous, **Ise-jingu**, to gaudy and life embracing at Nikko's **Tosho-gu**.

Red *torii* gates, such as this one in Kyushu, mark the entrances to Japan's Shinto shrines.

While in Tokyo, do not fail to visit **Meiji-jingu**. It gets left off many itineraries due to the wealth of things to see and do in the big city, but this leafy oasis in the middle of the city, with its stunning central shrine, is one of Tokyo's highlights.

As beautiful as it is, Meiji-jingu is not, however, one of the "three great" shrines of Japan. That honor is reserved for Nikko's **Tosho-gu Shrine**, **Ise-jingu Shrine** in Ise, and **Izumo-taisha Shrine** near Matsue. Izumo-taisha is Japan's largest Shinto shrine, and, according to some, the oldest.

CASTLES
Japan has so many relics of its feudal era that if you travel for any length of time in the country you will start to get tired of them. Nevertheless, some are nothing short of splendid. Castle towns, or *joka machi*, could be found far and wide as late as the Edo period (1600–1867), when the so-called "one-castle, one-domain" edict resulted in many being torn down. Even so, there were thought to be as many as 250 still standing afterwards. The Meiji restoration of 1868 led to the wide-scale destruction of most of these, and the bombing of World War II brought more bad news. Today, only 12 originals still stand, the rest being reconstructions that vary from inspired to lackluster.

If you visit only one of the originals, make it **Himeji-jo**, the "White Egret," an architectural triumph that conjures up the samurai past. It is contrasted by the "Black Swan" of **Matsumoto-jo**, which is also in good condition. The best of the reconstructions are **Osaka-jo** and **Kumamoto-jo**, both in the cities of the same name.

GARDENS
While Japan has many kinds of gardens, the "stroll" gardens and the Zen "dry landscape" gardens are the two most famous varieties. Completely different in style, stroll gardens generally make use of miniaturized views laid out along a walk, often incorporating "borrowed views" of nearby natural features or manmade structures like castles. Zen dry landscapes on the other hand are not walked through so much as viewed from different angles, and can often be quite mysterious collections of misshapen stones surrounded by raked pebbles, the deep significance of which scholars spend their lives debating.

In their characteristic quest for categorization and definition, the Japanese have identified three of the nation's stroll gardens as "great." **Kenroku-en Garden** in Kanazawa is the one that most foreigners get to see, but it is also worth making a whistle stop in western Honshu to see **Koraku-en** at Okayama. **Kairaku-en** at Mito is the other famous stroll garden.

The dry landscape (*karesansui*) derives its name from the use of sand and gravel to represent rivers and seas, with rocks usually representing islands. It is said to have evolved under the influence of Chinese brush and ink landscapes. The **East Garden** at Daisen-in Temple, a sub-temple of Kyoto's Daitoku-ji Temple, for example, uses sand and rocks to represent a cascading waterfall. In the same temple grounds is the famous dry landscape representing the "sea of nothingness."

Kyoto is home to Japan's most famous dry landscapes, and the most famous of them all is the raked sea at **Ryoan-ji Temple** with its randomly placed rock islands. Also highly rated is the garden at **Kinkaku-ji Temple**.

THEATER

Seeing a performance of one of Japan's theater traditions shouldn't be missed. *Kabuki* is the most famous, and is the easiest to catch a performance of, particularly if you are passing through Tokyo. *No* is less instantly accessible, though strangely haunting, and is less a fixture on the tourist trail, though it is sometimes possible to catch a show in Tokyo, Kyoto or Osaka. Similarly, performances of *bunraku*, Japan's traditional puppet theater, are infrequent, but well worth going to the trouble of seeking out.

Kabuki derives from the verb *kabuku*, which means "to flirt," or "to frolic," and indeed it began in the form of lewd performances by all-women troupes. It was banned by the Tokugawa shogunate due to its associations with prostitution, but quickly revived in the form of all-male troupes, whose young male performers landed the nascent tradition in similar hot water. In the end the all-male troupes were composed of older men, and *kabuki* shed its lewd associations.

It's very much a performance of spectacle, marked by flamboyant costumes, stylized gestures and noisy musical accompaniments. The revolving stage, wide and low, is equipped with traps and has every mechanical trick known to pantomime. The *hanamichi* or "flower walk," which runs from the stage to the back of the auditorium, allows the actors to make the most of their entrances, and allows the audience to fully appreciate the fabulous costumes. The **Kabuki-za** ((03) 5565-6000 in Ginza, Tokyo, is the best place to see *kabuki*.

The medieval *no* theater has had a big influence on the avant-garde theater of the West. Its beauty lies in its hypnotic, mysterious dancing, its masks — some serene, some demonic — and in the atmosphere induced by the music of drums and flute, punctuated by low wails and whoops. In this unworldly setting, where rules of time and space seem to

be in suspension, old tales of loyalty, jealous passion and reincarnation unfold.

In Tokyo, the **Kanze No-gakudo** ((03) 3469-5241 and the **Hosho No-gakudo** ((03) 3811-4843 are two excellent places to see *no*, though performances are infrequent. Check *Tokyo Journal* or with the TIC in Tokyo for details of upcoming shows.

In Kyoto several other traditional theater (and musical) forms can be tasted in small doses at the **Gion Corner Theater** ((075) 561-1119, though it is an anodyne, highly touristic experience and many come away disappointed.

MUSEUMS

Japan has a profusion of excellent museums, and the best of them are attractions that are easily worth half a day or more of your time. In Tokyo a number of them are clustered together in Ueno Park. The pick of the pack is the **Tokyo National Museum**, which if you visit no other museum in Japan is the one you should go out of your way to see. Housing the world's largest collection of Japanese art treasures, it represents the country's single best overview of Japanese artistic achievement.

OPPOSITE: While the world of Japan's legendary geishas is one that few foreigners venture into, it is possible to see tourist-oriented performances in Tokyo and Kyoto. ABOVE: The tea ceremony, such as this one in Kamakura near Tokyo, is a ritual in which minute attention to every detail is observed.

Also in Tokyo is the **Edo-Tokyo Museum**, a fascinating futuristic building that takes visitors on a journey back in time to old Edo. It's highly recommended, especially if you are traveling with children.

In Nara, the **Nara National Museum** is home to some of Japan's priceless ancient treasures from the Nara region, and the treasure hall of Nara's **Horyu-ji Temple** contains yet more.

Also essential stops are either of the museum memorials to victims of the atomic bomb in **Hiroshima** and **Nagasaki**. Both provide moving accounts of the destruction wreaked on these cities and the suffering that occurred in the aftermath — a salutary experience for all of us who live in the modern world.

WAY OF TEA

Tea was introduced into Japan, together with Zen Buddhism, in the twelfth century, and was used by Zen monks as a way of warding off sleepiness during their long periods of meditation. They brewed and drank it in a formalized and starkly simple manner, and it was this ceremony which was adapted by laymen and became a popular pastime of the upper classes.

There are many schools of *cha-no-yu* (literally "tea's hot water"), but essentially they all follow a formalized procedure for the brewing, serving and drinking of tea in an environment in which attention has gone into every tiny detail. Tourists are often treated to performances of it, but it is far better to experience the tea ceremony as a participant. One place you can do this is at the **Kenkyusha Eigo Center** ((03) 5261-8940 in Tokyo, where you can take an afternoon or morning course. The **Hotel New Otani** ((03) 3265-1111 in Tokyo also has tea ceremonies that you can attend.

Shop till You Drop

Even the Japanese know that Japan is *takai*, or expensive, and come vacation time the airports are crammed with people heading overseas to enjoy the fruits of a yen salary in destinations where the price is right. But don't think for a minute that this means shopping can be scrubbed off the itinerary on a Japanese trip. Because Japan is the shopping nation *par excellence*, where a cliché like "shop till you drop" takes on new meaning. If you doubt this, simply call into one of Tokyo's massive department stores and think again — the capital is the place to see Japanese consumer culture at fever pitch. Even before you start thinking souvenirs, or perhaps electronic goodies, take some time out to explore Japan's retail world. In Japan, shopping is an experience.

Much is made of the fact that visiting (non-resident) foreigners are entitled to tax-free privileges on a range of goods, including cameras, audio and electrical equipment, watches and pearls. Essentially this means Japan's five-percent consumption tax is waived. The downside is this only applies in certain stores (notably in Tokyo the **Imperial** and **Palace Hotels** and the **Sukiyabashi Shopping Center** in Ginza; in Kyoto the **Kyoto Handicrafts Center**). Furthermore, if you shop around you may actually find the same goods at cheaper prices *with* the tax added.

Shop around. If you do opt to buy tax-free, remember to take your passport, and hold on to any documentation of the purchase, as you will have to surrender them to customs on leaving Japan. Customs may also demand to see your purchases, or, failing that, mailing receipts to prove you have sent them on.

ARTS AND CRAFTS
If you are looking for souvenirs or arts and crafts, the first place to (especially if you are in Tokyo) is the department stores. All the big department stores have floors devoted to arts and crafts, and they are good places to get an overview of what's available and the price ranges. There are periodic sales at the department stores too, so keep an eye on the local newspapers and listings magazines like *Tokyo Journal* and *Kansai Time Out* for the latest.

You will find shops devoted to specialty arts and crafts all over Japan, but Tokyo and Kyoto are the best places to trawl through the plenitude of Japan's possible souvenirs. In Tokyo try the **Tokyo Folkcraft and Antiques Hall**, where you will find some 30 stores gathered together and offering something of everything, usually at very reasonable prices. The **Oriental Bazaar** in Tokyo's Harajuku is something of a tourist institution these days, but it's nonetheless well worth a trip. It's a fascinating place to poke around in, and prices can be

surprisingly cheap for certain items. See SHOPPING, page 99 in TOKYO, for more information about these places, and also for information about regular flea markets, which can also be good hunting grounds for unusual crafty souvenirs.

In Kyoto, be sure to check out the **Kyoto Handicrafts Center**, a vast space devoted not just to Kyoto arts and crafts, but to a range of goods that covers regional traditions from around the country. You can even take a look at artisans plying their trade. The **Kyoto Craft Center** is a similar set-up and also worth visiting. See SHOPPING, page 146 under KYOTO, in KANSAI for more information.

Ceramics are a big business in Japan, and you can buy beautiful examples at any of the places noted above. But if you want something unique, try the pottery town of **Mashiko** (see page 121 in AROUND TOKYO), where you can see potters at work and buy directly from them.

ELECTRICAL GOODS AND CAMERAS
Japan is heaven for gadget freaks. Tokyo is the best place to shop for electrical items, but all major Japanese cities have their electrical districts. In Tokyo head to **Akihabara**, where a sign at the station indicating the direction to "Electric Town" will lead you into a bizarre

OPPOSITE: Souvenir fans tempt tourists, while the bright lights of Osaka's Dotomburi ABOVE constantly remind the visitor of Japan's best buys.

warren of neon and electrical gadgetry. You'll find all the latest products here, many of which are tested on the Japanese market before making an international appearance. Be sure to check that anything you buy is compatible with electrical standards in your home country.

Most of the world's most famous brands of cameras are Japanese, making Japan a good place to stock up on gear. Again, Tokyo is the place to shop for camera gear. See SHOPPING, page 99 in TOKYO, for information.

BOOKS AND CDS

Once you leave the big centers of Tokyo, Osaka, Kyoto, and to a lesser extent Sapporo and Fukuoka, finding reading material is a frustrating exercise. Stock up on books either before you get to Japan, or in Tokyo and Osaka. Tokyo has the best range, with **Kinokuniya**, now with two branches in Shinjuku, leading the way. Kinokuniya also stocks selections in French and German, though the range is modest compared to the impressively well-stocked English section.

Even if you are not in the market for CDs, which are reasonably priced in Japan, at least venture down to Shibuya if you are in Tokyo and pop into the massive **Tower Records**, where you will find every CD imaginable as well as an extensive book and magazine section.

Short Breaks

Japan is a compact destination with one of the world's most efficient transportation systems. What this means is that on even the briefest trips there is no reason why you should be stuck in the immediate vicinity of the airport you touch down in. Even, say, with a layover of only a couple of days in Tokyo,

spending one of them in Kyoto is not out of the question if you are prepared to splash out some money on the Shinkansen.

TOKYO

Tokyo is a city with enough attractions in its own right to keep you busy for as long as you are able to stay. That said, as fascinating as it is, it is a city, and its diversions and sights are only part of the Japanese experience. Fortunately, if you are looking for a taste of rural Japan and only have a short space of time in Tokyo, there are any number of interesting day trips you can make to destinations where Tokyo, as little as 45 minutes away, will seem like a distant dream.

Pick of the pack, in terms of convenience, is the rustic temple town of **Kamakura**. This former Japanese capital is almost a tiny, wooded version of Kyoto, and without the crowds (midweek at least). From Kamakura, it's possible to continue on by train to **Yokohama**, and conceivable, in a long day, to combine the destinations in a day trip. While Yokohama is far less interesting than Kamakura culturally, its **Minato Mirai** portside development is a mind-boggling "city of the future" experiment, and the city's **Chinatown** is a good place to take lunch.

Farther from Tokyo, just under two hours to the north, is **Nikko**, one of the country's top cultural attractions. If you are pressed for time, have spent a couple of days exploring

the streets of Tokyo and want a breathtaking glimpse of Japan's cultural assets, Nikko should be your first choice. **Tosho-gu Shrine**, a heady memorial to the warlord who unified Japan and made Edo (now Tokyo) its capital, rates among the country's foremost attractions.

Tokyo is littered with suburbs that end with the suffix "fujimi," or "**Mount Fuji** view." They remind us that the air in Tokyo is not what it used to be. Nowadays, to get a view of Japan's iconic peak, you will need to get on a train and head out of town. In fine weather, the best destination is **Hakone**, an hour and half from Shinjuku station. A destination in its own right, Hakone offers a fun-filled day in which a circuit that takes in an outdoor art museum, a soaring cable-car journey, a jaunt across a lake and the possibility of some hiking is accompanied throughout by postcard views of Mount Fuji.

OSAKA

With the completion of the impressive Kansai International Airport, Osaka has now become Japan's second major international gateway. The thing to bear in mind is that this is Kansai airport, not Osaka airport, and while Osaka is the nearest major city, the airport has good rail connections with both **Kyoto** and **Kobe**. Indeed, flying into Kansai gives you a wide range of places to be based, probably the best of which is Kyoto, which has a greater range of foreigner-friendly accommodation than anywhere in Japan. But

you might equally choose to spend a couple of days in much quieter Nara. No matter. Wherever you base yourself in Kansai, the rest of the region is on your doorstep and easily reached for any number of fascinating day-trips. Consider the following Shinkansen times: Osaka to Kyoto, 17 minutes; Osaka to Kobe, 15 minutes; Osaka to Himeji, 35 minutes; and so it goes.

How you want to juggle your time between the major Kansai destinations is a matter of personal preferences. You might choose to spend all your time exploring the temples and shrines of Kyoto, or you might opt for dining and nightlife in Osaka, or a combination of both. But it's worth considering taking a day-trip or two away from the nucleus of Kansai out to some of the more far-flung sights. A good choice is the castle town of **Himeji**. Easily undertaken in a day or morning, Japan's best-preserved and most visually stunning feudal-era castle provides a welcome contrast with the reconstructed castle in Osaka.

Also worth visiting, and a far cry from the fortifications of Japan's samurai past, is **Ise-jingu**, the country's most famous Shinto-shrine. Reconstructed every 25 years,

OPPOSITE: Nagoya's castle may be a reconstruction but it still evokes old feudal Japan, particularly as here when its walls are draped in winter snow. ABOVE: Nikko's famous monkeys steadfastly hear no evil, speak no evil and see no evil.

the shrine is a modest structure, and yet there is an otherworldly quality about this place, which reaches far back into the soul of Japan before the arrival of Buddhism.

If you have time for an overnight stay somewhere outside the Kansai heartland and you are looking for a uniquely Japanese experience away from the crowds, consider **Mount Koya-san**, an ancient Buddhist temple retreat that now offers the opportunity to overnight in a temple. Some may balk at the idea of no meat, no alcohol, early to bed and up at the crack of dawn, but it's doubtful it will be an experience you will forget in a hurry — the kind of experience that is definitive of travel.

Festive Flings

The Japanese year is marked by a colorful roll-call of festivals far too numerous to enumerate in full — that is a subject worthy of a book of its own. They divide broadly into *matsuri*, which are local festivals usually of Shinto origin, and *nenchu gyoji*, the annual, nationwide festive days — many of them formalized as national holidays — that break up the calendar year.

NATIONAL FESTIVALS

The Japanese year kicks off with **O-shogatsu**, the New Year holiday, when nearly all shops and offices close for several days and people swarm by the million to popular shrines such as Meiji in Tokyo to pray for a good year. Special food is eaten — all prepared, in theory, before January 1, so that Mom can take a rest, too. Kites are flown, and an ancient form of battledore, or shuttlecock, is enjoyed. Around midnight on New Year's Eve the bells of Buddhist temples boom out 108 times across cities, towns and villages, marking the time to gulp down bowls of *soba* (buckwheat noodles).

On January 15, Japan erupts into color when girls and boys who have reached the age of 20 during the previous 365 days celebrate the event with shrine-visiting and parties, the girls dressed in traditional kimono. This is **Seijin-no-hi**, or Adult's Day.

Boys and girls who are yet to become adults have their own special days, girls on March 3 — **Hina Matsuri** — and boys on May 5 — **Tango-no-sekku**. In both cases traditional dolls are dusted off and admired. In the lead-up to boy's day, brightly painted cotton carp-shaped windsocks can be seen flying from high poles in many gardens. Boys are exhorted to be as brave as the carp, which fights its way upstream.

The spring and autumn equinoxes, *higan*, have a significance in Japan that they have long lost in most countries the West. At these times the sun sets dead in the west, which is the location of the heavenly Pure Land according to one school of Buddhism, so at *higan*, graves are visited and prayers offered for the repose of the dead.

The biggest festival in honor of ancestors, however, occurs in August and is called **O-bon**. This is the year's second major holiday, after O-shogatsu, and many millions of Japanese with roots in the countryside return to their home towns. The spirits of the dead are welcomed back into the home, the family taking lanterns to the graveyard to light their way. As part of the general party, made lively by the *bon-odori* dancing, small portions of the dead ones' preferred foods are set aside for them, and on the last night of the holiday, paper-lantern boats are set afloat on local streams and rivers to light the spirits' way back to the celestial world.

Another occasion for kimono-viewing is the **Shichi-go-san** (Seven-five-three) festival on November 15. On this day, girls of seven, boys of five, and three-year-olds of either sex are dressed up in finery — at vast expense — and taken to visit local shrines.

MATSURI

The big annual holidays described above can be interesting to observe for the foreigner visiting Japan, but for the most part they are family affairs during which the shops and many restaurants close, and transport around the country becomes clogged. Of far more interest are the hundreds of local *matsuri* that bring color and excitement to the passing year. They take on many forms, sometimes solemn, sometimes boisterous, but they are never dull.

It is the local shrine which, all over Japan, is the focus of such festivals. There, locked away behind heavy doors, are the *mikoshi*, the miniature portable shrines in which the shrine's deity is said to reside for the duration of its day out. Supervised by an aged priest, the young blades of the area, looking their most macho in sweat bands, *happi* coats and straw sandals, heave the weighty shrine aloft on poles and begin their long, cheerful and grueling parade around the neighborhood.

The biggest of the matsuri, broken down by region, are as follows.

Kyoto's Spring Boat Festival commemorates the frequent trips down the Oi River made by the Heian emperor and his court.

TOKYO

On January 6, **Dezome-shiki**, firemen parade through the streets at Chuo-dori, Harumi (Tsukiji subway station), giving displays of traditional acrobatics on top of tall bamboo ladders.

In mid-May of even-numbered years, **Kanda Myojin Shrine** (a short walk from Ochanomizu subway station) is host to one of Japan's big three festivals, with fantastic *mikoshi* displays and frequent performances of ancient dances.

For **Sanja Matsuri**, on the third Friday, Saturday and Sunday each May, Senso-ji Temple in Asakusa becomes a riot of activity, with parades, music and ceremonies by Shinto priests.

From June 10 to 16 in odd-numbered years, Hie-jinja in Akasaka hosts the other of Tokyo's two great *matsuri*, **Sanno Matsuri**, with dancers, wood-wheeled carts, *mikoshi* and gilded lions' heads.

Asakusa puts on Tokyo's greatest fireworks display from 7:15 PM to 8:15 PM on the last Saturday in July for **Sumida-gawa River Hanabi Taikai.**

NIKKO

The **Grand Festival of Tosho-gu Shrine**, held on May 17 and 18, is the occasion for a procession that recreates the days of the Tokugawa shogunate against the background of Japan's most gorgeous shrine.

KAMAKURA

Tsurugaoka Hachiman-gu Spring Festival is held from the second to the third Sunday in April, when Kamakura celebrates the cherry blossom season with costumed parades and performances.

Kamakura's biggest shrine hosts **Hachiman-gu Matsuri** in mid-September, with costumed performances of *yabusame*, the martial art of archery on horseback, held in the grounds of the shrine.

HAKONE

For **Hakone Daimyo Gyoretsu**, November 3, 200 to 300 people dress as feudal lords (*daimyo*) and parade through the streets of the handsome old spa town of Hakone-Yumoto, with a festival in the evening1.

SHIMODA

Held at Gyokunsen-ji Temple, Shimoda, **Kurofune Matsuri**, from May 16 to 18, commemorates the arrival of the American Commodore Perry's "black ships" (*kurofune*) in 1853, which resulted in Japan opening to international trade.

KYOTO

Aoi Matsuri is held on May 15 at Kamigamo and Shimogamo shrines, to celebrate a Heian period (794–1185) festival with a costumed procession of an imperial messenger and his retinue accompanied by a cart with huge wooden wheels decorated with wisteria flowers and drawn by a garlanded ox led by ropes of orange silk.

On the third Sunday of May, **Mifune Matsuri**, boats mounted with dragon heads and phoenixes sail down the River Oi bearing musicians, in commemoration of the river-borne excursions of the Heian court at the Oi River, Arashiyama, near Kyoto.

Gion Matsuri is held from July 17 to 24 in Yasaka-jinja Shrine in Gion. This is perhaps Japan's most famous festival, with towering, teetering carts dragged through the streets, all of ancient origin and each with a story to tell.

On August 15 to 16, **Daimonji Okuribi**, a great bonfire on Mount Nyoiga-dake burns in the shape of the character *Dai*, or "Great," visible for miles.

For **Jidai Matsuri**, held on October 22, Heian-jingu Shrine is host to the "Festival of the Ages," in which a long procession showcases the sartorial fashions of Japanese aristocracy, starting with the Meiji period (1868–1912) and working backwards to the nobles and archers of the eighth century.

NARA

On February 3 or 4, all 3,000 lanterns of Kasuga-taisha Shrine are lit for **Mando-e**, welcoming the coming of spring. The same lantern-lighting festival occurs again on August 14 or 15.

Onio-shiki is held near February 4 (it varies year to year). For the *Setsubun* (the annual festival in which demons are driven from homes) Kofuku-ji Temple is invaded by men dressed as demons, who are chased away by priests.

From March 1 to 14 for **O-mizutori Matsuri**, huge torches illuminate Todai-ji Temple and the eerie wailing of conches echoes through the air, culminating at midnight March 12, when holy water is drawn from the Wakasa well.

OSAKA

Tenjin Matsuri, held on July 24 or 25 at Osaka's Temman-gu Shrine, is one of Japan's major festivals, with lion dances and spectacular drumming performances.

A quiet moment in the lead-up to the pageantry of Nikko's Grand Spring Festival at Tosho-gu Shrine, one of Japan's most colorful festivals.

HI MEJI

Kenka Matsuri, October 14 to 15, is the occasion for *mikoshi*-bearing teams to do battle at Matsubara Hachiman-gu Shrine, jostling and barging one another in an effort to come in first — injuries are common.

MIYA-JIMA

For **Kangen-sai Matsuri**, held in mid-July, a fleet of brightly decorated boats makes a sea parade accompanied by *gagaku*, the ancient music of the imperial court.

TAKAYAMA

Twelve of Takayama's 23 enormous and fabulously ornate *yatai*, or festival wagons, are covered in carvings and tapestriesand dragged through the streets for **Sanno Matsuri** on April 14 and 15, some carrying mechanical figures that perform tricks. The other 11 Takayama festival floats get the same treatment for **Takayama Matsuri**, on October 9 to 10.

KANAZAWA

Hyakuman-goku-sai, on June 13 to 15, is when geisha and old-fashioned firemen parade through the streets, and demonstrations of the tea ceremony are held at Oyama-jinja Shrine.

SENDAI

Tanabata Matsuri, August 6 to 8, celebrates the annual reunion of two heavenly lovers, with colorful paper lanterns and street festivities.

MATSUSHIMA

The island-sprinkled waters of this famous bay become awash with thousands of tiny floating lanterns for **Matsushima Toronagashi**, held on August 16.

AOMORI

Two million people pour into Aomori from August 1 to 7 to witness **Nebuta Matsuri**, the spectacle of huge, beautifully painted and illuminated papier-mâché floats being hauled drunkenly through the city, followed by parades and traditional drummers — the last two days are the most dramatic.

AKITA

From August 5 to 7, for **Kanto Matsuri**, the boys and men of the city balance huge bamboo frameworks covered with lanterns and weighing some 60 kg (132 lb) on their foreheads, shoulders, hips, hands and even mouths as they parade the streets to the accompaniment of traditional music.

SAPPORO

In the first or second week of February, Sapporo takes advantage of its freezing winter with a famously kitschy festival of snow sculpture, **Yuki Matsuri**, plus a costumed parade and skating.

SHIKOKU

On August 15 to 18, the season of *O-bon*, Tokushima is host to three days of drinking and festivities, **Awa Odori**.

NAGASAKI

Suwa-jinja Shrine clebrates Chinese-influenced **Okunchi Matsuri** from October 7 to 9, with gaudy carts and dragon dances.

Galloping Gourmet

If you are prepared to be a little adventurous, one of the highlights of a trip to Japan is the food. It is a fascinating cuisine that has evolved through the convergence of many influences — among them Zen Buddhist, Chinese, Korean and latterly Western. There is little surprise that it has had a profound influence in the West, providing much of the inspiration for the development of nouvelle cuisine.

The Japanese diet has undergone some revolutionary changes from the Meiji period (1868–1912) onwards, with the introduction and acceptance of meat eating, previously taboo due to Buddhism, and the consequent development of dishes like *sukiyaki* and *tonkatsu*, which are now standards of Japanese cuisine but actually of only recent provenance. This is not to mention the invasion of Western standards like pizza, French fries, hamburgers and omelets, most of which Japanese are as much at home with as sushi nowadays. But, despite this, traditional Japanese cuisine still thrives in the form of *kaiseki* (banquet cuisine), sushi and sashimi restaurants, Zen vegetarian restaurants (often in temples), and in countless Japanese-style *soba* and *udon* restaurants across the country. Indeed, a journey to Japan is as much an adventure in food as it is in a foreign culture.

KAISEKI

The ultimate Japanese culinary experience is *kaiseki*, or imperial cuisine. At its best, it is served in an environment that replicates the simple and yet meticulously prepared qualities of the food — an echo from the genesis of *kaiseki* as an accompaniment to the tea ceremony. Today *kaiseki* is usually accompanied by sake (not drunk with rice, and hence you will get no rice with your meal, or not at least until the meal is all served), and while there may appear a fussiness in the presentation and delivery of the dishes, the idea in fact is that it should be a relaxing, convivial occasion in which a succession of nibbles and drinks are consumed amidst fine conversation.

The serving of dishes follows a strict order. First come the appetizers, usually sashimi, or perhaps pickles, with *suimono* (a clear soup). Steamed dishes usually follow, and after, or sometimes at the same time, will come simmered dishes and a dressed salad. More soup follows — always a miso soup — after which, finally, comes the rice with pickles (*tsukemono*) as an accompaniment. For many foreigners there is an effervescent quality to *kaiseki*, and it is easy to come away with the feeling of not having eaten to the full. The problem, in part, derives from the fact that *kaiseki* is less a sit-down meal than an occasion. For anyone focused simply on the act of eating and not on an entertaining evening accompanied by an unceasing flow of morsels, it can be a slightly disappointing experience — to enjoy it at its best, partake with a group.

SUSHI AND SASHIMI

As an island country, fish has been central to the Japanese diet for centuries. Due to the recent spread of Japanese restaurants around the world, raw fish is not the object of shock and horror it once was. As with many alien

foods — frogs' legs, snails — most of the difficulty is in the mind. Once the first sliver of really good *maguro* (tuna) has melted on your tongue, objections are likely to evaporate in the sweet smell of sake.

Sashimi is raw fish, plain and simple. Fine slices of a variety of fish are dipped in soy sauce flavored with *wasabi* (fiery-flavored Japanese horseradish). *Nigirizushi* are slices of raw fish, shellfish, shrimp or sweet Japanese omelet, laid on thumb-sized portions of sweetened, vinegared rice and presented in pairs. Ideally eaten in one bite, it can first be lightly brushed in a platter of soy sauce. It is usually accompanied by green tea and pickled ginger.

Sushi shops come in many grades of quality, though you are unlikely to come across one that is truly bad — such restaurants simply don't stay in business. For the budget conscious, try a *kaiten-zushi* restaurant, of which there are no end of in Japan — the sushi sits on plates that make circuits of a central bar area on a conveyor belt. Take the ones you want, and you will be charged at the end of the meal according to how many empty plates you have.

OPPOSITE: Koto players entertain the crowds below Japan's most perfectly preserved castle — Himeji — during the brief but widely celebrated blooming of the cherry blossoms. ABOVE: Many Japanese dishes are "do-it-yourself" requiring a certain adeptness with chopsticks.

FUGU

One fish eaten *sashimi*-style, though only at restaurants that specialize in it, is *fugu*, or globefish. The liver and ovaries of *fugu* contain a deadly poison, and in a much quoted incident in 1975 a *fugu* meal killed a famous *kabuki* actor. Nowadays *fugu* chefs are all licensed by the government and deaths are all but unheard of. Has this done away with the fun? Some gourmets say so, maintaining that the slightly mouth-numbing effect of the poison (taken in very small quantities) is part of the pleasure. *Fugu* is at its best — and safest — in the winter months, and is also eaten *nabe*-style, as part of a delicious stew.

SUKIYAKI AND SHABU-SHABU

With the Western influences of the Meiji period (1868–1912) came the dilution of long-maintained Buddhist strictures on the consumption of four-legged creatures. Nevertheless, when Japanese took to beef, they did it in unique style, finely slicing it and simmering it in a flavored stock. The dish is called *sukiyaki* (pronounced "ski-yaki") and along with *shabu-shabu* is among the Japanese dishes most commonly offered to foreign visitors. It might be a relative newcomer to the Japanese repertoire, but it is none the less delicious for that.

Sukiyaki is a particularly fine winter dish, cooked at the table with onions, mushrooms and other vegetables, jelly-like *konnyaku* or *shirataki* and tofu, in a delicious broth of stock, soy sauce and sweet sake. The same goes for *shabu-shabu*, a similarly thin-sliced beef dish in which diners dip ingredients for a few moments into a pan of boiling stock, before then dunking it in a soy-based sauce. Finally, *udon* — wheat flour noodles — are cooked in

the boiling water and similarly dunked, in place of rice. *Shabu-shabu* is an onomatopoeic word which is supposed to suggest the sound of the beef hitting the boiling water — "slap-slap."

TEMPURA

Tempura, another favorite with visitors, is the Japanese answer to fish and chips, minus the chips. The basic idea arrived with the Portuguese in the sixteenth century and has been Japanized into a crisp, deep-fried delicacy. Items which drop, fresh and battered, into the deep oil include eggplant, *shiso* leaves (perilla), slices of lotus root and carrot, as well as shrimp, *kisu* (a variety of salmon) and many other types of fish. Presented to the customer on absorbent paper which soaks up the grease, it is dipped in a soy-based broth before eating.

TONKATSU

Ton means "pork" and *katsu* is a Japanese approximation of the word "cutlet." Together they spell *"tonkatsu,"* another dish born of Western influence, and now a staple in the Japanese diet. A breaded, deep-fried chop, it is served either on a bed of rice, as *katsudon*, or as part of a *teishoku* (set meal) with raw cabbage, slices of lemon, *miso* soup and rice. At a good shop it's great.

Another cheap and popular *domburi*-style (served on rice) dish is *oyakodon* (literally "parent-and-child" — a mixture of chicken and egg).

ODEN

Few foreigners take to *oden*, a popular winter dish in which items such as *kamaboko* ("fish sausage"), *daikon* (Japanese white radish), deep-fried tofu and hard-boiled eggs are simmered in a pot and served on a plate with a dab of mustard. Look out for *oden* stands in tiny, portable, tent-like bars that can be found in the streets near train stations in busy parts of Tokyo and elsewhere. Make your selection from the bubbling pans of *oden* by pointing and wash it down with beer or cheap, hot sake.

NOODLES

Cup noodles may have wormed their way onto supermarket shelves the world over, but this shouldn't put you off sampling some of Japan's many varieties of noodles.

Basically they divide into Japanese-style (*soba* and *udon*) and Chinese-style (*ramen*). It's the latter variety that most foreigners take to the quickest. Not that there's much that's Chinese about them. The nearest equivalent would be the noodle soups of Guangdong. But the Japanese, in true Japanese style, have taken this poor-man's Cantonese dish and turned it in a uniquely Japanese, delicious meal that now has countless regional variations ranging from plain silly (try "milk *ramen*") to inspired (the now standard "*miso ramen*").

You'll find *ramen* restaurants everywhere in Japan, but notably in areas with nightlife, where they are invariably open late to accommodate the appetites of after-hours drinkers. Many *ramen* eaters will take a side order of grilled dumplings (*gyoza*), which together with the noodles makes for a substantial meal for around ¥1,000.

Soba and *udon* are both home-grown noodle varieties, and tend to be less filling than *ramen*, making them good options for lunch, less so for dinner. *Soba* are made with buckwheat flour, while the thicker *udon* are made with plain flour. The tastes of both are more subtle than with *ramen*, and to a Western palate can sometimes seem bland.

In summer, *soba* is often served cold on a bamboo screen, to be dunked into a cold sauce before eating The cloudy liquid in the lacquerware teapot that arrives with the cold *soba* is the water it was boiled in. When you've finished eating, pour this hot water into what remains of your dunking sauce and quaff it.

No matter what kind of noodles you eat, slurping is *de rigueur*. Japanese will tell you that noisy slurping makes noodles taste better. Try it if you like, but be sure to break yourself of the habit before you go home.

RED LANTERN BARS

A red paper lantern hanging outside a restaurant — or outside a little cart — means it's a *nomi-ya*, "drinking shop." But the Japanese never drink without eating at the same time, and that doesn't mean just peanuts. *Tsumami* is the word for an appetizer accompanying beer or sake — be careful not to say "*tsunami*" which is a tidal wave caused by an earthquake — and they come in all shapes and sizes.

At the **Nombe** chain, for example, which has numerous branches in Tokyo, appetizers include *atsuage* (deep-fried tofu), *nikuzume* (green peppers stuffed with meat) and *wakame-su* (vinegared seaweed salads). Add such items as fried chicken, *kawa-ebi* (fried shrimp) and *nabe-mono* (stew-like foods, marvelously warming in winter) and it's easy to see that your appetizer can swell into a full-blown meal. If it does, you may feel like finishing up with *o-chazuke*, boiled rice with pickled sour plum, *nori* (seaweed) and peppery spices, with hot green tea poured

over the whole lot. This dish is customarily prepared by long-suffering wives to help their tipsy husbands sober up, but you can enjoy it just as well in a restaurant.

Yakitori is a rough delicacy you will also find at the sign of the red lantern. *Yakitori-ya* restaurants, found by the dozen close to major railway stations in office areas such as Shibuya, Shinjuku and Yurakucho, are perhaps the closest Japanese equivalent to the English pub: down-to-earth, noisy, cheerful and relatively cheap. *Yakitori* are bits of chicken and other fowl such as quail, duck and sparrow, often taken from highly improbable parts of the bird's body, spitted on a stick, dipped in sauce and barbecued.

No particular *yakitori-ya* cries out to be recommended and phone numbers are beside the point. Just head for that friendly looking joint crowded with flush-faced salarymen and find a seat. Pointing to likely looking items being devoured by the people around you is a quite acceptable way to order.

Another cheap and cheerful dish worth knowing about is *okonomiyaki*, a favorite with students. It is a sort of do-it yourself filled omelet. The waiter brings the ingredients of the meal, which might include cuttlefish and vegetables as well as egg, and the diners cook for themselves on the hotplate built into the table.

LEFT: The classic Japanese breakfast. ABOVE: *Sake* is the national drink though beer and whisky are also very popular.

IZAKAYA

The atmosphere of an old country farmhouse in the middle of Tokyo — that's what the popular *izakaya*, or *robata-yaki* restaurants offer. Surrounded by tasteful reminders of country life — straw raincoats, bamboo snow-shoes, old farming implements — the diners sit at a counter or around an old wooden hearth. Like the hostelries described above, the focus of interest at *robata-yaki* is drinking, but the *tsumami* at the *robata* (grill) are varied and appetizing and include everything from french fries to *miso*-topped eggplant and bamboo shoots. All the evening's ingredients are displayed at the counter (as in a *sushi* shop), so if you sit there you can order merely by pointing. After it has been cooked, the dish of your choice may arrive on the end of a paddle with an immensely long handle. In most modern *robata-yaki* the grill is gas-fired.

DRINKS

Whatever the *nomi-ya* you wind up in, selecting your drink is not a problem. Beer, sake and whisky — these are the three options, wherever you go.

Beer usually means one of the excellent Japanese-made lagers, some of which have been on the market for a 100 years and more. All brands are drinkable but Kirin is the most popular, while Yebisu is probably the best. Bottled beer is usually known as "draft" or *nama*, just to confuse things.

Sake is the national drink: Chinese who visited Japan nearly two millennia ago noted that the Japanese were getting drunk on it even then. In those days the fermentation was set in motion by having shrine virgins chew mouthfuls of rice then spit the mushy result into casks, where the enzyme in human saliva set to work. Conditions of hygiene have improved a lot since then, but the price has gone up too. The protection offered for political reasons to Japanese farmers means that Japanese rice is three times the price it is anywhere else in the world, and sake is as a result a good deal more expensive than beer, which is mostly made from imported barley.

It's a splendid tipple all the same. Taken hot in the winter it is wonderfully warming, though the best-quality sake may be drunk cold in all seasons. If you don't mix it with other drinks, it should leave you with an uncannily clear head the next morning.

If it doesn't, you were probably drinking in a cheap place where the sake is cut, quite legally, with industrial alcohol and other additives to reduce the price. Sake made with rice and nothing else accounts for only one percent of national production, and most of that is made in small breweries in the country.

Sake sold in liquor stores in large *issh-o* bottles containing about half a gallon comes in three grades of quality: *tokkyu* (special class), *ikkyu* (first class) and *nikyu* (second class). Sweet sake is called *amakuchi*: the dry variety which most Westerners prefer is called *karakuchi*. If you are keen to try 100-percent rice sake ask for *kome hyaku-pa-cento*.

The history of Japanese whisky goes back to the beginning of this century. The best is fine, and contains a considerable proportion of malt whisky, imported in bulk from Scotland. Most Japanese drink it as *mizuwari* with ice and lots of water. Many pubs and "snacks" operate a keep-bottle system: the customer buys a bottle of whisky and writes his name on the label, and can come back and tipple from it whenever he likes, paying only for ice and appetizers.

LUNCH BOXES

A special treat unique to Japan is the *eki-ben* or station lunchbox. Japanese food fits the lunch-box format well: small quantities of a variety of different things agreeably presented. *Makunouchi-bento* is the version most commonly found nationwide and typically consists of small pieces of fried chicken and seafood, *kamaboko* (fish paste sausage), *shumai* (Chinese-style meat dumplings), boiled or vinegared vegetables, pickles and a field of boiled rice with a pickled plum (*umeboshi*) dead center, suggesting the Japanese flag.

But many other types are encountered when traveling, some presented in charming wooden cases or ceramic pots. Just ask for *bento* on the platform of any large station, study the photographs of the contents on display and try your luck. It's the cheapest and arguably the best way of eating on the move.

Note, too, that *bento* are also available from supermarkets, department stores, and even from stalls on the street. Be prepared for both disappointments and pleasant surprises.

ORDERING

The only serious problem for the adventurous gourmet out and about in Japan is language. Many is the time the grateful visitor has opened a menu, on the cover of which the restaurant's name and the word "menu" are boldly printed in flawless English, only to find that the dishes themselves are described only in flawless Japanese.

Snack time at the Asakusa Kannon Temple in Tokyo. Small sticks of grilled meat and fish balls bridge the gap between meals.

There is usually a way out of this fix. A great many restaurants have wax or plastic replicas of the food on offer displayed in the window. Just take the waitress out to the front and point. Pointing, this time at the actual ingredients, is also recommended in *sushi* shops and *robata-yaki* (though in the former there may be models of set dinners to help you as well). Sit at the counter as close as possible to the person in charge.

If there is nothing to point at and no one is willing to help you out, retire with dignity and, if it smells as if it's worth it, resolve to return to fight again another day with your secret weapon: a Japanese-speaking companion.

However warm and helpful the service, don't leave a tip on the table: more than likely your waiter will come down the street after you to return it. Tipping is not the custom in Japan.

Special Interests

More so than any other Asian destination besides perhaps China, many people go to Japan to study. Almost everything uniquely Japanese can be studied somewhere, providing you can afford the somewhat formidable living expenses. If your interests run to the arcane, or simply anything not covered below, your first stop should be the TICs in Tokyo or Kyoto, which have volumes of information on study and special interests in Japan.

JAPANESE LANGUAGE

Japanese language is the most popular study subject for foreigners in Japan. It's probably a good idea to get some grounding in the language before arriving, but it's also possible to start from the very basics in Japan itself. Schools abound in Japan, some good, some bad. If in doubt, get a copy of the TIC's *Japanese & Japanese Studies* brochure, which lists all schools that are government accredited. If you choose to study at a school that isn't, you take your chances.

Enumerating the myriad schools, colleges and universities offering Japanese language study is a subject that deserves a book of its own, and making recommendations of schools is difficult. A good place to start getting an overview of schools is the **Association for the Promotion of Japanese Language** WEB SITE www.rim.or.jp/nisshinkyo/mcntr.cgi, which has a list of approved schools with information about their courses.

If you are planning a long stay in Japan, you can put off making a decision about which school you want to study at until you arrive. Many smaller schools have flexible schedules that allow you to start classes almost immediately. The two best sources of information about such schools are the magazines *Nihongo Journal* and the *Hiragana Times*, both of which are also good magazines for learning and practicing Japanese. They're available in bookshops in Japan, and *Nihongo Journal* is available worldwide.

ZEN AND BUDDHISM

A good starting point for those interested in studying Zen or Buddhism in general in Japan is the **Buddhist English Academy** ((03) 342-6605, 802 Diamond Place, 3-5-3 Nishi Shinjuku, Shinjuku-ku, Tokyo, where English is spoken and where information is available on courses provided by all the main sects of Japanese Buddhism. Alternatively, before arriving in Japan, check the **Buddhist Asia Directory** WEB SITE www.buddhanet.net/abc_j.htm for contact details of many of Japan's temples offering courses.

The **Soto School of Zen**, which along with Rinzai is Japan's biggest, is the most open to foreign students, and most of its main temples around Japan offer one-day or longer courses. For a complete list of the temples around Japan, with contact details and times, check their WEB SITE www.sotozen-net.or.jp/kokusai/list.htm.

In Tokyo **Tosho-ji Temple** ((03) 3781-4235 offers accommodation and early morning (that's *early*) *zazen* meditation, for those who are very serious about experiencing Zen. In Kyoto, contact the **International Zen Center**

(0771) 23-1784, which is actually in Inukai, some distance from Kyoto. Accommodation and *zazen* is available for those who make arrangements by phone or by E-MAIL Genpo-HR-Doering@t-online.de beforehand.

TEA CEREMONY

Much better than simply watching it acted out on a stage is to actually participate in the tea ceremony. In Tokyo it's possible to do this at numerous places, notably at luxury hotels in the Akasaka area. The **New Otani** ((03) 3265-1111, the **Hotel Okura** ((03) 3582-0111, and the **Imperial Hotel** ((03) 3504-1111 in Ginza all offer tea ceremony classes on weekdays. For a more serious insight into the art, the **Kenkyusha Eigo Center** ((03) 5261-8940, in Iidabashi, Tokyo, not only offers one-day courses, but also month-long courses. In Kyoto the **Urasenke Tea Ceremony School** ((075) 451-8516 has an afternoon English-language course that provides an introduction to the art before allowing students to experience the ceremony itself.

CERAMICS AND POTTERY

Japanese ceramics and pottery are famous, and with good reason. Practiced in Japan for some 12,000 years, native traditions have coexisted with more sophisticated glazing techniques imported from China in the thirteenth century to create a particular rich range of crafts. Today potters and their kilns can be found throughout Japan, though notably in central and western Honshu, and in Kyushu.

OPPOSITE: A Kyoto artisan fashions noh masks for a theater group. ABOVE: The interesting showroom of Kei Tanimoto, a traditional potter working in Iga, near Kyoto.

Kyoto is a good place to get an overview of Japan's rich ceramic traditions. The **Tojiki Kaikan** ((075) 541-1102, in Higashiyama, mostly features local ceramics, but also has examples from farther afield, though the idea here is to sell you ceramics.

To try your hand at pottery or, if you have already studied, to take advanced classes, the most famous destination in Japan is **Mashiko** (see page 121 in AROUND TOKYO). A number of Western potters have gone to Mashiko and made it their home, and as a result some of the kilns have established courses for foreigners. Some of the more famous include: the **Mashiko Ceramic Art Center** ((0285) 72-7555; **Tsukamoto** ((0285) 72-5151; **Mashiko Togei Juku** ((285) 72-7521; **Hasegawa Toen** ((0285) 72-6161; and **Togei Mura Village** ((0285) 72-5955.

Taking a Tour

For a first-time visit to Japan, a tour can take a lot of the anxiety out of getting around, finding accommodation and ordering food, all of which can be stressful at first. Essentially, there are two ways to approach touring Japan. You might of course simply book a tour from home, and lists of recommended agencies for doing so are included below. Alternatively, you might pre-book your accommodation, and join a tour once you arrive. **JTB's Sunrise Tours** ((03) 5620-9500 runs a vast array of packages, ranging from straight-out knock-off-the-sights excursions to special-interest outings. Too numerous to list here, they are, however, listed in full on the JTB WEB SITE www.jtb.co.jp/sunrisetour/esunrisetop.html, where prices are included and it is also possible to make online reservations.

Some international tour operators are listed below.

UNITED STATES AND CANADA
Abercrombie & Kent International ((630) 954-2944 TOLL-FREE (800) 323-7308 FAX (630) 954-3324 E-MAIL info@abercrombiekent.com, 1520 Kensington Road, Oak Brook, Illinois 60523, is one of the big names of package tourism, and offers not only tours to Japan but to destinations all around the world. They have a good selection of Japanese tours, mostly along the conventional highlights lines, but also high-end tailor-made tours.

For a less conventional approach to Japan, try **Geographic Expeditions** ((415) 922-0448 E-MAIL info@geoex.com, 2627 Lombard Street, San Francisco, California 94123, which offers tours to less obvious destinations and also provides specia-interest tours.

For even more adventurous tours, including mountain trekking, **Worldwide Adventures** ((416) 633-5666 FAX (416) 633-8667 WEB SITE www.worldwidequest.com, Suite 45, 1170 Sheppard Avenue West, Toronto, Ontario M3K 2A3, is recommended. **Pacific Rim Travel Corporation** ((250) 380-4888 TOLL-FREE (800) 663-1559 FAX (250) 380-7917 E-MAIL pacrimtc@pinc.com, 8-1501 Glentana Road, Victoria, British Columbia V9A 7B2, is another Canadian operator with Japanese tours.

BRITAIN
One of the most knowledgeable agencies when it comes to touring Japan is **Creative Tours** ((020) 7495-1775 FAX (020) 7499-7699 WEB SITE www.jaltour.co.uk/index.html, Second Floor, No. 1 Tenterden Street, London W1R 9AH, an agent for Jaltour. They can organize Rail Passes, and have a selection of tours; from destinations such as Tokyo and Kyoto to some more unusual possibilities.

For specialist tours, try the **Nippon Travel Agency** ((020) 7437-2929 FAX (020) 7437-2946 WEB SITE www.nta.co.jp/english/index.htm, Third Floor, Academy House, 161-167 Oxford Street, London W1R 1TA, the world's longest-running Japan specialist, with offices worldwide.

The **Imaginative Traveler** ((0209) 742-8612 FAX (208) 742-3045 WEB SITE www.imaginative-traveller.com, 14 Barley Mow Passage, Chiswick, London W4 4PH, offers interesting alternatives to the fly-in, fly-out conventional tours, in the form of tours that approach Japan via the Trans-Siberian.

CONTINENTAL EUROPE

Swiss-based **Kuoni Travel** has tours not only of Japan but of other Asian destinations. They have many offices around the region, including one in the United Kingdom: Kuoni ((01306) 740500 FAX (01306) 744222, Kuoni House, Dorking, Surrey, RH5 4AZ, England; **Voyages Kuoni** ((01) 42 85 71 22 FAX (01) 40 23 06 26,

95 rue d'Amsterdam, F-75008 Paris, France; **Reiseburo Kuoni** ((089) 2311-1630 FAX (089) 2311-1650, Furstenfelderstrasse 7, D-80331 Munich, Germany; **Kuoni Travel** (Head Office) ((01) 277-4444 FAX (01) 272-0071, Neue Hard No. 7, CH-8037 Zurich, Switzerland.

AUSTRALIA

Adventure World ((02) 9956-7766, 76 Walker Street, North Sydney, offers tours of Japan, as does one of Australia's most well established tour operators, **Flight Centres International** — Sydney ((02) 9267-2999, Bathurst Street (corner of George Street), North Sydney 2090; Melbourne ((03) 9600-0799 TOLL-FREE 1800-679943, Level 7, 343 Little Collins Street, Melbourne 3000; Brisbane ((07) 3229 5917 TOLL-FREE 1800-500204, Level 13, 157 Ann Street, Brisbane 4000.

The peaks of the Japanese Alps become like Ginza during the climbing season.

Welcome
to
Japan

IN HIS INTRODUCTION TO *THE ROADS TO SATA*, ALLAN BOOTH WRITES SIMPLY: "The Japanese are 120,000,000 people, ranging in age from 0 to 119, in geographical location across 21 degrees of latitude and 23 degrees of longitude, and in profession from emperor to urban guerrilla."

That was in 1985; there are 127 million now, and it is reasonable to suppose that the 119-year-old is not among them. But the sentiments are as valid as ever. Despite the endless theorizing about Japan and "the Japanese," a journey to Japan is a journey to a place that is a composite of particulars. Just as Japan is a different place for every Japanese, so it is for every traveler.

This is all the more true because of the baggage we take with us. Few destinations invite more of it. The land of Walkmans, hatchbacks, Zen, sushi and company anthems is a place we all recognize in some way or another. People might scratch their heads at the mention of, say, Laos, but when it comes to Japan everybody has been there in their imagination.

The real Japan, however, is many things. It might very well be that much touted vision of gray-suited hordes, ground down by the overtime shift, commuting cheek-by-jowl to a rabbit-hutch "mansion." But then it's equally the rolling meadows of Hokkaido, an old farmhouse converted into an inn with hot-spring water piped in for the baths.

The only certainty about Japan is that it is everything you think it is and simultaneously everything you think it is not. In other words, the only certainty — besides the fact it's going to be expensive — you have as a traveler is that it will surprise. Provided you're prepared to have your preconceptions turned on their head one minute and confirmed the next, that element of surprise will soon become a state of wonder — and what more can one ask for from travel?

The novelist Mishima Yukio, looking at a map in which Japan was colored pink, was reminded of a shrimp hanging off the underbelly of Asia. Most Japanese concur (if not with the analogy then at least with its spirit), thinking of their island home as a place of puny proportions. This is little more than a myth, perhaps even an element of what Japan theorizers refer to as Japan's inferiority complex. Japan is larger than most of the countries of Europe — roughly one-and-a-half times the size of the United Kingdom, for example.

Small it may not be, but in relation to its landmass Japan certainly packs a lot of punch. Its attractions ecompass elegant and yet discretely fortified castles, isolated shrines, bustling temples, enigmatic raked-pebble gardens, smoking volcanoes, artificial beaches in buildings, perfectly preserved samurai-era villages, high-tech skyscrapers, museums devoted to noodles and beer, turn-back-the-clock traditional inns. The list goes on.

The truth is, even with the luxury of a month to explore Japan you can do little more than lift the lid and take a peek at what's inside.

No matter. Regardless of how short your trip is, Japan will reveal something of itself that dispels the clichés and turns it into a living place. After all, Japan may well be a destination with more than its fair share of preserved history, but the memories most travelers leave with are far more likely to be the thronging street scenes, the incandescent neon-lit nights, the legendary sardine-can crush on the rush-hour trains.

In the end, the magic of Japan reposes in something that doesn't fit into a guidebook — or at least it's all the things in the guidebooks and a lot more.

It's a sum of its parts: 127 million people living in a modern land with a long history, "across 21 degrees of latitude and 23 degrees of longitude." To go there is to plunge into its particularities and to come away with a new vision of its uniqueness.

OPPOSITE TOP: A traditional dance in celebration of the cherry blossom season. BOTTOM: The view of fashionable Shibuya in Tokyo from Shibuya railway station. ABOVE: Japan's rickshas are a thing of the past except in some tourist areas, such as here at Meiji-jingu Shrine in Tokyo.

The Country and its People

THERE'S NO DENYING JAPAN IS A PLUCKY LITTLE NATION. When Commodore Matthew Perry's "black ships" sailed into Edo bay in 1853, they were approaching the world's biggest city. But the city and the country it governed were closed off from the world by a policy of National Seclusion. In just 15 years all that changed. Perry's opening of Japan was the catalyst for a chain of events that toppled the Tokugawa shogunate, abolished feudalism, restored the authority of the emperor, and saw Japan take the first steps in its evolution into a modern industrial state. A little less than a century later, the country was in ruins, occupied by the Allied forces, most of its cities leveled by fire bombing, two of them by atomic devices. The response? Japan embarked on another stage of revolutionary change, embracing democracy, creating a new constitution, renouncing the divinity of the emperor and dismantling the industrial conglomerates that had previously powered its economy. A little over 50 years on, Japan is one of the world's richest and most powerful nations.

If nothing else, the Japanese are a people who can adapt to change and take on challenges. There are no doubt many reasons for this, but not least among them is the land they live in, a place of extremes of climate and protean seismic and volcanic forces of upheaval.

A slim string of islands arranged in an arc, more than 160 km (100 miles) of stormy sea from the nearest point on the Asian continent, Japan is a place of climatic extremes, both from season to season and from place to place. The narrow archipelago stretches from latitude 45 degrees north to about latitude 24 degrees north, with the result that while in March and April the people in the northwest of the country are still shivering in the tail-end of their bitter, snowy winter, the inhabitants of the southern islands might well be snorkeling coral reefs. In the Japanese heartland, the crucible of Japanese civilization in Honshu, stifling summers give way to icy winters that shut off mountain passes for months at a time. Come late summer, early autumn, the typhoons arrive. In the thirteenth century, typhoons aborted two invasion attempts of Japan by the Mongol hordes, but they are more likely to bring their own style of rape and pillage to the land. A typhoon in 1954 left more than 5,000 dead or missing, and every year typhoons continue to claim lives and cause widespread destruction.

Typhoons are no less frequent than earthquakes. Some 10 percent of the world's seismic energy is concentrated in the Japanese islands. The last big one struck Kobe on January 17, 1995, causing approximately 5,500 deaths and 35,000 injured. But even the devastation of the Kobe earthquake pales in comparison with the Great Kanto Earthquake of 1923, which caused the deaths of 140,000 people in Tokyo, mostly in fires that swept through the city in the quake's aftermath.

The Japanese, in other words, are accustomed to adversity, and they are also accustomed to periodically picking up the pieces and rebuilding their world. Visiting the historic sights of Japan involves reading up on a catalogue of reconstructions, whether it be castles, shrines or temples: founded in AD 707, rebuilt in 953, destroyed by fire two centuries later, rebuilt in the fifteenth century and so on. One of Japan's most important Shinto shrines, Ise-jingu has been faithfully rebuilt every 25 years since its founding in the third century AD. All but 12 of the country's numerous castles are reconstructions. Almost all the cities, with the exception of historical Kyoto, are essentially post-War creations.

Perhaps too this is why tradition is such a powerful force in Japan. In a land where the physical manifestations of culture are routinely shaken or blown or burnt to the ground, the Japanese obsession with form becomes almost a cultural imperative. Modern Japan may well be in many ways the most Westernized of all Asian nations, but it is also a place where time-honored rural festivals and ancient traditions such as the tea ceremony, calligraphy, and flower arranging (ikebana) are all alive and well.

Small surprise then that Japanese see themselves as a unique people. An island race separated from the Asian continent by a far greater distance than Britain is from the European continent, the Japanese are quick to jump on theories that validate their sense that their country and culture is a place apart. Young Japanese can be genuinely surprised that even something as universal as the changing of the seasons, sentimentally celebrated as definitive of the Japanese experience, is shared by other countries. It is, of course, as is much else that the Japanese consider hallowed. Despite attempts to block out the rest of the world, such as the Tokugawa policy of National Seclusion, Japan is a nation whose people probably came from somewhere else, and whose culture has evolved largely as a process of refinement of foreign influences, a process that continues to this day.

But to see how that has come to be, some history is in order.

THE JAPANESE TRIBE

Before the last Ice Age, for much of the Paleolithic period (30,000 to 10,000 BC), Japan was connected to the Asian continent by a land-bridge. The approximately 4,500 Paleolithic sites that have been discovered in Japan bear much in common with contemporaneous sites in China and Korea, suggesting that the earliest Japanese crossed from East Asia to the Japanese isles. Korea is the nearest point

The heavily made-up face of a Kyoto geisha.

to Japan on the continent and has perennially provided the most convenient jumping-off point for migrants and travelers. Certain elements of the culture, such as the flimsiness of the early wooden architecture, suggest that there was an early influx of migrants from more southerly regions, but no archaeological evidence to support this has been discovered.

The picture is complicated by the *Ainu*, the hairy hunting and fishing tribes who, until the eighth century, occupied the northern part of the main island of Honshu. They were pushed further and further northwards by the dominant Yamato Japanese, and as a distinct people exist now only in small communities in the northernmost island of Hokkaido. However, large numbers of them have probably been absorbed over the centuries, as is attested by the bushy eyebrows and deep-set eyes of some of the Japanese today.

By the eighth or ninth century, large-scale immigration to Japan had come to a halt. Since that time — soon after the dawn of the nation's recorded history — the Japanese have been, and have regarded themselves as, a single, unified and homogeneous people. With the exception of the arrival of some half million Koreans earlier this century, as slave workers in the Japanese war effort, nothing has occurred during the intervening millennium to disrupt that state of affairs.

CORDS AND MOUNDS

Early Japan emerged as a knowable place with the start of the Jomon period (10,000–300 BC). Archeologists divide it into six different periods, but the overwhelming single feature of this hunter-gatherer society for us is its "cord-marked" (which is what "Jomon" means) pottery, the oldest examples of which represent the world's earliest

Korean inspiration. In some cases they probably even came from China or Korea. Amidst these influences rose Japan's first important dynasty, the Yamato (*circa* fourth century to *circa* seventh century).

Yamato was the name of the region that is now Nara, and the chieftains here gradually grew in power. By the sixth century they controlled Japan from northern Kyushu to the area that is now Tokyo. By the time of Prince Shotoku (AD 574–622), Yamato was a sophisticated state. Shotoku instituted a 17-article constitution, established diplomatic relations with Sui-dynasty China, issued an edict that promoted the newly imported religion of Buddhism, and sponsored the construction of important temples such Horyu-ji, which still stands today (see NARA, page 156). Japanese civilization as we now know it was beginning to emerge.

THE GOLDEN AGE

During the early centuries of the Buddhist era, contact between Japan and the continent was frequent, and Chinese influence continually seeped into the country. But during the sixth century, as China approached her glorious Tang period, this influence became suddenly and dramatically stronger.

Buddhism, the Indian religion which the Chinese had made their own, was one of Japan's earliest cultural imports, bringing a host of artistic, architectural and administrative influences in its wake. Some Chinese ways were unsuited to the Japanese situation and faded away once the initial enthusiasm gave out. Others, such as the system of selecting civil servants by examination, were too democratic to be acceptable to the clannish Japanese. But in many ways they did an amazingly good job of transforming their nation into a miniature version of the Tang state.

As Japan was spared the waves of invasion that rolled across China, flattening her early achievements, Japan is the best place to see the architectural and artistic styles of the Tang today. The city of Nara, laid out in AD 710, was the country's first "permanent" capital (though it only lasted as a capital for 70-odd years). The temples and monasteries in the pleasant parkland at the city's old center reflect the purity of the Chinese influence at this time, and the fabulous achievement of the Japanese carpenters in mastering the foreign techniques.

In 784 Nara was abandoned to escape the increasing power of the Buddhist sects that had set up their bases there, and after a brief interregnum a new capital called Heian-kyo (present-day Kyoto) was built, in 794. Like Nara, Heian was laid out like a chessboard in imitation of the Chinese capital

pottery. By about 300 BC, a new culture with knowledge of bronze and iron technologies made its appearance. The Yayoi period (300 BC to AD 300) is marked by the wet cultivation of rice, a crop that was not native to Japan.

The cultivation of rice allowed the rise of a stratified society of aristocrats and commoners. By the late third century, extraordinary burial mounds for the elite of this society started to appear, providing the name for the following period of Japanese history, the Kofun (or "burial mound") period (AD 300–710). The mounds varied in size from a modest 15 m (50 ft) in diameter to the massive 32 ha (79 acres) of the keyhole-shaped burial mound of Emperor Nintoku (early fifth century) at Sakai, near Osaka.

About this time something important started to happen. The ruling-class burial mounds became increasingly ambitious, and the treasures buried with the dead seem more and more to be of Chinese or

A glorious autumnal setting, fitting for such an architectural gem, complements Kinkaku-ji, the Temple of the Golden Pavilion, Kyoto.

Chang-an, and this street-plan is still intact today. The city was to remain the nation's capital, at least in name, right up to 1868.

The founding of Heian-kyo marks the beginning of the Heian period (794–1185). It is regarded as the golden age of early Japanese civilization. Although swayed by China at its foundation, under the Heian court Chinese influence began to dwindle, and in its place blossomed a new indigenous culture.

Heian means "peace," and the Heian period was indeed a blessedly peaceful interlude. The imperial court, in accordance with Chinese practice, was supposed to be the center of government, but quite rapidly control devolved to the local clan

gangs of armed Buddhist monks who had begun to terrorize the capital. Two principal families, the Minamoto (also known as Genji) and the Taira (also known as Heike), competed for this role of guardian, and before long they were fighting each other as well.

Two major explosions followed. The second and decisive one shattered what was left of the court's authority and left the country in the hands of the leader of the Minamoto clan, a fierce young warrior called Minamoto-no-Yoritomo. He established his capital hundreds of miles from Kyoto in the obscure but easily defended fishing village of Kamakura, south of present-day Yokohama.

leaders throughout the country. This left the court with plenty of wealth but very little to do except enact the empty ceremonies of power. The rest of the time they plotted, made love, dashed off countless poems, held elegant contests of aesthetic sensitivity and wrote diaries. The world's first novel, *The Tale of Genji*, written at that time by the woman courtier Murasaki Shikibu, paints an unforgettably vivid picture of this foppish age.

ENTER THE SAMURAI

The Heian court was clearly too soft to last. The descendants of younger sons of the aristocracy, who had been sent into the countryside from the capital in earlier days, gradually acquired military as well as political power, and increasingly the most powerful of these tough, frugal warriors were called on by the court for protection from

The culture of the Kamakura period (1192–1333) saw some important developments that were to change the face of Japan. Chief among them was the emergence of a warrior class called *bushi*, or samurai, and the establishment of a military government. The period is also marked by the popularization of Buddhism, which had until this time been the provenance of the aristocracy.

It might be called the age of the cultured warrior. Unlike their medieval European counterparts, the Kamakura samurai did not despise learning, and, when Zen Buddhism was introduced from China at the start of this era, its discipline became the perfect complement to the Spartan military lifestyle. If the Heian period was a hot, perfumed bath, the culture produced by this union of warrior and monk was as bracing as an icy shower.

This fruitful relationship between Zen and the Japanese ruling class continued for hundreds of years, far beyond the Kamakura period, and left its mark on many different aspects of the culture, from the tea ceremony and tatami mats to garden design and flower-arranging.

Meanwhile, Buddhism was enjoying a boom among the lower classes, too, as new Japanese sects sprang up, offering salvation through the endless repetition of devotional phrases. With their emphasis on personal salvation in a literal heaven, some of these sects bear a closer resemblance to Christianity than to Buddhism as practiced in other parts of Asia. They owed much of their success to the political and economic confusion of the period.

The Kamakura shoguns survived the Mongolian menace at the end of the thirteenth century,

but the structural weakness of their administration, based on the loyalty of a few chieftains, spread throughout the country. When the quixotic Emperor Godaigo (1288–1339) attempted to seize power by force of arms, the regime succumbed. Godaigo had no great success, but his attempt ushered in an era of war and confusion which lasted more than 200 years.

FIRE FROM THE SOUTH

With the collapse of central authority in Kamakura, the old estate divisions began to break down. As strong warrior chiefs, some from old aristocratic families but many of common descent, forced their way to power and then, as *daimyo* (feudal lords) staked out defensible domains, Japan became a patchwork of tiny fiefdoms, who inevitably began to jostle for the position of top dog.

This process was hastened by the arrival in Japan of the first Europeans. Approaching the country from the south, and dubbed for that reason "southern barbarians," the Portuguese arrived in Japan in 1543. They amazed the natives by their appearance and their manners, and delighted them with their tobacco, sponge cake, clocks and spectacles; but it was their arquebuses (long-barreled guns) that left the deepest mark on Japanese history.

The military value of firepower was rapidly grasped, and within 20 years cannons and muskets were being widely and decisively used in battle. However, only the richest of the *daimyo*, or feudal lords, could afford to employ the new technology and to put up the monumental new castles which were the only effective type of defense against it. The struggle for power between the *daimyo* suddenly accelerated. Before the end of the sixteenth century, a resolution had been reached which was to last until the arrival of the next wave of destructive technology from the West, 300 years later.

Clambering out of the smoke of battle into the center of the picture came three great generals, one after the other. Between them they crushed or won over all who opposed them, unified the country politically and ushered in a long age of authoritarian calm that is one of the wonders of world history.

A TALE OF THREE GENERALS

The first, Oda Nobunaga (1534–1582), was a ferocious man, and the main objects of his ferocity were the Buddhist armies which had gained great power during the previous chaotic century. The enmity he had for them encouraged him to favor the Portuguese Jesuit missionaries, led by Saint Francis Xavier, who had begun introducing Christianity into the country. For many years they enjoyed great success, converting as many as 300,000 Japanese to the faith until, losing favor with a later shogun, they and their works were stamped out and Christianity effectively disappeared from the country.

Toyotomi Hideyoshi (1537–1598), the second and most interesting of the three, was a small and famously ugly man who rose to supremacy from the rank of foot-soldier. He was a general of Alexandrian ambition: in an attempt to conquer China he had his troops overrun Korea, thereby poisoning forever the feelings of the Koreans towards the Japanese. But he was also an administrator of genius, balancing the forces of antagonistic and loyal *daimyo* throughout the nation to ensure the stability of his rule. In order to prevent other

British soldiers march along The Bluff in Yokohama past the British Legation, preceded by a military band, in a late eighteenth-century print.

ambitious soldiers from treading in his footsteps he drew a strict and largely artificial line between samurai and commoners, and issued laws preventing members of different classes from changing their professions.

The third general, Tokugawa Ieyasu (1542–1616) is remembered for his patience and his cunning, and also for his fantastically gaudy mausoleum at Nikko, which illustrates how drastically the taste of the Japanese ruling class had changed since the somber tranquility of the Kamakura period. Tokugawa consolidated the work of his predecessors. He pre-empted opposition to his rule by insisting that *daimyo* spend alternate years at home and at his capital in Edo (modern Tokyo) — thus wasting much time and money on the road — and by keeping their wives as permanent hostages in Edo.

He also skillfully arranged for the succession to stay in his family, and the Tokugawas ruled Japan, at least in name, from 1600 to 1867. For all but the earliest years of that period the only contact Japan maintained with the Western world was through a tiny Dutch trading settlement on an artificial island in Nagasaki Harbor.

WARRIOR TO MERCHANT

Establishing his capital at Edo, Tokugawa Ieyasu, despite founding a repressively hegemonic government, ushered in an era of stability that allowed the growth of a money economy and a new merchant culture.

The merchant class, theoretically at the bottom of the social scale, grew enormously in wealth, and they expressed that wealth in a flamboyant and frivolous culture. Most of those forms by which the rest of the world defines the word "Japanese" — *kabuki*, geisha, woodblock prints, for example — were part of a great surge of mercantile confidence that began with the start of the Edo period (1600–1867).

However unpleasant the means by which it was brought about, the long peace was a great blessing. While nothing resembling an industrial revolution took place, craftsmanship in many different fields attained an extraordinarily high level. The common people's standard of living rose, and education, provided by schools in temples, improved to the extent that about 35 percent of the population was literate by the nineteenth century. Though deprived of the scientific advances enjoyed in the West, the Japanese were spared the humiliation and exploitation of colonialism. When the shogunate — a very ripe fruit by the end — finally fell, the Japanese were uniquely positioned to take up the challenges of the modern world.

THE EMPEROR STRIKES BACK

In 1854, under the threat of force from the American Navy, Japan grudgingly opened her doors to trade with the West. Six years later the first Japanese embassy was sent to Washington. A photograph survives from that mission: the ambassadors, posing with American naval officers and dressed in

their samurai finery — split-toed socks, divided skirts, kimonos, shaved scalps and topknots, and two swords each — look wildly outlandish. Their befuddled, faraway expressions convey deep culture shock. They are obviously unaccustomed to sitting on chairs. No delegation of painted Papuan tribesmen would look more exotic or more distant from the modern world.

Yet less than 70 years later, the grandsons of these men, dressed in collars and ties, were to sit across the table from the world's great powers and participate with them on terms of perfect equality in the peace conference which ended World War I — the only non-Western power to do so.

The transformation was close to miraculous. How did it happen?

In a sense it was a re-enactment, 1,200 years later and under radically different conditions, of Japan's experience with China. In both cases, recognizing her backwardness vis-à-vis the other country or countries, Japan set about learning with fierce determination what was necessary to even the score.

By the 1830s all was not well with Tokugawa shogunate. Between 1833 and 1836, unusually low rice yields led to a nation-wide famine. Peasant revolts broke out around the country, and Osaka was laid waste by a rebellion. At the same time, China's defeat by Great Britain in the Opium Wars (1839–1842) was a message to the educated elite that growing pressure from the West for Japan to open its doors to international trade could probably not be staved off for too much longer. A new movement called Western Learning began to take root. Perry's "black ships" arrived in 1853, and by 1854 the Treaty of Kanagawa had opened Japanese ports to foreign trade — the result was inflation and instability of the Japanese currency. Finally, to make things worse, the Tokugawa shogun died in 1858 without an heir. In 1860, in front of Edo-jo Castle, disaffected samurai cut down the appointed successor to the Tokugawa regime.

Meanwhile, Japan's feelings towards the new foreign intruders was one of revulsion, and anger against the weak shogunate for letting them in. A slogan emerged — "Honor the emperor and expel the barbarian!" It wasn't long before the powerful domains of Satsuma and Chosho unified in support of the emperor, who was cloistered in Kyoto. In 1866, besieged on all fronts, the last Tokugawa shogun applied to the emperor in Kyoto for the restoration of imperial rule. The enemies of the Tokugawa, however, were by this time baying for blood, and under demands that it relinquish not only office but all its hereditary lands too, the Tokugawa dispatched troops to Kyoto. The ensuing Boshin Civil War saw the utter defeat of the Tokugawas and in 1868 the official restoration of the Meiji ("enlightened rule") emperor. In 1869 he moved his court to Edo and renamed the city Tokyo, "Eastern Capital."

LOOKING WEST

With the Meiji restoration, Tokyo became a changed place. For a start, the "barbarians" did not go away. Indeed some of their inventions — lightning conductors, steam engines and cannons, for example — were genuinely useful. A new slogan, "A rich country and a strong military," was adopted, and the new government, composed of young and highly enterprising samurai from the southwest, set about implementing it with fantastic dispatch.

Japan's eagerness to learn during the last third of the nineteenth century contrasts starkly with China's painful confrontation with the choice between tradition and change. Carefully choosing the most appropriate teacher for each subject, the Japanese learned avidly how to build a modern army and navy, a railway network, a textile industry, how to create an education system, a law code, a constitution. Cheerfully discarding their own "primitive" culture, they hurried to embrace the accessories of Western civilization — Western clothes, Western music, ballroom dancing and more.

No country in history had experienced such a rapid and drastic transformation. The period was crowned by two victories in war against gigantic opponents: China in 1895 and Russia in 1905. These triumphs amazed the world, not only because Japan won, but because of the civilized way in which the Japanese treated prisoners and

civilians (a striking contrast to their behavior in World War II). Japan became the first Asian nation to be admitted as an equal to the counsels of the rich industrial nations — and remains the only one, even to this day.

Among the lessons Japan learned was parliamentary democracy. The alien concept was applied with care and caution, and the power of elected politicians checked in the early days by the strength of the military leaders and the "elder statesmen," founders of the new regime, who kept a keen, corrective eye on their juniors.

As the last of these elder statesmen died in the early 1920s, and politicians who were neither soldiers nor aristocrats rose to high office for the first time, there was an interval of calm and moderation which suggested to the optimistic that a peaceful, democratic future awaited the country. A new modern literature blossomed. The prince regent — the late emperor — traveled to Europe, the first member of the imperial family to leave the country, and came back with a lasting love for oatmeal and golf.

OPPOSITE: Early Japanese depiction of an Englishman on horseback (circa 1861).
ABOVE: Members of an early Japanese delegation, photographed in Honolulu. Photo courtesy of the *Mainichi Shimbun-Sha.*

THE ROAD TO WAR

By the end of the decade and with the onset of the Depression, however, people realized this pleasant prospect was a mirage. During the next 10 years the system collapsed, undermined by corruption and weaknesses within and violent insubordination without. Angry and self-righteous young army officers in the Japanese Imperial Army, fiercely patriotic, repeatedly seized the initiative to deepen the nation's military involvement with China and to assassinate balky or pacific politicians. In 1931 the Japanese military devised a flimsy pretext to attack Manchuria, installing Pu Yi, China's last emperor, as the head of a puppet state. By the mid-1930s the Japanese government was largely under the control of the Imperial Army, and Japan was being drawn into a much wider conflict in China.

In 1937 an incident in northern China initiated war with Chiang Kai-shek, followed in 1940 by Japan signing the Tripartite Axis Pact with Germany and Italy.

By 1940 war between Japan and the Allies had almost become inevitable. The United States had been steadily applying sanctions to Japan while building up its military in the Philippines. In 1939 the United States effected an embargo on the export of American goods to Japan and in 1940, as Japan moved into Indochina, the United States cut off Japan's oil supplies. Japan negotiated for better terms, but a tempting alternative was a pre-emptive strike on the United States before it could further build up its military might in the Pacific. Japan attacked Pearl Harbor on December 7, 1941, following with invasions of the Philippines, Malaya and Indonesia.

The initial successes in Japan's attempts to carve out what it called a "Greater East Asia Co-Prosperity Sphere" soon began to give way to defeats. In June 1942 the United States sunk four Japanese aircraft carriers in the Battle of Midway. By 1944 they had gained the island of Saipan, which put Tokyo and the rest of Japan within range of their B-29 bombers. The damage inflicted was staggering. All the great cities, with the exception of Kyoto, were destroyed. In all, 40 percent of the built-up area of 60 towns and cities was burned to the ground. Nearly 700,000 civilians were killed, including 100,000 on one night in Tokyo as a result of incendiary bombing. By the spring of 1945, 13 million were estimated to be homeless as a result of bombing. Even Japan's frequent earthquakes had never done damage on this appalling scale.

It was against a backdrop of such destruction that the Allies called for Japan's unconditional surrender in the Potsdam Declaration of July 1945. Japan's military government, however, clung to the idea that it could make further advances by the Allied forces so costly in terms of lives that something other than unconditional surrender could be achieved. It ignored the call. On August 6 an atomic bomb was dropped on Hiroshima; three days later another was dropped on Nagasaki.

On August 15, for the first time in Japanese history, the emperor, regarded by the people as a living god, spoke to his people. The war was over. Japan had lost everything it had gained, and at the cost of more than three million lives.

POST-WAR YEARS

After the war, General MacArthur and the allied army of occupation took over and ruled Japan until 1952. Under MacArthur's supervision the whole social and economic structure of the country was overhauled. A new constitution sheared the emperor of his divinity, while allowing him to remain a symbol of the nation. Farmers grew rich through land reform, and the educational system was remodeled along American lines. An attempt was made to dismantle the *zaibatsu*, the huge financial empires blamed for stoking the war effort. Then MacArthur's priority shifted to the creation of a staunchly anti-communist Japan. Article 9 of the new constitution renounced the use of force for aggressive purposes. Although the article remains in force today it has not prevented the country from re-arming.

Gradually, during the 1950s and early 1960s, as economic recovery got under way, the old strength and confidence returned. The Tokyo Olympic Games of 1964, the first ever to be held in Asia, signified that Japan was once again a full member of the community of nations, and the inauguration of the Shinkansen, the fastest train in the world, in the same year gave a hint of the technological prowess with which she has been dazzling the world ever since. Japan's rapid return to prosperity has been one of the wonders of the postwar-age.

MIRACLE TO BUBBLE

Japan, from the late 1950s through to late 1980s, went from strength to strength. Presided over by the Liberal Democratic Party, which fostered cozy relationships between government, business and bureaucracy, Japan proceeded to get rich on an export-driven economy whose own markets were fiercely protected. By 1964 Japan had joined the club of rich nations, the Organization for Economic Co-operation and Development (OECD).

Through the 1970s and 1980s the conservative LDP was plagued by a series of corruption scandals, but its continued ability to deliver on the economic front ensured its grip on power. Resentment built overseas, however, as Japan's huge volume of exports failed to produce any efforts to open its markets to imports. People began to talk of Japan Inc., a hegemonic money-making machine set on global domination. Not that such resentment did anything to slow the boom times: by the late 1980s soaring real estate values was making Japan the richest country in the world, and Japanese were talking openly about "*Nihon ichiban*" — Japan number one.

It was not long, though, before a new catch-cry was to enter the lexicon — the "bubble economy." By the late 1980s such was confidence in Japan that golf club memberships were worth millions of dollars; Tokyo real estate was the most expensive in the world, with the land that the Imperial Palace sits on reckoned to be worth more

than all of Florida. It seemed as if the good times would last forever. But all good things come to an end. When the market collapsed, banks found themselves sitting on huge bad loans on properties valued at enormously inflated rates. The bubble had burst.

The actual reasons for the bursting of Japan's bubble economy are complex to say the least, but whatever they may be the results created a new element of uncertainty in a country accustomed, since the setbacks of World War II, to success. In June 1993 the LDP, for the first time in 38 years, were ousted by a clean-up coalition government, though it lasted just a year before the LDP were back in control again in a bizarre — some say cynical — coalition with their old foes the Socialist Party.

The sense that old certainties were crumbling left, right and center in the 1990s was compounded by events like the Kobe earthquake of 1995, to

which the government response was universally judged to be fumbling, and the gassing of the Tokyo subway by a millenarian cult called Aum Shinrikyo headed by a blind visionary. By 1996 the LDP was back in power in its own right, only to be plagued ever since by leadership problems. By 1998 the government had officially admitted what everybody had known all along, that Japan was in recession, as the yen, along with other Asian currencies, took a drubbing. In the June 2000 elections the LDP continued to hold onto power in coalition with two small parties, having lost its previous prime minister to a heart attack in May. The current prime minister, Yoshiro Mori's hold on power is, however, commonly regarded as tenuous — although he survived a no-confidence vote in November 2000.

JAPAN TODAY

Japan has changed a lot in the last 10 years. A decade ago it was easy to think of the place in terms of the stereotypes of the "salaryman" and the "office lady," or "OL" as they are known in Japan, a formulation that perhaps sought to explain the Japanese miracle in terms of a ritualized static society. But with the miracle on hold, if only temporarily, such certainties become less tenable. Enormous changes are sweeping through Japanese society, and with them come, albeit more slowly, political and economic change. The job-for-life system that reigned for much of the post-War era is becoming a thing of the past, people are marrying later, if at all in some cases, the assurance that Japan was master of all it touched turned out to be hubris.

The jury is out on whether Japan's long-lasting recession will deepen into a full-blown depression — which will probably be bad news for the world economy — but it's worth bearing in mind that Japan, after all, is a plucky nation, with a strong tolerance for change. It has undergone revolutions before. If the past is anything to go by, the current adversities will eventually become an opportunity to learn and pick up the pieces.

In the meantime, for the foreign visitor it's business as usual. Japan may not be feeling completely itself these days, but the depreciated yen is nothing but good news for travelers, the food is as good as ever, the sights as compelling as they always have been, and the Japanese experience remains a unique adventure.

Fukuoka/Hakata, a major port and a central hub for exploring the island of Kyushu.

Tokyo

THE JAPANESE THEMSELVES HAVE BEEN HEARD TO WONDER WHETHER TOKYO IS JAPAN AT ALL. Modern, international, always fashionably one step ahead of the rest of Asia, Japan's capital has little truck with any of the cherished hearth-and-home values that the Japanese see as defining their homeland. Be that as it may, for the foreign visitor, Tokyo is very much a Japanese city. The trains run like clockwork, crime is virtually non-existent, neon *kanji* illuminates the bustling night, the frantic and uniquely Japanese sounds of a city forever on the move assault the ears at every turn. In short, Tokyo may be a far cry from the contemplative stillness of the Zen garden, the tea ceremony or a soak in a hot spring, but it is nevertheless the apotheosis of the modern Japanese

experience — a city that despite the setbacks of a massive, leveling earthquake in 1923 and the aerial firebombing of 1945 has risen up and declared itself a major metropolis.

And "major" is the definitive term — don't underestimate the size of the place. For many recent arrivals Tokyo can be an overwhelming experience, a confusing labyrinth of nameless streets, a spaghetti-tangle of overhead expressways and subway lines. Try not to panic and flee. Tokyo may not be rich in historical attractions — most were destroyed in the upheavals of the twentieth century — but it's the country's most vibrant city, and as such it's not to be missed.

First impressions can be disappointing. Coming in from Narita International Airport, Tokyo seems to go on forever. Somber, gray and brooding, seen from the overheard expressways that funnel traffic into the city, it looks like a blighted urban landscape, a futuristic dystopia. Descend to street level, however, in any of the city's commercial centers and such impressions are quickly dispelled. From the surging shop-till-you-drop crowds of Shinjuku to the refined al-fresco café life of Shibuya, Tokyo is far more than a bleak convergence of office and apartment blocks.

Depending on how much time you have and your interests, there are essentially two ways to approach the city: the whirlwind tour of the attractions, or a more measured exploration of the city. It's the latter, of course, that best yields up the city's secrets, and no matter how tight the schedule is, it's worth allocating at least one afternoon to an aimless stroll through one of the city's sections. The discoveries you make — often bizarre, always surprising — will be uniquely yours, something no tour can provide, and something certainly no other city can provide.

BACKGROUND

By Japanese standards, Tokyo is the new kid on the block. Officially founded in 1457, it was not until a century later, in 1590, when Tokugawa Ieyasu made what was then called Edo his base, that the city assumed any prominence. In making himself supreme among Japan's warlords and appointing himself shogun, Tokugawa transformed this erstwhile village on the mudflats of the Sumigawa River into Japan's power-base, even though imperial power lingered in Kyoto.

Tokugawa's Edo Castle, occupying the site that is now home to the Imperial Palace in Central Tokyo, was in its day Japan's grandest, and a century after the establishment of Tokugawa's shogunate the surrounding city had become the world's most populous.

Edo was the de-facto capital throughout the 260 years of the Tokugawa period. The capital in name, however, was still Kyoto. In 1867 the shogun was deposed and the emperor restored to his former position of prestige. He moved with his court to Edo Castle and the city was renamed Tokyo — "Eastern Capital."

A British envoy who visited the city at that time praised it as one of the most beautiful in the Orient. Earthquakes, bombs and the arrival of concrete have dated such kind words. Today, little remains of the glory of old Edo, though fascinating pockets linger on here and there.

But Tokyo is very much the hub of the nation — more so than many capitals — and it is the best and biggest showcase for the new Japan: for the electronics, the motorbikes, the cars, the fashion, the architecture. It has the most museums and galleries, the best stores, the best theaters and cinemas,

For the finest choice in state-of-the-art technology, Akihabara offers virtually wall-to-wall electrical goods stores.

many of the best restaurants and the most exciting and varied night life in the country.

GENERAL INFORMATION

Tourist information is readily available in Tokyo from the various offices of the Japan National Tourist Organization (JNTO) Tourist Information Centers (TICs), which are now known as "**Tokyo i**." The main office ((03) 3201-3331, open 9 AM to 5 PM weekdays, 9 AM to noon on Saturdays, closed Sundays and public holidays, is in the office of the Tokyo International Forum, a two-minute walk from Yurakucho station, 3-5-1 Marunouchi, Chiyoda-ku. Another branch, open daily from 10 AM to 6:30 PM, has recently opened on the first floor of the east exit podium of Shinjuku station. Terminal 2 of New Tokyo International Airport has another ((0476) 34-6251.

Tokyo has two 24-hour, English-language services. The **Tokyo Metropolitan Police** ((03) 3501-0110 can offer advice and help on any emergency — whether medical or otherwise — as can **Tokyo English Life Line (TELL)** TOLL-FREE (0120) 46-1997. The latter is a toll-free number that can be dialed from anywhere in Japan, though it is aimed at providing emergency information for foreigners resident in Tokyo.

The main branch of **American Express** TOLL-FREE (0120) 020-666, 4-30-16 Ogikubo, Suginami-ku, has a 24-hour cash machine. Elsewhere around Tokyo, despite the fact this is a modern city, it can be difficult to find cash machines that take foreign cards. The best bet is **Citibank** TOLL-FREE (0120) 50-4189, which has increasingly large numbers of branches around Tokyo, including one close to the A2 exit of Ginza station, opposite the Matsuzakaya Department Store on Ginza Dori.

Most of the world's major airlines are represented in Tokyo. Contact details are as follows: **Aeroflot** ((03) 3434-9681, Dai-ni Matsuda Building, 4-8 Toranomon 3-chome, Minato-ku; **Air Canada** ((03) 3586-3891, Sixth Floor New Akasaka Building, 2-3 Akasaka 3-chome, Minato-ku; **Air China** ((03) 3505-2021, Aoi Building, 2-7 Akasaka 3-chome, Minato-ku 107; **Air France** ((03) 3475-2211, Fifteenth Floor Shin Aoyama Building, Nishi-kan, 1-1 Minami Aoyama 1-chome, Minato-ku; **Air India** ((03) 3214-7631, Sixth Floor Hibiya Park Building, 8-1 Yuraku-cho 1-chome, Chiyoda-ku; **Alitalia** ((03) 3580-2181, Tokyo Club Building, 2-6 Kasumigaseki 3-chome, Chiyoda-ku; **All Nippon** ((03) 3272-1212, Kasumigaseki Building, 2-5 Kasumigaseki 3-chome, Chiyoda-ku; **British Airways** ((03) 3593-8811, Sanshin Building, 4-1 Yuraku-cho 1-chome, Chiyoda-ku; **Canadian Airlines** ((03) 3212-5811, Hibiya Park Building, 8-1 Yuraku-cho 1-chome, Chiyoda-ku; **Cathay Pacific** ((03) 3504-1531, 5-2 Yuraku-cho 1-chome, Chiyoda-ku; **China Airlines** ((03) 3436-1661, Matsuoka Building, 22-10 Shimbashi 5-chome,

Minato-ku; **Finnair** ((03) 3222-1691, NK Building, 14-2 Koji-machi 2-chome, Chiyoda-ku; **Garuda** ((03) 3593-1181, Fifteenth Floor Kasumigaseki Building, 2-5 Kasumigaseki 3-chome, Chiyoda-ku; **JAS** ((03) 5473-4100, No. 37 Mori Building, 5-1 Toranomon 3-chome, Minato-ku; **Japan Airlines** ((03) 5259-3777, Daini Tekko Building, 8-2 Marunouchi 1-chome, Chiyoda-ku; **Japan Asia** ((03) 3284-2666, Yurakucho Denki Building-South, 7-1 Yuraku-cho 1-chome, Chiyoda-ku; **KLM** ((03) 3211-5322, Yurakucho Denki Building-North, 7-1 Yuraku-cho 1-chome, Chiyoda-ku; **Korean Air** ((03) 5443-3311, Tokyo KAL Building, 4-15 Shiba 3-chome, Minato-ku; **Lufthansa** ((03) 3580-2121, Tokyo Club Building, 2-6 Kasumigaseki 3-chome, Chiyoda-ku; **Malaysia** ((03) 3503-5961, Hankyu Express Building, 3-9 Shimbashi 3-chome, Minato-ku; **Northwest** ((03) 3533-6000, 12-12 Toranomon 5-chome, Minato-ku; **Qantas** ((03) 3593-7000, Tokyo Chamber of Commerce & Industry Building, 2-2 Marunouchi 3-chome, Chiyoda-ku; **SAS** ((03) 2714-0820, Second Floor, SVAX TS Building, 1-22-12 Toranomon, Minato-ku; **Singapore** ((03) 3213-3431, First Floor Yurakucho Building, 10-1 Yuraku-cho 1-chome, Chiyoda-ku; **Swissair** ((03) 3212-1011, Room 410 Hibiya Park Building, 8-1 Yuraku-cho 1-chome, Chiyoda-ku; **Thai** ((03) 3503-3311, Asahi Seimei Hibiya Building, 5-1 Yuraku-cho 1-chome, Chiyoda-ku; **United** ((03) 3817-4411, Suite 228 Kokusai Building, 1-1 Marunouchi 3-chome, Chiyoda-ku.

ORIENTATION

Tokyo is such a vast, sprawling city that it is difficult for newcomers to orient themselves at first. For a start, though the imperial palace and surrounds are nominally the city center, Tokyo is actually a city with many centers. Fortunately most of them lie on the railway line that circles the city — the Yamanote-sen.

The Yamanote-sen is an overhead railway line that loops around the heart of Tokyo taking in almost all the city's main commercial districts en-route. Most of these can be found to the west of Tokyo station; the areas north and east of here, notably Ueno and Asakusa, have some fine tourist attractions, but represent what is sometimes referred to as the "low city," the Tokyo that sees its roots in the Edo of old.

Traveling north and west from Tokyo station takes you first to Kanda, an area that lies close to the city's second-hand bookshop area of Jimbocho. Next comes Akihabara, a bustling area that is renowned for its electronics bargains. Two stops north of here is Ueno, home to one of Tokyo's oldest parks, some of the city's best museums, and staging point for nearby Asakusa, one of the city's oldest districts and home to the lively Senso-ji Temple. The northern loop of the Yamanote line is relatively devoid of interest until Ikebukuro, a burgeoning commercial and nightlife area that has long been overshadowed by Shinjuku but is not without some interest. Shinjuku itself lies four stops to the southwest of here, and is home to some of the city's biggest hotels on its west side, and to one of the city's busiest shopping and entertainment areas on its east. Continuing on the loop, next comes Harajuku, celebrated for its youth shopping and Paris-style cafés, followed by Shibuya, which with its department stores and cinemas is something of a youth-oriented Shinjuku. Farther south, Ebisu was until a few years back a nondescript area, but has been given a massive face lift and now sports several worthwhile attractions, including a superb photography museum. From here the line continues

30 minutes) and Yokohama stations. The Limousine bus services offer the advantage of being dropped off at the door of one of Tokyo's major hotels (different buses cover almost all the major hotels); but traffic snarls are not uncommon, particularly at peak hours. Taxis, meanwhile, are not only horrendously expensive, but are no faster than the buses.

Tokyo's domestic airport is Haneda Airport. It has a more convenient location, and is connected to the Yamanote loop line by a 20-minute monorail journey to Hamamatsucho station.

In town, most visitors find the best way to navigate the city is on the overhead Yamanote line and on the subway system. Unfortunately the two

to Yurakucho, a mere hop, skip and a jump from high-flying Ginza, and then to Tokyo, administrative heart of the city and not far from the Imperial Palace.

GETTING AROUND

There is no denying it: Tokyo is a confusing city to get around in at first. It starts at New Tokyo International Airport, from where access to central Tokyo is available through several rail services, limousine bus or, should you feel like splashing out nearly US$200, by taxi. The trains are the fastest way to cover the 66 km (41 miles) that separate downtown Tokyo from its international airport. The relatively inexpensive Keisei line, runs to Ueno station in little over an hour, while the luxury Narita Express (N'EX) runs direct to Tokyo (one hour), Shinjuku (one hour and 20 minutes), and much less frequently to Ikebukuro (one hour and

operate under separate ticketing systems, and just to confuse things there are actually two separate subway systems. Don't be fazed. Get in line at the automatic ticket vending machines, and if puzzled simply buy the cheapest ticket and pay the excess when you reach your destination to one of the ticket gate guards — they're used to dealing with confused *gaijin*.

Tokyo's subway system virtually constitutes an underground city. At the larger stations there are kiosks, small restaurants, and even quite elaborate shops. Shinjuku Station, which serves both subway and overground rail systems, is the most heavily used train station on earth. Once you begin to understand your way around there, you can consider yourself an honorary citizen of the Japanese capital.

Japan's Shinkansen are better known in the West as "bullet trains," a name that aptly describes their bullet-like appearance and almost aeronautical speeds.

Finding your way around any of the Tokyo subway stations is made easier thanks to the color-coding system. Once you know the color for the line you are looking for, you will be unerringly led to the platforms by following that color on direction-pointing signs. Then all you have to do is decide which of the two platforms you need, a decision easily executed by looking at the list of stations served. Stations ahead are printed in black, those behind are in gray.

WHAT TO SEE AND DO

Think of Tokyo as a city of many centers, and approach it accordingly. Spend too much time dashing from one end of the city to another and exhaustion will soon set in. The following information has thus been broken down into the main areas of the city: take them one at a time, and within a week you will have a broad overview of how the city works. As for the order in which the areas appear below, it describes a loop, starting at the Imperial Palace, moving north through the older sections of the city, before moving south through the newer commercial sub-cities that lie on the Yamanote line and ending up at Akasaka, close to the Imperial Palace where the journey began. There is, of course, no need to follow such a route in your exploration of the city — pick and choose from the areas below according to your mood.

CENTRAL TOKYO

The **Imperial Palace**, nestled in the heart of Tokyo, may well be one of the city's most famous tourist attractions, but it's worth bearing in mind that beyond its ramparts and the parts of the grounds that have been turned into public parks, little of the palace can be seen. The reason is simple: it is still a functioning palace, home to the Japanese imperial family. On just two days a year does the public get a glimpse beyond the palace gates: December 23 (the emperor's birthday) and January 2, 9 AM to 3:30 PM. Expect a lot of company.

Fronting the palace is the sprawling **Imperial Plaza**, a somewhat sterile expanse bounded by moats to the north, south and east, and the palace walls to the west. The chief attraction is the southwest corner of the plaza, where the picture-perfect Niju-bashi Bridge can be glimpsed flanked by willows and the palace walls. The closest subway station is Sakuradamon.

North of here, close to Otemachi subway station, is **Higashi Gyoen** (East Garden) (9 AM to 3 PM, closed Mondays and Fridays). While there is little imperial about the garden, it is a pleasant place for a stroll, and a small museum houses a selection from the imperial art collection. The main entrance is the Ote-mon Gate, in the southeast of the garden.

Enter here, and then exit from the Kitabanebashi-on Gate in the northwest of the garden, as it provides access to another interesting park with some worthwhile museum attractions.

Kitanomaru-koen Park, northwest of the Imperial Palace, and easily reached by a stroll through the East Garden, may not be Tokyo's greenest urban escape, but it is worth visiting for the **National Museum of Modern Art** (10 AM to 5 PM, closed Mondays). For anyone with an interest in how Japanese modern artists have been expressing themselves from the Meiji period onwards, it is the best overall introduction in Tokyo, with both changing and fixed exhibits. Equally noteworthy is the museum annex, the **Crafts Gallery** (same hours), which features the work of some of Japan's most famous craftspeople. The nearby **Science Museum** (9:30 AM to 5 PM, daily) is arguably only worth a visit (entry is a little expensive at ¥600) if you have children with you or if you are a science buff — aimed mostly at Japanese schoolchildren, the museum suffers from a lack of English. Lastly, in the north of the park, not far from Kudanshita subway station, is the massive **Budokan** hall, built in the early 1960s to hold judo events, but now more famously the Tokyo venue for visiting big-name rock bands.

Opposite Kitanomaru-koen Park, on the other side of Yasukuni Dori,9 is Japan's most controversial shrine — **Yasukuni-jinja Shrine**. The name means "country at peace," and it started its days as a memorial to those who died in support of the Meiji imperial restoration. It has subsequently grown to accommodate the vast numbers who died in later conflicts, notably World War II, which claimed some three million Japanese lives. Herein, unsurprisingly, lies the controversy. Class-A war criminals have been enshrined here, and, despite a constitutional separation of religion and the state, politicians make a habit of paying their respects here on the anniversary of Japan's World War II defeat (August 15). On most days, however, the temple is a quiet and unassuming Shinto structure, with a fascinating, if at times disturbing, **Military Museum**. Along with displays of bullet-torn uniforms, pride of place goes to a display of a *kaiten*, a "manned torpedo," the submarine version of the more famous *kamikaze* attack planes.

From Yasukuni-jinja Shrine, it's a good idea to hop on the Tozai subway line at nearby Kudanshita station and backtrack three stops to Nihombashi station. Here is the other face of central Tokyo, the occasionally monolithic but nevertheless fascinating flipside to the gardens, museums and palace

TOP: Many of Tokyo's boldest architectural experiments are the work of Kenzo Tange; here, the Fuji Television Headquarters. BOTTOM: In contrast, Tokyo is also home to many traditional shrines, such as Kanda Shrine pictured here.

walls you have so recently explored. There may not be quite as much to see, but if the Imperial Palace and its surrounds are in a sense the spiritual heart of Japan, then **Nihombashi**, with its banks, trading bourses and brokerages, is the heart of the economic machine that powers Japan. It's worth a lunch-time visit, as much as anything, for the bustling torrents of suited workers who come pouring out of the office blocks lining the streets here.

The name Nihombashi means "Japan Bridge," and refers to an actual bridge that once marked the geographical center of Tokyo. The original wooden bridge, a favorite of artists in the days of old Edo, is long gone, and its Meiji-era replacement languishes in the shadow of the Shuto overhead expressway, but it remains an interesting sight.

From Nihom-bashi Bridge, walk east along the south bank of the river to the **Tokyo Stock Exchange**, where, between 9 AM and 11 AM and 1 PM

and 4 PM weekdays, it is possible to catch a glimpse of Japan Inc. in action. Also close by and worth a visit are the **Yamatane Museum of Art** (10 AM to 5 PM, closed Mondays) on the eighth floor of the Yamatane Securities Building, which exhibits recent examples of traditional Japanese art, and the **Kite Museum** (11 AM to 5 PM, closed Mondays) on the fifth floor above the Tameiken Restaurant, which exhibits a fascinating collection of kites from Japan and around the world.

Back at Nihom-bashi Bridge, to the north, on **Chuo Dori** (literally "Central Street") is Japan's most venerable department store. **Mitsukoshi** changed Japanese shopping forever when it opened in the early 1670s, introducing a gamut of consumer gimmicks that over the succeeding centuries have become standard practice: door-to-door delivery, flashy window displays, fixed prices. Little of the history remains today, but the

GINZA

Despite a widespread Western convention to the contrary, it is Ginza, not *the* Ginza, though in its day this was indeed *the* place to be seen. Times have changed. Ginza today may still have a certain ring to it, but other areas have emerged as more popular places to shop. Nevertheless, Ginza, which started its days in the early Edo period as home to a mint (hence the name "Silver Mint"), has always guaranteed a certain exclusivity and does so to this day. It houses some of Tokyo's most opulent department stores, some of the city's most expensive restaurants, and it remains the preferred place for artists, famous or otherwise, to exhibit and sell their art.

What Ginza has lost is its cutting edge. One of the first districts of Tokyo to modernize, Ginza in the late nineteenth century introduced Tokyoites to gas street lamps, brick buildings and department stores. Tokyo's first trams and subways ran here, and this was where the smart set came to drink coffee and show off their Western-style umbrellas and watches. Today, Ginza is mostly about respectability — it arrived long ago and no longer needs to show off like brasher parts of town such as Shinjuku and Shibuya.

Like many parts of Tokyo, while Ginza has some attractions that are worth seeking out, it is also a superb area to wander in aimlessly. The main streets follow a logical grid pattern, making it difficult to stay lost for long, and between them are fascinating alley-like streets that yield up many surprises. Look out in particular for hole-in-the-wall galleries — Ginza teems with them. Most of them are only too happy to have you wander in and take a look at the art.

If you have arrived from Nihombashi, then the corner of Chuo Dori and Harumi Dori is a good place to start exploring the area. This is known as the Ginza Yonchome intersection, and is where you will find the Ginza subway station, along with the massive **Wako** and **Mitsukoshi** department stores. To the west along Harumi Dori is another famous Ginza landmark — the **Sony Building**. Venture inside for hands-on displays of Sony's products, along with branches of some famous Tokyo restaurants.

East along Harumi Dori is the **Nihonshu (Japan Sake) Center** (11 AM to 6:30 PM, closed Thursdays), which throws light on the production of sake, its varieties, and even provides an opportunity for a tipple or two. A short walk away is Ginza's most famous tourist attraction: the **Kabuki-za**, Tokyo's foremost venue for *kabuki*. Performances take place twice daily for the first three weeks of every month and are highly recommended.

head store of what is now a major chain remains the most prestigious of them all.

Continuing south of Nihom-bashi Bridge along Chuo Dori look out for some more of Japan's famous department stores, successors to Mitsukoshi's pioneering example: **Tokyu** and **Takashimaya**, the latter announcing itself with its distinctive red awnings. **Maruzen**, on the other side of the road, was in its turn one of Japan's pioneers in the import of Western books, and remains a good place to stock up on English-language reading material.

Farther south on Chuo Dori, on the corner of Yaesu Dori, make a point of calling into the **Bridgestone Art Museum** (10 AM to 5:30 PM, closed Mondays), which has a small but highly recommended collection of Impressionist art.

Meanwhile, straight ahead from the Bridgestone Art Museum along Chuo Dori is that most famous of Tokyo districts, Ginza.

Once the height of fashion and now very much establishment Tokyo, Ginza is still home to some of the city's most prestigious department stores and art galleries.

On the next block north of the Kabuki-za is the **World Magazine Gallery** ((03) 3545-7227. While hardly a tourist attraction, it is all the same a relaxing place to escape the crowds and browse through some of the gallery's hundreds of current magazines from around the world.

On the western outskirts of Ginza, close to the Imperial Palace are several more sights worth seeking out if you still have energy. Chances are, if you have already made that obligatory stop at the main "Tokyo i" tourist center, you will already have seen the **Tokyo International Forum**, noted for its breathtaking 60-m-high (197-ft) atrium. Close by is the **Idemitsu Art Museum** (10 AM to 5 PM, closed Mondays), which has a small but superb collection of Japanese and Chinese antiquities. It is not, however, easy to find. Look for the Kokusai (International) Building next door to the Imperial Theater (Teikoku Gekijo) — it's on the ninth floor.

Hibiya-koen Park, to the south of here, is notable only as Tokyo's first Western-style park. Sunny days bring out the office workers in droves at lunch time, but at other times it is a peaceful getaway from the crowds in Ginza and the tourists at the Imperial Palace.

TSUKIJI

Two stops from Ginza on the Hibiya subway line, Tsukiji is famous as the place where almost all of Tokyo's daily fish intake starts the day. Actually the **Tokyo Central Wholesale Market** sells more than fish, but it's the fish market and the nearby morning sushi stalls that tug in the occasional early-rising foreigner for a look at the action. The day begins at 5 AM (before the subway starts running) with the wholesale auction of fish from destinations all over the world. By 7 AM the wholesalers are selling their purchases to Tokyo's restaurateurs. **Sushisei** ((03) 3541-7720 is one of the many sushi restaurants that open from the early hours outside the market, and is universally lauded as among the best, having inspired a chain that can now be found throughout Tokyo. The market and the restaurants are closed on Sundays.

Between the market and Tsukiji subway station, look out for **Hongan-ji Temple**, which is unique among Tokyo's Buddhist temples in having been inspired by Indian architecture. It's open from 6 AM, making it a good place to visit in combination with an early morning visit to the market.

Another Tsukiji highlight is the nearby **Hama Rikyu Teien Detached Palace Garden**, which lies a short walk east of the market. Once belonging to the Tokugawa shogunate, it is a charming place of ponds, a floating teahouse and manicured gardens. Ferries depart from the pier at the garden to Asakusa, a charming cruise on the Sumida-gawa River that is highly recommended, though boats don't start with any regularity until after 10 AM.

KANDA

Kanda ward, to the northeast of the Imperial Palace, encompasses a number of very different districts. Compelling sights are few and far between, but almost all Tokyo visitors find themselves wandering agape at some point or another through Akihabara's Electric Town, a cornucopia of modern gadgetry, and more and more are trekking to Ryogoku to visit the Edo-Tokyo Museum: one of the city's newest, and something of a marvel. Less take the time to wander through the second-hand bookshop warrens of Jimbocho or the Koishikawa Koraku-en Park. This is understandable given the scale of Tokyo and the vast number of attractions clamoring for visitors' attention, but unless you are on a very busy schedule it is worth spending perhaps a half day visiting Kanda's more notable sights.

Close to Suidobashi station and the **Tokyo Dome**, home to Tokyo's Yomiuri Giants baseball team (and a baseball museum, if you're a fan), is **Koishikawa Koraku-en Park** (9 AM to 5 PM, closed Mondays). A seventeenth-century stroll garden, its purpose is to take the walker on a journey, with contrived landscapes of miniature mountains and manicured views at every turn of the winding path. At the other extreme is the adjacent **Korakuen Amusement Park**, a thrills-and-spills experience of the traditional low-tech variety.

One stop from Suidobashi on the Toei Mita subway line is **Jimbocho**. It is a minor attraction, one of those areas that are notable for flavor more than sights, but it's worth an hour or so. Its main claim to fame is its second-hand bookshops, some of them several floors high, some of them seemingly little more than fronts for "adult" magazines. **Kitazawa** is the best English bookshop in the area — head upstairs for the extensive second-hand selection, though much of it is academic. **Kanda Kosho** is the biggest of the bookshops, with seven floors of books.

The next stop, after Jimbocho, is Akihabara, a journey that involves backtracking on the Toei Mita subway line to Suidobashi and changing there to the JR Sobu line. It's possible, if you are an indefatigable explorer, to stop en-route at **Ochanomizu**, where close to the station are the **Russian Orthodox Nikolai Cathedral** and the **Yushima Seido Shrine**. The former, dating from the 1890s, came about through the efforts of Nikolai Kassatkin, a Russian Orthodox missionary. The latter is a quiet and unimposing Confucius shrine.

At **Akihabara**, the next stop from Ochanomizu (two from Suidobashi) on the Sobu line, the atmosphere changes dramatically. Just as Jimbocho specializes in books — district commercial specialization is a feature of many Asian cities, and old Edo was no exception — in Akihabara the stock in trade is electronics. It all started as an "under the tracks" black market, but today it is a legitimate industry, a bustling place of blazing neon, ear-piercing advertisements and wall-to-wall gadgetry. Most of the larger stores have tax-free sections and should also be able to help with finding models that are compatible with your home electrical requirements and standards. To find the action, just follow the signs that start on the Akihabara station platform announcing **Electric** (or Denki) **Town**.

Take the Sobu line two more stops east, and you arrive at Ryogoku, famous for its **National Sumo Stadium**, and now home to one of the city's best museums. The stadium fills with fans just

museum allows you to take a grand tour of Tokyo's history, from its earliest days through its emergence as a major city in the Edo period to its embrace of the modern world in the Meiji period. The sections on the floating world are particularly good, and the scale models of street and festival scenes will be a winner with children.

UENO

While Ueno, just two stops north of Akihabara on the Yamanote line, is an interesting area to poke around in, its park, one of Tokyo's largest open spaces, is what pulls in the crowds. The attraction is not simply the park itself, which has some pleasant

three times a year — usually in January, May and September — and at other times the only way to get a taste of Japan's unique sporting obsession is to take a look at the stadium's attached Sumo Museum (9:30 AM to 4:30 PM, closed weekends). There's very little English labeling and the presentations are somewhat pedestrian, however. Don't be surprised if you come across sumo wrestlers wandering the street in *yukata* in the area — Ryogoku is still home to some *sumo-beya*, or sumo stables, where the big boys train.

But the real treat of Ryogoku is the **Edo-Tokyo Museum (** (03) 3626-9974 (10 AM to 6 PM, 8 PM Thursdays and Fridays, closed Mondays), a massive, futuristic structure (it is allegedly meant to represent a rice granary) on legs that covers 30,000 sq m (35,880 sq yards) — don't worry, the ticket enables you to come and go as you please for the whole day. Starting on the sixth floor, the

walks, but the concentration of museums in the park, along with a surprisingly good zoo — at least by Asian standards.

In fact, with so many attractions clustered together in the park, it is easy to forget the park itself. This is a pity. At almost any time of the year, it is a wonderful urban escape. It also has an interesting history: once home to Edo's major Buddhist temple complex (all that remains today is the shrine of Tokugawa Ieyasu), in 1868 it was the site of a last-ditch stand — now known as the Battle of Ueno — by Tokugawa loyalists against supporters of the Meiji restoration. Ueno Park is also, usually in April, the site of Tokyo's most raucous celebrations of the fleeting but colorful cherry-blossom season. Come nightfall, the cherry trees are

The wee hours of the morning see Tokyo's Tsukiji Fish Market come to life, as the city's restaurateurs haggle for their daily stock of fish.

strung with lanterns, and the revelers spread out picnics, quaff sake and make merry. Stay away if you don't like crowds.

For a tour of the park, take the Shinobazu exit at JR Ueno station. A flight of stairs leads from here to a curious statue of a samurai warrior walking a dog. The warrior in question is **Saigo Takamori**, a prominent leader in the Meiji restoration, who, having seen the emperor restored to power, became disillusioned in his hometown of Kagoshima with the modernizing influences sweeping Japan. In 1877 he led a rebellion against the imperial forces, but was beaten. He committed ritual suicide. Just 15 years later he was pardoned by imperial decree, and a statue erected here in his honor.

The main attraction, however, is **Tosho-gu Shrine**, which lies back in the park and farther along the path you have been following since you entered. Built in 1651, it is one of Tokyo's oldest structures. Like the shrine of the same name in Nikko, it is dedicated to Tokugawa Ieyasu, the warlord who unified all Japan and upon his death was declared divine. Perhaps there is some truth in the latter claim, considering the disasters his shrine here in Ueno has survived to make it unscathed into the twenty-first century.

Lastly, if you are not ready for the museums, just north of Tosho-gu Shrine is **Tokyo Zoo** (9:30 AM to 5:30 PM, closed Mondays). The star attraction is the pandas, but foreigners are as likely to take

A pathway leads from Saigo's memorial statue to the main tree-lined avenue that snakes through Ueno Park. Follow this path north and you arrive at the **Kiyomizu Kannon-do Temple**. The temple is modeled on its better known, and more impressive, Kyoto counterpart, Kiyomizu-dere and is dedicated to Kannon, the goddess of mercy, known in Chinese as Guanyin — here she is worshipped in her *senju*, or "1,000-armed" manifestation. Women wishing to have children leave dolls at the shrine here, and the dolls are ceremoniously burned once a year on January 25.

The path continues from here alongside the Shinobazu Pond. An interesting diversion is in store for those who look out for the red *torii* that announces a causeway out to an island in the pond. This is **Benten-do Temple** (Benzi-ten), an unassuming temple dedicated to Benten, patron goddess of the arts, among other things.

as much pleasure from the platoons of small children marching in formation, sketching the exhibits and listening respectfully to their teachers' lectures about the big outdoors.

But, when all is said and done, when you've explored the park, perhaps popped into the zoo, the real reason to come to Ueno is the museums. The **Tokyo National Museum** ((03) 3822-1111; 9 AM to 4:30 PM, closed Mondays) alone would be worth making an excursion to Ueno for. After all, the world's largest collection of Japanese art is a place even someone with a casual interest in Japanese culture could easily spend a couple of hours exploring. Not that the museum restricts itself only to Japanese art: one gallery features art from all corners of the Orient. There are five galleries in all, any one of which could easily eat up hours of contemplation. The **Honkan** (main gallery), for example, has 25 exhibition rooms displaying everything from arms and armor on the first floor to paintings and lacquerware on the second. The **Toyokan**, with three floors, exhibits east-Asian antiquities and art. The two-story **Heiseikan** is devoted to Japanese archeology. The **Horyuji Homotsukan** exhibits seventh- and eighth-century treasures from Nara's Horyuji Temple. Meanwhile, the **Hyokeikan**, a Meiji era structure, is an attraction in itself, and has been designated an Important Cultural Property.

The **National Museum of Western Art** (9:30 AM to 5 PM, 8 PM Fridays, closed Mondays) is a wonderful place to visit on a sunny day, as the courtyard in front of the main gallery (designed by Le Corbusier) is home to a small army of Rodin sculptures. Works inside include paintings by Renoir, Gauguin and Monet, and the museum is also frequently host to popular visiting exhibitions.

The **National Science Museum** (9 AM to 4:30 PM, closed Mondays) may not be in quite the same league as its neighbors, but it is a great place to come if you have children. English labeling is far more generous than at most other science attractions in Japan.

Easy to miss, but also recommended, is the **Shitamachi History Museum** (9:30 AM to 4:30 PM, closed Mondays) on the southeast corner of Shinobazu Pond. A recreation of life in Edo's old Shitamachi district, the museum provides a unique opportunity to doff your shoes and poke around in a merchant's house, a candy shop, and the home of an ordinary Shitamachi denizen.

Ueno has one more highlight, **Ameyoko Arcade**. This bustling market is opposite Ueno station and the park, having evolved from an under-the-tracks black market, and it is the perfect place to bring someone who thinks Japan is all stuffed-shirt scrapes and bows. Raucous, in-your-face, the salespeople who work the crowds here — no matter whether they're peddling fish or rip-off Gucci handbags — are anything but demure and retiring about their work. The range of products on sale is vast, making it a good place to shop, but in the end it's simply a fun place to browse and see the other side of Tokyo.

ASAKUSA

If Ueno provides some fascinating glimpses of the other Tokyo, a trip out to Asakusa, two stops away on the Ginza subway line, is a journey farther into the same territory. Asakusa is probably as close as contemporary Tokyo gets to the Shitamachi of times of past, and its focus is **Senso-ji Temple**.

For anyone who thinks of Buddhist temples, particularly Japanese Buddhist temples, as places of quiet contemplation, the approach to Senso-ji will come as a surprise. It starts with the jostling crowds at the **Kaminari-mon Gate**, next to the subway exit. Housed on either side of the "Thunder

Gate" are respectively the fierce gods of the wind and thunder — Fujin and Raijin. Ahead lies Nakamise Dori, a gaudy, permanent festival of stalls selling everything from soy-flavored crackers (*sembei*) to handmade dolls and *kabuki* wigs. At the end of the market street stands the **Hozo-mon Gate**, also guarded by fierce gods and housing holy *sutras* on its upper floors. Inside the temple compound there is invariably a crowd jostling for position around a huge incense urn, waving their arms in an attempt to waft the holy smoke over their bodies — it is said to bestow health-giving effects. The temple itself, a post-World War II reconstruction, provides little to see, though the spectacle of hordes of worshippers tossing coins and bowing at the altar is an attraction in itself. Legend has it that the temple houses an image of Kannon (goddess of infinite compassion and mercy) that was fished out of the nearby Sumida-gawa River nearly 14 centuries ago by two brothers. But the image, if indeed it exists, is too holy to be displayed.

The Shinto shrine on the temple grounds behind Senso-ji is **Asakusa-jinja Shrine**. Finding a Buddhist temple and Shinto shrine sharing the same temple grounds is not uncommon in Japan, and says a lot about how the two religions have coexisted for centuries. It was founded in 1649 in memory of the two fisherman brothers who discovered the Kannon image, though like Senso-ji it is a twentieth-century reconstruction.

If you have arrived in Asakusa by subway, a fine way to leave is via the Sumida-gawa River. Boats for the so-called **Sumida-gawa Cruise** leave from the dock below Azuma-bashi Bridge, departing approximately every half hour between approximately 9:30 AM and 5 PM for the Hama Rikyu Detached Palace Garden in Tsukiji, not far from Ginza. It may not be the world's most picturesque river cruise, but it provides a view of Tokyo you will never get from the subway.

IKEBUKURO

On the northwestern edge of the Yamanote loop, almost directly opposite Ueno, is Ikebukuro, a sprawling commercial district that acts as a commuter gateway to the far-flung suburbs north of the city. Be warned: along with Shinjuku, Ikebukuro has one of the most confusing stations in Tokyo; if you get lost, you will not be the first.

Like Shinjuku, Ikebukuro divides into east (*higashi*) and west (*nishi*) districts, the separating line being the vast station flanked by Tokyo's biggest department stores: Tobu on the west and Seibu on the east. Nishi Ikebukuro, with its Metropolitan

---

While much of Tokyo's historical heritage was destroyed in the Great Kanto Earthquake of 1913 or the aerial bombing of World War II, pockets survive, surrounded by modern architecture that sprouted up in the latter half of the twentieth century.

Plaza, countless restaurants and hide-away bars is the more interesting of the two to explore, but Higashi Ikebukuro, with its cinema complexes, pachinko parlors and discount electronics is also worth taking a look at. Bear in mind, however, that the attractions on either side are minimal, and Ikebukuro can safely be dropped from a busy tour of Tokyo.

The big attraction on the east side is the **Sunshine 60 Tower**, which at 240 m (787 ft) has Tokyo's highest viewing platform — a worthwhile excursion on a fine day — though rather expensive at ¥620, particularly given that Shinjuku offers free high-altitude views that are only slightly less lofty. Auto buffs should take a look at the **Toyota Amlux Showroom**, which offers high-tech displays of the latest Toyota offerings close to the base of the tower.

The **Tobu Department Store** dominates the west side of the station. Reportedly the biggest department store in the world, it is a city in itself. It includes the nearby **Metropolitan Hall**, which is more a collection of boutiques and restaurants than a department store. Step outside the Metropolitan Hall and you will be confronted by the windy expanse of the **Metropolitan Plaza**, which has become a gathering place for Japanese youth, and the **Metropolitan Art Space**, which has a small art museum with changing exhibits on the ground floor and a much celebrated escalator ride.

A recommended excursion from Ikebukuro — indeed it should be recommended above Ikebukuro itself — is to **Rikugi-en Garden** (9 AM to 4:30 PM, closed Mondays), three stops on the Yamanote line back towards Ueno, close to Komagome station. A beautiful example of a Japanese stroll garden, it dates back to 1695, and recreates celebrated scenes from Japanese poetry at every turn of its meandering paths. The literary allusions will be lost on the average walker — Japanese included — but no matter; it is enough to appreciate the garden as a garden.

SHINJUKU

Love it or hate it, Shinjuku is in many ways the ultimate modern Tokyo experience — Kabuki-cho, on the east side, is allegedly the inspiration for the sets of *Blade Runner*. Dividing, like Ikebukuro, into west and east sections, it has everything: soaring skyscrapers, lavish department stores, a neon-lit red-light district, a sprawling park, a secluded Shinto shrine, and more restaurants, bars and clubs than you could explore in a lifetime. For anyone with just a day to dip into the Tokyo experience, it would be difficult to suggest anywhere more apt to spend it than Shinjuku.

The east and west sides of the station are different worlds, each with its own merits, but it is the east side that conjures up all the excitement. The west side is somewhat monolithic, a showcase for some of Tokyo's best (and highest) architecture, while the east side pullulates with people getting and spending, laying waste their powers, and presumably having a lot of fun in the process.

The best way to approach Shinjuku's east side is to strike out and get lost, soaking up the atmosphere of the place. If you get *very* lost — unlikely — you can always plunge underground, where a sign-posted subterranean warren mirrors the above-ground action — the underground network connects with the subways and eventually JR Shinjuku station. Back on the surface, east Shinjuku's action fans out north and south of Yasukuni Dori. The wedge between Yasukuni Dori and Shinjuku Dori is mostly department stores, restaurants and boutiques, while the section immediately east of the station and north of Yasukuni Dori is Tokyo's infamous Kabuki-cho, its biggest and liveliest red-light area.

For orientation take Shinjuku station's east exit and look out for the **Studio Alta** building. It is easily identifiable by its huge television screen. Along with the Hachiko statue in Shibuya, this is one of the city's most popular rendezvous spots, making it a positively bad place to rendezvous with friends, though it helps if they are *gaijin*, who tend to stand out in the crowd. There is little as such to see in the vicinity of Studio Alta, though the nearby **Kinokuniya bookshop** is probably Tokyo's best-stocked supplier of English-language reading material, and the **Isetan Department Store** has an excellent art gallery with changing exhibits. The best idea is to walk north from Studio Alta, cross Yasukuni Dori and plunge into **Kabuki-cho**, which as red-light areas go offers an oddly wholesome form of seediness — at least on street level.

Foreigners are unlikely to be bothered much in Kabuki-cho, though occasionally single men may be offered guidance to strip shows by touts. Such offers are easily shrugged off, leaving you free to stroll around the area. The heart of the area is the **Koma Theater**, which is fronted by a square that is surrounded by cinemas and, come nightfall, is always packed with people. Note that Kabuki-cho is by no means wall-to-wall sleaze — the area is also packed with excellent restaurants and some fascinating hole-in-the-wall bars. But the overall ambiance is a bizarre confluence of shrieked recorded advertisements, crackling neon and heterogeneous crowds that contain everyone from Japanese punks to perm-topped *yakuza* tripping along in colorful sandals.

East of Kabuki-cho, along Yasukuni Dori, make a point of taking an alley that leads to **Hanazono-jinja Shrine**. It's a surprisingly restful spot, though the rebuilt shrine itself is a little disappointing. West of the shrine, a warren of alleys lead into a Tokyo establishment known as **Golden Gai**. Long a haunt of intellectuals and artists, Tokyo's demimonde, it is remarkable that this maze of hideaway bars has lasted as long as it has, and indeed for the last two decades reports of its imminent demise have been rampant. Nevertheless, it is still there. It's not a wise idea to do much more than wander through the area of an evening and look, however. Most of the bars, no matter how ramshackle looking, operate as members' clubs, and are not particularly welcoming to outsiders.

Farther to the east, and slightly south of Shinjuku Dori, is **Shinjuku-gyoen Park** (9 AM to 4:30 PM, closed Mondays). As Western-style parks go, this is probably Tokyo's best, and well worth an excursion after you have soaked up the frenetic atmosphere of east Shinjuku. It has some wonderful

building of the lot, the **Tokyo Metropolitan Government Building**, home to more than 13,000 city government workers, a cloud-scraping monster of a building that could have been snatched from the movie *Brazil*. This creation of Tange Kenzo, Japan's pre-eminent architect, despite what some consider to be its overbearing nature, is a marvelous structure. A free viewing platform on the forty-fifth floor provides stunning views of Shinjuku and the rest of Tokyo on a clear day.

HARAJUKU

Harajuku is synonymous in Tokyo with quirky youth fashion, and was the site until 1996 of a

walks, a number of gardens and an interesting hothouse, along with cafés offering set-lunches at affordable prices.

North of the park, in the area east of Gyoen Dori and wedged between Shinjuku Dori and Yasukuni Dori is **Shinjuku Nichome**, a nondescript area by day but Tokyo's gay district by night. Stroll through the area after 10 PM and you will find dozens upon dozens of bars, some welcoming, some less so, but none hostile.

The contrast between east and west Shinjuku is extreme. If the east side is a maze of congested alleys, the west side is all boulevards and soaring towers of steel and glass. Despite its crowdedness there's something intimate about the east side. The west side, on the other hand, is the place where Tokyo asserts itself as a place of power and wealth. As you emerge from the west exit of Shinjuku station, directly ahead of you is the most impressive

weekly counter-culture festival in the form of hundreds of bands cranking out music every Sunday. The fashions live on, but the bands are gone. Harajuku, meanwhile, is far more than retro punk and Hello Kitty chic. It is also home to Tokyo's most impressive Shinto shrine, and has some of the city's most charming al fresco cafés. In short, it's one of the most interesting parts of the city to spend an afternoon.

The main reason for visiting Harajuku is **Meiji-jingu Shrine** (8:30 AM to 5 PM daily), which lies next to Harajuku station on the Yamanote line. Like most other shrines in Tokyo it was destroyed in the aerial bombing of World War II, but unlike most of the other shrines it was re-built

Tokyo's Harajuku is the place to go to see the zany inventiveness of Japan's youth culture on display; here three girls showcase the bizarre fashions that can be found in Harajuku's boutiques.

in 1958 with absolute attention to detail, the cypress for the shrine's massive *torii* gates being famously imported from Mount Ali-shan in Taiwan. Take some time out on the way into the shrine area to visit the **Meiji-jingu Park**, which is especially beautiful in the early summer months when more than a hundred varieties of iris are in bloom. Behind the shrine is the **Meiji-jingu Treasure House**, which after the beauty of the grounds and the shrine itself comes as something of an anticlimax. The displays on imperial life can be missed unless you have a special interest in such things. A word of warning: Meiji-jingu is best avoided on January 1, when it is overrun with literally millions of visitors

Mondays). Dedicated to Japanese *ukiyo-e*, or woodblock prints, this is a rare opportunity to see originals by masters of the art such as Hiroshige and Hokusai.

If you backtrack again on Omotesando and start walking away from Harajuku station, you will notice that the farther you go, the more fashionable the area becomes. Shops to look out for include the **Oriental Bazaar** — a good place to shop for souvenirs — and **Kiddyland**, a great place to take children providing you are prepared to spend some money on them. But as you continue in the direction of Aoyama Dori, heart of fashionable **Aoyama**, smart boutiques like Comme des Garcons take over. Serious art buffs

— the occasion is Hatsumode, the first shrine worshipping of the year.

The adjoining **Yoyogi-koen Park** is of little interest now that the once-famous weekly battle of the bands are no more. Rather continue to Harajuku station and cross the road to **Takeshita Dori**, which is like a living gallery of Tokyo youth fashion. Best avoided on Sundays, when the narrow street is cheek-by-jowl with shoppers, at other times of the week it is a fascinating insight into how Tokyo's young dispose of their parents' incomes.

At the bottom of Takeshita Dori, it's time to do some backtracking. Turn right, walk past the La Foret Building, and turn right again onto **Omotesando**, Tokyo's most elegant boulevard. A little way back towards Harajuku station, down an alley to the right (behind La Foret in other words) is the highly recommended **Ota Memorial Museum of Art** (10:30 AM to 5:30 PM, closed

might continue walking on Omotesando past Aoyama Dori, looking out on the right for the entrance to the **Nezu Art Gallery** (9:30 AM to 4:30 PM, closed Mondays), which is one of Tokyo's most expensive with an entrance charge of ¥1,000. Still, this does give the place an air of exclusivity, making it a quiet place to browse the small collection of Japanese and Chinese antiquities, and explore the museum's delightful and surprisingly expansive traditional gardens complete with tea houses.

SHIBUYA

Shibuya is in many ways a trendier, more youth-friendly version of Shinjuku. It's not exactly brimming with things to see, but it is still an interesting area to plunge into. Take the exit signposted "**Hachiko**," which is a statue of a dog and also happens to be Tokyo's most famous rendezvous spot — out-rivaling even Shinjuku's Studio Alta, and making it even worse a place to actually find the people you are rendezvousing with. Why a statue of a dog? The story goes that in the 1920s Hachiko was in the habit of waiting in this spot for his master to come home, except that one day his master didn't, having died at work. Hachiko persisted in waiting for a total of nine years before passing away, the kind of loyalty that Japanese find particularly irresistible.

Opposite Hachiko, Shibuya fans away in a wide "V" shape. **Dogenzaka**, to the left, goes up to Tokyo's most famous enclave of "love hotels," while Bunkamura Dori cuts through the middle, leading up to the **Bunka Mura** (literally "Culture Village"), an arts center that is event-oriented but worth visiting to see if anything interesting is happening.

It's also worth striking off to explore the narrow streets between Bunkamura Dori and Koen Dori. Things to look out for are the enormous **Tokyu Hands Department Store**, the **Loft Department Store**, and so-called **Spain Dori**, a steep, snaking alley lined with restaurants and boutiques that has become a favorite youth haunt. At the intersection of Koen Dori and Meiji Dori, take some time out to explore the massive branch of **Tower Records**, the biggest in Asia and probably one of the biggest in the world. If you are in the mood for one of Tokyo's quirkiest museums, continue north up Koen Dori to the **Tobacco and Salt Museum** (10 AM to 6 PM, closed Mondays), which has surprisingly interesting exhibitions on, you guessed it, tobacco and salt.

EBISU

Ebisu is a recent arrival on the Tokyo tourist circuit. Even today, unless you happen to be a photography buff or a committed beer drinker, its attractions are not compelling, but it is, nevertheless, an up-and-coming sub-city on the Yamanote loop and, just one stop south of Shibuya, is worth a quick visit.

Deciding which of Ebisu's two main attractions to visit first could cause arguments: it's beer versus photography. Of course, you might leave the best for last and take a stroll through the **Tokyo Metropolitan Photography Museum** (10 AM to 6 PM, 8 PM on Fridays, closed Mondays) first. It's somewhat expensive at ¥800, but for anyone with an interest in photography it is a fascinating place to explore, featuring some of the world's best shooters and including all kinds of background information on the development of the art. No less interesting is the **Yebisu Beer Museum** (10 AM to 6 PM, closed on Mondays), which additionally happens to be free, unless you opt to sample some of the exhibits, for which you will be charged prices much lower than in most Tokyo bars.

MEGURO

Meguro should only be on the itinerary of visitors with oodles of time in Tokyo. It is a nondescript area with only a couple of attractions to claim your attention.

Foremost among these, is the **Tokyo Metropolitan Teien Art Museum** (10 AM to 6 PM, closed the second and fourth Wednesday of every month), and even this is an attraction less for its exhibits than the building they are housed in — an art-deco structure designed by French architect Henri Rapin in the 1930s. If you visit the Metropolitan Museum, be sure to also visit the **Nature Study Garden** (9 AM to 4 PM, closed Mondays) next door. This beautiful garden is notable for its enlightened policy on visitor numbers, which are restricted to no more than 300 at a time, and its mission to preserve the original flora of Edo-era Tokyo, making it a fascinating place to discover what Tokyo looked like before the concrete was poured.

AKASAKA AND ROPPONGI

While many travelers find themselves staying in Akasaka — like west Shinjuku it has many of the city's best hotels — few go there to see the sights. Not without reason: Akasaka has little to see. One of the area's few highlights is **Hie-jinja Shrine**, which has perhaps the most delightful shrine entrance of any in Japan — a narrow path lined with red *torii* gates that seem to stretch ahead of the climber like a dazzling tunnel. The shrine itself is unassuming but peaceful.

Roppongi, on the other hand, has fairly little in the way of hotels but does attract many visitors — mostly by night. Tokyo's most famous, if not notorious, nightlife district has in fact little to attract visitors by day. The only real exception to this is the nearby **Tokyo Tower** (although it is actually much closer to Kamiyacho station, one stop from Roppongi on the Hibiya subway line). The tower's opening hours depend on the season, but they are essentially from 9 AM to 8 PM for most of the year, and from 9 AM to 6 PM from December through February. Modeled on Paris's Eiffel Tower and built in the 1950s, Tokyo Tower is today something of an anachronism, but for some visitors that is part of the fun. Be warned though: the **Grand Observation Platform**, while undoubtedly high, at 250 m (820 ft), will set you back ¥1,400, which makes it a decidedly expensive overview of the city. Other attractions in the tower, such as an aquarium and a wax museum, are similarly expensive.

Tokyo never ceases to offer up surprises, such as this postmodern sculpture in Meguro, long a backwater on the circular Yamanote line.

ODAIBA

Odaiba, a manmade island in Tokyo Bay, is more popular with day-tripping Tokyoites than it is with visiting foreigners. In fact, it is so popular with day-tripping Tokyoites that a weekend jaunt out there is not recommended. It's reached from Shimbashi station on the Yamanote line, from where the Yurikamome monorail approaches the island. Its attractions are the **Rainbow Bridge**, which provides superb views of Tokyo Bay; **Tokyo Big Sight**, an international exhibition space fronted by four inverted pyramids on giant legs; the **Museum of Maritime Science**; and an **artificial beach**.

and novelty shops, cafés and restaurants, each carefully harmonized with the setting in which it is located.

The bad news for homesick Americans is that Tokyo Disneyland's lingua franca is Japanese. The good news, perhaps, is that the food available will at least be roughly similar to that at the original. The surprise for anybody unfamiliar with Disneyland in America is the attention given to detail in making this a seamless and self-contained four-dimensional theater, and the extravagantly high quality of the finish.

Fear of overcrowding led Tokyo Disneyland's management to stipulate, before the park opened, that all visitors must book in advance, but this

TOKYO DISNEYLAND

Tokyoites have had their own Disneyland for so long now they could be forgiven for forgetting that it all started across the ocean in California. In April 1983 Walt Disney Productions' third theme park, and the first outside the United States, opened its gates to the public. The huge amusement park, built on reclaimed land in Chiba, east of the city, is one-and-a-half times the size of the original in Anaheim, but its attractions are basically the same. The park's 58-ha (143-acre) area is divided into six "themed lands": Adventureland, Westernland, Fantasyland, Toontown, Critter Country and Tomorrowland. Within each of these environments are a number of rides, including a jungle cruise, a trip through Snow White's adventures and the much-praised space trip. The park is also crammed with performance areas, gift

policy has been abandoned as unnecessary. Now you are almost guaranteed entrance on any day in the year, though if it's really packed you may be asked to wait awhile. The management point out that mornings and evenings are relatively slack, and they also suggest that visitors consider eating before or after the regular lunch hour (noon to 1 PM in Japan): the lines outside the restaurants can be horrendous, and picnic lunches are not allowed inside the grounds. Admission costs ¥3,670 (adults), ¥3,260 (12 to 18 year-olds), ¥2,550 (4 to 11 year-olds), while a "Passport," including admission and access to all rides and attractions except the Shootin' Gallery, costs ¥5,200 (adults), ¥4,590 (12 to 18 year-olds) and ¥3,570 (4 to 11 year-olds).

To get to Tokyo Disneyland take the JR Keiyo line or Musashino line from Tokyo Station to Maihama Station. The trip takes 15 minutes.

TOURING TOKYO

Getting to know Tokyo's interesting ins and outs takes time. If you're in a hurry, why not join a tour? The Japan Travel Bureau (JTB) offers several, advertised as **Sunrise Tours** ((03) 5620-9500, with the foreign visitor in mind, and though the buses tend to get clogged in the capital's frightful traffic they will take you to places you would have trouble finding on your own. The following are a few of the regular tours.

Tokyo Disneyland is a full-day tour of the hugely popular theme park closely modeled on the versions in Anaheim and Florida. Fares run for adults ¥8,800; juniors aged 12 to 17 years old, ¥8,000; and children 4 to 11 years old, ¥5,700. Saturdays, Sundays and Public Holidays (with certain exceptions, including Disneyland holidays); year round.

Panoramic Tokyo is a full-day city tour, including Meiji Shrine, Imperial East Garden (or Imperial Palace Plaza), Asakusa, Tokyo Bay cruise, drive through Ginza. It runs daily, March through November (adults ¥9,350, children ¥7,150, lunch included).

Tokyo Morning Cityrama offers the above minus lunch and the Tokyo Bay cruise. It runs daily (except at New Year period) for ¥3,500 (adults) and ¥2,700 (children).

Kabuki Night provides dinner, a night ride through the city, and a *kabuki* theater show. The cost is ¥10,950 for adults and ¥8,800 for children. They run daily, except when there is no *kabuki* show sheduled.

Tokyo Wondernight is a monorail ride, a high-rise view of the city, dinner, and a topless dance show in Roppongi for ¥11,400 (over 18s only); daily except during the New Year period.

SHOPPING

Tokyo's reputation as one of the world's most expensive cities means that many visitors don't think of it as a city to shop in. But, while some things are more expensive than at home — wherever that might be — Tokyo is not without its bargains and reasonably priced souvenirs.

ARTS AND CRAFTS

All of Tokyo's big department stores have arts and crafts sections, and while obviously days could be spent trawling through these places it is worth taking a look at the selection in one or two of the bigger branches — the **Tobu** and **Seibu** department stores in Ikebukuro are good choices, as is **Isetan** in Shinjuku.

In Harajuku, a fixture on the tourist circuit — but none the less enjoyable for all that — is the

Oriental Bazaar ((03) 3400-3933, a bric-a-brac-strewn store with good bargains on everything from kimonos to paper fans. Prices are generally very reasonable, making it a perfect place to shop for interesting souvenirs. It's closed Thursdays. Also in Harajuku, a flea market is held at **Togo-jinja Shrine**, next to Takeshita Dori and directly opposite the JR station, on the first and fourth Sunday of every month — the market stalls open in the wee hours, and if you are a real bargain hunter this is definitely the time to come. **Hanazono-jinja Shrine** in Shinjuku has a similar flea market every Sunday.

A couple of spaces in town bring together groups of antique traders. The best is the **Tokyo**

Folkcraft and Antiques Hall ((03) 3982-3433, about five minutes walk from the east exit of Ikebukuro station in the basement of the Satomi Building. There are more than 30 different traders here, making it a wonderful place for a rummage. It's closed Thursdays.

CAMERAS AND ELECTRONICS

Shinjuku is Tokyo's hunting ground for cameras, and it is not a bad area to look for electronics either, though Akihabara is the place for cut-throat bargains. **Yodobashi Camera** in west

OPPOSITE: While Tokyo is packed with gargantuan department stores, many of the city's tiny specialist stores still do a busy trade, such as this camera store packed with lenses next door to a shop specializing in fans. ABOVE: Tokyo's crown jewel for travelers with children:Tokyo Disneyland.

Shinjuku claims to be the biggest camera store in the world, and though it is a massive place, it still manages to be cramped. In the back alleys of Kabuki-cho and east Shinjuku look out for hole-in-the-wall second-hand camera shops, some of which have very good deals on lenses and cameras. Ginza is another area to look for second-hand camera supplies.

In Akihabara, the massive **Laox** is one of the few stores where you will find English-speaking staff. Fortunately their prices are usually competitive with other stores in the area, though if you can memorize the name of the product you are after it always pays to shop around.

BOOKS AND MUSIC

For Tokyo's best selection of English-language books, go to the south exit of Shinjuku station and look for the **Kinokuniya Bookshop** behind the Takashimaya Times Square. There is another, also very well stocked, branch in east Shinjuku. In Nihombashi, Maruzen is another bookshop with English (and French and German) language reading material. Tokyo's biggest music store is **Tower Records** in Shibuya, which has six floors of mostly music. Shibuya also has branches of **HMV**, while **Virgin** has a large store in east Shinjuku. Bargains can be found on CDs if you shop around.

WHERE TO STAY

Tokyo has something for nearly every budget and taste, though it makes life much easier for those who are prepared to throw around some money and live in style. Also, more so than in most Asian cities, Tokyo is a city where reservations are extremely important. Hotels can be fully booked at the oddest of times. The **Welcome Inn Reservation Center** ((03) 3211-4201 can help with reservations for certain hotels.

LUXURY

Trying to come up with the best hotel in Tokyo is a near impossible task. A number of hotels vie for the number-one spot, each of them with outstanding characteristics of their own. But close to the top of anyone's list would be the **Park Hyatt Tokyo** ((03) 5322-1234 FAX (03) 5322-1288 WEB SITE http://tokyo.hyatt.com/tyoph/, 3-7-1-2 Nishi-Shinjuku, Shinjuku-ku, a relative newcomer. Located on the upper floors of the soaring Shinjuku Park Tower, an architectural wonder designed by Kenzo Tange, the hotel is aimed first at international business travelers, and this is reflected in the facilities provided in the hotel's 178 guest rooms — which come complete with two telephone lines, a modem socket, voice mail, CD player, walk-in wardrobe and a soak bathtub.

There are just four restaurants, but the New York Bar & Grill, towering 235 m (770 ft) over Shinjuku, is rated as among the best American restaurants in Tokyo, and has nightly live jazz performances, often by name performers.

Another top-notch Tokyo hotel is the **Hotel Okura** ((03) 3582-0111 FAX (03) 3582-3707 WEB SITE www.okura.com/tokyo.html, 2-10-4 Toranomon, Minato-ku, which possesses one of Tokyo's most prestigious addresses, near the United States embassy and Kamiyacho subway station, just a stone's throw from Roppongi if you want nightlife. It's a massive place, with 858 guest rooms, 12 bars and restaurants, gardens, its own art museum, and will even provide you with an e-mail address for the duration of your stay. The roster of celebrity guests who have stayed here is impressive, if the idea of being in good company appeals to you.

An interesting option is to stay in one of Ginza's luxury hotels. This puts you in the heart of the city, making sightseeing a breeze. The most exclusive of Ginza's hotels is the **Hotel Seiyo Ginza** ((03) 3535-1111 FAX (03) 3535-1110 E-MAIL hsgmktng @tkf.att.ne.jp, 1-11-2 Ginza. Every guest in this small, 72-room hotel has his or her own private secretary to organize sightseeing and business affairs, and each of the rooms is individually furnished and designed by, in some cases famous, designers. Obviously such attention is reflected in the room rates, which start at around ¥42,000. On the downside, not all rooms have modem services, though they are being phased in, and there is no swimming pool.

For a luxury hotel that provides respite from the push-and-shove, allowing you to dip into the big city from the oasis of a garden setting, the **Four Seasons Chinzan-So** ((03) 3943-2222 FAX (03) 3943-2300 WEB SITE www.fshr.com/locations/Tokyo/main.html, 0-8 Sekiguchi 2-chome, Bunkyo-ku, is set in nearly seven hectares (17 acres) of Japanese garden. The 283 rooms come in either Western or Japanese decor, and there is an Old World elegance about the entire hotel. Its location is not so much remote — it's not far from Mejiro station on the Yamanote line, between Ikebukuro and Shinjuku — as off the beaten track, allowing the hotel to provide much larger rooms than are the norm in Tokyo. The hotel claims they are the city's largest, but the Park Hyatt is a close contender.

MODERATE

Most of Tokyo's mid-range hotels are business establishments. Japanese business hotels are in a league of their own. Rooms are generally minuscule, check-out times may often be at the ungodly hour of 9 AM, and there may even be evening curfews. It goes without saying that you should not expect any character in such places. Tokyo is brimming with these hotels, and in a pinch they are perfectly reasonable places to spend a night, usually with rates from ¥8,000 and upwards for a single. The area immediately surrounding Ikebukuro station — both east and west — is a good place to look, but the same goes for Ueno and Asakusa stations. The following selection includes hotels that break the business hotel convention, and make for an interesting Tokyo stay without breaking the budget.

Highly recommended is the **Hilltop Hotel** ((03) 3293-2311 FAX (03) 3233-4567, 1-1 Surugadai, Kanda, a unique Tokyo establishment that dates back to the 1930s and was once a favored haunt of the novelist Mishima Yukio — don't worry, this is not where he ritually disemboweled himself. The hotel, which comes with restaurants and bars, and rooms that ooze character, is small (just 78 rooms) so it is wise to book ahead. It's close to Ochanomizu station. Be warned, however, that it only just creeps into the moderate category: room rates start at ¥15,000.

For that most unexpected of things, a moderately priced hotel in the heart of Ginza with room rates approximately half that of the Hilltop, the **Hotel Alcyone** ((03) 3541-3621 FAX (03) 3541-3263, 4-14-3 Ginza, is recommended. It's something of an odd place, having been converted from a Japanese-style hotel some time in the 1980s to a Western-style establishment with an attached Swiss restaurant. Some of the rooms have failed to make the full conversion, coming with tatami mats. The public bath is another unusual touch (don't worry, the rooms all have their own bathrooms). But there is little to complain about the service or the size of the rooms. The location, just a short walk from the Kabuki-za, is superb.

If you are only in Japan on a brief visit and Tokyo is your main port of call, it is good to know that even in Tokyo you can enjoy the legendary *ryokan* experience at a price nearly everyone can afford. The **Ryokan Shigetsu** ((03) 3843-2345 FAX (03) 3843-2348, 1-31-11 Asakusa, Taito-ku, is a superbly atmospheric location close to the heart of Senso-ji Temple's Nakamise Dori. It's a small place, with just 24 rooms, so advance bookings are essential, especially if you want one of the 10 Japanese-style rooms (recommended). The *ryokan* comes complete with male and female public baths, each of which have views of the nearby pagoda in the temple grounds. *Kaiseki* (banquet) dinners are available on request.

Lastly, for a hotel with character close to Ueno's Shinobazu Pond, the **Suigetsu Hotel Ohgaisou** ((03) 3822-4611 FAX (03) 3823-4340, 3-3-21 Ikenohata, Taito-ku, is a charming place, though it is wise to avoid the less charming Western-style rooms and opt for one of the Japanese rooms. Extra special touches include a garden, an attached sushi bar and a public bath.

INEXPENSIVE

Budget accommodation can be hard to come by in Tokyo, making advance bookings even more essential than in the other categories of accommodation. Very few hotels around town offer rooms for less than US$50 per person per night, and those that do can often be booked up for as much as a month ahead. Extremely low-cost accommodation for those staying more than a week can sometimes be found at short notice in the city's so-called *gaijin houses*, apartments, or sometimes even houses, in which rooms have been partitioned off for foreigners to use. Such places come and go in popularity, and often, because most are illegal, close almost as fast as they open. The best source of current information on *gaijin* houses is the free listings magazine *Tokyo Classifieds*, or the monthly magazine *Tokyo Journal* (which you will have to pay for).

The most popular of Tokyo's budget hotels, and justifiably, is the **Kimi Ryokan** ((03) 3971-3766, 2-36-8 Ikebukuro, on the west side of Ikebukuro station. It's extremely hard to find the first time, but the police box close to the western exit of Ikebukuro station is used to giving instructions, and may even have a map. Rooms are spotlessly clean, as are the shared bathing facilities. There is a lounge area downstairs that looks onto a small enclosed Japanese garden and is usually a focal point for gatherings of foreign and sometimes Japanese travelers in the evenings. Rooms are Japanese style, with roll-out futon.

Another extremely popular budget hotel is the **Asia Center of Japan** ((03) 3402-6111 FAX (03) 3402-0738, 8-10-32 Akasaka, though its popularity sometimes makes it a difficult place to secure rooms in. It's something like a college dormitory without the dormitories. Rooms, like the Kimi, are maintained spotlessly, and some of the more expensive ones come with their own bathrooms. There is also an inexpensive canteen here. For many, the location in Akasaka, just a 10 to15-minute walk to the bright lights of Roppongi, is another plus.

For a budget *ryokan* stay, the **Ryokan Sawanoya** ((03) 3822-2251 FAX (03) 3822-2252, 2-3-11 Yanaka, Taiko-ku, close to Nezu station, is quite a treat, mostly on account of its enthusiastic proprietor, Sawa San, who will induct newcomers into the mysteries of *ryokan*-style accommodation, and generally bestows a family-run atmosphere over the place. Again, rooms are in short supply (there are only 12 of them; two with bathrooms) so advance bookings are essential.

WHERE TO EAT

Tokyo is arguably Asia's most exciting dining experience. Though similar claims might be made of Hong Kong and Bangkok, Tokyo's diversity of cuisines makes it hard to beat … and then, of course, there is the fact that it has the best Japanese food in the world.

Admittedly, it is easy to be lazy in Tokyo, a city that perhaps has more fast-food outlets per capita than anywhere in the world, but try not to succumb. Japanese restaurants in particular can be intimidating to the newcomer, but you'll soon discover that ordering is not has hard as it looks — after all many restaurants have either photo menus, or plastic displays of the dishes in the front window; if worse comes to worst, you can always drag the waiter outside and make your order.

If you are watching your money, bear in mind that there are some great deals to be had around

the rustic Japan of far-away, for about ¥4,000 to ¥6,000. Despite the traditional appearance of the place, an English menu is available, though the set lunches are the easiest and cheapest to order.

If *kaiseki* sounds a little fussy, a Japanese dish that nearly every foreigner loves is sukiyaki, and if it is made with melt-in-the-mouth Kobe beef it is an experience that you won't forget. One of the most memorable places in Tokyo for this experience is **Sernya** ((03) 3344-6761, Fifty-second Floor, Sumitomo Building, 2-6-1 Nishi-Shinjuku. Perched high on one of west Shinjuku's highest sky-scrapers, the restaurant has terrific views of the city. Dinners are expensive, starting at around ¥10,000, but the weekday set-lunches cost a fraction of the price.

town come lunch time. Even some of Tokyo's best restaurants offer extremely good set-lunch deals, providing an opportunity to sample the best in Japanese cuisine at affordable prices.

JAPANESE

The ultimate in Japanese dining is maintained to be *kaiseki*, or banquet dining, but as fitting for Tokyo, **Kisso** ((03) 3582-4191, B1, Axis Building, 5-17-1 Roppongi, takes Japan's most traditional cuisine and puts a nouvelle spin on it. The decor too manages to bring together all that is best about Japanese design, with a thoroughly modern look. Expect to pay from around ¥8,000 for dinner, however. Kisso is closed on Sundays.

For a more traditional *kaiseki* experience, **Tatsumiya** ((03) 3842-7373, 1-33-5 Asakusa, is like being transported to the Japan of old, or at least

There are so many sushi bars in Tokyo they merit a guidebook all of their own. That said, they can be the most inaccessible of dining places for foreigners, as generally the format is a bar, a chef and diners shouting out the orders in Japanese. For a combination of sushi at its best in a foreigner-friendly yet authentic environment, **Fukuzushi** ((03) 3402-4116, 5-7-8 Roppongi, is highly recommended. Something of a Roppongi institution, the restaurant is meticulously designed, complete with a gravel path entrance, garden and pond, and there's even a cocktail area. Dinner ranges from around ¥7,000, but set lunches again are considerably cheaper.

Less expensive, but nevertheless quite highly regarded is **Sushisei** ((03) 3586-6446, 3-11-14 Akasaka, the Akasaka branch of a chain of sushi restaurants that have earned their reputation by serving the freshest cuts of fish at affordable prices.

Expect to pay around ¥4,000 for dinner, but lunches can be had for less than ¥1,000. The head branch ((03) 3541-7720 of this chain is in Tsukiji, home of Tokyo's biggest fish market, and is regarded as the best place for a sushi breakfast after touring the market. All branches close on Sundays.

Cheaper still and a long-running favorite with the after-hours crowd in Roppongi is **Bikkuri Sushi** ((03) 3403-1489, 3-14-9 Roppongi, opposite the Roi Building. It's a conveyor-belt sushi operation, making ordering easy — just take the plate you want from the conveyor; they're color-coded for price. It's as much an interesting place for people watching as it is for dining, and it is inexpensive — figure on less than ¥1,000 for dinner.

Japanese cuisine is far more diverse than many newcomers first realize, encompassing far more than sushi, tempura and sukiyaki. For an unusual experience, it is worth heading out to Kanda, which is home to some of Tokyo's longest-running traditional restaurants. **Botan** ((03) 3251-0577, 1-15 Kanda Sudacho, which is a few minutes from Awajicho station, specializes in just one thing — chicken. Dishes come either as *nabe*, which means literally "pot," meaning a stew, or as a form of sukiyaki. It's a delightfully traditional place in which diners eat in partitioned tatami rooms (not the place to come if you are dining alone) attended to by scraping, kimono-clad attendants. Dinners cost a little less than ¥7,000. It is closed Sundays.

Also in Kanda and equally renowned is **Yabu Soba** ((03) 3251-0287, 2-10 Kanda Awajicho, which is also close to Awajicho station. As the name suggests, the specialty here is Japanese buckwheat noodles, or *soba*. For many Japanese, this is the quintessential down-home dish, and there's an earthy, familial atmosphere to this restaurant, which often has lines snaking out of the door at peak dining hours. To complete the atmosphere the restaurant features its own garden. Prices are inexpensive.

Another unusual Japanese specialty is *tonkatsu* (breaded, deep-fried pork cutlets). In the hands of a chef who knows what he's doing, this can be quite a revelatory dish, and the place to go try *tonkatsu* at its best is **Tonki** ((03) 3491-9928, 1-1-2 Shimo Meguro. A charmingly chaotic place, it is, however, not a restaurant for an intimate meal. Somewhat frenzied in character, no on could accuse Tonki of being boring. The set course (*teishoku*) is the best way to order and it comes to less than ¥2,000 per person. Tonki is closed the third Monday of every month.

For many residents of Japan and repeat visitors, after trying the full gamut of Japanese cuisine, the variety they are most fond of — as much for the lively ambiance as the food — is the *robotayaki*, or home-style grill. One of Tokyo's most famous — and expensive — is Akasaka's **Inakaya** ((03) 3586-3054, 3-12-7 Akasaka, where the chefs

make a great show of cooking their dishes and passing them to the customers on giant-size wooden spoons. The ingredients are piled up high in baskets, in full view of the diners — in fact it's dining as a spectacle, and first-timers never fail to come away surprised and impressed. It's easily one of Tokyo's most fun evenings out, and well worth the bill, which can run up over ¥9,000 per person before you know it. Inakaya has two more branches in Roppongi.

For many who have never visited Japan, tempura is that side order of fluffy fried fish and shrimps. In Tokyo it's serious business, and restaurants that specialize in it serve nothing but. Tokyo's most famous is **Tsunahachi** ((03) 3352-1012, 3-31-8 Shinjuku, a restaurant that is so successful it has generated a chain with several dozen branches around town. This one, close to the Mitsukoshi Department Store in east Shinjuku, is the original, founded in the 1920s and still commanding lines at peak hours. It even has an English-language menu these days.

INTERNATIONAL

Tokyo has the best of nearly everything, and international cuisine is no exception. In the last two decades, Tokyo, which once had a reputation as a city where Western cuisines tended to be filtered for the Japanese palate, has become very serious indeed about the real thing. This means, no matter what you get a hankering for, chances are you can get it in Tokyo. The following wrap-up goes through some of the best of Tokyo's foreign food offerings, in alphabetical order according to cuisine.

American

Some call it Tokyo's most elegant restaurant, and it would be difficult to take issue with them. The **New York Grill** ((03) 5322-1234, on the fifty-second floor of the Park Hyatt Hotel in west Shinjuku, not only offers superlative views, it has nightly live jazz, an all-encompassing wine cellar (nearly 2,000 varieties) and what is perhaps Tokyo's best grilled steak, seafood and racks of lamb. Evening meals are of course expensive, starting at around ¥10,000, but it's possible to dine for less than half that at lunch. Reservations are essential.

The long-running **Spago** ((03) 3423-4025, 5-7-8 Roppongi, is something of a Tokyo institution. Hated by some, loved by others, it successfully imports a slice of Californian style and cuisine to the heart of Roppongi's club district. The menu tends to change fairly frequently, as the chefs come up with new ideas, but the pizza seems to be a constant fixture,

Even if you don't speak or read a word of Japanese, ordering is rarely a problem as so many restaurants feature window displays of their dishes, as at this Tokyo sushi restaurant.

and is regarded by some as the best in town. Reckon on spending around ¥10,000 per head.

For less expensive American cuisine, Roppongi's **Hard Rock Café** ((03) 3408-7018, 5-4-20 Roppongi, is a reliable, if not predictable, option. For anyone who knows the format, the Tokyo branch will be comfortingly familiar. It's also worth looking out for **Victoria Station**, a restaurant chain with branches too numerous to list that has long been celebrated by foreign residents of Tokyo for its salad bar. Other American standards feature on the menu at reasonable prices.

Australian

Not far from Roppongi subway station, on an alley off Roppongi Dori (in the direction of Aoyama), the **Oz Café** ((03) 3470-7734, 1--13 Nishi-Azabu, started as a small, unpromising restaurant that has subsequently been very successful and expanded. With its potted plants and bright interior decor it might have been spirited from inner Sydney. If you have ever felt like trying kangaroo or emu meat but thought you would have to wait for a trip to Australia, think again. Evening meals here cost from around ¥3,000.

Cambodian

Back in the old days, Tokyo's only Cambodian restaurant, **Angkor Wat** ((03) 3370-3019, 1-38-13 Yoyogi, operated out of a hole in the wall and was one of the city's ethnic pioneers. Nowadays, with Southeast Asian restaurants thick on the ground, it is still going strong, and represents a great opportunity to try a little known cuisine for those unlucky enough not to have visited Cambodia. The curries are vaguely Thai, coconut based but sweeter and milder. The menu comes in English, Japanese, Khmer and Chinese for easy ordering, and the staff, while always on the run, are friendly and will happily make suggestions for ordering. Meals cost around ¥2,000.

Chinese

Chinese cuisine is such a neighborhood fixture in Japan that in many places it has almost become an extension of Japanese cuisine — witness the *ramen* phenomenon. There are nevertheless plenty of Chinese restaurants in Tokyo that strive for authenticity. One of them is the famous **Din Tai Fung** ((03) 5361-1381 on the tenth floor of Takashimaya Times Square, which is close to the south exit of Shinjuku station — you can't miss it. It is a branch of a Taipei *dim sum* (or more properly *dian xin*) restaurant that achieved fame when some years ago the *New York Times* chose it — somewhat mysteriously, it must be said — as one of the world's 10 best restaurants. Whether you trust such accolades or not, the *dim sum* here are excellent and lines at meal times are de rigueur. A meal should cost from around ¥1,500.

Another restaurant with excellent dim sum, this time Cantonese style complete with trolleys, is **Tokyo Dai Hanten** ((03) 3202-0121, in the Oriental Wave Building on Yasukuni Dori in Shinjuku. Prices are moderate.

French

Harajuku started shaping up its reputation as the Paris end of Tokyo with its sidewalk cafés, and has continued the trend with some genuine French sidewalk restaurants. **Aux Bacchanales** ((03) 5474-0076 is the pick of the lot, with a wonderful people-watching location on Meiji Dori near the intersection of Takeshita Dori. Getting a place in the alfresco section may take a wait, but it's worth it. The restaurant serves French standards, and costs from around ¥2,000. By day it is a brasserie. Also highly recommended and not far away is **Flo** ((03) 5474-0611, on an alley off Harajuku's Omotesando (opposite the Hanae Mori Building), a moderately priced French restaurant that has built up a loyal following due to the authenticity of its offerings. It's worth making a weekday lunchtime visit for Flo's celebrated buffet lunch.

Shinjuku has a number of French restaurants. For a bargain meal, try **Metro de Paris** ((03) 3357-5655, part of a chain of French restaurants that started more than a decade ago offering daily fixed-course specials. It's a small place, but the food is consistently excellent, and won't come to more than ¥2,500 per person. It's one block north of Shinjuku Gyoen station. Closed Sundays. Similarly inexpensive and similarly good is **Canard** ((03) 3200-0706, another hole-in-the-wall with a loyal following. It is a little difficult to find, in the basement down an alley opposite the Marui Interior Department store off Meiji Dori.

Indian

Indian restaurants are very popular in Tokyo, with, according to some reports, more than 250 restaurants around town. One of the pioneers was **Moti** ((03) 3479-1939, just around the corner from Roppongi station on Gaien Higashi Dori. There are other branches around town, but the Roppongi original still commands lines at peak hours. The tandoori is particularly recommended. Figure on spending around ¥2,500 per person. The head branch in Akasaka ((03) 3582-3620 tends to be less busy and has more room.

Another popular Indian restaurant chain in Tokyo, with similar prices, is **Samrat**, with branches in Shinjuku ((03) 3355-1771, close to the Kinokuniya Bookshop on the seventh floor of the Seno Building; Shibuya ((03) 3770-7275, opposite the southern end of Spain Dori; Ueno ((03) 5688-3226, behind the ABAB Department Store, and Roppongi ((03) 3478-5877, on Gaien Higashi Dori, opposite the Hotel Ibis.

Claiming to be the first Indian Tokyo restaurant, **Ajanta** ((03) 5420-7033 now has a branch on the thirty-ninth floor of Ebisu Garden Palace, next to Ebisu station. It is popular for its wide selection of breads and the thoughtful addition of a wine list. Prices are similar to those of Moti and Samrat.

Italian

There are so many Italian restaurants in Tokyo, making recommendations is difficult. In fact, chances are as you explore the city, you will chance across several a day. In Shinjuku, an easy place to find is **Agio** ((03) 3354-6720, on the seventh floor of the Isetan Department Store. It's by no means the best in Tokyo, but fresh ingredients and a

simple approach to preparation combined with reasonable prices means that few come away disappointed. The wide-ranging menu takes in everything from seafood to pizza. Lunches are excellent value at a little over ¥1,000 per person. Agio is closed Wednesdays.

In Harajuku give **Il Carbonaro** ((03) 5469-9255 a try. It's close to Omotesando subway station behind the Kinokuniya International Department Store (a good place, incidentally, to pick up anything from home you might be missing). It's the grilled items that are the house specialty, but the salads are highly recommended too. Evening meals are slightly expensive — figure on around ¥5,000 per person — but the lunch specials are good value. Il Carbonaro is closed Sundays.

For a splash-out Italian meal, the place to go is — where else? — Ginza, where **Sabatini di Firenze** ((03) 3573-0013, a faithful copy of an

original in Florence, occupies a spot on the seventh floor of the Sony Building. Even lunch is expensive here, starting at around ¥4,000, while dinners start at ¥10,000 per person.

Thai

Thai emerged as Tokyo's favorite "ethnic" cuisine nearly two decades ago, and Thai restaurants can now be found dotted all over the city, ranging from informal Bangkok-style cafés popular with visiting Thais to sit-down restaurants serving royal cuisine. One of the pioneers, and still worth a visit, is **Chiang Mai** ((03) 3580-0456, which can be found just north of the Hibiya Chanter building (south of the Denki Building), close to Yurakucho station in the Ginza area. It's no great shakes on the decor front, but it serves reliable Thai standards at reasonable prices. Chiang Mai is closed Saturdays.

A wonderful Roppongi institution is **Maenam** ((03) 3404-4745, a trendy Thai restaurant and cocktail bar that stays open until 4 AM. The after-hours set can be seen in here in the wee hours slurping back *tom yam gung*, a fascinating sight to behold.

For a very authentic Thai dining experience, head over to Meguro, where close to Meguro station, on Meguro Dori, you will find **Keawjai** ((03) 5420-7727, which has a vast menu offering Thai royal cuisine. It's an intimate place, and it often seems there are as many Thais dining here as Japanese. Be careful with the Chang beer — it's stronger stuff than the average brew — and let the knowledgeable staff make some adventurous ordering suggestions for you. Costs are from around ¥3,000 per head. Keawjai is closed Mondays.

NIGHTLIFE

Like many Asian cities, Tokyo comes into its own by night. Much of the city is uncharming by day, but come sunset the neon starts to blaze and crowds start lining up at restaurant doors, by 11 PM it seems that half the passengers on the rail network have had a few too many.

Tokyo's main nightlife areas are Roppongi, Aoyama (mostly tucked away clubs) and Shinjuku, though pockets of activity can be found all over the city. But for the first-time visitor probably the best way to get an overview of Tokyo's nightlife is to spend an evening in Roppongi, which has something of everything.

Not that Tokyo's nightlife is just bars and clubs. Tokyo offers cultural entertainment by night too.

BARS

In Roppongi, as is the case in most of Tokyo, bars don't really get going until after 9:30 PM. An exception is convivial **Paddy O'Folleys** ((03) 3423-2239,

Shinjuku is the ultimate Tokyo experience, a warren of alleys lined with restaurants and bars.

an Irish bar in the basement of the Roi Building that pulls in the off-work crowd. It has Kilkenny and Guinness on tap, and a 6 PM to 8 PM happy hour. The alfresco tables are much sought after and make for great people watching. Similarly popular in the early hours and more of an American-style bar is **Motown House** ((03) 5474-4605, close to Roppongi subway station on Gaien Higashi Dori. Happy hours are the same as Paddy O'Folleys.

For a congregation of bars popular with the younger set, head down Gaien Higashi Dori and turn left into the cul de sac next to the Bikkuri Sushi revolving sushi restaurant. At the end of the lane, next to Roppongi cemetery, is **Deja Vu** ((03) 3403-8777. It has been running for long over a decade

Tokyo by storm. Take the west exit of Ebisu station and look out for a branch of Wendy's. What the Dickens is on the fourth floor of the Roob 6 Building close by. It features live music most nights of the week, has a warm, cozy interior, and a good selection of draft beers (including Guinness and Bass) and bottled beers. It's closed Mondays. Also worth checking out in the area is the sprawling **Yebisu Beer Station**, part of Yebisu Garden Palace, with its convivial beer garden — lots of fun in the warm summer months.

For the Tokyo Irish bar phenomenon, **The Dubliners** ((03) 3352-6606 in east Shinjuku, on the other side of Shinjuku Dori behind Yodobashi Camera, is a reliable choice, creating a tolerable

and has been through several face-lifts, but is still going strong, though the crowds don't begin to arrive until late in the evening. Close by, back towards Gaien Higashi Dori, is **Gas Panic** ((03) 3405-0633, the first in what is now a chain that can only be recommended to the very adventurous. Along with **Club 99 Gas Panic** ((03) 3470-7180, in the nearby Togensha Building, it is a late-night haunt of foreign men on the howl and Japanese women presumably willing to be prowled. More wholesome is the cavernous **Bar Isn't It?** ((03) 3746-1598 on the third floor of the MT Building. It has a cover charge Friday and Saturday nights, but is free the rest of the week and has perhaps the cheapest drinks in all of Roppongi.

Back in Ebisu, a pub with taking a look at is **What the Dickens** ((03) 3780-2099, an eccentric British-style bar that comes as a relief after the somewhat formulaic Irish pubs that have taken

faux-Irish atmosphere and offering Guinness on tap. It is extremely popular Thursday through Saturday, and tends to get packed from around 7 PM, making it a better place for starting off an evening. For an adventurous late-night excursion in east Shinjuku, the **Rolling Stone** ((03) 3354-7347 has been running for as long as almost anyone can remember. Loud, grungy, wall-to-wall leather on weekends, it is an interesting insight into the other side of Tokyo, though definitely not for the faint-hearted.

CLUBS

Tokyo's club scene is forever changing: for the latest in what's hip and what's not, the giveaway *Tokyo Classifieds* is good place to look. In the meantime, some long-running, dependable options include the following, most of which are in the Roppongi area.

Most Tokyo clubs have a cover charge of around ¥4,000, which will also buy you a couple of drinks.

For the standard Tokyo disco experience, the **Lexington Queen** ((03) 3401-1661 has long been the favored haunt of out-of-town celebrities, which ensures an interesting mix of locals too. The ultimate club experience can be found at nearby **Velfarre** ((03) 3402-8100, a uniquely Japanese experience — opulent, massive, teeming with the best dressed dancers in town by 9 PM, and then at midnight it is all over. To most foreigners it is a slightly mystifying place, but it has been packing people in for more than six years now, and is a fascinating place to take a look at. It's close to exit 4A of Roppongi subway station, roughly behind the Ibis Hotel.

Yellow ((03) 3479-0690 is another long-running club that amazingly has managed to stay at the cutting edge of Tokyo cool. Different events take place on every night of the week, and discriminating door staff mean that you will have to look the part to get a peak inside. It's a little hard to find: head down Roppongi Dori and look for a glimmer of yellow neon down an alley on the right just before the Nishi Azabu Crossing. Close by, on the opposite side of the road on the Nishi Azabu Crossing, is **328** ((03) 3401-4968, known as San Nippa. It's a cool, very relaxed DJ bar that is usually home to an interesting collection of regulars, with the occasional model thrown in for good measure; a good antidote to the more frenetic options in Roppongi central.

In Ebisu, in a basement of the same building as What the Dickens (see Pubs above) is **Milk** ((03) 5458-2826, which combines live music, a dance club and a kitchen (complete with sex toys — display only). A good place to check out Tokyo's live scene, it's also possible to escape the hubbub and chat in the kitchen or in a chill-out area.

For more live music, there are several perennial favorites that make for superb evenings out. **The Cavern** ((03) 3405-5207 is a recreation of the club that started it all for the Fab Four, and features impressive Japanese Beatles cover bands playing note-perfect versions of all the old favorites. It's on an alley west of the Roi Building parallel to Roppongi's Gaien Higashi Dori. Along similar lines is **Kentos** ((03) 3401-5755, where the music is 1950s rock'n'roll. It's virtually next door to the Cavern.

TRADITIONAL ENTERTAINMENT

Tokyo does not quite rival Kyoto as a destination to soak up traditional Japanese entertainment, but there are, nevertheless, performances worth taking time out to see.

The most popular traditional entertainment choice for Tokyo visitors is *kabuki*. Performances take place twice daily for the first three weeks of every month at the **Kabuki-za** ((03) 5565-6000 in Ginza. Performances last for hours, but it is also possible to buy discounted one-act tickets which give you around an hour, more than enough for most first-timers. It is worth renting the English earphone guide at the theater — the proceedings tend to be extremely confusing if you don't.

Occasional performances of *no* take place in Tokyo. The best place to check for upcoming performances is the giveaway *Tokyo Classifieds*, which is available at all English-language bookshops. Another place to look is the *Tokyo Journal*, or you can try calling Tokyo's main *no* theaters: the **National No Theater** ((03) 3423-1331 and the **Kanze No-gakudo** ((03) 3469-5241.

Less traditional — it started in Osaka in the early 1900s — is the all-girl, singing, dancing Takarazuka. It's another of those uniquely Japanese experiences, and should you visit you will find yourself in the rather odd situation of watching an all-female performance among an all-female audience. Regular performances take place at the **Takarazuka Theater** ((03) 3201-7777 opposite the Imperial Hotel in central Tokyo.

HOW TO GET THERE

All roads (and air routes, rail lines and sea lanes) lead to Tokyo. Unless you are in the southern islands and traveling by boat, the Japanese capital can be reached within a day from almost anywhere in Japan. Domestic flights lift off and touch down at Haneda Airport, which is easily accessed by monorail in around 25 minutes from downtown Tokyo. Domestic flights are a keen rival to Japan's extensive rail network, and it is always worth comparing prices and times, as it can often work out faster and not much more expensive to fly from Tokyo to more remote destinations than to travel by train.

Tokyo station is the city's main rail hub. Shinkansen services start from here on the arterial Tokaido route between Tokyo and the cultural heartland of Kansai (Kyoto and Osaka notably), before heading on to Western Honshu and Kyushu. Northern Tohoku services start and terminate at Ueno station, on the northeast quadrant of the circle Yamanote line. Some of Tokyo's nearby attractions (Yokohama, Kamakura, Hakone and Nikko, for example) are serviced by alternative Tokyo stations — see the relevant sections in the AROUND TOKYO, chapter below, for details.

Long-distance bus services — popular on the overnight routes with those who are looking to save on a night's accommodation while they get where they are going — start and terminate at various locations in Tokyo, depending on the service and the destination. Tokyo station is one of the main terminals, as is Shinjuku station (on the west side).

Kyoto is the heartland of Japan's geisha culture, though it is still possible to see performances — mostly tourist oriented — in Tokyo.

Around Tokyo

TOKYO MAY BE A VAST CITY, BUT THANKS TO ITS SPLENDID transportation network it doesn't take much work to get out of the city into its hinterland. It's easy to spend a week or more exploring the attractions around the city, and while few people have this much time, it's worth taking at least a couple of days to see the highlights. Deciding which highlights should take priority is the hard part.

For many first-time visitors, the temptation is to put Yokohama high on the list, usually due to its fame as a port city. But while Yokohama is not without its attractions, it is essentially another city — not quite Tokyo by the sea nor compelling enough for it to eclipse some of Tokyo's nearby more rural sights. Chief among these are Nikko, a beautiful mountain town with one of Japan's most captivating shrines; Kamakura, a former capital and now a splendid place for an afternoon of walking and visiting ancient Buddhist temples; and Hakone, a volcanic resort town with a stunning lake and equally — on a fine day — stunning views of Mount Fuji.

Of course, the Tokyo vicinity has many more attractions, but most of them fall into the category of getaways for residents of the city. Both the Izu-hanto and Boso-hanto peninsulas are picturesque and make for pleasant day trips, both can safely be dropped from a busy itinerary. The same goes for Narita and Kawasaki. While Mount Fuji is obviously a major attraction, as already noted, Hakone offers views of Japan's most famous peak, and it's by no means imperative that you trek out to the Five Lakes region to see it at its best.

The following round-up of Tokyo's nearby attractions starts in the southwest, moves north and then south, winding up at Mashiko.

YOKOHAMA

Just 30 minutes from Tokyo by train, the port city of Yokohama is a very different place from the capital. Less crowded than Tokyo, there's a spacious, cosmopolitan feel to the place that makes it pleasant to stroll around. It has few major attractions, however.

GENERAL INFORMATION

It would seem logical to get off at Yokohama station when traveling to Yokohama, but in actual fact the main station is inconveniently located to the north of the central hub and most of the city's points of interest. Bear in mind, if you take any train service other than the JR Keihin Tohoku (see GETTING THERE, below) you will need to change trains at Yokohama to travel on to either Sakuragicho or Kannai stations, both of which are more central. At the east exit of Sakuragicho station is **Minato Mirai 21 General Information Center (** (045) 211-0111, which is open daily. In Yokohama station **(** (045) 441-7300 there's

another helpful information kiosk and yet another in Shin Yokohama station **(** (045) 473-2895. All have copies of the giveaway *Yokohama City Guide* and can help with hotel reservations should you need, or perhaps want, to overnight in Yokohama.

WHAT TO SEE AND DO

Yokohama's newest attraction is the still-developing **Minato Mirai 21** (or MM21), a high-tech city of the kind beloved by Japanese. Many of its much-touted attractions are of the mall variety, but it is nevertheless an impressive sight, particularly when seen from a distance. The centerpiece is the **Landmark Tower**, Japan's tallest building, complete with the world's fastest escalator, which will rocket you up to the sixty-ninth floor for a truly spectacular view in clear weather, though the price is steep at ¥1,000. Next door is the **Landmark Plaza**, a huge

five-story shopping complex with nearly 200 restaurants and shops. In front of the tower, and a good attraction for children, is the **Yokohama Maritime Museum** (10 AM to 5 PM, closed Mondays) and the Nippon-Maru Memorial Park, where the *Nippon-Maru* sailing ship is permanently moored and can be explored. The nearby **Yokohama Cosmo World**, an amusement park with extremely complicated opening hours (essentially 10 AM to 9 PM, with all kinds of odd permutations seasonally) features the world's largest Ferris wheel (the London Eye is bigger but technically not a Ferris wheel, as it is supported on one side only) — great views when you finally reach the top. Also recommended is the **Yokohama Museum of Art** (10 AM to 6 PM, closed Thursdays), another building designed by Japanese architectural maestro Tange Kenzo (who seems to be designing half the new buildings in Japan these days), which has

changing exhibits usually of a high standard. The **Mitsubishi Minato Mirai Industrial Museum** (10 AM to 5:30 PM, closed Mondays) covers the history of energy, environment and communications, and usually has high-tech, hands-on exhibits that are winners with children. All this, to be honest, just scratches the surface — it would be easy to spend an entire day exploring MM21.

Southeast of Kannai station, on the northern edge of Yamashita-koen Park is the **Silk Museum** (9 AM to 4 PM, closed Mondays), a fascinating journey through the history of silk production. **Yamashita-koen Park** is the traditional spot from which to gaze out at Yokohama Harbor, but as a park it is relatively uninteresting. The ship moored

Yokohama's harbor is one of the fastest developing areas in the whole of Japan, featuring the Minato Mirai 21, a high-tech city of the future with a host of tourist attractions.

in the harbor here is the *Hikawa-Maru*, a passenger ship built in 1930 and now a tourist attraction. Regular harbor cruises set out from beside the ship between 9 AM and 9 PM. At the southern end of the park is the **Marine Tower**, a lighthouse and once Yokohama's tallest building, but now eclipsed by the Landmark Tower.

Southeast of the Marine Tower is **Harbor View Park**, which has good views of the harbor and leads to the **Foreigners' Cemetery**, where some 4,500 foreigners, mostly American and British, are buried. Some of the inscriptions on the headstones are very evocative, conjuring up impressions of a very different Yokohama from the up-and-coming city of the future that confronts the eye today.

AROUND TOKYO

Southwest of the park and cemetery is Yokohama's most famous attraction: **Chinatown**. Japan has only three Chinatowns to speak of — an odd thing when you consider how much Japan owes China culturally — the others being in Kobe and Nagasaki. But Yokohama's is the biggest, and it pulls in literally millions of (mostly Japanese) tourists annually to sample its stir-fries and steamed buns, and to gaze on its quaintified Chinese streetscapes. For anyone who's actually eaten authentic Chinese food, much of what is on offer here will taste somewhat adulterated, but it's an interesting area to explore all the same, and joining any of the lunch and dinner-time lines snaking out of the restaurants will give you an opportunity to try what Japanese call *chuka ryori* — Chinese food.

A couple of attractions on the outskirts of Yokohama are worth taking in, though one of them — **Sankei-en Garden** (open 9 AM to 5 PM daily)

— is difficult to get to unless you take a train to Negishi station and then jump in a cab. It's worth the trouble, however: a beautiful garden to stroll in, perfectly maintained, filled with ancient buildings that have been moved here from around the Tokyo region. At the opposite end of town, around five minutes from Shin Yokohama station, is one of Japan's quirkiest museums: the **Ramen Museum** (11 AM to 11 PM, closed Tuesdays). If you don't know what *ramen* are by now, this museum will fill you in, and perhaps even make you a fan. It's a fascinating blow-by-blow account of the history of a dish that started in southern China but now bears virtually no resemblance to anything eaten by the Chinese. When you're done with the history you can dine on the subject of the exhibitions in a recreation of mid-twentieth-century Tokyo downstairs.

WHERE TO STAY AND EAT

It's unlikely that you will need — or want — to stay in Yokohama. Tokyo, after all, is only 30 minutes away, and less than half an hour in the other direction is delightful Kamakura, a pleasantly rural place to overnight. If you do need to overnight here, the information counters around town (see GENERAL INFORMATION, above) can help with reservations and recommendations.

An atmospheric hotel that dates back to 1927, the **Hotel New Grand** ((045) 681-1841 FAX (045) 681-1895, 10 Yamashita-cho, Naka-ku, has 262 guestrooms, along with French, Italian and Japanese restaurants, a cocktail bar and a lounge coffee shop. Rates range from around ¥14,000 per person. Yokohama's best hotel is the **Royal Park Hotel Nikko** ((045) 221-1111 FAX (045) 224-5153 WEB SITE www.nikkohotels.com/japan/yokohama.html, which occupies the dizzying top floors of the Landmark Tower in the Minato Mirai 21 complex (¥25,000 and up). Complete with 10 restaurants, bars and lounges, including the Sirius Sky Lounge on the seventieth Floor, which has stunning views of Mount Fuji on a clear day. The hotel's 603 guest rooms are in the fifty-second to sixty-eighth floors and provide amazing views.

On the food front, most people head to Yokohama to dine in Chinatown, though there is a lot of good Japanese food in Yokohama too. The best bet is to wander through the area and get in line at whichever seems most popular. **Manchin-ro** ((045) 651-4004 is a long-running, inexpensive favorite, though it offers very much the same dishes as its neighbors. The nearby **Pekin Hanten** is also popular in the same price category. **Kaiin-kaku** ((045) 681-2374 is a tiny, unpromising looking place that doesn't get as crowded as some of its more lavish neighbors, but the food is inexpensive and good. Unfortunately it has no English sign — the *kanji* name means "Sailor's Pavilion."

Garlic Jo's ((045) 682-2870 is a popular Western restaurant with generic pizzas and other offerings inspired by garlic. The restaurant started in Yokohama and now has branches as far away as Shibuya in Tokyo. The latest branch is in Queen's Square in the Minato Mirai 21 Complex — it's an inexpensive, unpretentious place that is perfect for dinner or lunch.

HOW TO GET THERE

Four different train lines all head out to Yokohama from Tokyo, but the simplest option is to take the Keihin Tohoku line from Tokyo station. Taking slightly more than 30 minutes it stops at Yokohama, Sakuragicho and Kannai stations, while the other three lines all stop only at Yokohama station, which means you will have to change trains there. The cheapest option is to take the Toyoko line from Shibuya station, which takes around 45 minutes. Shinkansen trains, running between Tokyo, Kyoto and Osaka, stop at Shin Yokohama station, which is connected to Yokohama station by subway. To continue on from Yokohama to Kamakura, take the Yokosuka line from Yokohama station.

KAMAKURA

Tourists usually stop in Kamakura, a seaside town about one hour south of Tokyo, to see the Dai-butsu (Great Buddha). This is a good reason, for the 11.4-m-high (37-ft) bronze figure is strikingly beautiful, but there are many reasons for prolonging the visit beyond the customary half hour.

For one thing, Kamakura is the nearest really attractive town to Tokyo. Enclosed on three sides by small but steep and densely wooded hills, and on the fourth by the sea, its atmosphere is much older than Tokyo's, while its air is much fresher.

The hills and the sea made it marvelously easy to defend in the Middle Ages and this is why the first shogun, Minamoto Yoritomo, chose to raise it from a humble fishing village to capital of the country when he seized control in 1192. The Great Buddha was one of the greatest products of the Kamakura period (1192–1333) which ensued, but there are many others.

GENERAL INFORMATION

It makes a lot of sense to get off the train at Kita (North) Kamakura, one stop before Kamakura station, and walk the remainder of the distance into town, as this allows you to see some of Kamakura's most splendid temples en-route. There is an **information counter** at Kamakura station ((0467) 22-3350 but it's not a particularly useful source. Bicycles are available for rent around Kamakura station.

Kamakura's temples are open daily, and almost all are open roughly from 8 AM to 4:30 or 5 PM.

WHAT TO SEE AND DO

Immediately south of Kita Kamakura station lies **Engaku-ji Temple**, a Zen temple of the Rinzai sect, and one of Kamakura's best. Founded in 1282, the most ancient remaining part of the temple is its **San-mon Gate**, which dates from the late eighteenth century. A flight of stairs leads up from beside the gate to the temple's original bell, forged some 700 years ago in 1301.

Waking south from Engaku-ji towards Kamakura station, you pass a number of temples, all of which deserve closer inspection. **Tokei-ji** is a former nunnery where once women — if they sheltered

there for three years — could claim divorce from their husbands. A cemetery where some of the former nuns are buried lies behind the temple. No nuns inhabit the temple now.

Continue ahead and you will see **Hachiman-gu Shrine** — this is in fact the rear entrance to the shrine but entering this way is not a problem. Hachiman is the God of War and was the guardian deity of the Minamoto clan. An ancient gingko tree on the shrine grounds is said to be over 1,000 years old and was once witness to the assassination of a shogun.

From Hachiman-gu follow the main road through the center of town to Kamakura station. Take a train to Hase station on the private Enoden line, and from here it is a short walk to Kamakura's two most famous attractions: the Great Buddha

Kamakura's Hachiman-gu shrine.

and **Hase-dera Temple**, which contains a statue of the 11-headed (*juichi-men*) Kannon that is said to be some 1,300 years old. Two halls flanking the main hall contain respectively a Treasure Exhibition that features Hase-dera's original bell, which dates from the thirteenth century, and a striking carved Amida Buddha.

Several well-marked and well-tramped hiking trails follow the ridges of the town's hills. The **Daibutsu** trail, for example, goes from near Kita-Kamakura station to a spot near the Great Buddha. It's about an hour's pleasant stroll from end to end. On the way, you can drop in at **Zeni-Arai Benten**, a very popular shrine, to wash your money. It should then double in value — sometime.

As for the Great Buddha himself, it is a remarkable piece of work. Cast in bronze in 1252 it has survived the storms, typhoons and earthquakes which destroyed the temple building that used to enclose it. The rock-solid posture and the sublime calm of the face successfully embody the ideals of Buddhism.

Kamakura has a lighter side, too: the seaside, where Tokyoites flock in their thousands every summer weekend to swim, sail, windsurf and sunbathe. The lack of alternatives helps them to ignore the quantities of garbage that are continually washed up on the beach. Foreign visitors do not always find it so easy.

Along the scenic coast between Kamakura and the nearby city of Fujisawa runs the single-track Enoden railway line. Some 15 minutes from Kamakura it stops at **Enoshima**, and 10 minutes' walk away is the holy island of that name, reached by a bridge. It's small, steep and notably overdeveloped, but the shrines and tower at the top of the island are popular. If your legs ache by the time you reach the shrine precincts you can, for a small sum, take an escalator to the top.

WHERE TO STAY AND EAT

There is not a great deal of accommodation in Kamakura, but it is a pleasant place to overnight all the same. For basic but hospitable *ryokan* accommodation (at about ¥5,000), the **Ryokan Ushio** ((0467) 22-7016 is a tiny place that is almost impossible to find — call from the station, perhaps with the help of the information counter there, and have them pick you up. The **Kamakura Kagetsuen Youth Hostel** ((0476) 25-1238, 27-9 Sakanoshita, has 49 dormitory-style beds.

Ask at the information counter at Kamakura station about how to sample the cuisine associated with Kamakura's Zen Buddhist history — *shojin ryori*, a Buddhist vegetarian cuisine. It's served in a temple setting, not in a restaurant. Otherwise, the station area has a large number of economical if somewhat uninspiring restaurants, ranging from traditional *soba* outlets to the usual fast-food barns.

HOW TO GET THERE

The JR Yokosuka (pronounced "yokos'ka") line covers the distance from Tokyo to Kamakura in just over an hour. The platform at Tokyo is underground, on the Marunouchi side of the station.

If you wind up your visit in Enoshima, there are two other ways of getting back to Tokyo. The private Odakyu line runs between Odakyu Enoshima station and Shinjuku, in the heart of Tokyo. The fastest trains (*tokkyu*, limited express), which run roughly once an hour, cover the distance in 70 minutes. Like most private lines, the Odakyu line is much cheaper, and consequently more crowded, than JR.

Alternatively, you can take an exhilarating 13-minute ride on the Shonan monorail that swoops and climbs through the hills between Enoshima Shonan station and Ofuna, and catch JR's Tokaido line to Yokohama and Tokyo from there.

IZU-HANTO PENINSULA

A favored resort getaway for Tokyoites, Izu-hanto Peninsula offers some beautiful coastline views, hot-spring soaks in the area's spa towns, and a handful of historical attractions. It's really only an attraction if you find yourself based in Tokyo for any length of time, or if your travel in Japan is restricted to the Tokyo region and you would like to see some Japanese countryside that gets little foreign tourism. Bear in mind, if you decide to do a loop of the peninsula on your own steam, that it is as not as foreigner-friendly in terms of signposting and information as some of the more popular destinations close to Tokyo.

Most people approach the peninsula via the resort town of **Atami**, which lies on the JR Tokaido line, and is accessible in around an hour from Tokyo station. Its chief attraction is the **MOA Museum of Art** (9:30 AM to 5 PM, closed Thursdays), a fascinating, if expensive (¥1,600) collection of mostly Japan and Chinese art with a few masterpieces by Rembrandt and Monet thrown in for good measure. In fact, it is the building and setting which are as much the attraction as the art. Set atop the 220-m (722-ft) Mount Momo-yama, entry is via a series of four surreally futuristic escalators, which give way to gardens and the museum overlooking the sea. A Henry Moore sculpture greets visitors. One of the highlights inside is a full-size *no* theater featuring a thatched roof made from Japanese cypress bark. All things considered, the entry price is worth every yen.

The next stop on the peninsula is **Shimoda**, a picturesque town with enough things to see to while away an afternoon or so, and a good place to overnight if you are doing a circuit of Izu. Shimoda briefly entered history as the initial trading enclave settled by Commodore Perry, the American who prized open the tightly shut doors of Japan to the world in the 1850s. In 1854, after it became clear that isolated Shimoda was not exactly the ideal place for the trading community to do business, a supplementary treaty was signed here and operations moved to Yokohama.

For a fascinating glimpse into these times, take a visit to **Ryosen-ji Temple**, which is where the supplementary treaty was signed, and which now has a small museum (9 AM to 5 PM, daily) dedicated to Perry and his Japanese courtesan Okichi-san (perceived by Japanese as a sacrifice on the altar of internationalism) and sex in religion through the ages. A so-called "ropeway" (a funicular) heads up

Dogashima on the southwest of Izu. Dogashima is a small coastal town famed for its rock formations, which can be explored on foot, and its bay cruises that take visitors out to a cave with a hole in its roof. These cruises leave regularly throughout the day and cost a little under ¥1,000. From Dogashima, buses continue north to the hot-spring resort of Shuzenji, which is something of a tourist trap, but has direct access back to Tokyo via the JR Odoriko line.

HAKONE

Nestled on the flanks of Mount Fuji, the Hakone region is a wonderful day trip or even overnight

Mount Nesugata-yama next to the harbor, for good views and some pleasant walks.

There is a large amount of resort accommodation in Shimoda, all of which have hot-spring water piped into public bathing rooms — a wonderful experience mid-week when the hotels (and the baths) are usually deserted. One of the best of these is the **Shimoda Tokyu Hotel (** (0558) 22-2411 FAX (0558) 22-4970, 5-12-1 Shimoda-city. It has a swimming pool, hot-spring bathing, a restaurant, and room rates starting at around ¥14,000.

If you have stopped at Atami, it makes sense to switch to the private Ito line to continue to Shimoda. Otherwise, the JR Odoriko service runs direct from Shinjuku to Shimoda in a little under three hours.

From Shimoda, regular buses journey south, rounding the southern cape of the peninsula at the scenic **Iro-zaki** and then continuing north to

trip from Tokyo. It has a beautiful lake, incomparable views of Mount Fuji, bubbling volcanic springs, a historic walk and even a couple of impressive museums. If you are not heading north to the mountains, Hakone provides a splendid opportunity to see Japanese nature at its best, though it must be said that it is at times overrun with tourists.

Hakone, bordered by mountains and lying within the crater of an extinct volcano roughly 40 km (25 miles) across, is the most accessible and, along with Nikko, most rewarding, Tokyo getaway. Tokyo lacks gardens: Hakone is the compensation, paid in one splendid lump sum. Only one and a half hours from the capital by express train, half that by Shinkansen, it is the perfect place to relax and replenish your oxygen supply.

Atami on the Izu-hanto Peninsula is one of Tokyo's best loved hot-spring getaways, and is particularly favored by honeymooning couples.

GENERAL INFORMATION

An established one-day route takes in Hakone's many attractions, and while you will need to set off fairly early and will no doubt return to Tokyo exhausted, it is a fun journey. The best way to do it is to buy a **Hakone Free Pass** at Shinjuku Odakyu station, which costs ¥5,400. The pass essentially covers all your transportation for a three day period, should you need it, but still saves money even if you are doing the trip in one day. It also gives you discounts to some of the area's sights. Japan Rail Pass users should take a Shinkansen to Odawara, where you can change to the Hakone Tozan switchback railway to Gora in Hakone. From Gora, a funicular takes you to the summit of Mount Soun-zan, from where a cable car goes to Togendai on the northern lip of Ashino-ko Lake. "Pirate ships" ply the lake to the small tourist town of Hakone-machi, from where it's possible to return to Odawara by bus.

There is an "i" information counter ((0460) 5-8911 in Hakone, but it is at **Hakone Yumoto** station on the Hakone Tozan line, a station most travelers bypass en-route to Gora, though this popular hot-spring town has the most accommodation and is a good place to overnight. The staff here speak English and can help with hotel reservations.

WHAT TO SEE AND DO

From **Odawara**, the Hakone Tozan line puffs its way via many a switchback to **Gora**, in the heart of the mountains. Gora itself offers little in the way of diversions, though it does have several simple restaurants, if you are hungry (there is more food at Owakudani). Most travelers use it simply as a transfer point, taking the funicular straight up to the summit of Mount Soun-zan. Consider stopping one station before Gora station at the **Hakone Museum of Modern Art** (9 AM to 4 PM, closed Thursdays), which is also referred to by its Japanese name *Chokoku-no-Mori* — "Forest of Sculpture."

Entry to the museum is somewhat expensive at ¥1,500, and it is not included in the Hakone Free Pass, but for some the opportunity to see sculptures by Rodin, Henry Moore and many others — along with galleries featuring the art of Picasso, Miro and Renoir — all in a beautiful, landscaped setting, will be hard to pass up.

Getting back on the train and going to the end of the line you change to a cable car (or "ropeway" as the Japanese prefer) which carries you even higher to aptly named **Owakudani**, the "Valley of Greater Boiling." A foul stench of hydrogen sulfide fills the air. Vivid yellow gashes mark the places where the steam belches from the earth. In one or two small pools, strange gray material is indeed boiling away with great frenzy. It's all very impressive and

is said to be the only place of its type in Japan. Hot water from Owakudani is piped to hot spas for miles around. To learn more about the area's volcanic activity, pop into the **Owakudani Natural History Museum** (9 AM to 4:30 PM, daily).

One of the finest views of Mount Fuji — should it be visible at all, of course — is from the cable car, which swings you down the steep mountainside from Owakudani to **Togendai** on **Lake Ashino-ko**. Having arrived there you can continue this carnival of transportation by crossing the lake on a replica of a seventeenth-century English man-of-war, or "pirate" ship. Another boat plying the lake is modeled on a Mississippi steamer. The boats cross the lake to the small town of **Hakone-machi**.

The Tokaido, the old road which led from Edo (Tokyo) to Kyoto and Osaka, passed through Hakone. Near where the ferry docks at Hakone-machi is the old **Barrier Guardhouse** (8:30 AM to 4:30 PM, daily), where travelers in pre-modern days were searched and their documents rigorously checked. The guardhouse has been reconstructed in the original style and contains life-size models of travelers and guards. In the nearby **Hakone Materials Hall** are many old relics from those days.

If you want a taste of what transportation was like way back then, the course of the old road has been preserved for several miles east of the Barrier Guard house. Narrow, winding and precipitous, though paved for much of the distance with large stones, it inspires respect for the messengers of those days who, clad in loin cloths and straw sandals, dashed across the country along roads like this.

Ashino-ko is 723 m (2,372 ft) above sea level. On July 31 every year there's a Lake Festival there, with floating lanterns, and fireworks positioned so that they reflect on the lake's surface.

Formal parks are everywhere in Hakone. The **Wetlands Botanical Garden** is home to some 1,700 species of flowers, and in spring the azaleas that bloom close to the Hakone Hotel and the Barrier Guardhouse are famous. The **Hakone Detached Palace Garden** is situated on a promontory on the lake shore.

WHERE TO STAY AND EAT

One of Hakone's most luxurious hotels is the **Hakone Prince Hotel** ((0460) 3-1111 FAX (0460) 3-7616 WEB SITE www.princehotels.co.jp/hakone-e, 144 Moto-Hakone, Hakone-machi. It has a superb location on the wooded slopes that overlook Ashino-ko Lake, and room rates start at around ¥28,000 for a double.

Not quite as luxurious as the Prince, but a little more intimate and also set in beautiful surroundings, the **Hotel de Yama** ((0460) 3-6321 FAX (0460) 3-7419 WEB SITE www.nexus-co.net/yama-hotel, 80 Moto Hakone, is a hospitable four-star hotel that is highly recommended. The expansive gardens full of azaleas and other seasonal flowers are almost worth a visit in themselves.

For a delightful budget *ryokan* stay in Hakone, the **Fuji-Hakone Guesthouse** ((0460) 4-6577 FAX (0460) 4-6578, 912 Sengokuhara Hakone, is a good choice. Complete with a hot-spring bath, the traditional rooms with roll-out futon cost from ¥5,000 per person. The **Hakone-Sounzan Youth Hostel** ((0460) 2-3827, 1320 Gora, Hakone-machi, has 27 beds in dormitory-style accommodation.

Sakurai-jaya ((0460) 3-1131 is a restaurant that specializes in Kyoto tofu cuisine, served in a beautiful temple-style building that was moved to Hakone from Nara. Given the quality of the food and the beautiful surroundings, meals — they are

MOUNT FUJI FIVE LAKES

Every mountain in Japan is sacred, according to the Shinto view of things. And Mount Fuji (Fuji-san), the highest, at over 3,776 m (12,388 ft), and the most beautiful, is the most sacred of all.

After weeks of cloud and rain, the skies over the capital clear and suddenly the mountain appears to the southwest, astonishingly high and sharply defined. Sometimes only the peak is visible, hanging in the air like the Cheshire Cat's smile. Towards dusk it is often the mountain's silhouette that dominates the skyline, black against the deepening blue of evening. No matter how many

served in set courses — are reasonable at less than ¥3,000 per person.

For something a little less expensive, try the **Gyoza Center**, which lies between Gora and Chokoku-no-Mori stations. Despite the fact that these traditional Chinese dumplings are a favorite accompaniment to *ramen* noodles in Japan, finding a restaurant that specializes in them is unusual. Here they do more than a dozen different varieties — it's an inexpensive and delicious place to fill up and move on.

HOW TO GET THERE

Japan Rail Pass holders should take the Tokaido Shinkansen from Tokyo station to Odawara. It covers the 84-km (52-mile) distance in 42 minutes. At Odawara change for the Hakone Tozan line. See GENERAL INFORMATION, above, for information about the Hakone Free Pass.

pictures one has seen of it, the volcano never loses its ability to startle and impress.

Before modern times it was frequently visible from Tokyo, as the various place-names including the prefix Fujimi ("Fuji visible") attest. During the notoriously smoggy years of the 1960s and early 1970s, it disappeared almost entirely except for a few magical days in autumn and winter, and although things have improved since then, and in really fine weather you can see it all the way from Narita Airport, it is best to get a little closer.

A trip round the **Fuji-go-ko** (Fuji-Five-Lakes) area in the national park at the mountain's base provides pleasant scenery and diversions such as boating and fishing, should the mountain decline to put in an appearance. For those determined

Pleasure boats on the shores of Lake Ashinoko, one of the five lakes found in the Hakone region.

to sit it out there are plenty of hotels and *ryokan*, but be warned that really clear days are rare except in autumn and winter. **Kawaguchiko** is the name both of one of the five lakes and of the resort on its shore. Alternatively you can climb the great mountain itself. About 300,000 people do this every year, most of them during the open months of July and August.

CLIMBING MOUNT FUJI

Mount Fuji is the highest mountain in Japan and by far the most splendid. July and August are climbing season. Japanese like to make light of the difficulties of the climb, saying that an athlete could leave home in Tokyo in the morning, reach the peak and be home in time for dinner. This is nonsense. Be prepared for a tough climb to the summit. Take it at a leisurely pace, spending a night close to the top before rising early to greet the morning sun on the summit.

Here's how to tackle it. Find your way either to Go-gome (Fifth Station) on the north side of the mountain or Shin-go-gome (New Fifth Station) on the south side. Shin-go-gome is the more convenient, as quite a number of buses run there from Gotemba, Mishima and Fujinomiya stations on the Tokaido line from Tokyo.

From Fifth or New Fifth stations it takes five hours or more to the top. Although all sorts of people do the climb, including the blind and the extremely aged, the mountain demands respect. It's bitterly cold at the top, the wind can be fierce, part of the climb requires hauling oneself along by chains, while part of the descent is a sandy slide. Warm protective clothes, including gloves, are a necessity. Take water along unless you want to buy it on the mountain; take easy-to-carry food such as nuts and raisins, too — food and drink are available but they're not cheap.

At the top there are primitive stone shelters where a space on tatami mats may be rented from ¥3,000 a night. Alternatively, you can take a tent. It gets far too cold at the top to stay in the open all night.

To avoid having to sleep at the top, many people have taken to setting off long after dark and climbing through the night, arriving at the peak or at one of the higher stations — the eighth has been recommended — in time to greet the sun. Sunrise on the peak at the start of the mid-summer open season is at around 3:40 AM, becoming later as the season advances.

NIKKO

About 140 km (87 miles) north of Tokyo lies Nikko, the one attraction that is worth squeezing into even the busiest of tour schedules. The chief attraction is Tosho-gu Shrine, the gorgeous mausoleum of

the mighty shogun Tokugawa Ieyasu. Not that Nikko's history began with the Tokugawas. Long revered as a center for Shinto and Buddhism, it is home to a curious cult called Mountain Buddhism that mingles the two. Devotees scaled mountains, lived as hermits and immersed themselves in icy water, all as a means of attaining spiritual enlightenment. Clad in white, these men and women still congregate at Nantai-san, the conical mountain at the heart of the Nikko region, in early August each year.

GENERAL INFORMATION

The Tobu and JR Nikko stations are nearly next door to each other in the east of town, a little over a kilometer (half a mile) from Tosho-gu Shrine. It is not an unpleasant walk to the shrine, but there is little to see on the way. Taxis are available in front of Tobu Nikko station and frequent buses also run up to the shrine from the same area.

Nikko has two information offices, both of which have pamphlets in English and can help with hotel reservations. The **information desk** ((0288) 53-4511 at Tobu Nikko station, however, is less useful than the **Nikko Kyodo Center** ((0288) 54-2496, which is about half-way between the stations and the shrine area in a clearly signposted building on the left side of the road. The friendly, English-speaking staff at the latter can help with almost any problem.

WHAT TO SEE AND DO

As you approach the shrine area, the first sight you come across is the celebrated **Shin-kyo Bridge**. This 1907 replica of an original built in 1636 is extremely photogenic.

But it is the **Tosho-gu Shrine** itself that hogs visitors' attention, and justifiably so. Ieyasu was the first shogun of the Tokugawa line. It was he who, having united the country, fettered it so successfully that his heirs ruled for the next 250 years without serious challenge. The mausoleum built here at Nikko by his grandson, 18 years after Ieyasu's death, glorifies his achievement.

It can be a confusing place for the visitor. For a start, it is totally unlike any other shrine or temple in the country. Most Japanese Buddhist temples are somber, even gloomy places, with structures of unpainted wood and little decoration. Shrines are often painted — typically an orange-red color — but usually in a simple manner. The gorgeous colors and overwhelming richness of decoration and carving at Nikko are unique, more reminiscent of Chinese and Korean temples than of Japanese. In fact, many of the craftsmen who worked on the shrine were of Korean stock.

Spectacular views of Mount Fuji from the "ropeway," the Japanese term for a cable car.

The other respect in which Nikko is confusing is the carefree way it mixes elements of Buddhism and Shinto. The two religions are radically different, although early on they learned to live with each other. At Nikko, however, the two religions mingle architecturally in an effort to create a structure of superlative magnificence.

At the entrance to the shrine, for example, stands a huge *torii* gate, which survives from the original temple and which is, of course, a Shinto feature. On the left, meanwhile, stands a beautiful five-story Buddhist pagoda, a reconstruction that dates from the early nineteenth century. Ahead lies the **Sanjinko** (Three Sacred Storehouses) on the right, and to the left the **Shinkyusha** (Sacred

of the shrine is **Daiyuin-byo Shrine**, a more restrained version of Tosho-gu, dedicated to the third Tokugawa shogun, Iemitsu.

Slightly less than an hour (depending on traffic) west of Nikko is **Lake Chuzenji-ko** and the **Kegon Falls**. The lake is reached by one of two hairpin roads — the Irohazaka Driveway — each of them one-way. The scenery here is lovely, particularly in autumn, but it should be added that autumn is the area's busiest season and the roads are often clogged with traffic. **Chuzen-ji Temple**, above Chuzenji-ko Lake not far from the shrine, is recommended. The eighth-century statue of Kannon, goddess of mercy, enshrined here was carved from a living tree, and practically glows with spirituality.

Stable), where the famous "hear no evil, see no evil, speak no evil" can be seen carved in relief. Just before the intricately carved **Yomei-mon Gate** is the **Honji-do Hall**, which is famous for its ceiling fresco of a dragon in flight. There is usually a line of people waiting to stand beneath the dragon and clap — the echo produces a sound akin to a dragon's roar. Beyond the Yomei-mon Gate, a path leads to the diminutive (but wildly popular with Japanese tourists) **Nemuri Neko** (Sleeping Cat). Beyond, a path climbs up to the final resting place of the man who inspired this riot of color and architectural invention — Tokugawa Ieyasu. His mausoleum is surprisingly unostentatious after all that has preceded.

Directly to the east of Tosho-gu Shrine is **Futarasan-jinja Shrine**, a tranquil and unadorned shrine established nearly 1,200 years ago and dedicated to the god of Mount Nantai-san. Just south

Kegon Falls near the lakeside Chuzenji spa is also worth a visit. If you have time, take the lift down to the observatory at the bottom. The waterfall used to be a favorite spot for love suicides — something the guides don't tell you.

WHERE TO STAY AND EAT

Nikko's top accommodation experience is the **Nikko Kanaya Hotel (** (0288) 54-0001 FAX (0288) 53-2487, 1300, Kami-Hatsuishi-machi. Established in 1873 and one of Japan's oldest Western-style hotels, it still retains some of it's old Meiji era charm. The hotel has some moderately priced rooms, but most are in the expensive price bracket. Note that prices sky-rocket in the peak holiday months of May and October.

The **Turtle Inn (** (0288) 53-3168 FAX (0288) 53-3883 E-MAIL turtle@sunfield.ne.jp, 2-16 Takumi-cho, has long been a popular budget choice and is still going strong. It's an odd, red-pink building that looks something like a hobbit house. If you have come here from Tokyo, its peaceful location next to the Daiya-gawa River will seem like bliss. Rooms are simple and Japanese-style, and dinner and breakfast are provided upon additional payment. Rates start at ¥4,200 per person. The Turtle has a more modern annex called **Hotori-An** ((0288) 53-3663 FAX (0288) 53-3883, 8-28 Takumi-cho, if you are looking for moderately priced, Western-style accommodation. Rooms are about ¥1,000 per person more expensive than at the Turtle. It's beyond the Turtle, on the other side of the river. The **Nikko Youth Hostel** ((0288) 54-1013, 2854 Tokorono, has 48 dormitory beds.

Most of the hotels, pensions, *ryokan*, and even the youth hostel provide meals for their guests, and in the case of the Turtle, Hotori-an and the youth hostel these are consistently excellent, often incorporating local specialties that are hard to find in the restaurants. The Japanese restaurant **Yashio** in the Nikko Kanaya Hotel has highly recommended lunches and dinners, though they are somewhat expensive — reckon on around ¥2,500 for lunch and ¥5,000 for dinner per person.

HOW TO GET THERE

You can get to Nikko either by Japan Rail (JR) or the private Tobu line (for which, however, your Japan Rail Pass will not be valid). The private Tobu line is cheaper and more convenient, as it runs direct to Nikko. Traveling JR requires a change of trains at Utsunomiya.

For the Tobu line, go to Asakusa. Standard *kaisoku* (rapid) do the journey to Nikko in around two hours and cost ¥1,330. If you want to shave 15 minutes off the trip you can take a *tokkyu* (limited express) train, though this will double the price to ¥2,750.

JR trains leave from Tokyo and Ueno stations, taking 90 minutes, plus the time you have to wait when changing at Utsunomiya. The fare, if you don't have a Japan Rail Pass, is ¥5,430.

Tours to Nikko are heavily promoted in Tokyo, but there are several disadvantages to them, the main one being that most are too ambitious, and don't leave travelers enough time to savor the sights. Tours that include Mashiko (see below), for example, rarely provide the opportunity to try your hand at throwing some pottery.

MASHIKO

A popular side-trip on the way to or on the way back from Nikko is the traditional pottery town of Mashiko. This was for many years the home of Shoji Hamada, a great potter whose vigorous and simple work, decorated with a rapid technique that became his trademark, helped spread the fame of

Japanese folk ceramics throughout the West. Hamada's home has been moved to the **Toge Messe Center** ((0285) 72-7555 (9 AM to 4:30 PM, closed Wednesdays). Although the center has an interesting museum with exhibits of works by famous Mashiko potters, the highlight for most is the studio, where you get to try your hand at throwing your own pot. It's essential you book for the latter.

Mashiko has been a pottery town for 150 years, and the town to this day is packed with potters' kilns. Hamada moved there because of his admiration for the rough, folksy forms the town's potters produced, but he became so famous that, ironically enough, many of them are now producing

rather uninspired imitations of *his* work. Nevertheless, this is by no means true of all the town's artisans, many of whom are purists, deeply committed to their art.

The easiest way to get Mashiko is take a bus from Utsunomiya station. It takes about 50 minutes. See the HOW TO GET THERE, above under NIKKO, for details about how to get to Utsunomiya.

OPPOSITE: Evening light picks out Nikko nestling between the hills. ABOVE: Fall foliage in mountainous Nikko heralds the onset of winter.

Central Honshu

CENTRAL HONSHU — KNOWN IN JAPAN AS CHUBU — became much more accessible in 1998 when a new Shinkansen line was built connecting Tokyo and Nagano for the Winter Olympics. It is a spectacular region, and while it is often dropped from tight itineraries — and justifiably so — in favor of the more famous cultural attractions of Kansai, it is worth trying to fit in at least a trip over the Japan Alps, perhaps squeezing in the delightful village of Takayama en-route to Kyoto or Osaka.

Other notable attractions in Central Honshu include the Kenroku-en Garden in Kanazawa, Eihei-ji Temple near Fukui, the castle town of Matsumoto, and another castle town, Inuyama, that is famed for its cormorant fishing, or *ukai*. In all, there are enough sights to keep a traveler busy for a week or more, though should you take such a trip you would be guaranteed to see few other foreigners on the way.

NAGANO

Nagano occupies a special place in Japanese history, as the home of the first Buddha image to touch shores on Japan. Nagano's **Zenko-ji Temple**, an object of pilgrimage for millions of Japanese Buddhists every year, is alleged to house the image, though it is so holy that 1,300 years ago, when the temple was built, the emperor decreed that only a copy could meet the public eye, and that only once every seven years during the Gokaicho festival (the next one is in 2006).

Zenko-ji is the only real reason to set foot in Nagano, though it is far from being an unpleasant town. With the new Shinkansen line putting Nagano just one and a half hours from Tokyo, it's feasible to breeze in, visit the temple and either head back to Tokyo or continue onwards, deeper into Japan.

There is a useful English-language **Tourist Information Counter** ((026) 226-5625 inside Nagano station, where they will ply you with pamphlets and arrange somewhere to stay should you need it.

Zenko-ji Temple lies directly north of the railway station up Chuo Dori, a walk of little over one kilometer (half a mile). Walking is considered the way to approach this holy place, though no one will stop you if you jump into a cab.

Part of Zenko-ji's popularity is its multi-denominational character. It accepts believers from all sects of Buddhism, and is notable for its acceptance of women well before other Buddhist temples did. The approach is through a series of gates: first **Dai-mon**, then the **Nio-mon**, the way between these first two lined with shops selling Buddhist accessories, to the colossal **San-mon Gate**, which gives onto the **Hondo**, a 1707-reconstruction of an original built some 1,300 years ago. Beneath the Hondo is a dark — actually pitch black

— tunnel, which pilgrims grope their way through in search of the "key of salvation." If you're game, follow the example of the crowds and fumble your way through the dark, keeping to the right side of the wall, and you should be rewarded with the a touch of the holy key — it is said to guarantee salvation in the afterlife.

If you plan to spend the night in Nagano, try and get a room at the **Gohonjin Fujiya Hotel** ((026) 232-1241 FAX (026) 232-1243, 80 Daimon-cho. It's not the best hotel in town, but it certainly has the most character. The rooms are traditional, with tatami and futon, and some of the better ones look out onto gardens. Meals are optional. Rooms range from ¥6,000 per person. For a slightly better class of business hotel, try the **Hotel Sunroute Nagano Royal** ((026) 228-2222, 1-28-3 Minami-Chitose, which has above-average rooms and service. Rooms range from ¥7,000 per person.

Nagano is accessible directly from Tokyo via the JR Hokuriku Shinkansen line. The JR Shinonoi line connects Nagano with Matsumoto in 55 minutes. For long distance buses to other destinations in central Honshu and farther afield, take the west exit of Nagano station and look for the Nagano bus terminal immediately outside the station.

KARUIZAWA

Travelers arriving at Nagano by Shinkansen might want to hop off the train two stops before their final destination at Karuizawa, one of Japan's most famous hot-spring resort towns. For anyone who knows Japan, "famous" and "hot spring" in the same sentence is rarely a recommendation. And Karuizawa — trendy, crowded and often tacky — is no exception. Still, there's no denying that it, like Beppu in Kyushu, makes for an interesting insight into the Japanese hot-spring obsession, and some of the surrounding landscape remains remarkably pristine.

Oddly enough, given how Japanese the place looks today, it was "discovered" by foreigners over a century ago. One Archdeacon A.C. Shaw popularized the place in 1896. His legacy can be seen in a wooden church that stands at the end of the busy, boutique-lined mall known, appropriately, as Ginza Dori.

Of more interest is the nearby active volcano **Mount Asama-yama**, the slopes of which Karuizawa sits on. For a good view of the volcano, take a bus from Karuizawa station (around 30 minutes) to Onioshidashi-en, where a volcanic eruption of 200 years ago has left a bizarre plastic-appearing landscape of boulders and rock.

It's best to avoid staying in Karuizawa, as the hotels are almost uniformly resort-style monsters that cater to holidaying Japanese. It's better to head to Nagano, or perhaps farther afield to Matsumoto to overnight.

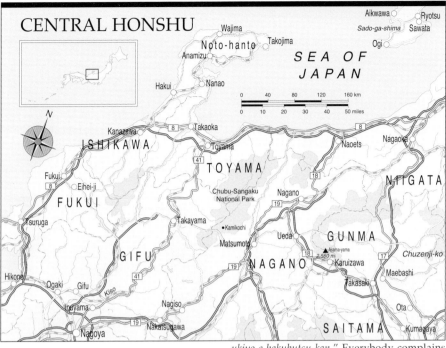

CENTRAL HONSHU

SEA OF JAPAN

MATSUMOTO

Two and a half hours direct from Shinjuku in Tokyo or 55 minutes from Nagano, Matsumoto has one of Japan's finest castles. This and an excellent *ukiyo-e* museum are its chief attractions, but the castle alone is enough to warrant at least a flying visit.

The **Matsumoto City Tourist Information Office** ((0263) 32-2814 has an office at the southern end of the concourse of Matsumoto station. The staff can help with reservations for accommodation in Matsumoto.

Matsumoto Castle (8:30 AM to 4:30 PM, daily), or Karasu-jo (Crow Castle) as it is also known, is the one attraction that should not be missed. It's keep, built in the 1590s, is Japan's oldest. It's possible to climb all the way the keep's top, sixth floor, which provides great views over the city. Come back to the neighboring park in the evening if you are still in town, when the castle is floodlit and makes for a grand backdrop to an evening stroll — it is evidently a popular pursuit for many locals too.

Adjoining the castle grounds is the **Japan Folklore Museum** (same opening hours as the castle), where artifacts from the museum are displayed along with exhibits relating to Matsumoto of old — not to mention a collection of old clocks and a menagerie of stuffed birds.

About three kilometers (just under two miles) west of central Matsumoto is the **Japan Ukiyo-e Museum** (10 AM to 5 PM, closed Mondays). The best way to get there is by taxi — tell the driver "*nihon ukiyo-e hakubutsu-kan*." Everybody complains about the building — the tourist literature usually describes it as "ultra modern" — but the real attraction is inside. The private collection of the Sakai family, who amassed over 100,000 woodblock prints and paintings, allegedly the largest private collection in the world. Unfortunately only a tiny fraction of the total collection is on display at any given time. But, then, perhaps this is a blessing — 100,000 *ukiyo-e* would probably exhaust the patience of even the most ardent scholar.

Lastly, and one of those idiosyncratically Japanese items of note, the view from the footbridge above the tracks in Matsumoto station provides a famous panoramic view of the Japanese Alps, weather permitting.

In the downtown area look out for a couple of shops that are renowned for their local arts and crafts: **Chikiriya Kogen-tei** ((0263) 33-2522 and the **Chuo Mingei Showroom** ((0263) 33-5760.

WHERE TO STAY AND EAT

Matsumoto has a good range of accommodation. The best of the Western-style hotels is the **Hotel Buena Vista** ((0263) 37-0111 FAX (0263) 37-0666, 1-2-1 Honjo, a sleek, glass-fronted building where reasonably spacious rooms start from around ¥9,000 per person. It also has a good range of restaurants — two Japanese, one Chinese, one Continental, along with a bar and a coffee lounge. Cheaper, and typical of Japan's station, business hotels is the **Hotel New Station** ((0263) 35-3850

FAX (0263) 35-3851, 1-1-11 Chuo, where small but well-maintained business rooms start at less than ¥7,000 per person.

The charming, three-story **Nunoya Ryokan** ℂ (0263) 32-0545 FAX (0263) 32-0545, 3-5-7 Chuo, which looks modeled on the famous castle not far away, is a pleasant Japanese-style alternative to the less personal business hotels. It's fairly basic — washing facilities are in the *ryokan* public bath — but clean and cheery. Room rates start at ¥4,500 per person. Meals are available at an extra cost.

Asama Onsen Youth Hostel ℂ (0263) 36-1335, 1-7-15 Asama Onsen, is a good 20 minutes out of Matsumoto by bus at the spa town of the same name. It has basic dorm beds.

HOW TO GET THERE

To get to Matsumoto directly from Tokyo, go to Shinjuku station, from where Asuza *tokkyu* (limited express) services do the trip in a little over two and a half hours. Onward trains to Nagoya are via the Chuo Honsen line and take a little over two hours. It's possible to continue on to Osaka in around three and a half hours. Trains to Nagano take just under one hour. The bus terminal is in front of Matsumoto station, and has direct services to most major cities in the region.

KAMIKOCHI

One of Matsumoto's most famous side-trips is to Kamikochi (1,500 m/4,921 ft), center of the **Chubu-Sangaku National Park** and one of the most attractive parts of the northern Alps. The tiny village has a special relationship with the popularization of the Japanese Alps as a tourist destination, because it was here that Walter Weston was based when he first started exploring the mountains of Japan in the 1890s, publishing a book in Britain in 1896 called *Mountaineering and Exploration in the Japanese Alps*. A century or so later, he would no doubt be shocked at the results. Once considered holy and untouched by human feet, from June 1 (on the nearest Sunday to which Kamikochi celebrates the "Weston Festival"), the summer climbing onslaught begins. Indeed, the trail up nearby Mount Yariga-take gets so crowded it has been dubbed the "Ginza Traverse."

The message here is that if you want to enjoy Kamikochi, and it is indeed a beautiful spot, it is best to avoid the peak summer months of June through August. From late October until early April it is usually snowed in and inaccessible, but there are two brief windows in May and October when the area is accessible and not over-run.

The best way to explore the Asuza Valley surrounding Kamikochi is on foot. A free guide — the *Kamikochi Pocket Guide* — is available at the information counter at the bus stop before the village

(no vehicles are allowed to enter Kamikochi) and has a good map for following some of the valley's trails. The walk into the village takes you to a collection of hotels and a wooden suspension bridge called **Kappa-bashi**.

Most of Kamikochi's accommodation is clustered around the Kappa-bashi Bridge, but if you want to stay in style you will have to go about a kilometer (half a mile) out of town to the **Kamikochi Imperial Hotel** ℂ (0263) 95-2001 FAX (0263) 95-2006, a beautiful four-story wooden structure with an authentic fireplace in the lounge. It is the lap of luxury in the Japanese Alps.

It takes a little under two hours by train and bus from Matsumoto to Kamikochi. Take the

Dentetsu line to Shin-Shimashima (half an hour), and there transfer to a bus to Kamikochi.

KISO VALLEY

A detour in a southwesterly direction, half-way to Nagoya, is a journey back in time to a wooded valley that is home to three of Japan's best-preserved villages. Nowhere else in all of Japan gives a better impression of what life must have been like in old rural Japan.

The three towns — Narai, Tsumago and Magome — were once post towns on the Nakasendo, an alternative route between Edo (Tokyo) and Kyoto to the Tokaido highway. Unlike other post towns on the route, they have been perfectly preserved; reminders of Japan's feudal past.

As many of the travelers were of high caste, including the *daimyo* (feudal lords) and their retinues doing the obligatory commuting between their home province and the shogun's capital, the standard of some of the inns was very high. Interspersed among the inns were teahouses and craft workshops turning out exquisite souvenirs and everyday articles. In fact, the villages were quite different from the typical farmer's villages in the countryside and more like fragments of the metropolis set down in the wilds.

The villagers have rather miraculously managed a smooth transition from feudal days to the present. Their economic activity remains almost exactly as it was — inns, crafts and tea (and now coffee) — but today the clients are ordinary modern Japanese in search of history.

small front doors covered with *shoji* paper and the narrow wooden bars on the upper windows.

You can deepen your understanding of the place the following morning by dropping into one of several *shiryokan*, houses typical of the village, whose antique appearance has been preserved inside as well as out. The kettle hangs over the hearth, the abacus is ready by the desk, the second floor is full of silk-weaving equipment. Craftsmen, including makers of lacquered vessels and combs, are still at work in the villages.

While Narai is out on its own, Tsumago and Magome are connected by the old Nakasendo road. The walk between them takes about three hours and is pleasant, particularly if you go from

Some wise souls have realized that the survival of the villages depends on their maintaining their historical appearance, and this is what they have done. Modern-looking structures are very few, and when a new building goes up — a post office in Narai, for example — it's in the traditional style and made with traditional materials. And very charming it is, too.

A night in a *minshuku* or *ryokan* in one of these villages is perfect time-travel. After a hot dip in one of the tiny bathrooms, in which everything is made of *hinoki* (Japanese cypress), there may be time for a stroll before supper. Array yourself in the *yukata* (cotton kimono), *haori* (half-coat) and *geta* (wooden shoes) provided by the *ryokan* (take a parasol if it's raining) and explore the village's single street. Note how narrow the houses are at the front, but how deep: houses were taxed according to the width of their frontage. Note also the

Tsumago to Magome, as that way the road is largely downhill.

Accommodation in all three towns is of the *minshuku* variety — traditional Japanese inns — and rather than make recommendations it is better to go through the information desks that are easily found in all three towns. They will help smooth the way for nervous inn-keepers unused to dealing with *gaijin*.

Although all three old post towns are in the Kiso Valley, Narai doesn't combine with Tsumago and Magome as an excursion, and most travelers choose one or the other. The latter — Tsumago and Magome — is the more attractive option, as the towns are more perfectly preserved (traffic runs

OPPOSITE: In contrast to the light and airy castle at Himeji, the black yet equally ornate castle at Matsumoto is called the Crow Castle. ABOVE: The snow-capped peaks of the Japanese Alps near Kamikochi.

through the main street of Narai) and they also offer the opportunity to hike the trail between them. They are, however, harder to get to. From Nagoya (55 minutes) and Matsumoto (one and a half hours) take the Chuo line to Nagiso station and change to a bus for Tsumago (10 minutes); for Magome, get off at Nakatsugawa station, from where buses take half an hour.

Narai is 50 minutes from Matsumoto by train.

TAKAYAMA

One of Japan's most charming rural towns, and easily accessible from either Matsuyama or the Kiso Valley, Takayama is a "little Kyoto" (like Kanazawa, described below) that almost everybody falls in love with when they visit. The area surrounding Takayama is known as Hida.

GENERAL INFORMATION

Takayama is no stranger to foreign tourism, as you will discover when you stop at the **Hida Tourist Information Office** ((0577) 32-5328, in front of the station. Useful maps of the town and the area are available, as is help reserving accommodation. Most of the town's attractions are easily reached on foot in the center of town. The only real exception is the Takayama's number one attraction, the Hida Folk Village, which is around 10 minutes west of town by bus.

Takayama is an ideal size for exploring by bicycle. There are bike rental shops near the station — ¥300 for the first hour, ¥200 for subsequent hours — and the Tourist Information people in the station will point you in the right direction.

WHAT TO SEE AND DO

Takayama's premier sight is the **Hida Folk Village** (8:30 AM to 5 PM, daily). Pick up an English map of the village when you buy your ticket (¥700), though it will probably be given to you as a matter of course.

Some complain that the 20 buildings are not lived in, that a "village" not lived in can hardly qualify as a village. This is true, but the village does nevertheless bring together fascinating examples of folk architecture (dismantled and put back together here) from around the region, also providing opportunities to explore the buildings, which would not be likely if people were living in them. Of particular interest are the examples of *gassho-zukuri* architecture, houses with precipitously sloped straw roofs that the Japanese name alludes to as "hands in prayer." Buses run to the village from Takayama station.

If you find yourself wondering about the golden roof topped with a red ball in the distance, it is the **Main World Shrine**, headquarters of the

Sukyo Mahikari religious sect. Visitors are free to enter and take a look if they like. It is an almost disconcertingly strange place.

Back in Takayama itself, walk east of the station down Hirokoji Dori, turn right at the Miyagawa River and look out **Takayama-Jinya** (9 AM to 4:30 PM, daily) on the right. The original building dates from 1615, and although most of what can be seen today was reconstructed 200 years later, it is nonetheless worth a visit. It is a great rarity, being the only one of 60 administrative offices of the Edo period still standing. Here was where the appointee of the shogun in Edo once administered the Hida region. It's a large, rambling building with a garden full of trees swathed in straw bandages

(in winter). Admire the roof of cypress bark, the storerooms for rice (the unit of currency and taxation), the large tatami-matted reception rooms. Regular English-language tours of the buildings are available, and recommended for a full understanding of all that is on display here.

Over the river from here is the **San-machi Suji** district, a journey back in time. It is an excellent place to find souvenirs: sake (from the brewery), *miso* (from the factory), fine textiles, wooden objects, antiques. The town is dotted with small sake factories, and if you approach them politely (and ideally in Japanese) the owners of some may be willing to show you around — a fascinating experience. This district also has perhaps more museums per square meter than anywhere else in the world, and you could spend a small fortune in entry fees were you to visit them all, but most can be safely left to their own devices.

Magnificent festivals are held in Takayama every April and October (see FESTIVE FLINGS, page 50 in YOUR CHOICE). Four of the huge and gorgeously decorated festival wagons (*yatai*) are on permanent display in the **Takayama Yatai Kaikan** (9 AM to 4:30 PM, daily) in the grounds of **Hachiman Shrine**, near the center of town.

WHERE TO STAY

For the best in Takayama accommodation, the **Hotel Associa Takayama Resort** ((0577) 36-0001 FAX (0577) 36-0188 WEB SITE www.associa.com/english/tky/, 1134 Echigo-cho, has a peaceful setting in the forested hills not far to the southwest of town. With three restaurants, a bar and a Jacuzzi, it's a fully international hotel. It has both Western and Japanese rooms that are considerably larger than is average in Japan. The deluxe Japanese-style rooms are highly recommended.

In the west of town is the charming **Pension Anne Shirley** ((0577) 32-6606 FAX (0577) 36-0650, 87-1297-1 Yamaguchi-cho, looking for all the world like a chalet and having both Japanese and Western rooms with attached bathrooms inside. It has a family atmosphere, making a stay here a wonderful interlude if you have been staying in big, impersonal business hotels. The pension also has its own hot spring baths. Rates range from ¥10,000 per person.

The **Rickshaw Inn** ((0577) 32-2890 FAX (0577) 32-2469 E-MAIL rickshaw@gix.or.jpis, 54 Suehiro-cho, is everything you could look for in an inexpensive to moderately priced *ryokan*. It's immaculately maintained, has oodles of atmosphere, the staff are welcoming and speak English, and there are also guide services and information provided. Unlike many budget *ryokan*, along with the usual common bathroom basic singles and doubles, the Rickshaw Inn also has some more expensive rooms with bathroom attached. The Inn is in the heart of town, and rates range from ¥4,000 to ¥10,000 per person.

Hida Takayama Tenshoji Youth Hostel ((0577) 32-6345 FAX (0577) 35-2986, 83 Tenshoji-machi, is an improvement on the average Japanese youth hostel for a few reasons. First, it is set in temple surroundings; second it has a central Takayama address, being directly west of the station on the far side of the Enako-gawa River; and third, besides the usual dormitory beds, it also has private rooms from around ¥3,500 per person.

WHERE TO EAT

Like any self-respecting regional tourist destination, Takayama has its share of local delicacies. The chief one here is *sansai*, which means "mountain vegetables." This essentially refers to fresh vegetables — it's highly unlikely they were picked

wild in the mountains — and you can expect them to appear in most of the dishes offered by the dozens of restaurants serving lunch (rarely dinner — the tourists have all gone by then) in the San-machi Suji part of town. A popular dish is *sansai soba*, a simple dish of buckwheat noodles topped with green vegetables — a good light lunch, but rather unsubstantial as a dinner.

If you are staying at either the Rickshaw Inn or Pension Anne Shirley — see WHERE TO STAY above — consider eating in for dinner. Many of the local restaurants close after lunch, and if you venture into town of an evening for dinner you will be mostly at the mercy of generic *izakaya* (Japanese pub) restaurants around the station.

A well-known place to sample the regional cuisine is **Suzuya** ((0577) 32-2484, 34 Hanakawa, which is not far west of the station, close to Kokubunji Dori. An atmospheric place to dine, it has the famous *sansai soba*, along with some other Hida favorites including the distinctive *hoba miso* (vegetables roasted with miso sauce), which tastes much better than it sounds. It is open for both lunch and dinner, though it closes early in the evenings. An English menu makes for easy ordering.

In the grounds of Shoren-ji Temple, which lies southwest of the station on the far side of the Miyagawa River, is **Kannenbo** ((0577) 32-2052, where the Hida region's vegetable obsession comes into full play. This vegetarian restaurant is a delight, mostly on account of the setting, and is open daily from 11 AM to 5 PM.

HOW TO GET THERE

Takayama has a direct connection with Nagoya on the Takayama line, and trains take around two and a half hours. Buses run direct from the bus terminal immediately west of Takayama station to Kamikochi, where, if you are headed for Matsumoto,

OPPOSITE: A vermilion bridge in Takayama.
ABOVE: Takayama's morning market

you will need to change buses again for Shin-Shimashima station (see under KAMIKOCHI, above, for details). To travel to Kanazawa, take a train to Toyama and change there — the total journey takes around two and a half hours.

KANAZAWA

Once one of Japan's great cities, Kanazawa still likes to think of itself as a special place, something of cultural haven along the lines of Kyoto. This is not so far from the truth. Kanazawa has a wealth of things to see and do, has a fascinating history, and at least one stand-out attraction: the famous Kenroku-en Garden, one of Japan's famous top three.

Kanazawa's place in history was earned by a revolt against the Togashi family in the fifteenth century that toppled the ruling elite and established what was then called the Kaga region under Buddhist autonomy. This state of affairs lasted remarkably for nearly 100 years until Oda Nobunaga, the warlord who unified Japan, installed one of his men to rule the region.

GENERAL INFORMATION

Most of the city's major attractions are clustered within walking distance of each other a 10-minute bus ride from Kanazawa station, which is inconveniently located in the far northwest of town. Take a bus to Korinbo from in front of the station.

One thing Kanazawa does not lack is information for foreigners. Inside the station look out for the **tourist information counter** ((076) 231-6311, where English-speaking staff can load you down with tourist pamphlets, help with making reservations for accommodation, and even organize a free guide to show you around. The **Kanazawa International Exchange Foundation** ((076) 220-2522 is in the Kenshukan Hall in the Nagamachi area, and also provides guides and can arrange for you to stay with a Japanese family in Kanazawa.

WHAT TO SEE AND DO

Kanazawa's famous sight is **Kenroku-en** (7 AM to 6 PM, March 1 to October 15, 8 AM to 4:30 PM the rest of the year), a large and exquisite landscaped garden near the city center. With its ponds and streams, grotesque pines, charming views and tea cottages, it is possibly the most beautiful garden of its type in Japan. Just one caveat: Kenroku-en is arguably too beautiful, too famous, for its own good. It is perhaps self-indulgent to complain about all those *other* tourists at popular tourist attractions; but it is difficult not to do so here, where the tourist numbers — many in brigades led by megaphone-touting guides — often overwhelm the garden's undeniable charms. The answer: get

here as early as possible — preferably at the 7 AM opening in the late spring, summer and the early autumn months.

Inside the garden, just east of the **Kasumiga-ike Pond** (it is usually translated as "lake") is the **Seison-kaku Pavilion**, a ravishingly beautiful traditional villa, well worth the separate admission fee (¥500). Wander through its rooms, admire the bold decorative scheme upstairs, sit on the veranda and enjoy the placid garden: the lifestyle of the aristocrats who used to live here is quite easy to imagine — and quite enviable. An English-language guide comes with the price of the entry ticket and gives useful background information.

The scanty remains of Kanazawa Castle can be seen across the road to the north of Kenroku-en, but more interesting is the small but very well-defined area of samurai houses called **Nagamachi**. It is a 10-minute walk west of Kenroku-en, behind

the Korinbo 109 Department Store (perhaps Kanazawa's number-one landmark), and is easily recognized by the long, high walls of packed earth which enclose the houses. There are old tea shops in this small section and a silk-dyeing workshop. You can watch the craftsmen and craftswomen at work.

Another 10-minute walk southwest of here, on the other side of the Sai-gawa River, is the **Tera-machi** (temple district) area. Numerous small temples can be found here, but the chief attraction is **Myoryu-ji Temple**, which is better known as **Ninja-dera**. Despite their fame in the West, *ninja* — those men-in-black agents of stealth — rarely make an appearance on the Japanese travel trail. Here they have a temple, complete with hidden doors, traps, the usual *ninja* ruses. To look around the temple, it is necessary to join a Japanese-language tour. For reservations (essential) call ((076) 241-2877.

WHERE TO STAY AND EAT

Kanazawa's most luxurious hotel is the 254-room **Hotel ANA Kanazawa** ((076) 224-6111 FAX (076) 224-6100 WEB SITE www.ananet.or.jp/anahotels/e/direct/japan/tokan/kana.html, 16-3 Showa-machi, directly in front of Kanazawa station. It has Japanese, Chinese and Continental restaurants, as well as a bar, and other amenities include a swimming pool, gym and sauna. It's slightly far away from Kanazawa's main attractions, but not so far as to be a major inconvenience.

For Japanese-style accommodation, try the **Murataya Ryokan** ((076) 263-0455 FAX 263-0456, 1-5-2 Katamachi, in the Katamachi district just south of Nagamachi. This is a small place, and the rooms are a little pokey, but it's fine for an

Kanazawa's Kenroku-en Garden is one of Japan's three most celebrated "stroll gardens."

Central Honshu

overnight stay. The bathing facilities are shared and per-person costs are ¥4,500.

The **Matsui Youth Hostel** ((076) 221-0275, 1-9-3 Kata-machi, is one of the chain's better examples, having a good central location in Katamachi and also offering inexpensive rooms along with the usual dormitory accommodation.

Kanazawa's famous contribution to Japanese cuisine (though not famous outside Japan) is *jibuni*, a stewed duck dish prepared with seasonal vegetables. A good place to try it is **Shiki-no-Table** ((076) 265-6155, 1-1-17 Nagamachi, a quaint restaurant run by a local expert in the cuisine of Kanazawa, which specializes in banquets based on the local specialties. It is closed on Wednesdays.

HOW TO GET THERE

Kanazawa is just two and a half hours from Kyoto on the JR Hokuritsu line (see under TAKAYAMA, above, for information on how to get there). From Tokyo the fastest rail route is to take a Shinkansen to Nagaoka and then transfer to a *tokkyu* (limited express) direct to Kanazawa, a trip that takes approximately four hours.

NOTO-HANTO PENINSULA

Kanazawa is the gateway to the placid and rural Noto-hanto Peninsula. As is often the case when

North of Korinbo 109 Department Store is the bustling Omicho Market, which mostly provides fresh fish, meat and vegetables for the people of Kanazawa, but is also home to a couple of famous restaurants that draw on the fresh ingredients so close at hand. A unique variation on this is provided by **Shamoji-ya** ((076) 264-4848, 3 Jukkenmachi, where the restaurant cooks ingredients bought by shoppers in the market. It should be an interesting experience if you hook up with one of Kanazawa's local guides (see GENERAL INFORMATION, above). Also in the market is **Genpei**, a famous sushi restaurant.

Lastly, for a wide-range of dining alternatives, head over to the **Korinbo 109 Department Store** itself, where on the fourth floor you will find a gourmet section brimming with restaurants offering everything from sushi to pizza. Prices are reasonable, making it a good place for lunch.

you get out into rural Japan, however, the transport system is less than reliable, and long waits for buses can end up being the order of the day. But the peninsula is popular with cyclists, and residents of Japan often explore the area in rented cars.

Information about the peninsula can be picked up at Kanazawa station. Don't expect any English information on the peninsula itself. The JR Nanao line goes as far as **Nanao** in the southeast of the peninsula, after which the private Noto line takes over, traveling to the northeastern tip of the peninsula at **Takojima**. A branch of the Noto line crosses the peninsula at **Anamizu** to **Wajima**, Noto's main tourist attraction. For those who don't have time to spend a couple of days following the peninsula's coastline, a day-trip to the port of Wajima is a worthwhile excursion. It's a pretty port town with an interesting lacquerware center. A tourist information center in Wajima — no English spoken — can help find inexpensive *minshuku* or *ryokan* accommodation.

An alternative way to take a quick look at the peninsula is to get off the train before Nanao (on the west side of the peninsula) at **Hakui**, and then board a bus for **Monzen**, and you will find **Soji-ji**, a most serene Zen temple. Much of the way there the bus runs along the coast. The fantastic rock formations — phalluses, doughnuts, pinnacles joined by holy rope — and the old-fashioned prosperity of the little villages with their shiny black roofs, the *wakame* (seaweed) drying by the roadside, the sleek-prowed fishing boats, all help to make the journey a memorable one. Buses continue, though irregularly, on to Wajima, from where you can travel back to Kanazawa by train on the route described above, but in reverse.

FUKUI AND EIHEI-JI TEMPLE

Fukui, slightly over 70 km (43 miles) south of Kanazawa, is the center of the Echizen area, celebrated far and wide for its crafts. Lacquerware (*Echizen-Shikhi*), hand-made paper (*Echizen-Washi*), pottery (*Echizen-Yaki*) and high-quality cutlery (*Echizen-Uchihamono*) are all made nearby, and can be found on sale in Fukui itself. Fukui, however, has little else to offer travelers, and most make, at best, a whistle-stop here en-route to the area's most interesting attraction: Eihei-ji Temple (5 AM to 5 PM, daily). Note that the temple closes at certain unpredictable times of the year, so check with the Kanazawa tourist information counter in Kanazawa station that it is open before heading out there.

To get to Eihei-ji you will have to change trains at Fukui (one hour from Kanazawa on the JR Hokuriku line). At JR Fukui station change to Keifuku Denki Tetsudo station (they're connected), from where Eihei-ji station is 35 minutes.

Eihei-ji is the main temple of the Soto Zen sect, founded in 1244 by Zen Master Dogen, who brought the teachings of Soto Zen to Japan and whose famed sayings include "The landscape of the mountains/The sound of streams/All are the body and voice/of Buddha." He is regarded as a saint in Japan.

The temple's location among great cryptomeria trees (Japanese cedar) is awe-inspiring; the only pity is that its fame has turned it into something of a machine for tourists. The temple does accept students, and even overnight stays, but both involve complicated procedures that can take up to a month to accomplish.

NAGOYA

The major urban aggregation of central Honshu and Japan's fifth most populated city, Nagoya is the only stop the fastest Tokaido Shinkansen train, the Hikari, makes between Tokyo and Kyoto.

With a population of just over two million, Nagoya sits uneasily between the somewhat nondescript provincial cities that litter urban Japan and cosmopolitan centers like Tokyo and Osaka. A place of big boulevards and big-city pretensions, it somehow fails to convince. Add to this a relative shortage of compelling sights and it is not difficult to understand why, while the Hikari may indeed stop here, few foreign travelers get off the train.

This said, Nagoya has enough of interest to make it worth a brief stop, and it is also a useful gateway to Kanazawa, Takayama and nearby Inuyama.

BACKGROUND

In the seventeenth century, the great shogun Tokugawa Ieyasu built a major castle where Nagoya Castle now stands, and as so often happened in Japan, a city grew up around its skirts. Crafts, which had been practiced in the area since ancient times — especially pottery — flourished in Nagoya, and the city quickly became a major cultural center.

Unfortunately, nearly all vestiges of this culture were destroyed in the war, but the people of Nagoya took advantage of the disaster to rebuild the city on a grid plan. In 1959 they also rebuilt the castle, prudently in Ferro-concrete (reinforced concrete). The old trades — porcelain, cloisonné and textiles — flourished again, but were overtaken in importance by modern heavy and chemical industries: iron and steel, automobiles, ship-building, plastics, fertilizers, drugs. Ideally located on the Pacific, and in the center of the great Tokaido industrial belt, well-watered Nagoya is one of the modern world's most massive and smoothly turning dynamos.

GENERAL INFORMATION

Nagoya has a logical layout, making it difficult to get lost in. Nagoya station is in the west of town, and Sakura Dori cuts more or less straight through the city center west to east. A color-coded subway system with four lines has stops that take in most of the city's major tourist attractions — there is no need to resort to the less accessible bus system if you are on the regular tourist route.

The **Nagoya Tourist Information Center** ((05) 2541-4301 is in the central section of the massive Nagoya station and is open daily from 9 AM to 7 PM. Also useful, though aimed more at international residents of Nagoya than at visitors, is the **Nagoya International Center** ((05) 2581-0100 WEB SITE www.nic-nagoya.or.jp/index-e.htm, Nagoya

Eihei-ji Temple, not far from Kanazawa, is one of the country's most ancient Buddhist structures, having been founded in 1244 by the Soto Zen sect.

International Center Building, 47-1 Nagono 1-chome, Nakamura-ku. It has a library and televisions screening CNN, and is a good place to pick up tips on what is happening in Nagoya. It should be possible to pick up a copy of *Nagoya Avenues* here, a free listings magazine for the Nagoya area.

WHAT TO SEE AND DO

Nagoya Castle (9 AM to 4:30 PM) is Nagoya's biggest attraction. Although the main building is less than 25 years old, it is a faithful copy of the original (unlike Osaka Castle, for example, which is smaller than its model) and some of the gates and turrets around it have survived from the seventeenth century. It's a little too obvious that it is made of concrete, but the lift that whisks visitors to the fifth floor will be appreciated by anybody who has trudged up the hundreds of steps in a genuine Japanese castle.

On the way down there are weapons, armor, painted screens and, on the fourth floor, cases of beautiful paper dolls representing the city's October parade of feudal lords. The nearest subway station is Shiyakusho on the Meijo line. Entrance costs ¥500, for which you also get an informative and well-written leaflet.

East of the castle, close to Ozone (pronounced "or-zor-nay") subway station, is the **Tokugawa Art Museum** (10 AM to 5 PM, closed Mondays). It's expensive at ¥1,200, but the displays of the accumulated treasures of the Tokugawa are well worth seeing. The museum's most treasured possession — the original manuscript of *Tale of the Genji* — is unfortunately not displayed, but there are exhibits relating to the famous proto-novel.

Atsuta Shrine, the most important in the city, is one of the oldest in the country and draws streams of pilgrims. It's five kilometers (just over three miles) south of town and lies in wooded grounds. Its buildings are reminiscent of those at Ise, and its importance as a shrine is underscored by the fact that it is home to one of the Japanese imperial family's three "imperial regalia" — the others are the "sacred jewels" and the "sacred mirror." The regalia here is the *kusanagi-no-tsurugi*, or the grass-cutting sword, though, if indeed it exists, it is not on display. A museum in the shrine precincts has a collection of less sacred swords donated to the shrine over the ages. The nearest subway station is Jingu Nishi on the Meijo subway line.

It may not sound wildly exciting, but the **Toyota Commemorative Museum of Science and Technology** (9:30 AM to 5 PM, closed Mondays) is a great place to take kids. Touting itself as a place where young people "can learn the importance of making things," it has a fascinating section on the automated production of motor vehicles, as well as a section on textiles, which is what Toyota started out its days producing. It's east of Nagoya station,

and the easiest way to reach it is to take a train to Sako station on the Nagoya Meitetsu line.

There is little else to see in Nagoya, though the city center, **Sakae**, dominated by the 180-m-high (590-ft) television tower, and the garden-cum-boulevard in which the tower stands, Hisaya-odori Park, is worth taking a stroll to look at.

WHERE TO STAY

Leading the pack is the 28-story **Nagoya Hilton Hotel** ((05) 2212-1111 FAX (05) 2212-1225, 3-3 Sakae 1 Chome, a monster of a luxury hotel in the heart of the bustling Sakae district. It's the first choice for most business and luxury travelers, and features such as its tennis courts and indoor swimming pool give it the edge over the competition. Rates start at ¥29,000 for a double.

For something a little more intimate, the **Century Hyatt Nagoya** ((05) 2541-1234 FAX (05) 2569-1717 WEB SITE www.hyatt.com/japan/nagoya/hotels/hotel_nagoy.html, 2-43-6 Meieki Nakamura-Ku, offers true international standards (not Japanese business approximations) in the heart of Nagoya. Small by Hyatt standards, with just two restaurants and 115 guest rooms, it has all the amenities you would expect of a five-star establishment.

Not quite in the same league, but with great views of Nagoya Castle and spacious rooms, is the **Westin Nagoya Castle Hotel** ((05) 2521-2121 FAX (05) 2531-3313 WEB SITE www.castle.co.jp, 3-19 Hinokuchi-cho, Nishi-ku. It's next to Sengencho subway station on the Tsurumai line.

For a basic but reliable business hotel, the **Nagoya Green Hotel** ((05) 2203-0211 FAX (05) 2211-4434, 1-8-22 Nishiki, Naka-ku, is centrally located and is part of a chain of hotels that specialize in no-frills comforts from around ¥8,000 per person.

Inexpensive *ryokan* accommodation is found at the **Ryokan Meiryu** ((05) 2331-8686 FAX (05) 2321-6119 E-MAIL meiryu@japan-net.ne.jp, 2-4-21 Kamimaezu, Naka-ku, which is a three-minute walk from Kamimaezu station on the Meijo subway line. It's a traditional place, with a welcoming family atmosphere, and meals are provided for an extra charge. Rates are from ¥5,000 per person.

The **Aichi-ken Seinen Kaikan Youth Hostel** ((05) 2221-6001 FAX (05) 2304-3508, 1-18-8 Sakae, has one of the best locations of all Japan's youth hostels, right in the center of Nagoya's downtown Sakae district, and it also has inexpensive private rooms along with dormitory beds.

WHERE TO EAT

Nagoya's most famous regional specialty is *kishimen*, or flat noodles served in soup. *Misonikomi udon* is a thick noodle dish served in a miso-based

Nagoya is a thoroughly modern city, but monuments such as this Buddhist temple evoke times past.

sauce. *Temmusu* are tiny balls of rice half-wrapped in seaweed with a small shrimp inside.

Kishimen is available in restaurants all around the Sakae business district but for an easy way to try it, head up to the seventh floor of the **Matsuzakaya Department Store** next to Nagoya station, where you will find a host of restaurants offering this and other local specialties. For *misonikomi udon* the place to go is **Yamamotoya ℂ** (05) 2241-5617, 12-19 Sakae 3-chome. There are actually three other branches around town, but this one, in Sakae, is the most centrally located.

For Thai cuisine, try the popular **Sawasdee Sumiyoshi ℂ** (05) 2261-6781, which is next to Exit 6 of Tsurumai subway station, above a branch of Watsons. It's authentic, the menu covers all the Thai standards, and it should not cost much more than ¥2,500 per person.

For the usual recipe of American food, drinks and loud sounds, the Nagoya **Hard Rock Café ℂ** (05) 2218-3220 is next door to the Hilton Hotel in the ZXA Building in the heart of Sakae. Also not far away (call for directions) is **Across The Border ℂ** (05) 2201-4300, a popular haunt for local expats, with Mexican food and drinks — it is a good source of information for what's hot in Nagoya if you are looking to go out late.

HOW TO GET THERE

Nagoya airport is around 12 km (seven and a half miles) north of town, and is connected with most major domestic destinations and an increasingly large number of international ones too.

By train, Nagoya is one hour 55 minutes from Tokyo, 50 minutes from Kyoto (and one hour from Shin-Osaka) by the Hikari Shinkansen, the fastest train available on a Japan Rail Pass. The super-express Nozomi takes one hour, 36 minutes. All Shinkansen trains running west from Tokyo stop at Nagoya.

The JR Chuo rail line connects Nagoya with Matsumoto and Nagano. It's also possible to get to Takayama by train — take the Meitetsu Inuyama line to Inuyama and change there for the Takayama train line.

INUYAMA AND GIFU

Close to the big city of Nagoya are several attractions that can be seen as daytrips. Inuyama is famed for its castle and for its *ukai*, or cormorant fishing. Not far from Inuyama is Meiji Mura, a sprawling collection of Meiji-era buildings and one of Japan's most interesting open-air museums. Farther west is the city of Gifu, which, like Inuyama, has a castle and is another center for *ukai*. There is little point in going to both Inuyama *and* Gifu, and given that Inuyama is the more charming of the two and closer to Meiji Mura, it is the logical

choice. Bear in mind that the *ukai* season runs only from June 1 to September 30.

Inuyama is just 30 minutes from Nagoya via the private Meitetsu line. The main attraction is the diminutive **Inuyama-jo Castle** (9 AM to 5 PM, daily), which is around 10 minutes' walk from the station. Rarely visited by foreign tourists, the surprise is that this is in fact Japan's oldest surviving castle. There is not a great deal to see, but it's a pleasant walk through an old part of town to get to it, and the castle provides views over the town and surrounding countryside. In the summer months, *ukai* can be seen in the Kiso-gawa River just south of the castle from 6 PM.

It's well worth seeing the *ukai* ritual. Suspended from the prow of the boats is a fiery torch; and each boat also contains a number of cormorants on leads. Lured by the light, *ayu* (delicious sweetfish) rise to the surface, where the cormorants snap them up and bear them to the boats. This very ancient ritual takes place under the eyes of hundreds of spectators, almost all of them river-borne too, and most of them enjoying snacks or full-blown picnics washed down with quantities of sake.

Meiji Mura (9:30 AM to 5 PM, daily), seven kilometers (four miles) southeast of Inuyama, is a little expensive at ¥1,500, but it is one Japanese tourist attraction where the sheer scale of the place and the effort that has gone into creating it justifies the expense. It can be reached by buses that leave from Inuyama station or directly by bus from Nagoya's Meitetsu bus terminal.

Unique in Japan, the large hillside park is home to more than 50 of the most significant buildings of the Meiji period (1868–1912). Like all such parks, it rates nil for atmosphere, but as a series of vivid demonstrations of the way the Japanese variously imitated, adapted and resisted Western architectural styles, it is unbeatable. Among the attractions are a prison, a bathhouse, a small *kabuki* theater and the house occupied in turn by the novelists Mori Ogai and Natsume Soseki. The park fronts onto a lake, Iruka Pond (rowboats for hire). Electric buses ferry sightseers around the village grounds.

Nagoya is also close (40 minutes by the Meitetsu line) to the old city of Gifu. No longer very picturesque (blame the bombs), Gifu is nonetheless a center of picturesque trades — parasol and and lantern making. It is also, more significantly, the center of the ancient sport of *ukai*. **Gifu-jo Castle** (9 AM to 5 PM, daily) is accessible via cable car, offering splendid views of the Ngara-gawa River, where Gifu's cormorant fishing takes place in the summer.

Takayama is noted for the brewing of fine quality *sake*. Tourists can visit the breweries to see its production then buy attractive souvenir bottles, or kegs

Kansai

THE KANSAI REGION IS THE JAPANESE HEARTLAND. In terms of cultural treasures, nowhere else in Japan compares. Japanese history started here, and it was here that Japanese culture evolved into what it is today. Arguably, of course, Tokyo has been the great arbiter since the Meiji restoration, yet Kansai, with its modern cities of Osaka and Kobe, has had its part too in defining the modern Japanese experience.

This, in the end, is what is so compelling about Kansai. While the Tokyo region is overwhelmingly modern and urbanized, with scant pockets of tradition, Kansai has both — the high-tech future and the lingering past.

Kyoto, with its temples, shrines, tea houses, faded pleasure districts, *kabuki* performances and geisha, at first glance seems defining of the region. But try telling that to an Osaka-jin. The two cities may be barely half an hour away from each other by train, but they're worlds away in style and substance. Osaka is a forward-looking, impatient town, a place on the go, a city where the inhabitants famously greet each other with the words: "Making money?"

But there is more to Kansai than the old Osaka-Kyoto rivalry (both of which see Tokyo as a young upstart). Kobe is a cosmopolitan city that has for the most part put that devastating earthquake behind it and is back to business. Meanwhile Nara, now a sleepy backwater studded with Buddhist temples, has even a longer history than Kyoto, and was the nation's first capital. And this is not even to mention the Buddhist mountain-top retreat of Mount Koya-san or Japan's grandest Shinto Shrine, Ise-jingu, dedicated to Amaterasu, the Sun Goddess, from whom, according to legend, the Japanese imperial family is descended.

Indeed, it would be possible to spend every annual leave for the rest of your life exploring Kansai, and you would probably never run out of things to do and see.

KYOTO

If you had time for just one destination in Japan, it should probably be Kyoto. It's all the bad things people say it is — frequently overrun with tourists, blighted by ugly modern architecture, and exclusive to the point of snootiness. But, for all that, it is still the defining Japan experience in many ways.

Capital of the country for more than a thousand years, it is the cradle of almost everything that is uniquely Japanese, and though designed along Chinese lines, it is the place where the medieval Japanese first shook off that tradition and started to go their own way. As the only Japanese city of substance to escape wartime bombing — at the plea, it is said, of a highly placed American Japanophile — a great deal of this ancient beauty

survives: in temples, shrines, palaces, castles and aristocratic villas. There are also theaters, craft workshops and museums, geisha houses, and the most refined cuisine in the country.

It's possible to take in Kyoto's major attractions in a day, but you should stay longer if you can. It is an elusive city, and with its modern steel and Ferro-concrete and snarled-up traffic it doesn't at first seem anything out of the ordinary. Much of the charm is on a delicate scale: give yourself time to drop in to that little temple you would otherwise march right past, to get lost in the geisha district, to follow the winding course of a city stream. There are no grand European-style prospects in the city, and the view from the 131-m (430-ft) Kyoto Tower outside the station (the proprietors claim it harmonizes well with classical Kyoto) is banal in the extreme. You have to get close to the city and become a part of the picture before you can start to relish it.

BACKGROUND

Kyoto was founded in AD 794 as the capital of Japan. Like nearby Nara, the capital for the preceding 70-odd years, it was designed according to Chinese concepts, with nine broad streets running from east to west, intersected by a number of avenues running from south to north. This street plan persists to the present day and makes the city a blessedly easy place to get about in.

Heian-kyo — "Capital of Peace" — was one of its early names, and its golden age was the Heian period, from its foundation to the twelfth century. During these years the imperial court lived in great splendor and the city's artisans developed the skills necessary to satisfy the courtiers' luxurious tastes. These were the centuries when Kyoto was the country's true capital.

From the twelfth century onwards, Kyoto's fortunes waxed and waned, periodically swept by fires, at times near forgotten as provincial warlords fought among themselves for supreme influence over Japan. But throughout Kyoto remained a potent force. Conceivably the city might have become history when Tokugawa Ieyasu moved his government to Edo in 1603, but the imperial family didn't follow until nearly three centuries later. When they did, in 1869, the city survived, its old trades shored up by modern industries.

Like most great cities, Kyoto has seen its fair share of turmoil and change, and like other great cities its spirit is undaunted. It remains as refined and aristocratic — snobbish, many Japanese say — as ever. And why not? Tokyo might be the big smoke, but the elaborate enthronement ceremonies for new emperors still take place in Kyoto. Kyoto, after all, is the imperial home, the heart of Japan the nation.

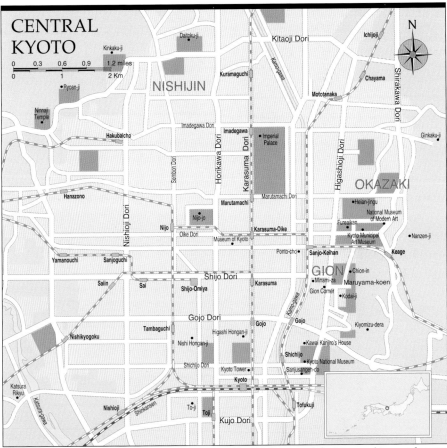

CENTRAL
KYOTO

0   0.3   0.6   0.9   1.2 miles
0   1   2 Km

N

GENERAL INFORMATION

Like Tokyo, Kyoto has its own large, and very well organized, tourist information center. The **Kyoto Tourist Information Center** ((075) 371-5649 is in the Kyoto Tower in front of Kyoto station — take the Karasuma exit. Opening hours are 9 AM to 5 PM, 9 AM to noon Saturdays, closed Sundays and public holidays. The staff are invariably rushed off their feet but do their best to help. The center's hotel reservation desk can be used for reservations not just in Kyoto but farther afield too.

Inside Kyoto station, on the second floor, is the **Kyoto City Information Office** ((075) 343-6655, which is open daily from 8:30 AM to 7 PM. It is less geared to foreigners and depending on who is staffing the desk there may be slight communication problems.

The **Kyoto International Community House** ((075) 752-3010, in Higashiyama, near Nanzen-ji subway station, is a center that has been established for foreigners living in Kyoto, and as such is not a tourist office. Nevertheless, it's an interesting place to call into: it has a library, notice boards,

English language television, and is a good source of information about the city that few first-time visitors would otherwise stumble upon.

For current information about what's happening around town, where to eat, where to party and so on, look out for the long-running *Kansai Time Out*, a monthly listings magazine. Tourist offices and hotels around town should also have copies of the free *Kyoto Visitor's Guide*, another good source for the latest events and things to do in Kyoto.

ORIENTATION

Commentators sometimes seem to make heavy weather of Kyoto's Chinese-style layout. But anyone who has ever visited a Chinese city will quickly realize they are right. To this day, Kyoto preserves a grid-like north-south orientation that makes navigation of the city straight forward.

Look at a map of Kyoto and you will soon see that the city center — its banks, shopping, entertainment — lies in the center, midway between Kyoto station in the south and the Imperial Palace in the north. Apart from the Imperial Palace itself, the city center is for the most part of little interest. Kyoto's sights — the "real" Kyoto — are scattered around the outskirts of town. The Kamo-gawa River, which runs north–south, is the natural boundary of eastern Kyoto, where most of the city's temples can be found. Everything north of the Imperial Palace and west of Nijo-jo Castle is western Kyoto.

GETTING AROUND

It's possible to travel direct from **Osaka International airport** to Kyoto by taking the JR Haruka *tokkyu* (limited express) service, which takes around one hour. Like all trains, it pulls into Kyoto's new station.

Kyoto on the buses, a free *Bus Route Map* is also available at the KTIC. Ask also at the KTIC about the books of bus coupons, some versions of which can combine with the subway system. The *Kyoto Journal* is not exactly a source of practical information on Kyoto. But, with poetry, sophisticated photographs and art-work, it is a useful source of information on the best Kyoto has to offer.

WHAT TO SEE AND DO

Kyoto has so many sights that it is easy to become paralyzed by indecision over where to start. The best idea is to pick an area and explore it. The city breaks down logically into central, eastern and

The city has two subway lines: the **Karasuma line** runs north-south past Kyoto station and the Imperial Palace, while the newer **Tozai line** runs west to east, starting at Nijo and continuing past Nanzen-ji. The two lines connect at **Karasuma Oike**, which is pretty much the center of town. Together they amount to a very convenient way of getting around the key points of the city, and given that central Kyoto is not a particularly attractive place, you are not missing too much by moving around underground.

Unlike many Japanese cities, Kyoto's bus network is a relatively simple proposition, and even first-time visitors usually find themselves using the buses far more than they have in other Japanese destinations. The simple bus route map that comes with the giveaway Kyoto map provided by the KTIC is more than enough for the average user, but if you want to get serious about exploring

western sections, and ideally you should give yourself at least three days, with one for each. Even this will only allow you scrape the surface of what the city has to offer, but at least you will have an overview of Kyoto and will have seen the most famous attractions. If you have only one day, rather than race around, it is best to spend it exploring eastern Kyoto, which has the highest concentration of sights. With two days to look around, you would be best served by spending the second visiting some of western Kyoto's more far-flung attractions.

Central Kyoto

The first thing that strikes the newcomer to Kyoto is the **Kyoto station**, a controversial structure in a city full of controversial structures. At least, say some, it has stopped people complaining about the **Kyoto Tower**, which was erected here to continuing outcry in the 1960s. The complaints — at least in the case of the station — are probably undeserved. Downtown Kyoto succumbed to urban blight long ago, and buildings like this one at least bring some imagination to the city.

Straight ahead of the station is **Higashi Hongan-ji Temple** (6:30 AM to 4:30 PM, daily), the city's largest wooden building. The victim of many fires, it was most recently rebuilt in 1895. Two of the halls are open to the public, and entry is free.

Directly west is **Nishi Hongan-ji Temple** (6 AM to 5 PM, daily), which was founded in 1591. An interesting story lies behind these two temples, the "west" and the "east" Hongan-ji. Nishi (west) Hongan-ji was established as the headquarters of the popular Jodo Shinshu (True Pure Land) sect of Buddhism, which maintained that salvation could be achieved through the chanting of a simple mantra. A decade later, Hideyoshi Toyotomi, afraid of the sect's enormous popularity, had a rival *higashi* (east) headquarters built, hoping to splinter the faith doctrinally. Nishi Hongan-ji remains the more splendid of the two architecturally, though unfortunately guided tours only take place a couple of times a month and require a written request for permission to join beforehand.

North of the Hongan-ji Temple lies the true central Kyoto, the downtown area. There is not much to see, but it is an interesting area to wander around. Directly opposite **Takashimaya Department Store**, on Shijo Dori, look out for the **Teramachi** and **Shinkyogoku arcades**. They are good places to look for souvenirs. Parallel to them, next to the Kamo-gawa River, is the charming street of **Pontocho** with its small canal — come back at night, when the lanterns light up.

About a kilometer (half a mile) northwest of here is **Nijo-jo Castle** (8:45 AM to 4 PM, daily), once the Kyoto residence of the great shogun Tokugawa Ieyasu, and the best place to get a glimpse of his luxurious (and highly security-conscious) lifestyle. The castle, designed as a lavish habitat rather than a fortress, is crammed with invaluable works of art and craft, including carvings, paintings, metal work and furniture.

The single most famous feature of the castle is the *uguisubari*, the "bush warbler floor" of the corridor in the first building, which warbles under the lightest tread. This was to warn guards that an intruder — perhaps a would-be assassin — was on the premises.

The castle is surrounded by a pleasant garden but the trees in it are new: in the old days there were none. The sight of falling leaves was said to be too depressing for the resident samurai.

Around two kilometers (one mile) northeast of the castle is Kyoto's **Imperial Palace**, which covers a large area in the center of the city. It was the emperor's home before the Meiji restoration. Getting to see it, however, is not a simple matter of buying an entry ticket and presenting it at the door.

The procedure for gaining access to the Imperial Palace and all other "restricted" sights in Kyoto is firstly to go the offices of the **Imperial Household Agency** ((075) 211-1215 (8:45 AM to noon, 1 PM to 4 PM, closed weekends and holidays), near the northwest corner of the Imperial Park, fill in an application form, show your passport and wait for a short while. It's usually possible to get access to the palace the same day, though the agency prefers you apply two days in advance. Tours, in Japanese, begin at 10 AM and 2 PM.

Eastern Kyoto

About a kilometer (half a mile) east of Kyoto station, is a remarkable temple known as **Sanjusangen-do**

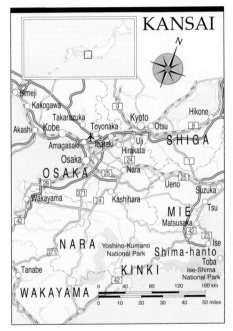

(open 8 AM to 5 PM April to November, 9 AM to 5 PM the rest of the year, daily), which glitters with the reflected light of 1,001 small images of Kannon, the goddess of mercy. The tall "thousand-handed" image of Kannon around which they cluster was carved in 1254. The temple is a great favorite with Japanese visitors.

Directly north of Sanjusangen-do is the **Kyoto National Museum** (9 AM to 4:30 PM, closed Mondays). It is not an essential stop, given the cultural treasures that lie ahead in eastern Kyoto — for museum buffs only.

Continuing north of here, you enter Kyoto's well-known pottery-producing area, and potters can be seen at work in several of the shops here. One of the greatest of them, Kawai Kanjiro, lived in this neighborhood, and his house is now open

Rich in color, the Heian-jingu Shrine is on the top of the list for most visitors to Kyoto.

to the public. **Kawai Kanjiro's House** (10 AM to 5 PM, closed Mondays and August 10 to 20 and December 4 to January 7) has examples of his work and the traditional "climbing kiln" in which he fired it.

Northwest of here lies one of Kyoto's famous attractions: **Kiyomizu-dera Temple** (6 AM to 6 PM, daily), founded in AD 798 but re-erected in 1633. It is easily one of the city's most splendid temples. Its veranda projects over a cliff and is supported by 139-m-high (456-ft) wooden columns: vertigo is assured. A miracle of wooden engineering, it offers great views of the city.

The approach to the temple is via a stiff, but rewarding, 10-minute walk up through narrow streets where much of Kyoto's characteristic pottery is produced and sold. The way back, down the cobbled **Sannen-zaka** and **Ninen-zaka** ("Three-year Slope" and "Two-year Slope"), is no less interesting. Many of the old shops along the way have been there for as long as two centuries.

At the end of Ninen-zaka you should see **Kodai-ji Temple** (9 AM to 4:30 PM, daily), a small temple that is worth visiting as much for its garden as for the temple itself. The area west of here is **Gion**, once the heart of Kyoto's "floating world." Some of the famous old geisha houses still operate, and it's an interesting area to wander through as dusk falls. Directly north of Kodai-ji is **Maruyama-koen Park**, where you will find **Chion-in Temple**, headquarters of the Jodo (Pure Land) sect of Buddhism and founded in the twelfth century. Everything from its San-mon Gate to its huge bell is built on a massive scale.

Directly north again is another of Kyoto's famous sights: **Heian-jingu Shrine** (8:30 AM to 4:30 PM, daily). This monumental piece of work was built in 1895 (though the current structure dates from the late 1970s) to commemorate the 1,100th anniversary of the city's foundation. Every year it is the locus for the city's **Jidai Matsuri** (Festival of the Ages), a historical costume parade on a grand scale held on October 22. Despite its enormous proportions, Heian-jingu is in fact a smaller replica of a much older shrine, built in AD 794.

In front of Heian-jingu is a towering red *torii* gate, to the south of which is a small cluster of museums. Most of them can be skipped in favor of a continued tour of the temples, but the **Kyoto Museum of Traditional Crafts**, or the **Fureaikan** (10 AM to 5:30 PM, closed Mondays), is worth visiting. Completely rebuilt in 1996, this museum is in the Miyako Messe Building. It has a great collection of traditional craft products as well as a reproduction of a traditional Kyoto house. To its south is the **National Museum of Modern Art** (9:30 AM to 5 PM, closed Mondays), which has changing exhibits, and the **Kyoto Municipal Art Museum** (9 AM to 5 PM, closed Mondays), which features modern Japanese art.

Uphill to the east of here is **Nanzen-ji Temple** (8:30 AM to 5 PM, daily). This enormous temple, which contains several subordinate temples, is noted for its *fusuma* (sliding door) paintings and its exquisite gardens. It is a Zen temple, and is the headquarters of the Nanzen-ji school of the Rinzai sect.

Like several other large Kyoto temples, Nanzen-ji's sub-temples have separate entry fees, and thus they tend to be less crowded than many other temples in eastern Kyoto. If you visit no other, at least take some time to see **Konchi-in's** beautiful "dry garden."

North of Nanzen-ji is the start to the **Path of Philosophy**, which is mostly residential, but a pleasant stroll all the same, with the occasional coffee shop along the way beckoning you in for a rest. At the end of the walk is **Ginkaku-ji Temple** (8:30 AM to 5 PM, daily), the "Temple of the Silver Pavilion" and not to be confused with Kinkaku-ji, the "Temple of the Golden Pavilion," which lies in the northwest of Kyoto. Hedges lead the way into the pavilion grounds, where the attraction is less the celebrated pavilion (modeled on the golden one in the northwest) than on the raked sand "dry garden," which looks like an exercise in modern minimalism.

Western Kyoto

Daitoku-ji Temple is another enormous Rinzai Zen establishment with numerous subsidiary temples. Pretty gardens and artworks of great age and beauty abound. Some of the sub-temples are open to the public, but an entrance fee must be paid for each one. It is generally worth it: they are full of charming surprises. If you visit no other, at least pay a visit to its **Daisen-in** sub-temple, which is celebrated for its two allegorical gardens, the first representing the "river of life" and the second the "nothingness" into which the soul must submerge to escape the cycle of rebirth.

In the grounds of Daitoku-ji there is also a restaurant which specializes in Kyoto's vegetarian cuisine. It does not look like a restaurant so much as another temple, and the atmosphere is appropriately hushed and meditative. The dishes may be too fussily presented for some people's tastes, but it is an interesting experience all the same, and a good place to sample Kyoto cuisine.

Daitoku-ji is open 9 AM to 5 PM daily. Regular buses leave from central Kyoto to Daitokuji-mae.

West of Daitoku-ji is the famous **Kinkaku-ji** (9 AM to 5 PM, daily), the "Temple of the Golden Pavilion" of Yukio Mishima's eponymous novel (take a bus to Kinkakuji-mae, one stop west of Daitokuji-mae). The pavilion of this temple, situated on a small lake, has two claims to fame aside from its extraordinary beauty: its walls are entirely covered in gold leaf, and it was burned to the ground by a deranged priest (the hero of

Mishima's novel) in 1950. It was rebuilt exactly as before — and not, for once, in Ferro-concrete — in 1955.

A couple of kilometers (about a mile) southwest from Kinkaku-ji is **Ryoan-ji Temple** (8 AM to 5 PM, daily). It's possible to walk there from Kinkaku-ji in around 20 minutes, or alternatively hop in a taxi or take a No. 59 bus from in front of Kinkaku-ji.

The temple is noted for its austere and simple stone garden, composed of a few mossy rocks arranged in a sea of gravel which is carefully raked into place daily. It is the most famous of its kind in Japan. This can lead to disappointment. The crowds can be overwhelming and broadcast

Katsura Rikyu is a mansion in the old English sense — a country pile. But it has none of the grandiloquence or pomposity of some Western equivalents. With its clean lines and masterly proportions, Katsura Rikyu is almost a modern building, except that the quality of the craftsmanship which greets the eye at every turn is beyond the dreams of any modern architect.

In the spring of 1982 the building was reopened to the public after six years of work, during which it was reconstructed from scratch. The fact that it was possible to reproduce the seventeenth-century craftsmanship of the original to the same high standards speaks volumes for the strength of Japanese craft traditions.

announcements and explanations of the deep meanings hidden beneath the garden's nuanced surface do little to enhance what some expect to be a deep metaphysical experience. The best advice is to arrive as early as possible, and remember that amidst the endless debate about the "riddle" of its significance, it is in the end just an arrangement of rocks and sand — very nicely done, though.

Rather a long way from the other attractions of western Kyoto is **Katsura Rikyu** (by appointment only), another of Kyoto's "restricted" sights. The procedure for gaining admittance is the same as that for the Imperial Palace (see EASTERN KYOTO above), though applications need to be made two days in advance. It is worth going to the trouble. Katsura Rikyu is regarded by many scholars as the crowning glory of Japanese domestic architecture.

Touring Kyoto

Once you've arrived, several lightning tours are available to give you a taste of the city.

The **JTB** ((075) 341-1413 Kyoto Morning Tour visits Nijo-jo Castle, the Imperial Palace, Kinkaku-ji and the Kyoto Handicrafts Center, and Nishijin Textile Center on Sundays and holidays. Departing from major city hotels between 8:20 AM and 9 AM, it returns at noon. The adult fare is ¥5,300. Also offered is an Afternoon Tour, calling at Heian-jingu, Sanjusangen-do and Kiyomizu Temple. The adult fare is ¥5,300. See Kyoto TIC for leaflets giving details of other tours, including full day tours and night tours.

The imposing lines of vermilion-laquered cyprus *torii* gateways, at the Fushimi Inari Shrine in Kyoto. Most Japanese pay their respects at both Shinto shrines and Buddhist temples, although the two religions are world's apart.

SHOPPING

Many cities, towns and villages in Japan boast of one particular craft which has been practiced in that place for generations and cannot be found in exactly the same form anywhere else. Kyoto, however, has not one craft but a whole spectrum, including silk weaving, dyeing, embroidery, pottery, lacquerware, cloisonné, woodblock prints, bamboo ware and others.

Some of these — silk weaving, for example — date back to the foundation of the city in the eighth century. Some — again, with weaving and dyeing as examples — have developed into modern industrialized concerns with an annual output worth hundreds of millions of dollars. But even in these cases the traditional craft techniques are maintained as a relatively small but vital part of the industry.

An excellent place to get an overview of Kyoto's rich craft traditions is the **Kyoto Handicrafts Center** ((075) 761-5080 (10 AM to 6 PM, daily) close to Heian-jingu. Not only is it a great opportunity to see craftsmen at work, it also conveniently brings together under one roof (and over five floors) a mind-boggling range of crafts for sale. On Shijo Dori in Gion is the **Kyoto Craft Center** ((075) 561-9660, which also carries a wide range of products — everything from lacquerware to textiles.

Kyoto is also home to a large number of specialty stores selling everything from clay dolls to Japanese stone lanterns. The best place for a comprehensive listing of such stores is the free *Kyoto Visitors Guide*, available at hotels and at the TIC.

WHERE TO STAY

Kyoto has the best range of accommodation in all of Japan. There are inexpensive youth hostels, tucked-away budget *ryokan*, business hotels, Japanese-style inns housed in historic buildings and, of course, luxury modern hotels. Despite the huge range of hotels, do not underestimate the popularity of Kyoto — it is always essential to book ahead if you want to be sure of a good place to stay in a good location. A last-minute search for accommodation can end up being an unpleasant and costly experience.

Luxury

The most convenient area to be based in is the center of Kyoto, and here two grand traditional Japanese inns vie for top position. Both are very old, very traditional, provide a *ryokan* experience you will never forget, and are, most importantly, welcoming to foreign guests (this is not true of all traditional *ryokan*).

The **Hiiragiya Ryokan** ((075) 221-1136 FAX (075) 221-1139, Oike-kado, Fuyacho, Nakakyo-ku, lies

north of Takashimaya Department Store, close to the Shiyakusho-mae subway station, and is almost definitive of the *ryokan* experience. Somehow, despite modern touches, like televisions and mini-bars in the rooms, this inn transports the visitor back to the world of samurai and shoguns. Art decorates the walls, the paper *shoji* doors slide back to reveal a manicured Japanese garden. When dinner is served — in your room — it is a *kaiseki* masterpiece of refinement, the service straight out of Hollywood Japan. Soak up to your neck in your own private tub. Perhaps it is the same one Charlie Chaplin used when he stayed here. This is perhaps as close as Japan gets to paradise. Advance bookings — and not just a few days, but weeks

preferably — are essential but absolutely worth the foresight.

Across the street is the even older **Tawaraya Ryokan** ((075) 211-5566 FAX (075) 211-2204, Fuyacho, Oike-Saguru. With a 300-year history, this *ryokan* has no doubt been host to real samurai. There are fewer concessions to the modern world here — the emphasis is more on the authentic inn experience — but the guest list is like a roll call of the great and famous. Rates at both *ryokan* start at between ¥35,000 and ¥40,000, more with meals, which should not be missed.

For luxury Western-style accommodation in the heart of eastern Kyoto, the **Miyako Hotel** ((075) 771-7111 FAX (075) 751-2490 E-MAIL yoyaku@miyako hotel.co.jp, Sanjo, Keage, Higashiyama-ku, next to Keage subway station, is a good choice. It's set amidst Japanese gardens complete with a bird-watching trail and has six restaurants, a swimming pool and sauna. The rooms come in either Western or Japanese-style, though compared to some of the traditional *ryokan* in Kyoto the Japanese-style offerings look very watered down. The room rates start at ¥19,000.

Moderate

Although there are plenty of mid-range business hotels in the station area of Kyoto, it is far more enjoyable to stay in *ryokan* accommodation. The Hiiragiya (see above), for example, has a less expensive annex about a five-minute walk north of Shiyakusho-mae subway station in central Kyoto called the **Hiiragiya Bekkan (** (075) 231-0151 FAX (075) 231-0153, Gokomachi, Nijo Dori, Nakagyo-ku. It

style hotel that has it hands down over the average Japanese mid-range hotel in terms of character. Rooms are not particularly large, but they're quiet. The hotel's location, in the heart of downtown Kyoto, makes it ideal for both sightseeing and nightlife.

Inexpensive

Yuhara ((075) 371-9583 FAX (075) 371-9583, 188 Kagiyacho, Shomen-agaru, Kiyamachi Dori, is a small place that seems to generate almost all of its business out of foreigners. This is not such a bad thing. It makes it a useful place to be based in terms of finding information about Kyoto. Nobody could fault the homey atmosphere of the

manages to achieve most of what the original Hiiragiya achieves in newer surroundings, and represents an opportunity to have the legendary *ryokan* experience at half the price of the more famous branch. Kaiseki dinners and Japanese or American breakfasts are available, but you are not obliged to order.

Yoshi-ima ((075) 561-2620 FAX (075) 541-6493, Hanimikoji-Nishi, Shinmonzen Dori, Gion, deserves a recommendation, first because of its location in the heart of old Gion, Kyoto's former geisha district, and second because it is accustomed to the errant ways of foreigners. Ask for a room overlooking the garden. Some of the better rooms here are definitely not moderately priced, but even the less expensive rooms are a delight to stay in.

A little east of Karasuma-Oike subway station, is the **Hotel Gimmond (** (075) 221-4111 FAX (075) 221-8250, Takakura Oike Dori, an elegant Western-

inn. Rooms are all Japanese style, and rates start at ¥4,000 per person.

Another long-established inn that is popular with foreigners is the **Ryokan Hinomoto (** (075) 351-4563 FAX (075) 351-3932, 375 Kotake-cho, Matsubara-agaru, Kawaramachi Dori, which is a few minutes south of the Takashimaya Department Store next to the canal. It's another homey, family-run place. The location, in the heart of Kyoto's action, makes it tempting to stay out later than you should — if this happens be sure to let the owners know, as they tend to lock the front doors before midnight.

Tani House ((075) 492-5489 FAX (075) 493-6419, 8 Daitokuji-cho, Murasakino, Kita-ku, is a Kyoto

Cherry trees lining this Kyoto canal are covered with a froth of pink, announcing the arrival of spring. The cherry blossom season is celebrated across Japan with costumed parades and performances.

institution — cheap, sometimes rowdy, a far cry from the elegance of many of the city's *ryokan*. Still for young travelers looking to save money on accommodation and avoid the disciplined atmosphere of the youth hostels, Tani is an attractive option. From the station, take a No. 206 bus to Kenkun-jinja-mae stop. Rates range from ¥3,000 per person.

Kyoto's youth hostels are strict places, with 10:30 PM curfews and books of rules. If you can tolerate such surroundings, the **Higashiyama Youth Hostel** ((75) 761-8135, 112 Shira Kawabashi-goken-cho, Sanjo-dori, is the most conveniently located, next to Higashiyama subway station.

WHERE TO EAT

Kyoto is famous as having the most refined cuisine in all Japan. It's called *kyoryori*, literally "capital cuisine," and if you can afford it you should splash out on at least one Kyoto-style feast while you are in town.

Hyotei ((075) 771-4116, 35 Kusakawa-cho, Nanzenji, is one of the most famous places indulge in Kyoto's best. Be served in your own small "hut" in a leafy garden with a pond, at this restaurant that first opened its doors for business three centuries ago. Even lunch time takeaways here will set you back more than the average expensive lunch (approximately ¥4,000). A *kaiseki* dinner can cost as much as ¥20,000 per person. Reservations are essential.

If Hyotei is beyond the means of your budget, **Tagoto** ((075) 221-1811, Shijo-Kawaramachi, Nishi-iru, is an excellent alternative. More than a century old and located in a quiet courtyard near the corner of Kawaramachi Dori and Shijo Dori, it has set courses of *kyoryori* from less than ¥4,000. It even has an English menu.

Yamatomi ((075) 221-3268, Ponto-cho, Shijo Agaru, has long been a popular place for foreigners, especially during the summer months, when it's possible to dine on a terrace overlooking the Kamo-gawa River. An English menu offers a good selection of generic Japanese dishes at very affordable prices.

Some of Kyoto's temple's have vegetarian restaurants on their grounds, some of which have been in business for centuries. One of the best is **Izusen** ((075) 491-6665, which is at Daitoku-ji Temple — actually in Daiji-in, a sub-temple on the Daitoku-ji precincts. As it is a Buddhist temple, it serves only vegetarian cuisine, in this case Zen vegetarian cuisine. It's a wonderful place to visit in the summer, when meals are served in the temple gardens. Meals start at around ¥3,000 per person. There is another, less expensive, branch on the second floor of the Kintetsu Department Store next to Kyoto station, though the surroundings cannot compare with Daitoku-ji — the latter is closed on

Tuesdays. Nanzen-ji Temple, as already noted above (see WHAT TO SEE AND DO), is another temple offering Zen Buddhist vegetarian cuisine: go to the **Chosho-in** sub-temple of Nanzen-ji. Please note though, that it is only open during the day and is closed on Tuesdays.

For a lively *izakaya* (Japanese pub) experience with Kyoto's student crowd head behind the Hankyu Department Store on Kawaramachi Dori to **Chikyu-ya**. Something of a dive, the food, beer and sake are cheap, the atmosphere rowdy, and there's even an English menu. It's a good place to meet people, though there should at least be two of you.

If you need a break from Japanese cuisine, Kyoto is a very cosmopolitan city, with a huge number of restaurants offering non-Japanese cuisines. Look out for branches of the popular Italian chain **Capricciosa**. Connoisseurs of regional Italian cuisine are advised to avoid it, but if you need a hearty meal in uplifting surroundings it can't be beat — the portions are nothing short of huge. There's a branch in the **Porta Restaurant Zone** (generally a good place to seek out inexpensive restaurants) ((075) 343-3499 in the basement of Kyoto station, and another branch on the second floor of the **Vox Building** ((075) 221-7496, on Kawaramachi Dori, close to the southeast corner of Sanjo Dori. There were five more branches around town at last count.

For more inventive Italian cuisine (with a Californian twist) **Fiasco** ((075) 415-0989, just north of the Imperial Palace on Karasuma Dori, is well recommended for an evening meal. Reckon on spending around ¥3,000 per person. Fiasco is closed Wednesdays.

Ashoka ((075) 241-1318, in the Kikusui Building on Teramachi Dori next to the intersection with Shijo Dori, is one of Kyoto's better Indian restaurants, popular for its tandoori and naan, and also offering vegetarian sets.

Homesick Americans should head up to Kitaoji Dori, where a small distance west of Daitoku-ji Temple, on the other side of the road, is the long-running **Knuckles** ((075) 441-5849, a relaxed (if this is not too much of a contradiction) New York-style restaurant that specializes in sandwiches and bagels and good coffee — though there's beer should you need it to.

NIGHTLIFE

Kyoto may not be Tokyo but it has an active nightlife scene all the same. It is a more pleasant city to explore by night too. Drift around the **Gion** section on the east bank of the Kamo-gawa River, admire the quiet elegance of the old town houses there, in a number of which geisha still live and work. Cross the bridge at the Minami-za Theater, home of Kyoto's *kabuki*, back to the west bank, then turn right up the narrow street closest to the river and parallel to it running north. This is **Ponto-cho** and it's the heart of the city's amusement quarter. Many bars and restaurants line the street, some forbiddingly traditional or expensive (remember to check before ordering), others welcoming and relatively cheap. The ones on the right look out over the river, and many have al fresco dining during the warm summer months.

For an evening drink, a good place to mingle with Kyoto residents — foreign and Japanese alike — is the **Pig & Whistle** ((075) 761-6022. Like its counterpart in Osaka, it's a fixture on the expat scene, and along with draft and bottled beer does homesick meals like fish and chips. Take the subway to Kawabata Sanjo station exit onto Sanjo Dori and look for the Shobi Building; it's on the second floor.

Bar Isn't It? ((075) 221-5399 is a popular chain with branches in Osaka, Kobe and Tokyo. The theme is simple: lots of room, minimal decor and cheap drinks. Not surprisingly it is popular with the foreign set and really pulls in the crowds Friday and Saturday nights, when it stays open until dawn. It's off Kiyamachi Dori near the intersection of Sanjo Dori, in the heart of Ponto-cho.

For traditional entertainment, **Gion Corner** (also known as **Gion Kaburenjo Theater**) ((075) 561-1119 is where you can catch one of the twice-nightly presentations of traditional arts and drama. The tea ceremony, flower-arrangement and *bunraku* puppet plays are among the arts demonstrated. While popular, many complain that the proceedings are overly touristy.

Unfortunately Gion's **Minami-za Theater** ((075) 561-1155 has only very occasional performances of *kabuki* nowadays, though it is worth checking at the TIC or in one of the local listings magazines such as *Kansai Time Out* to see whether anything is showing. You are more likely to get an opportunity to see a performance of *no*, which happens fairly regularly at Kyoto's **Kanze Kaikan** ((075) 771-6114.

HOW TO GET THERE

The quickest way is by Hikara Shinkansen from Tokyo station, which stops at only one station on the way (Nagoya) and covers the 513 km (319 miles) in two hours 37 minutes. (Japan's fastest trains, the all-reserved Nozomi Shinkansen, take two hours 15 minutes, but they are not available on a Japan Rail Pass). The stopping Kodama takes over four hours.

For those on a tight budget, JR runs convenient night buses, leaving the Yaesu side of Tokyo station at 10 PM and 11 PM and getting to Kyoto station at 6 AM and 6:50 AM.

Alternatively, you can fly to Kyoto, either from within the country or from overseas, landing at Osaka's domestic airport (Itami) or the Kansai International Airport.

OSAKA

Seemingly a world away from Kyoto is Osaka, Japan's third largest city, after Tokyo and Yokohama. Osakans are less reserved than the people of Kyoto, and have more of a zest for the good life — where Kyoto shuffles, Osaka bustles. Like Tokyo, Osaka is a window into modern Japan. Unfortunately, apart from its big city atmosphere, it has few compelling attractions, and for those on a whirlwind tour of Japan it can be safely dropped in favor of, say, Kyoto or Nara.

The city's main attraction is Osaka-jo Castle. Also worth a visit is the teeming nightlife area of Namba — indeed, even if you are based in Kyoto, it is worth heading into Osaka for an evening to stroll around the bright lights. Osaka Aquarium, in the Osaka Bay area, is an excellent place to take children.

BACKGROUND

Osaka has been a settlement of importance for some 1,500 years, but it was the great sixteenth-century warlord Toyotomi Hideyoshi who fashioned its modern character.

He not only built his castle, Japan's greatest, on the site where imperial palaces had stood in former times, but he also induced merchants from

The *taiko bashi* (drum bridge) of Osaka's Sumiyoshi Shrine, threshold of the sacred ground.

neighboring areas to move into the city and set up shop there. As a result, during the Edo period it became the most important distribution center in the country, and so it remains today.

Osaka enjoyed fantastic growth in the first half of this century: between 1889 and 1940 the population soared from 500,000 to 3,250,000. Although flattened during the war, it has more than regained its previous prosperity. Though it no longer teems in quite the way it used to, its carnal, mercantile character is unchanged.

GENERAL INFORMATION

Osaka may not be as high on most visitors' list of things to do as Kyoto and Nara, or even Tokyo for that matter, but it still has Japan's best tourist information network. The **Osaka Visitors Information Center** has offices at Shin-Osaka station ((06) 6305-3311, for those who arrive by Shinkansen; at JR Osaka Station ((06) 6345-2189. There are also tourist information counters at Namba station ((06) 6643-2125 and Tennoji Station ((06) 6774-3077.

Kansai International Airport is now a major gateway to Japan, and consequently most international airlines have offices in Osaka. They can be contacted on the following numbers: **Air France** ((06) 6641-1411; **Air India** ((06) 6264-1781; **Air New Zealand** TOLL-FREE (0120) 30-0747; **Alitalia** ((06) 6341-3951; **ANA** TOLL-FREE (0120) 02-9333; **Ansett** ((06) 6346-2556; **Asiana** ((06) 6229-3939; **British Airways** TOLL-FREE (0120) 122-881; **Canadian Airlines** ((06) 6346-5591; **Cathay Pacific** ((06) 6245-6731; **Delta Airlines** TOLL-FREE (0120) 33-3742; **Garuda** ((06) 6445-6985; **JAL** TOLL-FREE (0120) 25-5931; **Japan Air System** TOLL-FREE (0120) 71-1283; **KLM** TOLL-FREE (0120) 86-8862; **Korean Air** ((06) 6264-4311; **Lufthansa** ((06) 6341-4966; **MAS** ((06) 6635-3070; **Northwest** TOLL-FREE (0120) 12-0747; **Qantas** TOLL-FREE (0120) 20-7020; **Swiss Air** TOLL-FREE (0120) 66-7788; **Thai** ((06) 6202-5161; **United** TOLL-FREE (0120) 11-4466.

A reasonably inexpensive place to get on-line in Osaka is **Bean's Bit Café (** (06) 6766-3566, 6-2-29 Uehon-machi Tennoji-ku. Take exit 11 of Kintetsu Uehon-machi station, walk north and take the first on the left.

ORIENTATION

Like Tokyo, most of Osaka is contained within a JR loop line — the Kanjo line. Shinkansen pull into **Shin-Osaka station**, which lies north of JR Osaka station; the two stations are connected by the Mido-suji subway line. The city's two major commercial districts are **Umeda** (or Kita) in the north, and **Namba** (or Minami) in the south. They are quite different in character. Namba has a more intimate quality to it, while Umeda is more a place of towering office blocks and underground shopping malls. If you are pushed for time, Namba is the more interesting area to explore on foot. Osaka-jo Castle is in the east of town, close to the JR station of the same name. Osaka Bay, with its excellent aquarium, is in the west.

GETTING AROUND

Osaka has such a good rail network, that — unless you are out very late — there is no need to use any other kind of transportation to get around town. For a quick visit to the city, most travelers find themselves using a combination of the JR loop line and the Mido-suji subway line, which runs north–south connecting the commercial districts of Umeda and Namba. English sign-posting is reliable, and the system is relatively easy to use.

Osaka's Kansai International Airport (KIX) is some 35 km (about 22 miles) south of Osaka on an artificial island. There are a number of ways to get into Osaka from the airport, the least expensive being the Nankai Express, which takes around 40 minutes to Nankai Namba station, which is connected by subway to the rest of the city. JR services are more expensive, but useful if you have a Japan Rail Pass — passes can be validated at the airport on arrival. The JR Haruka limited express service runs to Tennoji station (30 minutes), Shin-Osaka (45 minutes) and then on to Kyoto.

WHAT TO SEE AND DO

It may be a reproduction, but **Osaka-jo Castle** (9 AM to 5 PM, daily) is still an impressive sight, and has been improved upon in recent years. The castle has been destroyed twice since Toyotomi Hideyoshi built it in 1586: first in 1615, the second time in the civil fighting of 1868, and it was rebuilt in 1931 using Ferro-concrete. Don't let this put you off visiting. The castle grounds provide great views of the castle, and inside the castle itself are eight floors of exhibits documenting the life and times of Toyotomi Hideyoshi, as well as panoramic views of the city from the eighth floor of the keep, which is accessible by two elevators.

The best way to approach the castle is via the Ote-mon Gate, a survivor from the second reconstruction of the 1620s. The gate is a short walk east of Tanimachi-4-chome subway station. **Osaka City Museum** (9:30 AM to 5 PM, closed Mondays) on the castle grounds is a somewhat underwhelming round-up of Osaka's history, and can be skipped unless you have a serious interest in the subject.

Usually touted as one of the city's prime attractions, **Shitenno-ji Temple** (9 AM to 4:30 PM, daily) is an unusually disappointing attraction. Theoretically it is the oldest temple in Japan, having been built in AD 593, 14 years before Horyu-ji (see NARA, below), but with the exception of a sole *torii* gate, the buildings are all of recent provenance, and there is a desolate, uninspiring air to the place. If it's temples you want, Kyoto is only 32 minutes down the track. The temple is close to Shitennoji-mae subway station.

There is very little to see in Umeda, although the **Umeda Sky Building**, just north of Osaka station, is certainly impressive, and has the **Floating Garden** observation deck at 170 m (558 ft) slung between two towers. It is a little expensive at ¥1,000. One stop to the south on the Mido-suji subway line (Yodoyabashi station) is **Nakanoshima**, a wedge of land between the Tosabori-gawa and Dojima-gawa rivers. It is a pleasant place for a walk, and is notable for its **Museum of Oriental Ceramics** (9:30 AM to 5 PM, closed Mondays), specializing not in Japanese, but in Chinese and Korean exhibits.

The Namba, or Minami, area is notable less for its sights — there are none — than as an area to stroll in and soak up the atmosphere. Walk the length of **Shinsaibashi-suji Arcade**, which is lined with shops and restaurants, to the **Dotomburi Canal**, which by night is Osaka's most famous picture-postcard view. **Dotomburi Dori** is a little like the east side of Tokyo's Shinjuku — Osaka at its *Blade Runner* best. North of here, on the east side of Mido-suji Dori, is **Amerika Mura**, or America Village, a trendy enclave of import clothing boutiques, cafés and bars that is reminiscent of Tokyo's Harajuku.

In the far south of the city, to the north of Dobutsuen-mae station, two subway stops south of Namba, is the area known as **Shin Sekai**, or New World. Once a rollicking pleasure quarter, today it has a shabby air about it, but is interesting and safe to explore all the same. It centers on the 103-m-high (335- ft) tower, **Tsutenkaku**, which is a popular symbol of the city and has an observation deck (9:30 AM to 6:30 PM, daily) that is now dwarfed by the Floating Garden in the Umeda Sky Tower but still pulls in the crowds probably for nostalgic

reasons, much as Tokyo Tower does. The surrounding streets are the domain of bingo parlors, hole-in-the-wall bars, X-rated cinemas and marvelously cheap restaurants specializing in dangerous delicacies like blow fish.

Farther south again, next to the station of the same name, is **Sumiyoshi-taisha Shrine**, one of Japan's oldest and one of the few that pre-date Buddhist architectural influences. It is by no means a grand Shinto shrine, but is of definite curiosity value for its distinctive stable-like buildings with gabled, cypress-bark roofs, and its red and white coloring.

West of town, on the Chuo subway line, is **Osaka Bay**, where you will find the imaginatively designed **Osaka Aquarium** (10 AM to 7 PM, daily), one of the world's biggest — the main tank is nine meters (nearly 30 ft) deep, and there are 13 others. It covers the marine life of the entire Pacific, including both poles, all of America and Australasia. It is a relatively expensive outing though, with entry prices starting at ¥2,000.

The aquarium is inside **Tempozan Harbor Village**, which is bordered by a massive Ferris wheel. Also in the village is the **Suntory Museum** (10 AM to 7 PM, daily), which has rotating modern art exhibitions.

A curious theatrical experience awaits you at Takarazuka, the terminus of the private Hankyu railway, 25 km (16 miles) or 34 minutes by express from Umeda station — the daily matinee performances of the **Takarazuka** all-female vaudeville troupe. In 1913 an entertainment tycoon named Kobayashi Ichizo decided to give the spa resort town of Takarazuka a kick-start by establishing an all-female revue. It was a huge success. Before the long the troupe was touring the country and by 1934 had is own theater in Tokyo.

Members of the troupe have to undergo a two-year course at the Takarazuka Music School, and the big stars are the women who play the roles of men. Most of the company's fans are teenage girls. The **Takarazuka Grand Theater** ((0797) 86-7777 has three performances daily except Wednesdays. Don't worry about "understanding" the performances — they're in the language of grand spectacle, which everyone understands.

Takarazuka Family Land (9:30 AM to 5 PM, closed Wednesdays), in which the theater is located, has an imaginatively designed zoo, a monorail, hot springs, a botanical garden and an "Age of the Dinosaurs" feature, among other lures. It's one of the best places in the Osaka area to give the kids a treat. Admission is ¥1,400, which does *not* include entry to a Takarazuka show. Also in the grounds is the **Tezuka Osamu Manga Museum** (same hours as Family Land). Tezuka (1926–1989) is Japan's king of *manga* (comics) and the creator of *Astro Boy* and *Kimba the White Lion*, among many other enormously successful comic series and later animation.

WHERE TO STAY

All things considered, unless you have business in Osaka, it's worth staying in Kyoto and visiting Osaka as a day trip. Osaka generally does not offer such good value for money on the accommodation front, and there is less variety. Budget travelers in particular will find Osaka a trying destination.

The Umeda area has seen the arrival of some very opulent new hotels in recent years, and pick of the crop is the **Ritz-Carlton Osaka** ((06) 6343-7000 FAX (06) 6343-7016, 2-5-25 Umeda, Kita-Ku. It has both Japanese-style and Western-style rooms, along with French, Cantonese, Japanese and Mediterranean restaurants.

A highly recommended mid-range hotel is the **Hotel California** ((06) 6243-0333 FAX (06) 6243-0148, 1-9-30 Nishi-Shinsaibashi, which is next to Shinsaibashi subway station in the heart of Minami's shopping and nightlife. Don't be put off by the somewhat love-hotel looking exterior, or the potted palms and stuffed parrots in the lobby — the rooms are larger-than-usual business-style and range from ¥7,000 per person. The lobby restaurant is recommended.

Cheaper still is the Japanese-style **Ebisu-so Ryokan** ((06) 6643-4861, 1-7-33 Nishi-Nipponbashi, which is a 10-minute walk from Namba station and conveniently located in the Minami area. It costs from ¥5,000 per person for simple tatami rooms with shared bathing facilities: definitely not a memorable *ryokan* experience, but perfectly acceptable if you need a place to spend the night in Osaka.

Osaka has two youth hostels, but both are inconveniently located, so for true budget accommodation you are better off staying in Kyoto.

WHERE TO EAT

Osaka is famed for its food, though for different reasons than nearby Kyoto. While Kyoto is renowned for its delicate *kaiseki* cuisine, Osaka is known as a place of culinary indulgence. Some of the regional specialties include *okonomiyaki* — a pancake filled with cabbage and whatever else happens to be on hand; *takoyaki*, or squid dumplings; *udon-chiri*, an interesting noodle dish in which the noodles and other ingredients (usually chicken or seafood) are simmered in broth; and *hako-zushi*, which is the delicious Osaka variation on traditional sushi.

Osakans are also very keen on that most dangerous of Japanese cuisines: *fugu* (blow fish) (see GALLOPING GOURMET, page 54 in YOUR CHOICE).

An Osaka restaurant advertizes its vast array of freshly caught seafood.

In actual fact the risks are negligible, though Osakans like to make jokes about it tasting so good it's worth risking your life for a nibble. Try the long-running (no deaths so far) **Zuboraya** ((06) 6211-0181, which is on Dotomburi, not far east of the Dotomburi Canal bridge. Renowned as a place to try *fugu* without breaking the budget, there are now branches all over town. Courses cost ¥5,000.

Another popular chain is **Ganko** ((06) 6644-4151, which is famous for its *tonkatsu*, or pork cutlets. There is a branch close to the Hard Rock Café, behind (south) of the Nankai Namba station, in front of Osaka Stadium.

Minami's famous restaurant, and perhaps most representative of the excess Osakans are so well known for, is **Kuidaore** ((06) 6211-5300, 1-8-25 Dotomburi, which lies on Dotomburi Dori and cannot be missed due to the mechanical clown who beats an attention-grabbing rhythm at the door, beckoning customers inside. With eight floors of cuisine, the restaurant not only has all the Osaka specialties, it also has almost every other conceivable cuisine available. It's a lively place for an evening meal and a few beers; it comes highly recommended.

If you want to try that famous cook-it-at-the-table-yourself Osaka *okonomiyaki*, one of the most authentic places to do so is **Tombei** ((06) 6213-9689, the sort of place where you impress the locals simply by being there — don't worry if you have trouble ordering, someone will help you out. It's behind the Nakazawa Theater in Namba, not far from Kuidaore.

Osaka has a branch of the successful Indian restaurant chain **Ashoka** ((06) 6346-0333, B2 Maru Building, 1-9-20 Umeda. The vegetarian *thali* (a number of small dishes served together) are extremely popular, as is the restaurant, which usually has lines of people waiting at peak meal times — it's worth the wait.

For generic Western food at rock-bottom prices in convivial surroundings, head to the **Bar Isn't It? Super Café** ((06) 6366-5514 on Shin Mido-suji Dori, south east of Higashi Umeda subway station. For anyone who has experienced the Bar Isn't It? concept in Tokyo or Kyoto, it will be familiar — ¥500 buys anything on the menu.

In Minami, for inexpensive drinks and excellent food (though there is no categorizing it), try the **Agave Café** ((06) 6213-8110, a charming, tiny place that gets packed late at night, making it a good place to meet interesting locals and ex-pats. It is a little tricky to find the first time. From Shinsaibashi subway station, walk south down Mido-suji Dori and make a right into Suomachi Dori, walk ahead until you pass a small park (known colloquially as the triangle park), and then make a right. Agave is on the right, three blocks down. It's open *late*.

NIGHTLIFE

Osaka's nightlife is mostly either in Kita or in Minami, but Minami is the more interesting to explore. Even if you give the bars a miss, make a point of exploring the Dotomburi Canal area, which is always awash with milling crowds under the blinking neon.

For a familiar formula, try the **Hard Rock Café** ((06) 6646-1470, which is close to exit 5 of Namba station. Probably Osaka's longest-running pub is the British-style **Pig & Whistle** ((06) 6213-6911, on the second floor of the Across Building on Suomachi Dori, not far from Shinsaibashi subway station. It has the usual favorites — Kilkenny and Guinness on tap, as well as good British-style pub grub. It's a good place to meet people.

Slightly tricky to find but worth the effort is **Murphy's** ((06) 6282-0677, an Irish pub that has a bit more character than the average. It's on the street that runs one block north of Suomachi Dori, east of Mido-suji Dori four blocks on the sixth floor of the Lead Building.

Osaka is Japan's center for *bunraku*, and seasonal performances (January, April, June, August and November) take place at the **National Bunraku Theater** ((06) 6212-1122, next to Nipponbashi station in Namba. Check the monthly *Kansai Time Out* for more details.

HOW TO GET THERE

Hikari trains of the Tokaido Shinkansen take two hours 53 minutes from Tokyo to Shin-Osaka. Kodama trains take four hours 20 minutes (the price is the same). From Shin-Osaka you have to board a local train to make the five-minute journey to Osaka station.

The whole Kyoto-Osaka-Kobe area is crisscrossed with railway lines. The private Hankyu line takes around 40 minutes from Umeda station to Kyoto, and is the least expensive way to get there, though if you are traveling on a rail pass, you may as well take the subway to Shin-Osaka station and switch to the Shinkansen, which takes just 16 minutes. For Nara, the Kintetsu line runs from Kintetsu Namba station, taking around 30 minutes.

KOBE

Kobe is a vibrant, cosmopolitan port town some 30 km (19 miles) west around the bay from Osaka. It is in many ways Kansai's answer to Yokohama, and shares many similarities with Tokyo's famous neighbor, mostly due to a history of foreign contact and an openness to outside influences.

More recently it was the victim of a 1995 earthquake that left more than 5,500 people dead and many more homeless. Not that you would guess it to look at the city today. Japan is a country that takes earthquakes in its stride and quickly gets back to business. Kobe is no exception, and you have to look hard for the scars now.

This, of course, assumes you visit the city at all. Even more than nearby Osaka, Kobe — while a charming city — is a place of modest assets from the point of view of the traveler. It has a pair of interesting museums, some pleasant harbor views, a small Chinatown, but other than that little to detain you.

GENERAL INFORMATION

Shinkansen stop in the far northwest of Town at Shin Kobe station, which is connected with Sannomiya station, in the center of town, by subway. In front of Sannomiya station, on Flower Road is the **Tourist Information Office** ((078) 322-0222.

WHAT TO SEE AND DO

It is often said of Kobe that it's a great place to live but not much fun to visit. A highlight for Japanese visitors, but less so for most foreign visitors, is the collection of foreign houses built in **Kitano**, a hillside district around one kilometer (half a mile) north of Sannomiya station. In good weather, however, it is worth taking a steep stroll through the area to the top, where the Shin Kobe Ropeway whisks visitors to the top of **Mount Rokko**, Kobe's highest peak at 932 m (3,057 ft). The views of the harbor and, on a clear day, the mountains of Shikoku make it worth the effort.

Back in town, the area directly south of Hanshin Motomachi station (around 10 minutes' walk west of Sannomiya station) is **Nankin-machi**, or Nanjing Town, a local way of saying Chinatown. It's not as big and bustling as its Yokohama equivalent, but it has some good restaurants and is usually packed with diners at meal times.

South of here is the Kobe port area, with its **Meriken Park**, which is notable mostly for the architecturally intriguing **Kobe Maritime Museum** (open from 10 AM to 5 PM, closed Mondays). While interesting, the museum will capture the most attention from maritime buffs and children, who will enjoy the scale model ships and interactive displays. Directly east, and a legacy of a 1981 expo, is **Kobe Port Island**, a manmade island in the harbor that, apart from a fairground with a massive Ferris wheel, is of little interest. A more worthy attraction is another manmade island, **Rokko Island**, which is farther to the east, and features the **Kobe Fashion Museum** (open from 11 AM to 6 PM and until 8 PM Fridays, closed Wednesdays). It's a massive complex featuring a permanent exhibition of European costumes from the eighteenth century through to up-to-the-

moment fashion displays. The museum also has an auditorium that is regularly used for anything from fashion shows to movies, and a resource center for fashion designers. Access to Rokko Island is by the Rokko Monorail.

WHERE TO STAY

Budget travelers are advised to avoid Kobe. Unlike Kyoto, there has never been a demand here for budget accommodation for foreigners and consequently you won't find any.

If you don't mind being in the somewhat sterile surroundings of Rokko Island, the **Kobe Bay Sheraton Hotel & Towers** ((078) 857-7000 FAX (078) 857-7001 E-MAIL info@sheraton-kobe. co.jp, 2-13 Koyochonaka, Higashinada-ku, is a world-class hotel with five restaurants and a sports bar. Rates for the spacious rooms start at ¥24,000 for a double. Of comparable standard and impeccably appointed is the **Hotel Okura Kobe** ((078) 333-0111 FAX (078) 333-6673 E-MAIL info@kobe .hotelokura.co.jp, 2-1 Hatoba-cho Chuo-ku, which has a great downtown location in Motomachi. The higher rooms in this 35-floor hotel have amazing views of the harbor.

For something less expensive, and also in the Motomachi district, the **Kobe Plaza Hotel** ((078) 332-1141 FAX (078) 331-2630 on Motomachi Dori, is a functional business hotel with easy access to Nankin-machi, Kobe's small Chinese enclave.

Kobe-Tarumi Youth Hostel ((078) 707-2133, 5-58 Kai gan-dori, Tarumi-ku, is rather a long way out of town, near Tarumi station on the San-in line, but along with the usual dormitory beds has rooms from ¥4,500.

WHERE TO EAT

Kobe is of course renowned for its beef. Kitano, the area famed for its Western-style buildings, oddly enough is the place to go for a Kobe beef dinner. One place you can try the famous dish, which features beef from beer-fed, massaged cows, served sukiyaki-style is **Iroriya** ((078) 231-6777. Meals cost ¥5,000 per person and upwards.

The **Gaylord Indian Restaurant** ((078) 251-4359 is one of Kobe's longest running Indian restaurants. It's on Nakayamate Dori just west of Kitano Dori, on the seventh floor of the Bacchus Building. The tandoori and naan, cooked in a traditional Indian clay oven, are recommended.

For good pub grub and a few pints, head to **Dubliners** ((078) 334-3614, a branch of the Sapporo beer chain, which is an excellent place to meet people. It's in a basement opposite the Daimaru Department Store, south of Hanshi Motomachi station. Kobe's other Irish pub is **Ryan's** ((078) 391-6902, seventh floor, Kondo Building, 4-3-2 Kano-cho, Chuo-ku.

How to Get There

Jet foils connect Kobe with Kansai International Airport (KIX) in just half an hour. For onward travel to Himeji, the JR San-yo line heads there from Sannomiya station, before continuing on into Western Honshu. JR lines and the private Hanshi line connect Kobe with Osaka in half an hour or less, depending on the service.

HIMEJI

Just over 50 km (31 miles) west of Kobe is the castle town of Himeji. Even if you don't have time to see Kobe, at least try and stop in Himeji long enough to explore **Himeji-jo Castle** (9 AM to 4 PM, daily), the most splendid surviving Japan castle.

Also known as **Shirasagi-jo**, or "White Egret," a reference to its preponderant color and its soaring appearance. The castle was first built in the 1300s, and in 1580 came under Toyotomi Hideyoshi, who set about expanding it, adding 30 turrets. A later lord of the castle added more turrets, making it second only to Osaka-jo Castle in size.

A great many Japanese castles were "restored" in Ferro-concrete during the 1950s and 1960s, some of them in places where nothing but a plan of the castle remained. This was doubtless good for civic pride (and the construction industry), but it's often a little depressing for visitors, especially when the interior is decked out with lifts and air conditioning. There are no such disappointments in store at Himeji. The eight-year repair job completed in 1964 was done with care and tact, and the lavish lifestyle of the original sixteenth-century inhabitants can be readily imagined. The castle is a 15-minute walk from Himeji station.

Himeji is about 40 minutes from Osaka and one hour from Kyoto by Shinkansen. From Kobe the trip takes 20 minutes. The castle is directly north of Himeji station up Otemachi Dori, around 10 minutes on foot. A **tourist office** ((0792) 85-3792 operates in the station, though it is only open from 10 AM to 3 PM.

Visit in October and you may be lucky enough to catch the town's **Kenka Matsuri** (Fighting Festival). See FESTIVE FLINGS, page 50 in YOUR CHOICE.

NARA

Before Kyoto there was Nara.

Many travelers visit Nara as a day trip from Kyoto. If possible give it longer. It's a fascinating place to explore, and also has some splendid walks. But it is Nara's temples and art treasures that draw most visitors. Horyu-ji Temple is the chief attraction, but Todai-ji, which has what is said to be the world's largest wooden building, and Kofuku-ji temples are also superb.

Background

In early Japanese history it was the custom for each new emperor to choose a new capital. In AD 710, however, Empress Gemmei (661-721) decided to pitch camp for good: a city was laid out — though never more than partially constructed — along rectangular Chinese lines. Although it only lasted 74 years, those years encompassed the reigns of eight successive emperors and a miracle of creativity that is now seen as marking the emergence of Japanese civilization. The city was called Heijokyo.

In 784 the capital was transferred to the southwest of present-day Kyoto and Heijokyo's tide began to recede. The process has been going on ever since. Of Japan's old capitals, Kyoto is still thriving in its own quiet way, and the population of Kamakura is almost exactly the same as it was

in the thirteenth century, but Nara has slipped, almost to the point of becoming a grassy ghost town. Many of the temples and shrines are still standing, but the people who once populated them have been replaced by tame deer and tourists.

GENERAL INFORMATION

Nara's attractions are spread over quite a large area, although the most famous — Todai-ji Temple — is close to the town the center. There are two train stations: the JR Nara station in the west of town; and the more convenient Kintetsu Nara station in the city center, close to Kofuku-ji Temple and around one kilometer (half a mile) west of Todai-ji Temple. To get to the far flung attractions like Horyu-ji Temple, you will need to take a bus or, if you don't mind spending the money, a taxi.

Nara's most useful tourist office is the **Nara City Tourist Information Center** ((0742) 22-3900, on Sanjo Dori, four blocks west of Kofuku-ji Temple. It can help with accommodation, supply maps and also put you in touch with "goodwill guides." At **Kintetsu Nara station** is another tourist information office ((0742) 24-4858, and there are more at **Sarusawa-ike Pond** (opposite Kofuku-ji) ((0742) 26-1991, and at **Horyu-ji Temple** ((0745) 74-6800.

A large number of tours are available for Nara from Osaka and Kyoto, but in general these JTB tours are rushed and tend to skip key attractions. The Nara-based **Nara Kotsu** ((0742) 22-5263 tours are altogether a better option, as they stick to Nara and its surrounds and don't waste time getting there and back. Ask at the Kyoto or Osaka TICs for more information before leaving for Nara.

Himeji's "White Egret" Castle seems to float above the town with the same grace as the local egrets do.

WHAT TO SEE AND DO

Whether you arrive in Nara by JR or by private Kintetsu, the best course of action, after calling into one of the tourist offices and loading yourself down with giveaway brochures and maps, is to head east through town along Sanjo Dori. This leads to the 528-ha (1,304-acre) Nara Park, which is home to two of Nara's most famous temples and a museum — as well as a lot of tame deer.

The first temple you come across approaching the park this way is **Kofuku-ji Temple** (9 AM to 5 PM, daily), one of Nara's great landmarks, famous for its two pagodas, one five stories and one three. It was founded in AD 669 by the powerful Fujiwara family, and by the tenth century had grown to the point that it had its own army of warrior monks — which it employed in conflicts with nearby Todai-ji Temple. It was raised in 1180, rebuilt during the Kamakura period (1192–1333), but then succumbed to a disastrous fire in 1717. Despite this turbulent history, there is still a lot to see, particularly in the attached **Kokuho-kan** (National Treasures Hall), which has some of the most splendid extant Japanese statuary from the seventh century through to the Kamakura period.

More superb Japanese statuary is on display at the **Nara National Museum** (9 AM to 4:30 PM, closed Mondays), a Meiji-era Western-style building that has been classified as an Important Cultural Property. The exhibits change as various art treasures from temples around Japan are loaned to the museum for display.

As is the case with Kyoto, much is made of the Chinese influence in the layout of old Nara, and this is very clear in the case of Nara Park's most famous temple — **Todai-ji** (7:30 AM to 5 PM, daily), the world's largest wooden building, containing the world's largest bronze figure, the *Daibutsu*, or Great Buddha.

The head temple of the now small Kegon sect of Buddhism, Todai-ji was built in the early eighth century by order of Emperor Shomu (who reigned AD 724–749), and became Japan's foremost religious institution. The temple's famous Nara *Daibutsu* was completed in 752 and was housed in an equally massive hall named appropriately the **Daibutsu-den**, or the Great Buddha Hall. Todai-ji records show that some 50,000 carpenters, 370,000 metal workers and more than two million laborers brought this complex into being. It's construction is said to have nearly bankrupted the state.

The Great Buddha himself is 16.2 m (53.1 ft) high, compared with the 11.4 m (37.4 ft) Great Buddha in Kamakura. It is certainly impressive, and somehow the temple's gloom makes it seem even more huge than it is. It has had an unhappy history, however — decapitated in earthquakes,

partially melted in fires and patched together numerous times — the last time from 1692 to 1709. The Great Buddha we see today is said to be less stylistically uniform and accomplished than the one originally made in the eighth century.

Kasuga-taisha Shrine is hidden away deep in the woods in the east of Nara Park and is a place to experience the tranquility of Shinto: you can almost smell the sanctity. It was founded in AD 709 by the Fujiwara family. There are 3,000 lanterns at Kasuga and they are lit twice a year (see FESTIVE FLINGS, page 50 in YOUR CHOICE).

From Kintetsu Nara station buses run to **Horyu-ji Temple** (8 AM to 5 PM, daily), along with Todai-ji Nara's chief attraction, and yet oddly one that does not feature on most of the Nara tours — a good reason for visiting on your own steam. Founded by Prince Shotoku (AD 574–622), the man on the 10,000-yen note, in the first decade of the seventh century, the temple burned down in 670 but was rebuilt on a massive scale, mostly as a tribute to Shotoku, around whom a reverential cult had coalesced. Many of the temple buildings from this 670 rebuilding still survive, making it the oldest surviving temple in all Japan.

The five-story pagoda, inner gate and main hall, all of which were rebuilt over the three decades following the fire of 670, constitute the world's oldest wooden buildings. As valuable as the buildings themselves are, the Buddhist statuary they contain is some of the most beautiful in Japan. It's perhaps just as well that no tours, at least no English speaking ones, call here, for these things deserve lingering over. Many of the best are preserved in the Ferro-concrete safety of the temple's **Great Treasure Hall** (Daihozo-den).

Close to Horyu-ji, almost like an annex (though it's separate and an admission fee must be paid) is the **Chugu-ji Convent** (same hours as Horyu-ji). Legend has it that the convent first came into being as a mansion built by Prince Shotoku for his mother in 596, but the main attraction is a statue that brings the Horyu-ji tour to a fine conclusion, the **Miroku Bosatsu**. This slender, youthful lacquer-on-wood carving depicts Maitreya, or the Buddha of the Future. Head tilted forward as if listening, eyelids lowered, fingers of the right hand poised near the cheek, he is meditating on the sufferings of mankind. Also in the convent are two pieces of a famous embroidered tapestry known as the **Tenjukoku Mandala**.

On the way to or from Horyu-ji, if you go by bus, get off at the Yakushiji Higashi-guchi stop for **Yakushi-ji Temple**. Dedicated to the Buddha of Healing, the temple was founded in 680 by Emperor Temmu (?–686) for his ailing mother, and completed in 687. It was relocated to its present position and rebuilt in 720. Its plan, with a central hall flanked by east and west pagodas is based on a Korean model, and is unusual by Japanese standards. The

East Pagoda dates from 730; the **West Pagoda** is a 1981 reconstruction. The East Hall, built in 1285, has a celebrated Kannon image.

WHERE TO STAY

Few travelers do, but it is worth staying overnight in Nara. It's a sleepy place with some excellent restaurants, and makes for a quiet alternative to Kyoto.

The pick of Nara's accommodation, with a splendid location right in Nara Park, is the **Nara Hotel (** (0742) 26-3300 FAX (0742) 23-5252. Housed in an 80-year-old Meiji-era structure, the rooms come with high ceilings. There's *kaiseki* dining in the main building as well as a very good French

WHERE TO EAT

Like Kyoto, Nara is renowned for its *kaiseki* cuisine, though in the town center you will find the usual fast-food barns, *ramen* shops and "Western-style" restaurants serving generic pizza and pasta dishes.

Nara's most famous *kaiseki* restaurant is **Tsukihitei (** (0742) 26-2021, which is set among the trees by Kasuga-taisha shrine. The set courses are the most economical way to order — at around ¥6,500 per person. Reservations are a must. At **Capricciosa (** (0742) 24-1072, Konishi Dori - Iseiya Biru 2F, the servings are large. The ¥1500 to ¥2000 price includes coffee or tea. An English menu is available.

restaurant and, of course, the hotel is perfectly located for sightseeing. Rates start at around ¥18,000 per person.

The **Ryokan Matsumae (** (0742) 22-3686 FAX (0742) 26-3987, 28-1 Higashi Terabyashi-cho, a memorably popular *ryokan* — it's friendly, spotlessly maintained and quiet. The Japanese-style rooms come both with and without private bathrooms, though those without give you more space to spread out.

Similarly priced and very charming is the **Ryokan Seikanso (** (0742) 22-2670 FAX (0742) 22-2670, 29 Higashi Kitsuji-cho, which has a garden and tatami-style rooms with shared bathing facilities. Rates are ¥4,000 per person, and breakfast and dinner are available.

The **Nara Youth Hostel (** (0742) 22-1334, 1716 Horen-cho, has 200 dormitory beds. It's not one of Japan's best, and imposes a strict 10 PM curfew.

HOW TO GET THERE

Nara is best approached from either Kyoto or Osaka. From Kyoto, the quickest and most convenient route is with the private Kintetsu line (also known as the Kinki Nippon line), which takes around half an hour by limited express. The JR Nara line is slower. From Osaka, the Kintetsu Nara line leaves from Namba station and takes around 30 minutes. The JR Kansai line is slower, but does provide the advantage of stopping at Horyu-ji Temple en route, from which it is a 20-minute walk to the temple.

Nara, laid out in AD 710, was Japan's first "permanent" capital (though it only lasted as a capital for 70-odd years). The ancient temples, shrines and monasteries in the pleasant parkland at the city's old center reflect the purity of the Chinese influence at this time.

MOUNT KOYA-SAN

One of Japan's holiest Buddhist retreats and long a place of pilgrimage — not opened to women until 1872 — Koya-san is little visited by foreigners, but is an intriguing destination for those who have the time to take it in. The great attraction, apart from exploring the mountain-top's many temples, is the opportunity to actually spend a night in one of them. Operated on a commercial basis, Koya-san's temples throw open their bedroom doors to anyone with cash nowadays, though many visitors are still pilgrims.

The mountain became a holy place in AD 816, when Emperor Saga granted the mountain to Kukai (774–835), more commonly known as Kobo Daishi, the priest who established the Shingon sect of Buddhism, as a place for monks to practice esoteric Buddhist meditation. It is in great part Kukai who has made Koya-san such a revered place. Kukai is credited with having devised the *hiragana* and *katakana* syllabaries used by Japanese to complement Chinese characters. He is also said to have written Japan's first dictionary, and his teachings did much to promote the wide acceptance of Buddhism in Japan. The complex of temples that arose as a result was called Kongobu-ji. The name is now reserved for the nineteenth-century reconstruction of the area's main temple. It is the head temple for around 3,600 temples that belong to the Koya-san Shingon sub-sect (Kukai's Shingon Buddhism now has some 45 sub-sects with a total of more than 12,000 temples).

The main attraction is **Kongobu-ji** (8:30 AM to 4:30 PM, daily) itself, although it is the small precinct opposite here, the **Danjo Garan**, where Kukai founded his first monastery, that is the holiest place on the mountain. East of the Danjo Garan is the somewhat eerie **Okuno-in Cemetery**, where, it is said, more than 200,000 stupas litter the forest floor. Some of Japan's most famous historical figures have their final resting place here. The cemetery leads on to the **Hall of Lanterns** and the **Mausoleum of Kukai**. The Hall of Lanterns maintains the creepy effect, with its thousands of flickering candles.

If, after all this, you still have the courage to spend the night — among so many of Japan's illustrious (and notorious) dead — some 50 monasteries offer accommodation in what are called *shukubo*, or temple lodgings. These are not hotels, and you shouldn't expect the service you would get in one — they keep strict hours (early to bed, early to rise), no alcohol is allowed, and the meals are all strictly vegetarian. If this appeals, and it *is* a worthwhile experience, the best way to organize accommodation is to ring ahead to the **Koya-san Tourist Association** ((0736) 56-2616, which has an office at the head of the ropeway station at Koya-san. This office can usually accommodate those who turn up without a reservation, but it is safer to book ahead. Expect to pay around ¥10,000 per person with meals, possibly more depending on the monastery.

The easiest way to get to Koya-san is from Osaka's Namba station, from where the Nankai Dentetsu line goes to Gokurakubashi station, taking around one and a half hours. From Gokurakubashi station, a cable car, or ropeway, will whisk you to the top of the mountain. Bear in mind that if you ask for Koya-san at Namba station, you will be sold a convenient combined rail/cable car ticket.

SHIMA-HANTO PENINSULA

Like a nose on the face of southeast Kansai, the Shima-hanto Peninsula would probably see very little tourist traffic at all if it weren't for two famous attractions on its northern coast. The most compelling is Ise-jingu Shrine, the very heart of Shinto, the native religion of Japan. The peninsula's other notable attraction is Toba, famed for its women divers and its pearl industry.

ISE-JINGU SHRINE

The Victoria Cross (VC) is the highest military honor that can be awarded in Britain, but the medal itself is only made of gunmetal. Similarly the two shrines that comprise Ise-jingu, Japan's Holy of Holies, are utterly plain, unpainted and undecorated. They are built in the style which prevailed in the country before Chinese techniques of temple-building were transmitted — with protruding poles, thick thatch roofs and unshaped, though perfect, knotless beams. These two shrines represent the most primitive architecture in the land, yet the workmanship is sublimely good, and the atmosphere of sanctity and harmony that pervades the forested precincts like a breeze leaves nobody unmoved.

Strangest of all to Westerners coming from the lands of Stonehenge and Chartres, is the fact that the buildings are less than 20 years old. Every 20 years since they were first built — the inner shrine probably sometime in the third century, the outer in the fifth — they have been reconstructed on adjacent sites. Despite the huge expense it is intended to maintain this custom indefinitely. The last time it happened was in 1993 — the next rebuilding will take place in 2013.

Two separate shrines, **Naiku** (the inner) and **Geku** (the outer), about six kilometers (four miles) apart, constitute the Ise shrines. While the outer is dedicated to Toyouke-Omikami, the goddess of farms, harvest food and sericulture, the inner is dedicated to the supreme deity of the Shinto pantheon and mythical forebear of the emperor, the Sun Goddess, Ameterasu-Omikami.

In both shrines the holiest spot is surrounded by four fences and the public is allowed to penetrate only the first. No photographs are permitted and hats and overcoats should be removed. The area within is reserved for the emperor and shrine officials.

In the inner shrine is preserved the sacred mirror, one of the three sacred treasures of the imperial family — mirror, sword and jewel. The myth goes that the mirror was given by the Sun Goddess to her grandson when he came down to rule Japan and to father the ancestors of the present emperor.

It is evident that the Ise shrines mean a lot to the Japanese, even the very large number whose belief is faint or non-existent. The grounds of the shrines are immaculately clean and quiet — no litter, no signs, no Coke machines, no cotton-candy merchants. The Japanese can create a spotlessly beautiful environment when they try; one only wishes they tried more often.

A small but much-loved sideshow in this area is the sight of the **wedded rocks** in the sea, about a kilometer (just over half a mile) from Futami-no-Ura station on the JR line between Ise and Toba. They are linked by a length of sacred straw rope which is replaced in a ceremony on January 5 every year. They are taken to symbolize Izanagi and Izanami, mythological creators of Japan. They look fine with the sun rising behind them — patriotic imagery which requires no explanation.

It is best to visit Ise as a day trip, perhaps in conjunction with nearby Toba. Ise city itself is dull and has no recommendable accommodation .

The access point for Ise's shrine area is Ise-shi station. JR services run here from Kyoto and Osaka (and Nagoya) in just over one and a half hours, but it's quicker to travel from all three cities to Ise-shi by the private Kintetsu line. Note that not all Kintetsu trains, however, stop at Ise-shi station — many stop one station south at Uji-Yamada station, where it is possible to transfer and backtrack to Ise-shi.

TOBA

Toba's claim to fame is as a center for the cultivation of pearls, and unless you have a particular interest in pearls it can safely be dropped from your itinerary. Toba's other point of interest is its *ama*, which means literally "sea people," a term that is used for people throughout Japan who dive for a living, collecting abalone (*awabi*), edible seaweed and other more obscure harvests of the sea. Here in Toba the divers are women and, while they no longer dive for pearls, around 2,000 of them still make a living the traditional way, a ritual that pleases the tourists.

You can watch them, by an irony which seems to have passed the Japanese by, at **Mikimoto Pearl**

Island (8:30 AM to 5 PM, daily), a shrine, if you like, to the memory of Mikimoto Kokichi (1858-1954), the father of the cultured pearl — the man who did more than anyone to put them out of business. They dive there every 40 minutes.

Pearl Island, however, is interesting for more than the women divers. Mikimoto made his first attempt to cultivate pearls in 1883 by using pearl oysters. At first it produced mixed results — the pearls were not perfectly round. It was not until 1905 that he succeeded in producing perfectly round cultivated pearls, an achievement that was initially met with some scorn internationally, due to allegations that they were nothing more than "imitation pearls" — science proved them to

be the real thing. The museum here documents his life and achievements in detail, and there is plenty of English information available.

Like Ise, there is little in the way of accommodation in Toba, and the town is best treated as a day trip from either Kyoto or Osaka. It's a short run east of Ise-shi station on the Kintetsu line to Toba station.

Toba, on the Shima-hanto Peninsula, is famed for its women divers, or *ama*, and its pearl industry. *Ama*, which means "sea people," is a term used throughout Japan for people who dive for a living, collecting abalone (*awabi*), edible seaweed and other more obscure harvests of the sea. Until the advent of the cultured pearl industry, Toba's women *amas* specialized in diving for pearls. While today they no longer dive for pearls, around 2,000 *amas* still make a living the traditional way. Tourists can watch *ama* dive at Mikimoto Pearl Island every 40 minutes during the day.

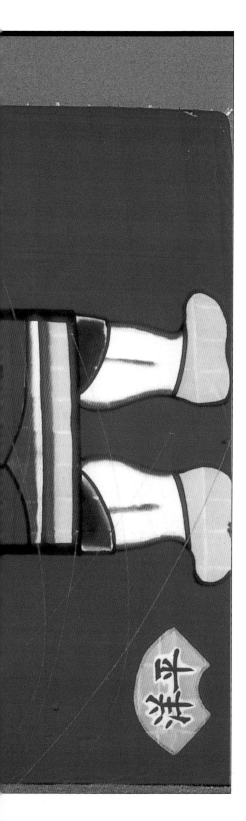

Western
Honshu

WESTERN HONSHU, the finger that points to the island of Kyushu, is neglected by many travelers. Some stop at Hiroshima, the world's first victim of an atom bomb attack, but otherwise most travelers breeze through en-route to Kyushu.

The reasons are obvious enough: Chugoku — the Middle Kingdom — as the Japanese call western Honshu, is for the most part an area of scattered and minor attractions. The southern San-yo Coast is densely populated and highly industrialized, and from the window of a passing train rarely beckons for you to disembark. The less traveled northern San-in Coast, on the other hand, is, as many lucky travelers have discovered, another world — the old Japan of small towns and villages, and some surprisingly unspoiled rural landscapes.

But, realistically, unless you have oodles of time to explore Japan, it is best to restrict your stops to the obvious highlights: the old merchant town of Kurashiki, with its canal, granaries and merchant homes; Hiroshima, reborn and with some poignant memorials to the devastation wreaked upon it; and perhaps the floating *torii* gate of Miya-jima. Those with more time will be rewarded by stopovers at Okayama, home to one of Japan's three famous gardens, and at the old castle towns of Hagi and Tsuwano on the north coast.

From Osaka it takes less than an hour to get to Okayama by Shinkansen. If you are traveling by Shinkansen and want to visit Kurashiki, you will have to stop here and change to the JR San-yo line, which takes 15 minutes.

OKAYAMA

Okayama is a dull prefectural capital with just one reason to stop: **Koraku-en Garden** (7:30 AM to 6 PM April through September, 8 AM to 5 PM the rest of the year, daily). The garden is one of Japan's three most famous landscaped stroll gardens. Established in 1702 by the local lord, it has winding paths, tea houses, ponds, a *no* stage and of course some famous "borrowed scenery" in the form of Okayama-jo Castle, which unfortunately nowadays is built of Ferro-concrete, but still deceives from a distance.

The park is a brief one-and-a-half-kilometer (about one-mile) bus ride from the station. After the obligatory stroll, if you have time, you might take a look at **Okayama-jo Castle** (9 AM to 5 PM, daily), on the other side of the Tsukimi-bashi Bridge in the south of the park. A 1966 reconstruction, in its day (its founding dates back to the 1570s) it was known as **U-jo**, or Crow Castle, for its black color, a jab at the more famous White Egret Castle (Shirasagi-jo) in Himeji. There are fine views from the top of the keep.

There is an **information counter** ((086) 222-2912, where English is spoken, in JR Okayama station. While the city has no shortage of hotels — mostly of the business variety — there is no need to stay here. Just 15 minutes farther west by train is the charming old town of Kurashiki, which is a delightful place to spend a night.

KURASHIKI

Kurashiki, a small city of slightly less than half a million, came to prominence as a trading town during the Edo period (1600-1867). The legacy of its Edo trading days, when it became a center for the transportation of rice, is a granary-lined canal area in the south of town. The canal once connected to a network of such canals, that in turn connected with the Inland Sea.

This lone canal has earned Kurashiki — at least locally — the dubious title "Venice of Japan." Venice, unfortunately, it ain't, but it is one of the San-yo Coast's few truly worthwhile stops, and is a good place to break a journey farther west with an overnight stop.

GENERAL INFORMATION

Kurashiki is not a very big place, and it is easy to get around in. Essentially, ignore the JR Kurashiki station area — which looks much like any other small-town station area — and head south down Kurashiki Chuo Dori to the **Bikan** district. The latter is where all the sights are, and is where you will find the city's most appealing accommodation.

There's a Tourist Information Office ((086) 426-8681 in Kurashiki station, while the Kurashiki-kan Hall Tourist Information Office ((086) 422-0542 can be found in the Bikan district.

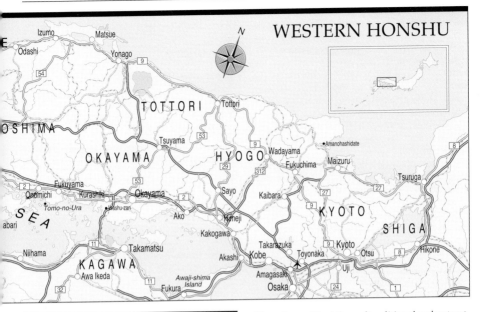

WHAT TO SEE AND DO

Kurashiki's attractions — and charm — are all concentrated in the Bikan district, where a willow-lined canal is the center point. At the northern end of the canal is the **Ohara Art Gallery** (9 AM to 5 PM, closed Mondays). Established in 1930 by local industrialist Ohara Magosaburo, the collection was actually created by Kojima Torajiro (1881–1929), an artist. It was one of Japan's first galleries to exhibit Western art. The surprise is the excellence of the pieces gathered together here — including works by El Greco, Rodin, Picasso, Pollock, Warhol, Kandinsky and many others. The attached Craft Gallery has a superb exhibition of ceramics, while an Asiatic Gallery features an impressive collection of Far Eastern antiquities.

The **Kurashiki Museum of Folkcraft** (9 AM to 5 PM, closed Mondays) close by is housed in four granaries. Exhibits include folkcraft from Japan and elsewhere.

Several other minor attractions clamor for the attention of the visitor, but they're equally easy to eschew in favor of a stroll around the canal area to check out the souvenirs and the cafés. Souvenirs include basketwork, woodwork and pots. There is also a delicious local preserve: persimmons (*kaki*) bound tightly in rope. The locally produced sake is also recommended.

WHERE TO STAY

Kurashiki has some delightful Japanese-style inns, and the best of them is the **Ryokan Kurashiki** ((086) 422-0730 FAX (086) 422-0990, 4-1 Honmachi, in the heart of the Bikan district, right on the canal.

If you haven't had the real traditional *ryokan* treatment yet, this is an excellent place to do so — an ancient, time-worn building with devoted staff who look as though they may have been around as long as the inn. With meals, and the *ryokan* prefers you eat in, expect to pay from arund ¥20,000 per person.

At the northern end of the canal area is the less expensive **Naraman Ryokan** ((086) 422-0143 FAX (086) 425-8585 E-MAIL naraman@kurashiki.or.jp, 2-22-3 Achi, a charming place that is housed in a granary with more than 200 years of history. English is spoken, and the *ryokan* welcomes foreign travelers. It also has a restaurant — an unusual feature for a Japanese inn — though you may elect to eat in your room.

Much cheaper and highly recommended is the **Minshuku Kamoi** ((086) 422-4898 FAX (086) 427-7615, 1-24 Honmachi, a new but still atmospheric "people's lodge" just east of the canal area at the southern end of Tsurugatayama-koen Park. The reasonable rates, which start at ¥5,500 per person, include meals.

The **Kurashiki Youth Hostel** ((086) 422-7355, 1537-1 Mukoyama, is one of the chain's more pleasant places to stay, though it only has dormitory accommodation. It's in the far south of town, about a 10-minute walk from the Bikan district.

WHERE TO EAT

If you are not eating in at your *ryokan* or *minshuku*, take a stroll along the canal area and take your pick from around a dozen good places to eat. The ivy-clad building at the head of the canal is the long-running **El Greco Café** ((086) 422-0297, which, while an extremely pleasant place to sit and watch the world go by, doesn't really offer anything besides expensive coffee. A better option, if you are looking for a meal, is to go to the other side of the canal, where, diagonally opposite El Greco, you will find **Kamoi** ((086) 422-0606. It's run by the same management as the *minshuku* of the same name, and is housed in an old granary overlooking the canal. The specialty is sushi.

Kiyu-tei ((086) 422-5140 is a steak house that is just north of the canal area — look for it on the left as you enter the Bikan district. Like other restaurants in the area it is housed in the atmospheric former home of a former merchant's house. The evening grill is good, and set lunches are also available.Close by and also recommended is **Azumi** ((086) 422-8970, 1-1-8 Chuo, a rustic-looking *soba* shop that specializes in buckwheat noodles prepared Nagano-style. It's a good place for a light lunch.

HOW TO GET THERE

Kurashiki is just 15 minutes from Okayama on the JR San-yo line.

TOMO-NO-URA AND ONOMICHI

Continuing west along the San-yo Coast, there are a couple of sights between Kurashiki and Hiroshima worth making a stop for if you are not pressed for time. The best of them is Tomo-no-Ura, a small port town that oozes Old World charm. A close second is Onomichi, another fascinating port town, this time with a celebrated 25-temple walk that is best enjoyed in part rather than in full.

Tomo-no-Ura is a destination that offers more atmosphere than specific sights. Indeed most of the fun of exploring the small port's few attractions is the exploring itself.

Up on the headland, overlooking the town are the ruins of **Taigashima-jo Castle**. Climb up and on the way you will pass **Empaku-ji Temple**, dedicated to the poet Basho (1644-1694). Back in town, the small **Tomo-no-Ura Museum of History** can be skipped, though given the inexpensive entry fee it is as easy to pop in for a look.

Frequent buses from the nearest rail junction, Fukuyama (on the San-yo line), take around 30 minutes, dropping you off at the ferry pier, where English maps of the small town are available.

Onomichi's celebrated 25-temple walk is overkill to all but the most ardent temple watcher, but it's fun to do part of the walk. Onomichi itself is a charming town, framed by wooded hills, which can be "climbed" with a ropeway that goes up to Mount Senkoji-san.

The temple walk starts east of JR Onomichi station, which is conveniently located on the San-yo line. The station has a small information counter that can provide an English map that marks all the important temples on the route.

HIROSHIMA

World over, the word "Hiroshima" (it means "broad island") is synonymous with "the Bomb." It is the reminders of Hiroshima's terrible leveling that make the city an essential stop on any tour of Japan.

GENERAL INFORMATION

Hiroshima's main tourist information office is the Hiroshima City Tourist Association and Information Counter ((082) 247-6738, which is in the Rest House at Peace Park. It's open daily, though hours vary seasonally — the core hours are 9:30 AM to 5 PM. There is another tourist office at the south exit of Hiroshima station ((082) 261-1877, and yet another ((082) 263-6822 at the Shinkansen entrance to the station. Both are open daily from 9 AM to 5:30 PM and can provide maps and English brochures, and can help with making reservations for hotels.

The city is not so difficult to get around in once you get into town, where most of the sights are within walking distance. Hiroshima station, however, is around two kilometers (just over a mile) east of the city center. The city's easiest form of public transportation to master is its trams, which are boarded through the middle door and disembarked by the front — there's a ¥130 straight fare for all destinations, which is paid as you leave the tram.

WHAT TO SEE AND DO

On August 6, 1945 at 8:15 AM a single American bomber dropped an atomic bomb over the city. When it exploded at a height of about 500 m (1,600 ft) the temperature in the vicinity rose to 30,000°C (54,000°F). The city center was destroyed instantly and, of the population of 344,000 (1940 census), about 200,000 died. Many who survived were later to die prematurely of leukemia and other radiation-induced diseases.

These facts and a great many others, along with paintings, models, video-taped testimonials from survivors and debris from the blast, are gathered together in the **Peace Memorial Museum** (9 AM to 6 PM May through November, 9 AM to 5 PM the rest of the year, daily) in **Peace Park (Heiwa Koen)**, and this is the place for which visitors should make a beeline (take a bus or tram from the station). The entrance fee is very low, the captions are in English, and the display is vivid.

Also in Peace Park is the **Children's Peace Monument**, which depicts a young girl holding aloft an origami crane. The crane, or *tancho*, in

Japanese iconography symbolizes long life, and in this case the reference is to the famous case of a young A-bomb victim, who, dying of leukemia, folded paper cranes in the hope that they would cure her. She died, though, and today the monument is inevitably decked with paper cranes folded by Japanese school children in her memory.

The **Memorial Cenotaph** is an unassuming arch sheltering a stone coffin that contains the names of all the victims of the bomb. Beside it is the ever-burning **Flame of Peace**, which will not be extinguished until the last atomic bomb is eradicated.

North of the park is **Hiroshima Museum of Art** (9 AM to 5 PM, daily), which has an interesting

collection of mainly French Impressionist art with the addition of some Picasso too. Just north of the museum is **Hiroshima-jo Castle** (9 AM to 4:30 PM, daily), a reconstructed Edo era (1600–1867) castle with some interesting exhibits in its keep, but not worth a special trip, especially if you have already had your fill of castles elsewhere. It incidentally, like other Japanese castles, has its own nickname — in this case Ri-jo, or Carp Castle.

Take a tram east of the castle and get off at the Shukkeien-mae stop for a stroll around the admirably reconstructed **Shukkei-en Garden** (9 AM to 5 PM, daily). This seventeenth-century garden is modeled on the famous Xihu Lake in Hangzhou, China, and the name means "shrunk view garden" — a reference to its attempt to recreate Xihu and its surroundings in miniature. The museum adjacent to the garden is the **Hiroshima Prefectural Museum of Art** (9 AM to 5 PM, closed Mondays),

which exhibits modern art — both Japanese and Western, and has some famous works by Dali.

WHERE TO STAY

Hiroshima is a good place to break up a journey along the west coast of Honshu, and can be used as a base to visit nearby Miya-jima. Most of the accommodation around the station area are typically dull business hotels, but there are some more interesting places to stay in town, including some economical *ryokan*.

The **Rihga Royal Hotel Hiroshima** ((082) 502-1121 FAX (082) 228-5415 WEB SITE www.rihga.com/hiroshi/, 6-78 Motomachi, Naka-ku, is a luxury 491-room hotel with a good location next to the Hiroshima Art Museum in the heart of town. The executive rooms on the thirtieth and thirty-first floors providing sweeping views of the city. With nine restaurants and bars, and a slew of amenities, it is the best of Hiroshima's luxury accommodations. Rates start at ¥12,000 for singles.

Slightly cheaper and also well located just minutes from Peace Park on foot is the **ANA Hotel** ((082) 241-1111 FAX (082) 241-9123, 7-20 Nakamachi, Naka-ku, a 22-story hotel with Japanese, French and Chinese restaurants.

Good mid-range accommodation is available across the road from the ANA Hotel at the **Tokyu Hotel** ((082) 244-0109 FAX (082) 245-4467, 10-1 Mikawa-cho, Naka-ku. It's part of a popular chain that, while unexciting, is ever reliable.

For excellent budget accommodation, the **Minshuku Ikedaya** ((082) 231-3329 FAX (082) 231-7875, 6-36 Dobashi-cho, Naka-ku, has been welcoming foreigners for years now, and provides comfortable accommodation in spacious Japanese-style rooms. English is spoken. It is on the other side of the Hon-kawa River, a short walk from Peace Park.

Hiroshima Youth Hostel ((082) 221-5343, 1-13-6 Ushita-shin-machi, Higashi-ku, will win no prizes on the atmosphere front, and its inconvenient location involves a long bus ride out of town. Only dormitory beds are available, and an early-to-bed curfew will curtail any revelry you might have planned otherwise.

WHERE TO EAT

Hiroshima's famous local specialty — as in Osaka — is its *okonomiyaki*, which according to locals is more refined than the Osaka version. In all honesty, *okonomiyaki* is a cuisine that few foreigners take to — it all too often seems little more than a

Hiroshima's atomic bomb dome and arched cenotaph. Despite it being devoid of traditional tourist attractions, Hiroshima remains firmly on most people's itineraries, if no more than a place to contemplate the atrocities of atomic warfare.

cabbage pancake smeared with mayonnaise. But to try it at its best, head to the inexpensive **Mitchan Okonomiyaki** ((082) 82-221-5438, 6-7 Hatchobori, Naka-ku, in the center of town. It even has an English menu, though the lines waiting at the door can be formidable. It's closed Mondays.

A popular *izakaya* (Japanese pub) is **Suikoden** ((082) 542-0270, which is in the basement just off Hon Dori, around the corner from the Parco Department Store, and comes complete with a picture menu for easy ordering. Prices are very reasonable — it's possible to eat and drink your fill here for less than ¥2,000 per person.

Nanak ((082) 243-7900 is one of Japan's many chains of Indian restaurants, and is justly popular for its economical lunch specials and reasonably priced evening meals. The tandoori dishes are recommended. It's in a small street south of the Honmachi Arcade in the center of town.

Close to Nanak is the popular **Mario Espresso** ((082) 241-4956, a three-story Italian restaurant that does generic pasta and pizza dishes. Prices are reasonable, and the restaurant can be very lively on weekends.

If you want to mingle with Hiroshima locals — ex-pat and Japanese — **Mac** ((082) 243-0343, 6-18 Nagarekawa-cho, Naka-ku, is a long-running institution that now has a smart new location. It's celebrated throughout town for its CD collection, which is nothing if not extensive. It's open until the wee hours.

HOW TO GET THERE

By Shinkansen it takes around four and a half hours to get to Hiroshima from Tokyo. Osaka and Kyoto are less than two hours away.

MIYA-JIMA ISLAND

Miya-jima, also known as Utsuku-shima, is a wooded and mountainous island with more monkeys and deer than people. Its most famous feature is visible from the ferry when you embark: a large and elaborate red *torii* gate set in the sea. One of Japan's most famous postcard scenes, and rated by the Japanese themselves as one of Japan's *sankei*, or three best views, this is the gateway to **Itsukushima Shrine** (6:30 AM to 6 PM, daily), the island's main attraction.

The shrine is thought to have been established in AD 593. It is dedicated to Ichikishimahime no Mikoto, the Shinto deity who looks after seafarers. In the twelfth century the shrine was expanded under the patronage of the Taira family, and the now famous "floating" *torii* gate erected.

After exploring the shrine — its *no* stage is the oldest in Japan — wander through the park that covers the hill immediately behind it. Full of Japanese maples, this area is supremely beautiful in autumn, but at any season when it's not too crowded

the meandering walks, the cries of birds and the heavy scent of flowers make it a charming place.

A two-stage ropeway takes visitors close to the summit of 530-m (1,739-ft) **Mount Misen-san**, the highest point on the island. The base station is at **Momiji-dani Valley** (or Maple Valley). Ask for "ropeway" and you will be pointed in the right direction. It's not cheap — ¥1,500 round trip — but the views can be splendid on a good day: Hiroshima on the way up and the silvery waters of the Inland Sea from the top. There's a monkey park at the top, too, while down near the harbor the shrine deer wander freely, as at Nara. Take care with the monkeys — they are not all friendly.

There are a number of ways to get to Miya-jima from Hiroshima. Most travelers take the No. 3 tram to Miyajima-guchi station, where a ferry makes a quick 10-minute run to the island. Direct high-speed hovercraft also run from Hiroshima, for about three times the amount it costs by a combination of tram and ferry. JR trains also run to Miyajima-guchi station.

THE INLAND SEA

The sea dividing Honshu, Shikoku and Kyushu is the birthplace, they say, of the Japanese sense of beauty. In the scaly seas, the mists, the fishing boats, the shifting perspective of pine tree-prickly islets and islands, there is certainly something quintessentially Japanese, something that invites depiction in *sumie* ink rather than oils.

But, as Donald Richie lamented in his marvelous book *The Inland Sea*, much of the area's beauty is vanishing under a slick of industry. Nothing has happened in the decades since the book was written to reverse that trend. Vast suspension bridges now straddle the sea, linking Honshu and Shikoku. They may help to revive the economy in this backwater of Japan, but they will not help to restore the Inland Sea's lost tranquility.

Several spots offer views of the Inland Sea, notably **Miya-jima** (see above), **Onomichi** (see above) and **Washu-zan Hill**, on the eastern edge of Shimotsui, south of Kurashiki (see above).

WEST OF HIROSHIMA

While most travelers making their way along the San-yo Coast make Hiroshima and Miya-jima their last stops before continuing on to Kyushu, there are a couple of possible stopovers en-route.

Just 44 km (27 miles) southwest of Hiroshima is the laid-back castle town of **Iwakuni**, which is famous for its **Kintai-kyo Bridge**, one of Japan's top three. The elegant, five-arched bridge was first built in the 1670s, and survived until it was finally done in by a typhoon in 1950. It was promptly rebuilt, and the results represent one of Japan's more faithful recreations.

Northeast of the bridge, over the Nishiki-gawa River, is **Kikko-koen Park**, once a samurai family estate, while behind the park a cable car (or ropeway) rattles up **Mount Shiro-yama**, from where you can walk to the 1960s reproduction of **Iwakuni-jo Castle**, which is in a photogenic but inauthentic location some distance from its original site.

From Hiroshima, Shinkansen travel to Shin Iwakuni station in less than 20 minutes, from where frequent buses head to the bridge area and take around the same time. JR limited express (*tokkyu*) services take a little over 40 minutes and stop at JR Iwakuni station, from where buses also head out to the bridge.

they would later be persecuted, many of them executed, by the Tokugawas.

Cycle north of here to the picturesque **Ruriko-ji Temple**, with its striking five-story pagoda. A couple of kilometers to the east is Yamaguchi's most worthwhile attraction: **Shesshu-tei Garden** (8 AM to 5 PM, daily). Designed by the renowned ink painter Sesshu Toyo (1420–1506), this moss Zen garden is a treat and can often be quite deserted — something that anyone who has visited the famous gardens of Kyoto will appreciate.

The nearest Shinkansen stop to Yamaguchi is Ogori, where it is necessary to change to the Yamaguchi line for the 15-minute journey to Yamaguchi itself. For all onward travel from

The other San-yo Coast attraction worth making a brief stopover in is **Yamaguchi**. It's a relatively sleepy place whose attractions are mostly the legacy of upheaval in Kyoto during the sixteenth century, when Yamaguchi emerged as a refuge for Kyoto aristocracy. When Francis Xavier (Francisco de Javier, 1506–1552) came to Japan, he settled here briefly, having unsuccessfully attempted to gain an interview with the emperor in Kyoto.

The best way to see the sights is to rent a bicycle at Yamaguchi station. From here, peddle directly north up Eki-mae Dori for the **Saint Francis Xavier Memorial Church**. Don't expect a crumbling old church — the very modern structure is only a few years old, replacing an original that was built in 1951 to commemorate the 400th anniversary of Xavier's Yamaguchi sojourn, which saw the conversion of several hundred Yamaguchi residents —

Yamaguchi, you will either have to return to Ogori, or choose to travel onwards to the northern San-in Coast of Western Honshu by taking a JR bus to Hagi, a journey of a little over an hour. Alternatively, it is possible to stay on the Yamaguchi line and continue inland to the interesting castle town of Tsuwano.

HAGI

The thriving pottery city of Hagi is renowned for the delicate gray glaze of its teaware, which grows richer and deeper with use. But the city, easily one of the San-in Coast's premier attractions, is also home to some interesting castle ruins and an old samurai quarter.

A view over the very distinctive shrine on Miya-jima and back to the mainland.

GENERAL INFORMATION

Hagi is one of those slightly confusing Japanese cities where the main station is not the handiest for seeing the sights. JR Hagi station is in the south of town, but it is a far less convenient place to alight than is Higashi Hagi station in the east of town. For Hagi-jo Castle, Tamae station in the west of town is the more convenient.

Higashi Hagi station has a **tourist information counter** ((0838) 25-3145, but only limited English is spoken.

WHAT TO SEE AND DO

From Higashi Hagi station head west across the Matsumoto-gawa River and then straight ahead through the area called **Tera-machi** (literally "Temple Town," on account of its many temples) to Joka-machi. To the north of here is **Kikuga-hama Beach**, which is only open for swimming in the height of summer (mid-July to mid-August). Meanwhile, Joka-machi itself is the old samurai quarter, a picturesque district that is one of Hagi's main claims to fame and is immensely popular with Japanese tour groups — be warned.

The most famous of the old samurai homes in this part of town is **Kikuya House** (8:30 AM to 5 PM, daily), which dates from 1604 and is actually a merchant home rather than a samurai one. Small matter: it is still a fascinating place to look at, and has a splendid small garden. Close by, and more authentically a samurai residence, is **Takasugi Shinsaku House** (9 AM to 5 PM, daily). Takasugi (1839-1867) was a leading opponent of the Tokugawa shogunate, but he died tragically of tuberculosis on the eve of the Meiji restoration. Also close by, but only for aficionados of Japanese tea, is the small **Ishii Chawan Museum** (9 AM to 5 PM, closed Mondays and for lunch), which is nominally devoted to Hagi's famous tea bowls but which in fact features everything tea-related.

Farther east of Joka-machi, and close to Tamae station, is **Shizuki-koen Park** (9 AM to 5 PM, daily) and the ruins of **Hagi-jo Castle**. There is not much left of the castle, but it's pleasant to stroll around the walls that remain and to reflect, perhaps, on how ruins can make a change from Ferro-concrete reproductions.

Another worthwhile Hagi excursion is to **Shoin-jinja Shrine**, which is southeast of Higashi Hagi station. Hagi's largest, it was built in honor of Yoshida Shoin (1830–1859), a major inspirational force in the anti-Tokugawa movement of the late Edo period (1600–1867). There is a small museum in his honor on the shrine precincts, but without a Japanese interpreter its exhibits are of little interest.

WHERE TO STAY AND EAT

Hagi's most famous *ryokan* is the **Hokumon Yashiki** ((0838) 22-7521 FAX (0838) 25-8144, 210 Horiuchi, which is just west of the castle ruins mixing Western and Japanese styles almost willy-nilly. It's not quite the *ryokan* experience of yore, but it is all the same an inn with impeccably high standards. Per person costs start at ¥20,000.

From outside the **Hagi Grand Hotel** ((0838) 25-1211 FAX (0838) 25-4422, 25 Furuhagi-cho, looks like a monstrosity, but inside it maintains good upper mid-range to luxury standards, even if it does look to have seen better days. Rates range from ¥13,500 for a single. Doubles start at ¥17,000.

The **Hotel Orange** ((0838) 25-5880 FAX (0838) 25-7690, 370-48 Hijiwara, Hagi-shi, is a standard business hotel close to Higashi Hagi station, but its rooms are larger than most of the others in the area, and rates are reasonable.

The **Pension Hagi** ((0838) 28-0071 E-MAIL pension@joho-yamaguchi.or.jp, 3328 Ohi Hagi, is a wonderfully welcoming place. It's two stops from Higashi Hagi station, but if you ring the owners they will come and pick you up from Hagi. Bed and breakfast is ¥6,900 person.

If you are feeling adventurous, try ringing the **Hagi Minshuku Association** ((0838) 25-1534, which can arrange inexpensive (usually from ¥5,000 per person upwards with meals) accommodation in a people's lodge. Many of them are located picturesquely along Kikuga-hama Beach.

The cheapest accommodation in town is at the **Hagi Youth Hostel** ((0838) 22-0733, 108-22 Horiuchi, which is close to the ruins of Hagi-jo Castle, near Tamae station. It only has dormitory accommodation.

The best place to go to seek out food is the central **Tamachi arcade**, where you will find dozens of places to eat with the usual plastic food displays outside for easy ordering.

HOW TO GET THERE

Hagi is connected with other north coast attractions such as Tottori by the JR San-in line. For Tsuwano, take a bus from the Bus Center, which is just south of the eastern end of Tamachi Arcade. The journey takes around one and a half hours.

TSUWANO

Tsuwano, like Hagi, is another castle town with an intact samurai quarter. In some ways it is more picturesque even than Hagi, a particular famous feature being its canals, which are thick with tens of thousands of carp.

The famous *torii* gate in the sea.

Orientation is a less of a problem in Tsuwano, a more compact destination than Hagi. Tsuwano station is in the north of town, and long-distance buses stop in front of the station. Next door to the station is a small **tourist office** ((08567) 2-1771, where the staff can do little more than provide an informative English leaflet on Tsuwano's attractions but are friendly.

First stop, after leaving the station area, should be the **Tono-machi district**, which is a short walk to the south. Once the samurai quarter, it still sports some splendid buildings, and the canal-lined streets are a treat to wander aimlessly through. Attractions in the area include a **Catholic church** that dates from 1930, and the **Yoro-kan** (9 AM to 5 PM, daily), once a school for samurai and now a small museum exhibiting local crafts. North of here is the **Hokusai Museum of Art** (9:30 AM to 5 PM, daily). Hokusai (1760–1849) was perhaps the greatest master of the *ukiyo-e* woodblock print, but was a master of many things during his life. His most famous series is his *36 Views of Mount Fuji*, which includes the almost iconic picture of a boat dwarfed by massive spumy waves, snow-capped Fuji-san in the distance, entitled *Beneath the Wave off Kanagawa*.

Almost directly west of the Catholic church and the Yoro-kan is **Taikodani Inari-jinja Shrine**, a colorful shrine approached by a "tunnel" of vermilion *torii* gates. Inari is the Shinto deity of grains, and his association with rice has led him to become linked to success in business. His messenger is the fox, statues of which can be found at all Inari shrines, usually dressed with a red bib — donated by someone in gratitude for prayers answered.

Head south from the shrine and you will come to a cable car that heads up to the ruins of **Tsuwano-jo Castle**. There are fine views up here, but the castle itself is off bounds due to structural instability following an earthquake — check to see if repairs have made it safe yet.

Tsuwano is connected to Yamaguchi by the Yamaguchi line, a 50-minute trip. For onward travel along the San-in Coast, continue on the Yamaguchi line to Masuda, where you can change to the JR San-in line for travel either east to Matsue or west along the coast to Shimonoseki, Western Honshu's gateway to Kyushu.

MATSUE

Yet another castle town with small canals and a samurai district, Matsue makes a good place to overnight and take a breather on the San-in Coast. Its attractions can easily be explored in an afternoon of walking, but it has a major attraction around 30 km (19 miles) west of town in Izumo-taisha Shrine, which justifies lingering a little longer here.

GENERAL INFORMATION

Matsue station is in the south of town, while most of the city's sights are in a compact area to the north of the Ohashi-gawa River. There's a very good **tourist information counter** ((0852) 21-4034 at Matsue station. English is spoken and maps and other material are available. It's possible to rent bicycles at the station for ¥1,000 per day or ¥500 per two hours.

WHAT TO SEE AND DO

Matsue's main attraction is **Matsue-jo Castle** (8:30 AM to 5 PM, daily), built in 1611 and still standing. As such it is well worth a visit, representing a unique opportunity to see an original wooden castle. There are exhibits of armor and so on inside. Inside the surrounding park is the **Matsue Historical Museum** (same hours as the castle), which has a modest collection of local arts and crafts.

The street directly north of the castle is called **Shiomi Nawate** and is the center of Matsue's old samurai district. Walk northwest along here and you will come to the **Lafcadio Hearn Memorial Museum** (8:30 AM to 5 PM, daily) and after it the former residence of **Lafcadio Hearn** (same hours). Hearn (1850–1904), a reporter of Anglo-Irish / Greek extraction, arrived in Tokyo in 1890, married the daughter of samurai, took up Japanese citizenship under the name Koizumi Yakumo, and wrote some influential, if romantic, accounts of Japan, including the beautiful *Glimpses of an Unfamiliar Japan*. The museum is curated by Hearn's grandson, and the residence is the former home of a samurai, though Hearn's stay here was relatively brief.

WHERE TO STAY

A reliable mid-range choice is the **Matsue Tokyu Inn** ((0852) 27-0109 FAX (0852) 25-1327, 590 Asahi-cho, which is directly in front of Matsue station and has comfortable singles and doubles ranging from around ¥7,000 per person. It's part of a chain of hotels.

Cheaper and long a popular choice for budget travelers is the **Business Ishida** ((0852) 21-5931, 205-11 Tera-machi, a no-frills Japanese-style hotel that is directly east of Matsue station. Don't expect much in the way of creature comforts in the plain tatami rooms, but it's an inexpensive place to spend a night.

HOW TO GET THERE

Matsue is connected with other north-coast destinations via the San-in line. For Izumo-taisha, it

172   *Western Honshu*

is necessary to change at JR Izumo station to the private Ichihata line for Izumo-taisha station. It is also possible to travel south to Okayama and Kurashiki by JR in just over two hours.

IZUMO

Izumo-taisha Shrine is one of Japan's grandest and most important Shinto shrines. It is dedicated to Okuninushi no Mikoto, a heroic, civilizing god who is responsible for fashioning the world of mortal men. The legend has it that upon creating this world he turned it over to the grandson of Ametarasu Omikami, who was so touched she founded this shrine here in his

TOTTORI AND AMANOHASHIDATE

Farther east along the northern coast is Tottori, famous for its 16-km (10-mile) strip of sand dunes east of the city, the uncanny atmosphere of which lent such power to the classic Japanese film *Woman in the Dunes* (based on the novel by Kobo Abe, available in translation).

West of town there is bathing and surfing at Hawaii Beach (accessible via JR's San-in main line; get off at Kurayoshi, then it's 20 minutes by bus).

Farther east again is Amanohashidate (the name means "Bridge of Heaven"), which is also accessible by train from both Kyoto and Tsuruga.

honor. October 11 to 17 is a major festival, the Kamiari Matsuri, in which all of the Shinto gods from across the land gather here — in times past other parts of Japan called October the "month without gods."

The sweeping roofs of the shrine are in the *taisha-zukuri* style, which is the oldest of Japan's shrine architectural styles, and there is an understated dignity about the buildings here. The **honden**, or main hall, dates back to 1744 and is said to have been rebuilt on this spot 25 times prior to that, although its actual founding is shrouded in myth.

The easiest way to get to the shrine is to take a train on the private Ichihata line, which is at Matsue Onsen station, a kilometer (about half a mile) northwest of Matsue station, and just south of Matsuejo Castle. The trip involves a change of train at Kawato and takes just under an hour.

It's one of Japan's *sankei*, or three most famous views, along with Miya-jima (near Hiroshima) and Matsushima (near Sendai). The attraction lies in the pine tree-dotted sandbar that stretches across the entrance of Miyazu Bay and which, when inspected upside down looking through one's legs, is indistinguishable from the sky. It's a *frisson* which may well be overrated, but it is amusing to watch Japanese tourists all doing the obligatory heads-between-the-legs maneuver, some of them even taking photographs as they do so.

The sign on this building's roof announces the view at Amanohashidate to be one of Japan's three most famous — Japanese appreciate it by bending over and putting their heads between their legs.

Northern Honshu

PROBABLY THE LEAST VISITED REGION OF HONSHU, by foreigners and Japanese alike, to Japanese ears Tohoku, or northern Honshu, rings of battles, long, snow-bound winters, and remote mountainous villages. The last part of Honshu to come under central control, many Japanese see it as a somewhat barbarous region compared to the rest of the main island. When Matsuo Basho (1644–1694) undertook a 2,400-km (1,500-mile) walk through the region in 1689 he published the resulting poetic diary tellingly as *Oku no Hosomich* (*The Narrow Road to the Deep North*), a title that simultaneously conjures up the remoteness and dark depths of the region he was exploring.

One of the reasons the region sees so little tourist traffic is that, unlike Tokyo, Kansai, Central Honshu and Kyushu, its attractions are scattered, often elusive and, for much of the year, snowbound. In fact, it is not a good idea to travel around northern Honshu from the beginning of November until mid-April, as most tourist facilities tend to shut down.

JR railway lines run north-south along both the east and west coasts of Northern Honshu, while the Shinkansen runs as far as Morioka, via Sendai.

AIZU WAKAMATSU

The first of northern Honshu's major attractions, at first glance Aizu Wakamatsu looks like any other far-flung Japanese city. But it has several historical sights that make it worth a stopover.

The city is spread out, and the main attractions are several kilometers from JR Aizu Wakamatsu station, where you will find a useful **tourist information counter** ((0242) 32-0688. Ask here about the city buses, which take in all three of the city's main attractions: the castle, a samurai home and Mount Iimori-yama.

The main attraction is **Mount Iimori-yama**, which you have the option of climbing on foot (around 15 minutes) or ascending with the help of an escalator. At the top are the graves of 19 Bakkotai, or members of the White Tiger Brigade. Organized in 1868 by the local pro-Tokugawa Aizu clan in defense of the besieged Tokugawa government, 20 members of this youth brigade were cut off from their fellows during an attack by pro-Meiji forces on October 8 of the same year. Believing all to be lost, they committed *seppuku*, or ritual disembowelment, here on the hill and have been revered as models of "loyalty, determination and courage" ever since. There are only 19 graves because one of the youths survived his attempt at disembowelment — to, it is said, his everlasting shame.

Of more interest to foreign visitors is the fascinating reconstruction of a samurai villa that can be found at **Buke Yashi** (9 AM to 4:30 PM, daily). The original was destroyed by pro-Meiji forces but not before the family inside committed *seppuku*.

Tsuruga-jo Castle (8:30 AM to 5 PM, daily) is a reconstruction of a castle that was destroyed by Meiji forces.

For somewhere good to stay, the **Washington Hotel** ((0242) 22-6111 FAX (0242) 24-7535, 201 Byakko-machi, is recommended. It is a quality mid-range hotel, not far from Aizu Wakamatsu station, and part of the reliable Washington chain. For something less expensive, the **Green Hotel Aizu** ((0242) 24-5181 FAX (0242) 24-5182, 3-7-23 Chuo, has reasonable rates (from ¥5,500 per person) and a mixture of both Japanese-style and Western-style rooms. It is also well located, just south of Aizu Wakamatsu station.

From Asakusa in Tokyo, the Tobu line runs to Aizu Tajima, where you can change to the Aizu line for Aizu Wakamatsu, a route that also allows a visit to Nikko. Alternatively, the quickest way to get here is to take a Shinkansen to Koriyama and then change to the JR Ban-Etsu line as far as Aizu Wakamatsu.

BANDAI KOGEN

In 1888, the volcanic **Mount Bandai** exploded with stupendous violence, destroying 11 villages and killing hundreds of people. The discharged rock blocked the courses of local rivers, creating an area of ponds and marshes. This is of peculiar beauty because the water of each of the ponds is a different color. A pretty nature course runs around and between five of them.

This area, called **Goshikinuma**, is very popular with Japanese tourists and should be avoided on weekends and national holidays. The main attraction is a four-kilometer (two-and-a-half-mile) nature trail.

The Bandai-Azuma Skyline toll-road, which covers the distance between Goshikinuma and Fukushima, features spectacular scenery.

SENDAI

Around 350 km (220 miles) north of Tokyo, Sendai is effectively the gateway to Tohoku, and the largest city in the region. While not an unpleasant place, nobody could accuse it of being wildly exciting either. Its attractions are modest and there is a sedate quality to its broad, tree-lined streets. Nevertheless it makes a good place to overnight, and it is the obvious base for visiting Matsushima, the last of Japan's *sankei*, or three big v iews (for the other two, see MIYA-JIMA ISLAND, page 168, and AMANOHASHIDATE, page 173 in WESTERN HONSHU).

GENERAL INFORMATION

Sendai station is in the east of the city, and the city center sprawls away westwards. There's little to do in the station vicinity except shop, eat and drink,

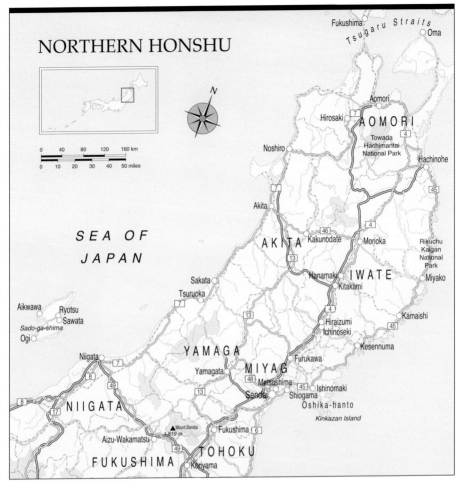

NORTHERN HONSHU

and most of the sights, such as they are, are in the far west of town. The city center was reconstructed from scratch after World War II. The Loople Sendai bus service, with its colorful, rather antique-looking buses, does a loop around the city's main attractions, and for ¥600 you can buy a ticket that allows you to embark and disembark at will for one day.

The **Sendai Tourist Information Center** ((022) 222-4069 is on the second floor of Sendai station and is staffed by friendly English-speakers.

WHAT TO SEE AND DO

Sendai's real attraction is not in Sendai itself but at nearby Matsushima (see below). But there are a few sights around town that can be used to kill a few hours. The best place to start is **Aoba-yama-koen Park**, which was once home to Sendai's **Aoba-jo Castle**, built in 1601 and once the focus of the city. All that remains today of what was a great castle are some ruins. Look for the statue of

Date Masamune (1567-1636), the founding father of Sendai. Known as Dokuganryu, or "One-Eyed Dragon," he was awarded the Sendai domain by Tokugawa Ieyasu for his support in the decisive Battle of Sekigahara (1600) that led to the Tokugawa unification of Japan. He built Aoba-jo Castle and made Sendai an important castle town in the Edo era (1600–1867).

For more on Masamune and Sendai's history, walk north of the park to the **Sendai City Museum** (9 AM to 5 PM, closed Mondays). It actually has displays of Sendai history that take you back into the mists of prehistory, but the interesting displays relate to Sendai at its height during the Edo period.

East of the museum and the park, in a bend in the Hirose-gawa River, is Masamune's mausoleum, **Zuiho-den** (9 AM to 4:30 PM, daily). The other two mausoleums here belong to successors of Masamune, and while they are recent reconstructions are none the less impressive for it. There is an attached museum.

WHERE TO STAY

If you turn up in Sendai without accommodation, there is a **hotel booking service** ((022) 222-4069 at Sendai station, though usually finding something at the last minute here is not a problem, as Sendai is not a city that sees large volumes of tourist traffic.

Sendai's most luxurious hotel is the **New World** ((022) 277-3111 FAX (022) 277-3122, 25-5 Nakayamaminami, Sanezawa, Izumi-ku, but it is inconveniently located around 20 minutes out of town — the hotel has a pick-up service — which leaves you at the mercy of the hotel facilities. It's popular with tour groups. Per-person costs start at ¥15,000.

Although rather unpromising from the outside, a more convenient luxury option is the **Sendai Hotel** ((022) 262-2411 FAX (022) 262-4109, 2-9-25 Ichiban-cho Aoba-ku, a looming 302-room monster opposite the station. Inside standards are near international in this long-running hotel. It has Japanese, Chinese, Italian and Continental restaurants, and singles start ¥12,000, twins at ¥16,000.

A simple mid-priced business hotel is the **Hotel Universe Sendai** ((022) 261-7711 FAX (022) 261-7745, 4-3-22 Ichiban-cho, Aoba-ku, which has a great location in the center of town at the northern end of the Chuo Dori Shopping Mall. If you have stayed in business hotels elsewhere in Japan, it's a familiar concept — smallish, functional rooms with rates from ¥6,500 per person.

The **Aisaki Ryokan** ((022) 264-0700 FAX (022) 227-6067, 5-6 Kitame-machi, Aoba-ku, is one of the least expensive places to stay in Sendai and is accustomed to receiving foreign guests. Rooms are either Japanese-style with shared bathing facilities for ¥4,000 or more expensive Western-style with attached bathrooms. It's a 15-minute walk southeast of the station.

The **Sendai Dochu-an Youth Hostel** ((022) 247-0511 FAX (022) 247-0479, 31 Onadakitayashiki, Taihaku-ku, is rated as one of Japan's best. Housed in an old farmhouse, the accommodation — all shared unfortunately — is traditional, and superb meals are available on site. It's a 10-minute walk from Tomizawa subway station.

WHERE TO EAT

If you are simply on a flying visit to Sendai, strolling around the city, and need a place for lunch, the obvious place to go is the central **Chuo Dori Shopping Mall**, where you will find dozens of restaurants to choose from. The local specialty is less appealing to most foreigners than some other local specialties around Japan. *Gyutan* is smoked or salted calf tongue, which actually tastes better than it sounds, and is traditionally eaten as an accompaniment to the local sake.

A place to try *gyutan* in style is **Tasuke** ((022) 262-2561, 1-6-19 Ichiban-cho, Aoba-ku, which is in the basement of the Ichiban-kan Building, just off Kokubuncho Dori, parallel to the northern end of the Chuo Dori Shopping Mall. Gyutan here is prepared every way imaginable, and lunchtime sets start at ¥1,200. Dinner sets cost just under ¥3,000.

Another recommended, centrally located restaurant is **Steak House Iseya** ((022) 221-2747, 3-10-15 Ichiban-cho, Aoba-ku, where you can try Sendai beef (not as famous as the Kobe variety, but highly rated in Japan all the same).

HOW TO GET THERE

Sendai's international airport is around 40 minutes by bus from downtown Sendai. The JR Tohoku line connects Ueno in Tokyo with Sendai, and continues on to Morioka and beyond. Shinkansen do the journey in a little over two hours.

MATSUSHIMA

It's official: Matsushima, along with Miya-jima and Amanohashidate, is one of Japan's three most beautiful places. In fact the accolades hung about Matsushima, as with Japan's other official beauty spots, are something of a yoke, and arrival can be anticlimactic. It's a pleasant bay, surrounded by wooded hills and harboring some 260 islets. By all means visit. But chances are, once you have left Japan, there will be other far less famous scenes more firmly fixed in your memory than this one. It's best to avoid weekends and public holidays, when the crowds here reach Tokyo proportions.

The big "must do" is a cruise around the bay. Regular 45-minute trips set out from the ferry pier, which is a short walk northeast of Matsushima Kaigen station.

Before leaving Matsushima, there are several sights within walking distance of the station that are worth giving some time to. Foremost among these is **Zuigan-ji Temple** (8 AM to 3:30 PM, daily), which was founded in the ninth century and rebuilt by Date Masamune in 1606 as a family temple. Be sure to include the **Seiryu-den**, or Treasure House, which contains originals of the temple's renowned screens.

South of the station, a bridge leads to **O-jima Island**, once a retreat for monks and priests.

From Sendai trains take approximately 40 minutes to Matsushima Kaigen station on the Senseki line. There is a Matsushima station on the Tohoku line too, but it is inconveniently located to the north of the main sights.

Ready for the annual Hollyhock Festival, this young girl is dressed in her best festival wear.

KINKAZAN

Some two hours by train and half an hour by ferry from Sendai is the small island of Kinkazan, at the tip of the Oshika-hanto Peninsula. The name means "Gold Flower Mountain," a reference to the days, long gone, when it was a magnet for gold prospectors. Today, it's a tranquil place of forests, with monkeys and deer running free. A large shrine, **Koganeyama-jinja**, attracts many visitors, and the overall atmosphere of the island is rather like that of Miya-jima, near Hiroshima — without the crowds of tourists. The island makes an excellent retreat for anybody wanting a weekend away from urban

A military stronghold from as long ago as the eighth century, Hiraizumi rose to prominence when the Fujiwara clan settled here in 1094. Chushon-ji Temple was founded at this time, and the town grew into an important provincial center.

A small place with around 10,000 inhabitants, Hiraizumi is not difficult to get orientated in. Motsu-ji Temple and its garden is just under a kilometer (half a mile) to the west of JR Hiraizumi station, while the famous Chuson-ji Temple lies just over a kilometer (half a mile) to the north. There's a small **tourist information office** ((0191) 46-2110 in the station, and bicycles — a good way to get around the sights — can be rented immediately to the right of the station.

frenzy. Accommodation is limited; the best way to make reservations is to ring the **tourist office** ((0225) 93-6448 in Ishinomaki, though you will need the help of Japanese speaker to do so.

During the summer months there are hourly ferry services to Kinkazan from the port of Ayukawa, reached by bus from Ishinomaki, terminus of JR's Senseki line from Sendai.

HIRAIZUMI

The small town of Hiraizumi is not promising at first glance. But in the nearby hills is the legacy of its far more illustrious past, Tohoku's premiere cultural attraction: the Golden Hall of Chuson-ji Temple. Also worth visiting are the ruins of Motsu-ji Temple, where a Heian period (794–1185) garden can be seen. Nearby are two gorges that offer hiking and boating opportunities.

While legend has it that the famous Buddhist priest Ennin (AD 794-864) founded **Chuson-ji Temple** (8 AM to 5 PM, daily), temple records only indicate that Fujiwara no Kiyohira (1056–1128) rebuilt an earlier temple that was on this spot, starting construction in 1105. In its day the temple complex comprised more than 40 temples. A fire in 1337 destroyed many of them. The **Konjiki-do**, or **Golden Hall**, however, was spared and is a breathtaking vision of gold leaf statuary, beneath which lies the mummy of the man who commissioned it. If you are expecting literally a "golden hall," however, you will be disappointed — the gold is all inside. One other building — it is behind the hall — is a survivor from the original temple complex: the **Kyozo**, or Sutra Repository.

Nothing remains but the foundation stones of the ninth-century **Motsu-ji Temple** (8:30 AM to 5 PM, daily), also said to have been founded by

Ennin. But the Heian-era Jodo-teien gardens are a captivating spot to stroll around. The chief feature is a lake studded with artificial "islands."

Hiraizumi's two gorges are only worth visiting if you have oodles of time on your hands. If you elect to visit them, go to **Geibi-kei Gorge** (the other, confusingly, is called **Gembi-kei Gorge**), which can be reached by bus or train from Hiraizumi station in around half an hour. Boat rides through the gorge are a little expensive but are highly popular with Japanese tourists.

In the Motsu-ji Temple precincts is the atmospheric **Motsuji Youth Hostel** ((0191) 46-2331, which has accommodation in both dormitories and in Japanese-style private rooms. For other accommodation, it is recommended that you ask the information counter (see above) staff to make reservations in one of Hiraizumi's *ryokan*.

Hiraizumi is easily reached from Sendai. Take a Tohoku train to Ichinoseki and change there either to a bus for Chuson-ji or a train for Hiraizumi — the former is usually quicker. Total travel time should be between one and one and a half hours depending on connections.

MORIOKA

The terminus of the Tohoku Shinkansen trail, Morioka is, while not unpleasant, a place with little to recommend it. It has virtually nothing in the way off attractions. But it does make a convenient stopover en-route to more interesting destinations, either in Tohoku or in Hokkaido.

JR Morioka station sits on the west side of the Kitakami-gawa River, while the city proper sprawls east on the other side. O-dori cuts east-west through the center, passing, about a kilometer (half a mile) from the station, what is left — virtually nothing — of the city's erstwhile castle in Iwate-koen Park. The **Kita-Tohoku Sightseeing Center** ((019) 625-2090 is in Morioka station, and is a useful source of information.

Only if you are pressed for something to do take a 20-minute walk east across town to **Iwate-koen Park**. Morioka's castle was destroyed in the battles immediately preceding the Meiji restoration.

For acceptable moderately priced to expensive accommodation, the **Morioka Grand Hotel Annex** ((019) 625-5111 FAX (019) 622-3527, 1-9-16 Chuo Dori, has a good location in the center of town, and has rates from ¥17,000 for doubles. The **Hotel New Carina** ((019) 652-2222 FAX (019) 625-2244, 2-6-1 Saien, is extremely good value and also has a central location. Complete with Japanese, Chinese and Continental restaurants, rates start at ¥8,000 per person.

The **Ryokan Kumagai** ((019) 651-3020 FAX (019) 626-0096, 3-2-5 Ohsawakawara, is in the center of town, around 10 minutes by foot from the station. It is a Japanese Inn Group member that offers Japanese-style rooms from ¥4,000 per person. It's not one of the group's best, but it is adequate for an overnight stay.

AOMORI

Like Morioka, Aomori is a somewhat characterless city, but a place that sees a fair amount of tourist traffic en-route to Hokkaido. It makes an alternative stopover to Morioka on the road north, and in many ways is a preferable option to Morioka, being a little more compact and easier to get around in. Its one big attraction is the annual **Nebuta Festival** (from August 1 to 7), though getting accommodation at this time is a nightmare and reservations should be made well in advance. Aomori is also a jumping off point for the nearby castle town of Hirosaki.

Aomori station is in the far west of town next to the Aomori Passenger Terminal which, before the construction of the Seikan tunnel, was the main access point for Hakodate in Sapporo. There are several **tourist offices** in town but the most useful is the one in Aomori station ((0177) 23-4670. There is another in the ASPAM building ((0177) 39-4561 in the nearby harbor area.

For something to do, the first stop should be the harbor with its impressive **Bay Bridge** and post-modern **ASPAM** building. The **Aomori Prefectural Folklore Museum** (9 AM to 4:30 PM, closed Sundays), or the Kyodo-kan, is of minimal interest, with displays of archeological digs from around the vicinity.

The best of Aomori's hotels is the **Hotel JAL City Aomori** ((0177) 32-2580 FAX (0177) 35-2584 WEB SITE www.nikkohotels.com/jal/jal1.html, 2-4-12 Yasukata. This new, 163-room hotel has larger-than-average rooms and even has a British-style pub — something unexpected this far afield. The hotel also has an excellent *izakaya* (Japanese pub) restaurant.

The **Hotel Sunroute** ((0177) 75-2321 FAX (0177) 75-2329, 1-9-8 Shin-machi, is just a few minutes walk east of the station and is a recommended member of a reliable chain of business hotels. Rates start at ¥7,000 per person.

Aomori is two hours from Morioka on the JR Tohoku line. The JR Tsugaru Kaikyo line continues north from Aomori to Hakodate in Hokkaido via the Seikan tunnel in around two and a half hours, more than one hour of it deep beneath the sea.

HIROSAKI

The city of Hirosaki is another of those Japanese destinations in which first impressions are deceiving. While the area around JR Hirosaki station looks much like any other provincial city station area, to the east of town are the remains of the old castle and a charming samurai district.

Tofu, fish and vegetables are grilled over charcoal.

Take a bus (to Shiyakusho-mae) or a taxi (to Hirosaki-koen Park) to the east of town, where the attractions are. There is a tourist information booth where some English is spoken at the station and another at the entrance to **Hirosaki-koen Park**.

Just outside the northeast corner of the park is the **Neputa Mura Museum** (9 AM to 4 PM, daily), which is dedicated to displays relating to Hirosaki's Neputa Matsuri (August 1 to 7), a close relative in timing, name and activities to Aomori's more famous Nebuta Matsuri. It features drumming, floats and even some pottery making. North of here is the former **samurai district**, which is mostly modern residential nowadays but still harbors a few old samurai residences.

It takes just over half an hour to reach Hirosaki from Aomori on the JR Ou line, making it perfectly feasible to visit as a morning or afternoon excursion.

AKITA AND KAKUNODATE

Southwest of Hirosaki, and the only sizeable city on Tohoku's northwest coast, is Akita, a modern city that sees very few foreign visitors. The only real reason to go there is to nearby Kakunodate, which makes up for Akita's lack of historical interest with a small samurai district.

There is no need to linger in Akita unless you have to. The JR station is in the east of town. A short walk to the west is the **Shenshu-koen Park**,

In the park stands all that is left of **Hirosaki-jo Castle**: a small but charming three-story tower that was built in 1810 to replace an earlier castle that burned down.

South of the park, a 20-minute walk takes you to the **Tera-machi district**, or "Temple Town," a pleasant area for a stroll in which the most interesting of many temples is the seventeenth-century **Chosho-ji Temple**.

The station area has the usual collection of business hotels, but for something closer to Hirosaki-koen Park, try the **Hotel Hokke Club** ((00172) 34-3811 FAX (0172) 32-0589, 126 Dote-machi. This moderately priced chain offers unexciting but reliable single and double rooms from ¥7,000. The **Hirosaki Youth Hostel** ((0172) 32-1515, 11 Mori-machi, is directly south of the park and perfectly located for exploring Hirosaki's older districts. Only dormitory accommodation is available.

once home to Akita's now absent castle. In the southern part of the park is the **Hirano Masakichi Art Museum** (10 AM to 5 PM, closed Mondays), which has an interesting collection of Western and Japanese modern art. There is an **information office** ((0188) 32-7941 in the station that can help with accommodation bookings. In a pinch, the **Hotel Metropolitan** ((0188) 31-2222 FAX 31-2290, a smart business hotel next to the station, is a reasonable place for an overnight stay, though nearby Kakunodate is a preferable overnight destination.

Kakunodate, a small town of around 15,000, is worth a visit for its well preserved **samurai district** and its streets lined with cherry trees. The station is in the southeast of town, and it is just under a kilometer (half a mile) to the samurai district. There is a **tourist information office** ((0187) 54-2700 next to the station, and the staff here can help with bookings for a hotel or *ryokan* should you want to stopover. Bicycles can be hired a little down the road leading west from the station.

The most worthwhile of the samurai homes (at least five are open to the public) is the **Aoyagi-ke Residence** (9 AM to 5 PM, daily), which has an eclectic mix of different-themed museum rooms. The nearby **Densho-kan Museum** (9 AM to 5 PM, closed Thursdays) has some interesting exhibits relating to Kakunodate's samurai past. There are other samurai homes to explore in the area.

Stay in the **Hyakusui-en** ((0187) 54-2700 FAX (0187) 55-2767, a traditional *ryokan* that it seems nearly every foreigner who overnights in Kakunodate stays in. It's a convivial place in a splendid old building. The owner speaks English. Rates start at ¥7,000, more with meals, which are highly recommended.

TSURUOKA AND DEWA SANZAN

The former castle town of Tsuruoka is now notable mostly as the gateway to the Dewa Sanzan trio of holy Shinto mountains that are famous as the haunt of *yamabushi*, Japan's high-altitude ascetics. Very few foreigners get this far afield, and even Japanese tourism here does not attain the frenzied proportions it does in many other parts of Japan. In other words this is a good opportunity to take a peek at a rarely seen Japan that combines beautiful scenery and some interesting cultural attractions.

Tsuruoka, while sporting a few sights, is an essential pit stop if you are on your way to Dewa Sanzan, as the **information counter** ((235) 24-7678 can provide time tables for buses (not very frequent) to the two main peaks — **Mount Haguro-san** and **Mount Gas-san**. The information counter can also organize lodgings at one of the mountains' *shukubo* — monastery inns — which provide the only accommodation on the mountains.

The **Haguro Trail**, which starts at Haguro-machi bus stop and ends at the Haguro-sancho bus stop — a total of a little more than an hour's walking — is a popular short hike (there are some very long ones). The walk on from here to Mount Gas-san is a far more serious 20-km (just over 12-mile) hike.

Tsuruoka is just under two hours from Akita on the JR Uetsu line.

NIIGATA AND SADO-GA-SHIMA ISLAND

Niigata, the capital of the prefecture of the same name, is an important port but otherwise of little interest to travelers accept as a gateway to the remote and unique island of Sado-ga-shima.

Niigata station, which is amazingly connected to Tokyo by Shinkansen, a journey of less than two hours, has a useful **information desk** ((025) 241-7914 that can assist with hotel bookings for Niigata and ferry bookings for Sado-ga-shima.

If you need to overnight in Niigata, the usual collection of business hotels can be found clustered around the station. The **Niigata Tokyu Hotel** ((025) 243-0109 FAX (025) 243-0401, 1-2-4 Benten, is directly opposite the station, and has the usual upper mid-range Tokyu standards, with rates from ¥8,000 per person. The **Niigata Green Hotel** ((025) 246-0341 FAX (025) 246-0345, 1-4-9 Hanazono, is next to the station and is a cheaper option, with rates from ¥5,000. It's another branch of a nationwide chain.

Sado-ga-shima, also known simply as Sado, is Japan's fifth largest island. It was an independent province for most of Japanese history (until 1876), and a place of exile from the mid-twelfth century through the sixteenth century. The discovery of gold and silver and the opening of mines (the first in 1601) made the island rich. Such times are long gone, and now the island lives off fishing and tourism drawn in by its reputation as a place where Japan is somewhat different — even for Japanese, this island is a place apart, with a unique cultural heritage and customs.

The most important gateway for the island is the small city of **Ryotsu**, where the island's only useful tourist information office is located in front of the ferry pier, which is the arrival point for jetfoils from Niigata. This is the place to organize accommodation and perhaps island tours.

There is little to see in Ryotsu, but the nightly performances of the local folk music — *okesa* — at the **Ryotsu Kai-kan Hall** are justly popular.

On the other side of the waist of the island is **Sawata**. It's mostly a transport hub. North of here is the former bustling gold-rush town of **Aikwawa**. With the closure of the last gold mine in 1989, its fortunes are far cry from those of the seventeenth century, when it became one of the biggest towns of Edo Japan, but it's worth visiting the **Sado Kinzan Gold Mine** (8:30 AM to 4:30 PM, daily), where an Edo-era mine has been turned into a museum.

Far in the south is **Ogi**, which is host to a major annual festival in mid-August — the **Earth Celebration** organized by Sado's own Kodo Drum Troupe (see WEB SITE www.kodo.or.jp) — and is famous for its *tarai-bune*, or **tub boats**, literally tubs that locals paddled out to sea in to collect edibles such as abalone.

The best way to get around the island's scattered sights is to take a tour. Bus tours operate out of both Ryotsu and Ogi, and are easy to join at short notice.

Jet foils cross from Niigata's Sado Kisen Terminal in around an hour, and less frequently (and only from April to November) from Naoetsu to Ogi.

A collection of vessels, both ceramic and glass, for that most beloved of Japanese tipples — sake.

Hokkaido

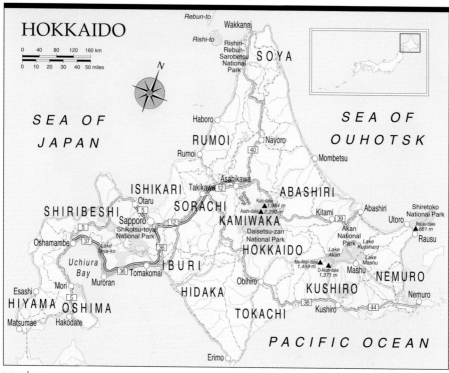

HOKKAIDO

Rebun-to
Wakkanai
Rishi-to
Rishiri-
Rebun-
Sarobetsu
National
Park
SOYA

0 40 80 120 160 km
0 10 20 30 40 50 miles

N

SEA OF
JAPAN

Haboro

RUMOI

Rumoi

SEA OF
OUHOTSK

Nayoro

Mombetsu

40

Asahikawa

ISHIKARI Takikawa 12
Otaru
SORACHI
SHIRIBESHI
Sapporo
Shikotsu-toya
National Park
Oshamambe 37
Lake
Toya-ko
Uchiura
Bay
Esashi Mori Muroran
HIYAMA OSHIMA
Matsumae Hakodate

5

12

36

36 Tomakomai

5

IBURI

HIDAKA

TOKACHI

Erimo

Kuro-dake
1,984 m
Asahi-dake 2,290 m
KAMIWAKA
Daisetsu-zan
National Park
HOKKAIDO

ABASHIRI

Kitami Abashiri

39

Akan
National
Park Lake
Kushiro
Lake
Akan

Me-Akan-dake
1,499 m
O-Akan-dake
1,371 m

Obihiro

KUSHIRO

38 Kushiro

Shiretoko
National Park
Utoro
Rausu-dake
661 m
Rausu

Lake
Mashu
Mashu

NEMURO

Nemuro

44

PACIFIC OCEAN

JAPAN'S NORTHERNMOST AND SECOND LARGEST ISLAND, Hokkaido (formerly Ezo) was, until the end of the Edo era (1600–1867), not even considered part of Japan. With the Meiji restoration, however, efforts began in earnest to bring the big northern island into the ambit of Japanese rule, and a colonial office was established there.

Hokkaido is home to the Ainu, the Japanese archipelago's indigenous people, whose domain in prehistoric times covered much of Honshu. Almost all are now integrated into mainstream Japanese society. In the eyes of some, however, they have suffered the fate currently being handed out to the Tibetans: dilution by immersion in the large-scale immigration of the numerically much larger neighboring ethnic group. Either way, Ainu culture today is mostly spectacle put on for tourists.

Hokkaido's lack of historical interest is made up for by its dramatic topography and its wide open spaces — it has 22 percent of the nation's total land area but only five percent of the population — and its pleasant reminders, for Westerners, of home: rolling green meadows spotted with cows and waving fields of grain. The towns seem as American-inspired as the agriculture: they spread on and on.

Due partly to the spaciousness, the people of Hokkaido enjoy a reputation for being looser and franker than other Japanese. Another reason for this is that, drawn as the population is from all parts of the country, the old-fashioned, soil-rooted clannishness prevalent elsewhere has been unable to survive.

The island is great for hiking and camping holidays, particularly in summer when the weather is pleasantly cool compared to the rest of the country. In winter, though, it's cold. Temperatures can go down to minus 15°C in Sapporo, below minus 20°C inland, and ice-flows stand off the east coast (i.e. in the Sea of Ouhotsk) every winter. But skiers flock here. Sapporo, the capital, was the site of the Winter Olympics in 1972, and its 90-m (300-ft) Okura-yama Jump Hill is the longest ski-jump in Japan.

Hokkaido is in places very wild, in so far as anywhere in Japan is ever permitted to be wild. Seventy percent of its surface is covered by forest — an astonishing figure. Dangerous Hokkaido brown bears can be found, especially in Daisetsu-zan National Park, swans migrate from nearby Siberia to the east coast, Japanese cranes arrive in villages in the Akan and Kusharo lake areas, and sea-eagles fish off the ice-flows.

HAKODATE

On the instep of the boot that extends southwest of Hokkaido island, the port city of Hakodate is usually rail travelers' first experience of Japan's northern wilderness. Established as a fishing port in the 1740s, it was one of Japan's first ports to open to foreign trade under the conditions of the Kanagawa Treaty (1854). The result is a smattering of interesting Western buildings, and like other port cities such as Yokohama, Kobe and Nagasaki, a cosmopolitan air that makes it a pleasant place to sojourn for a day or two.

GENERAL INFORMATION

Hakodate is a sprawling town, and its sights are spread out. Getting around is easy enough, however, due to a simple to navigate tram network. Hakodate station is in the northeast of town next to the harbor and the lively Asa-ichi, or Morning Market. Most of the city's more interesting sights lay in the west of town, four or five stops by tram from the Eki-mae tram stop in front of the station.

Hakodate's main **Tourist Information Center** ((0138) 23-5440 is in front of the train station — there are several around town. Staff speak English and can help with hotel reservations. In the Motomachi sightseeing district there is another branch of the **Tourist Information Center** ((0138) 27-3333, at 12-18 Motomachi.

WHAT TO SEE AND DO

It doesn't matter who you talk to, if you are overnighting in Hakodate, they will tell you to start your day with a tour of the pungent, rambunctious, never boring Morning Market, or **Asa-ichi**. It's actually a lot of fun, and if you are the adaptable sort who can stomach an Asian-style savory breakfast, there are a lot of places to nibble at sushi and the like — not to mention the squid-ink ice cream (see WHERE TO STAY AND EAT, below).

Hakodate's best known attraction — especially for its night views — is the 334-m (1,096-ft) **Mount Hakodate-yama**, which of course has a cable car (10 AM to 10 PM, daily). Whether or not, as the tourist literature would have us believe, the diminutive mountain looks like a supine cow, on a fine day the views are indeed splendid and worth the slightly expensive round-trip cable-car fare (¥1,160).

At the foot of the mountain is the Motomachi district, with its cobbled streets and Western-style buildings. Buildings worth taking a look at include the **Old British Consulate of Hakodate** (9 AM to 7 PM), which has a functioning tea room, the **Hakodate Orthodox Church** (10 AM to 4:45 PM, to 3:30 PM Saturdays, and 1 PM to 3:35 PM Sundays), and the delightful blue wooden **Old Public Hall of Hakodate Ward** (9 AM to 7 PM, daily). Also in the area and highly recommended is the **Hakodate City Museum of Northern Peoples** (9 AM to 7 PM, daily), which features fascinating exhibits on the Ainu people of Hokkaido. There are several other museums in the Motomachi district, of which one of the most interesting is the **Hakodate Museum of Photographic History** (9 AM to 7 PM, daily).

It's debatable whether it is really worth making a special trip out to the **Goryo-kaku Fort** (8 AM to 7 PM, daily), though you will undoubtedly hear a lot about it in Hakodate. It was Japan's first Western-style fort, and as such is of great interest to Japanese tourists. There is not a lot left to see here, as much of it was destroyed in a Tokugawa last stand against Meiji forces in 1869. To get there, take a 15-minute tram ride from Hakodate station to Goryokaku Koen-mae.

WHERE TO STAY AND EAT

The **Hotel JAL City Hakodate** ((0138) 24-2580 FAX (0138) E-MAIL jalcity@host.or.jp, 27-2581, 22-15 Horai-cho, is Hakodate's top hotel, located in the center of the more interesting western part of town and close to the Horai-cho tram stop. Rates start at around ¥15,000. Less expensive and less luxurious, the **Hakodate Kokusai Hotel** ((0138) 23-5151 FAX (0138) 23-0239, 5-10 Ote-machi, has harbor views and is not far from the station, just west of the Morning Market. It has a splendid *teppan-yaki* restaurant with views, and the rooms, which range from around ¥10,000 per person, are spacious by Japanese standards.

For an interesting mid-range stay, try the **Auberge Kokian** ((0138) 26-5753 FAX (0138) 22-2720, 13-2 Suehiro-cho, which is situated on the eastern fringe of the historic Motomachi district, close to the harbor. The Japanese-style rooms are not the best you will come across in Japan, but the building, which is over 100 years old, has some character, and the hotel is close to the attractions. Rates are from ¥8,000.

The **Niceday Inn** ((0138) 22-5912, 9-11 Ote-machi, has become Hakodate's most popular inexpensive accommodation in recent years. A family-style place, it has four-bed dormitory rooms and rock-bottom rates. It's immediately north of the Shiyakusho-mae tram stop, between Hakodate station and Motomachi.

Hakodate has no shortage of places to eat, as you will see when you start exploring the city. A good place to start looking is the Daimon district, which adjoins Hakodate station and by night becomes a busy strip of neon.

One of Hakodate's most popular places to dine out is the simply named **Hakodate Beer** ((138) 23-8000, 5-22 Ote-machi, which is directly north of the Uoiichiba Dori tram stop, west of the station — a huge place, you can't miss it. The specialty is locally brewed Hakodate Beer, of course, but it also has an extensive menu that ranges from seafood snacks and raw squid to pizza and pasta.

Another extremely popular place to eat out is **Beelong's** ((0138) 26-1122, which is right on the waterfront, not far from the west exit of Hakodate station, and like Hakodate Beer is a microbrewery. It specializes in seafood.

In Motomachi, wander over to the delightful ivy-clad, foreign-run **Raymond House** ((0138) 22-4596, where the specialty is sausages and sandwiches, European style—an exceptional lunch-time treat if you have been in Japan for any time. If the tastes of home are not what you are looking for, be adventurous at the Morning Market and head to **Ore-no-Hakodate** ((0138) 27-5656 for a taste of their unique "squid-ink ice cream." It opens at 4 AM — possibly the perfect start to an interesting day.

How to Get There

There are direct flights from Haneda airport in Tokyo to Hakodate airport, which is 20 minutes north of

Hakodate by bus. From Aomori, JR trains plunge beneath the Tsuguru Kaikyo Straits that separate Honshu and Hokkaido, and stay down there for more than hour (not a journey for the claustrophobic), taking about two and a half hours in all to cover the distance between Aomori and Hakodate. There are also JR sleeper services from Tokyo and Osaka. It's a little over three hours by JR to Sapporo.

SHIKOTSU-TOYA NATIONAL PARK

The most accessible of Hokkaido's five national parks, Shikotsu-toya can be reached easily from either Hakodate or Sapporo, though it makes sense to visit it en-route between the two cities. Despite its accessibility it is a stunning, beautiful destination, a place that verges between European Alpine views and Pacific protean forces of nature. The breathtaking **Lake Toya-ko**, for example, has no fewer than four volcanic islands rearing out of its waters, while close by is the fascinating **Mount Showa Shin-zan**, a so-called "parasitic volcano" of **Mount Usu-zan**, which started growing in 1943 and did so until 1945, reaching a height of 403 m (1,322 ft). The area continues to be very active, as an eruption of Usu-zan in April 2000 proved. It would be wise to check the current situation in either Hakodate or Sapporo before heading out

there, if it is Showa Shin-zan or Usu-zan that you are particularly interested in seeing.

The best way to approach the park is by train from either Hakodate or Sapporo to Toya station, from where buses make a short run to Toya-ko Onsen, a spa resort with expensive accommodation and lots of tourist shops. Mount Showa Shin-zan lies two kilometers (about a mile) to the south of here, and until recently could be combined with a somewhat nerve-wracking cable car ascent of its parent, Mount Usu-zan, which has been puffing and blustering and occasionally erupting for the last 60 years. Needless to say, the recent volcanic activity here has put the cable-car jaunt out of action — whether temporarily or for good is uncertain.

SAPPORO

Japan's fifth largest city is superficially much like other large Japanese cities. But take a closer look, and it starts to assert its identity. It's something like a well laid out, less-bustling version of Osaka: purposeful, practical and down to earth. It's a city that enjoys the good things: dining out, partying. This, combined with a smattering of modest but interesting attractions, makes it more than just a transportation hub from which to tackle Hokkaido's great outdoors. Give the city a day or two, and it is unlikely you will regret it.

One of the city's main attractions is its annual **Yuki Matsuri**, or Snow Festival, which is held in February. Be sure to book accommodation well in advance, however. At other times of the year, the Sapporo Brewery, home to Hokkaido's famous brew, is well worth a visit, as are the city's Botanical Gardens. Farther afield, but within easy striking distance, is the Historical Village of Hokkaido, an attraction that recreates the northernmost island's legendary (for Japanese) frontier days — Japan's "wild north" if you like.

General Information

Of all Japan's major cities, Sapporo is the easiest to get around and find where it is you want to go. The reason is simple: a grid plan and a sensible addressing system that actually works — if only the rest of Japan would follow suit. Indeed, it's accessibility is almost "un-Japanese." Ground zero is the TV Tower in Odori-koen Park, from where numbered blocks roll away in the four cardinal directions: The Seibu department store, just south of Sapporo station, for example, is thus located in North 4 West 3 (written as "N4 W3").

Sapporo station is in the north of town; the commercial center and almost everything of interest lies south of here. Most of the sights are within walking distance of each other, but three subway lines make getting around even easier. The Namboku and Toho lines run parallel to each other north-south from the station, while the east-west Tozai line intersects them both, at Odori station, under Odori-koen Park.

On the information front, for some odd reason, Sapporo is one of Japan's best organized destinations when it comes to assisting foreign travelers. Information outlets are thick on the ground, though the best of them is the **Sapporo International Communication Plaza "I"** ((011) 211-3678, First Floor, MN Building, N1 W3, Chuo-ku, which with a lobby, magazines and so on is more than just an information center. In Sapporo station is the **International Information Corner** ((011) 213-5062, another good place for the usual pamphlets, advice and help with accommodation.

the flora of Hokkaido, but they also contain several museums. The pick of them is the **Ainu Museum** (same hours as the gardens), also known as the Batchelor Memorial Museum. John Batchelor (1854-1944) was a British Anglican missionary who spent more than 60 years in Hokkaido among the Ainu, studying their language and culture, and even writing the *Ainu English Japanese Dictionary* in 1889. The museum features rotating exhibits of its large collection of Ainu artifacts. The **Natural History Museum**, also in the gardens, is less interesting, featuring a somewhat higgledy-piggledy collection of Hokkaido-related items.

Opened in 1876, the original **Sapporo Brewery** has now metamorphosed into the **Sapporo Beer**

It's on the western side of the station in the Lilac Paseo Arcade.

WHAT TO SEE AND DO

The center of Sapporo is **Odori-koen Park**, a block-wide strip, stretching from east to west, at the east end of which is the 147-m-high (481-ft) **TV Tower** (9:30 AM to 6 PM, daily). One block northwest of here is the symbol of Sapporo, the one place that every self-respecting Japanese tourist simple *has* to have a picture taken in front of, the **Toke-dai**, or the Clock Tower. Do not expect too much of this modest wooden structure, which is in its way emblematic of the enigmas of Japanese tourism.

Of more interest is the **Botanical Gardens** (9 AM to 4 PM, daily), a 10-minute walk southwest of Sapporo station. The gardens are a good place to get to know more (or perhaps something) about

Garden and Museum (9 AM to 5 PM, daily), and is probably Sapporo's most popular attraction. A special bus (not the Beer bus, unfortunately) runs from the Seibu Department Store, to the brewery, where guided tours end with samples of the product, after which patrons are turned loose on the restaurants and bars in the premises. Best of all, and that rarest of things in Japan, it's all free.

Along with the brewery, Sapporo's other must-see attraction is the **Historical Village of Hokkaido** (9:30 AM to 4:30 PM, closed Mondays), 14 km (just under nine miles) east of the city. Opened in 1971, it's a massive place with some 60 buildings in four different "regions" that together recreate frontier Hokkaido. It's possible to race around it

OPPOSITE: Figurines carved by Japan's indigenous people, the Ainu, who now live in small numbers in Hokkaido. ABOVE: Hokkaido's famous brew, Sapporo Beer, advertises its "Black Label" product.

in a morning or an afternoon, but to fully appreciate all it has to offer, give yourself a full day. Buses go to the village from Sapporo and Shin Sapporo stations — check with the information centers in Sapporo for the latest schedules.

WHERE TO STAY

Sapporo may be brimming with hotels, but there can still be a tight squeeze on accommodation during the high summer months and during the winter Snow Festival. Be sure to book ahead.

Combining an excellent location close to the Toke-dai Clock Tower in the center of town with first-class standards, the **Hotel New Otani** ((011)

511-7531 FAX (011) 511-7562, S7 W5, a standard business hotel with rates from ¥6,200 per person.

The **Nakamuraya Ryokan** ((011) 241-2111 FAX (011) 241-2118, N3 W7, has been popular with foreigners for many years now. Rates are slightly higher than many of the other Japanese Inn Group inns around Japan, but if you simply can't face another night in a business hotel the Nakamuraya has large Japanese-style rooms and meticulous service.

The most popular budget place to stay in Sapporo is the **Sapporo Inn Nada** ((011) 551-5882 FAX (11) 551-0303 E-MAIL nada@sapporo.e-mail.ne.jp, S5 W9, which is well located just south of Susukino and has dormitory accommodation in tatami rooms at ¥3,500 per person.

222-1111 FAX (011) 222-5521, N2 W1, is one of Sapporo's stand-out hotels. Rates start at ¥25,000. Not quite in the same league, but nevertheless a sound choice in the expensive category is the **Keio Plaza Hotel Sapporo** ((011) 271-0111 FAX (011) 221-5450, N5 W7, which is just north of the Botanical Gardens. Doubles start at ¥26,000.

Worth considering is the **Sapporo Prince Hotel** ((011) 241-1111 FAX (011) 231-5994 WEB SITE WWW .princehotels.co.jp/sapporo-e, S2 W11, which is not far west of Susukino. Like the New Otani and the Keio Plaza, it's part of a reliable Japanese luxury chain and has first-class amenities and rooms.

For something less expensive, **Sapporo Tokyu Inn** ((011) 531-0109 FAX (011) 531-2387, S4 W5, is perfectly located in the heart of the Susukino entertainment district, perfect for nightlife and dining, is good value from ¥8,000. Cheaper again, and in the same part of town, is the **Chisan Hotel** ((011)

WHERE TO EAT AND NIGHTLIFE

Sapporo is famous for its *ramen*, that inexpensive noodle dish found all over Japan. For the complete *ramen* experience head down to **Ramen Alley**, or Ramen Yokocho, S5 W3, next to Susukino subway station, where you can eat your fill for ¥1,000 or less at any of around a dozen bustling *ramen* joints. None of them will win any points for decor, but the bustling atmosphere is enjoyable.

Not surprisingly — Japanese like to call Sapporo the "spiritual home of Japanese beer" — beer halls are big in Sapporo, and are fun places have a meal and a few drinks. At the **Sapporo Beer Garden** ((011) 742-1531, N7 E9, you can make a pig of yourself with the all-you-can-eat-and-drink Genghis Kan Barbecue for ¥3,400 per person, though you are restricted to 100 minutes — fun if you are with a group. Genghis Kan, *jingisu-kan*, is regarded as a

Sapporo specialty, and you will find it offered at numerous other places around town, where it is invariably washed down with gallons of beer. Other popular places to try it include **Yoyotei**, on the fifth floor of the Matsuoka Building, S4 W4, and the **Kirin Beer Garden**, S10 W1.

Sapporo people like to say that their nightlife is second only to Tokyo's. They're up against some stiff competition in Osaka, but it's true that the Susukino district is packed with late-night action. A great place to start an evening (or finish one) and meet some local residents is the rough-and-ready **Mugishutei (** (011) 512-4774, S9 W5, in the basement of the Onda Building. Foreign-run, by local Sapporo legend Phred, it stocks a mind-boggling selection of beers, and prices are reasonable. Under the same management is the **Gaijin Bar (** (011) 272-1033, S2 W7, a second-story bar, that attracts the kind of clientele you would expect from the name.

For late-night club action, check out the massive **King Xhmu (** (011) 531-1388, S7 W4, which is very close to the Gaijin Bar, and is a long-running dance venue. The interior is exotic, to say the least.

How to Get There

New Chitose Airport is connected with all major (and many minor) destinations around Japan. The airport is 40 km (25 miles) northeast of Sapporo, and is linked to Sapporo by rail in around 30 minutes.

Direct sleeper trains from Tokyo to Sapporo take around 16 hours, and from Osaka 22 hours, about as long as you can spend on a direct train in Japan. Hakodate is three and a half hours away from Sapporo by JR limited express.

DAISETSU-ZAN NATIONAL PARK

Daisetsu-zan National Park, right in the center of the island, offers mile after mile of fairly undemanding and very enjoyable hiking. **Asahikawa**, Hokkaido's second city and one hour 34 minutes from Sapporo by Japan Rail, is the gateway to the magnificent area.

Two mountains in the more accessible northern part of the park are **Asahi-dake** (2,290 m or 7,634 ft, and the highest summit on Hokkaido) and **Kuro-dake** (1,984 m or 6,614 ft).

To climb Asahi-dake, take an Asahikawa Denki Kido bus from Asahikawa JR Station to Asahikawa Ropeway bus stop (one and a half hours), take the cable car to Sugatami Station, and then walk — two hours — to the summit.

Going up Kuro-dake is easier. From Kamikawa JR station (a short distance east of Asahikawa), take a Dohoku bus to Sounkyo, and then a cable car or lift to the peak. Sounkyo, incidentally, in the Sounkyo Gorge, is the place to stay in this more frequented part of the park.

Daisetsu-zan (sometimes spelled Taisetsuzan) is very popular with young Japanese, and hostels are often crowded in summer. Skiing, of course, takes place here in winter.

RISHIRI-REBUN-SAROBETSU NATIONAL PARK

The two islands of **Rishi-to** and **Rebun-to** lie to the west of the northern tip of Hokkaido, and are accessible from the small port of **Wakkanai**. This is about as remote as you can get in Japan, and a visit to the islands is really only feasible for travelers with a lot of time on their hands. Rishi-to, with its rearing 1,721-m (5,646-ft) volcanic peak, is the more interesting of the two topographically, and the hike to the summit of the volcano, Rishi-dake, is the most popular activity. Rebun-to, where alpine flowers are a feature, is a popular hiking destination in summer. It's possible to organize ferry tickets to the island on arrival at Wakkanai, and there are also 15-minute flights to the islands. **Sarobetsu**, just under 40 km (25 miles) south of Wakkanai, is a haven for wetland flowers on the mainland nearby.

SHIRETOKO NATIONAL PARK

Shiretoko National Park, in the extreme east of Hokkaido, is a narrow but mountainous peninsula. **Mount Rausu-dake** rises to 1,661 m (5,570 ft), and **Rausu** is the resort (hot springs) at its foot. But there are other peaks — **Io-zan** (1,560 m or 5,200 ft), **Omnebetsu** (1,331 m or 4,438 ft) and **Shiretoko** (1,254 m or 4,180 ft), as well as other spas — **Utoro**, for example. Boat trips can be taken to see the fine coastline.

AKAN NATIONAL PARK

The dramatic remains of past volcanic activity dominate the area in the north of Akan National Park in east Hokkaido. This park features three main lakes, Kusshāro, Mashu and Akan, and two smoldering volcanoes, Mount Me-Akan-dake at 1,499 m (4,995 ft) and Mount O-Akan-dake at 1,371 m (4,570 ft). The spa resort town of **Akan Kohan** to the west of Lake Akan has a small Ainu community, members of whom perform dances and sell Ainu clothing.

The park is usually approached from Kushiro on Hokkaido's south coast, four and a half hours by train from Sapporo; the park itself is two hours by bus, or JR's Semmo line, to the north.

The wintry snow-dusted slopes of Furano in Hokkaido, one of Japan's most famous skiing destinations.

Shikoku

SHIKOKU IS THE SMALLEST OF THE FOUR MAIN ISLANDS of the archipelago and is separated from Western Honshu by the picturesque but much-exploited Inland Sea (*Seto Naikai*). It is a placid, unhurried island with some marvelous festivals and a beautiful south coast, which is popular with divers. There are not as many tourist draws as in Honshu or Kyushu which means that, like the northern coast of southern Honshu, it is an ideal place to get off the beaten track and get a feel for the texture of every day rural life. Shikoku is far from being an unspoiled paradise, however, and the light industrial skirts of the towns and cities sprawl as badly as anywhere else.

Not surprisingly, Shikoku is probably the least visited by foreigners of all the main islands. It's tempting, as guidebook writers will do, to deplore this state of affairs, but the reality is, unless you are a repeat visitor to Japan, Shikoku has little to merit a special visit. There are no great sights, and its charms are mostly of the subtle variety.

TAKAMATSU

Shikoku's main gateway, Takamatsu is very much a one-sight town, though it does have a couple of nearby attractions in **Shikoku Mura**, another open-air museum of traditional houses, and the interesting shrine of **Kotohira-gu**. Originally a castle town under the Kagawa clan, established during the rule of Tokugawa Hideyoshi (1537–1598), it was laid level by bombing in World War II. The postwar years have seen a major rebound, helped not in small part by the building of the Seto-O-hashi Bridge in 1989, which connects Takamatsu with mainland Honshu.

JR Takamatsu station is in the north of the city, next to the harbor and the private Kotoden Chikko station. The city center is immediately south of here, while two kilometers (about a mile) to the south is Ritsurin-koen Park. Not far to the east of Takamatsu station is the Prefectural Pier, where

high-speed ferries connecting Shikoku with Osaka depart and arrive. There's a **Tourist Information Center (** (087) 851-1335 inm Taka matsu station, which has English brochures and can help with accommodation inquiries.

Ritsurin-koen Park (7 AM to 5 PM, daily) is easily the city's foremost attraction. Established in the early seventeenth century, this stroll garden was added to by various Takamatsu lords before falling into the hands of the powerful Matsudaira family. It was opened to the public in 1895. Inside you will find the **Sanuki Folkcraft Museum** (9 AM to 4:30 PM, daily), which has a modestly interesting display of local crafts. One of the garden's highlights is the teahouse in the south garden, where views of the garden can be seen through open *shoji* doors across tatami rooms.

Just east of the station and facing the Inland Sea is **Tamamo-koen Park** (open 9 AM to 5 PM, daily), where what's left of the city's castle stands — not very much, unfortunately.

A good mid-range hotel in Takamatsu is the **Rihga Hotel Zest Takamatsu (** (087) 822-3555 FAX (087) 822-7516 WEB SITE www.rihga.com/kagawa/, 9-1 Furujin-machi. The 133-room hotel has Japanese, Chinese and French restaurants, a shopping arcade, and a good location in the city center, just south of the Hyogo-machi Arcade. Rates start at ¥7,000 per person. Closer to Takamatsu station, on Seto-O-hashi Dori, is the **Takamatsu Terminal Hotel (** (087) 822-3731 FAX (087) 822-0749, 10-17 Nishinomaru-cho, a standard business hotel with rates from ¥6,000.

Takamatsu's local specialty is *sanuki udon*, another variation on the buckwheat noodle theme. The place to try this dish is the famous **Kanaizumi (** (087) 821-6688, 7-21 Daiku-machi, which is five minutes to the southwest of Kotoden Kawaramachi station on Ferry Dori.

Tenkatsu Honten ((087) 821-5380, 7-8 Hyogo-machi, is a famous Takamatsu seafood restaurant where the hapless creatures are snatched from a tank and dispatched at the customers' behest. If you find such scenes disturbing, it is best not to go, but the fish is, however, fresh. It's at the western end of the Hyogo-machi Arcade, just south of Takamatsu station.

Should you want to travel direct from Tokyo to Takamatsu, the quickest way to do it is to take a Shinkansen to Okayama and change there for Takamatsu, a journey of just under five hours. From Okayama, trains take an hour to Takamatsu.

YASHIMA

The main reason to visit Yashima, 20 minutes from Kotoden Takamatsu Chikko station, is the **Shikoku Mura Village** (8:30 AM to 5 PM, daily). An interesting collection of more than 20 traditional buildings collected from around the island and reassembled

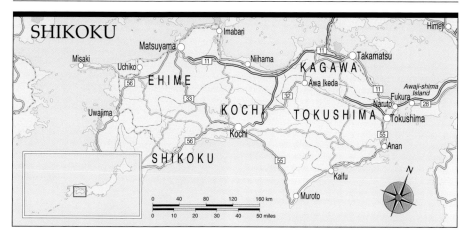

here, it is well worth spending a couple of hours to visit. If you do visit, you may as well take some time out to take a cable car (8 AM to 5:30 PM, daily) up to the **Yashima Plateau**. At the summit is the small **Yashima-ji Temple**, which on a fine day has wonderful views of the Inland Sea.

KOTOHIRA

The small town of Kotohira, with its **Kompira-san Shrine**, is Shikoku's major attraction. It's just 30 minutes from Takamatsu by JR train, and is easily visited as a morning or afternoon trip.

Approached by more than 700 steps — you can resort to a palanquin if you are not feeling up to the climb — the shrine, also known as Kotohira-gu, is dedicated to Omonushi no Kami, the patron deity of fishermen. Originally both a Buddhist and Shinto place of worship, with the separation of the two religions at the beginning of the Meiji restoration, the shrine is now exclusively Shinto.

There are a couple of other minor attractions at the base of the ascent to the shrine. Particularly interesting is the **Kinryo Sake Museum** (9 AM to 5 PM, daily) at the base of the steps, which takes you through the sake-making process and sells samplers at the end.

TOKUSHIMA

Tokushima has several attractions in its vicinity but few in its own right. Its major draw is the annual **Dance Festival**, or Awa Odori, which is held August 15 to 18 — book a long way ahead for accommodation if you plan to visit at this time, as the city's population of just over 250,000 swells nearly five-fold at this time.

Tokushima is also the starting point of Shikoku's famous pilgrimage course, which takes in 88 of the island's temples. The pilgrimage was originated by **Kukai**, or **Kobo Daishi** (774-835), a native of Takamatsu and the founder of the Shingon sect

of Buddhism (see MOUNT KOYA-SAN, page 160, in KANSAI for more on Kukai). The pilgrimage starts at **Ryozen-ji Temple**, near Naruto, and ends up, after circling the island in a clockwise direction, at **Okubu-ji Temple**, near Takamatsu.

People usually embark on such a pilgrimage after retirement. In the old days pilgrims used to hike from temple to temple and the whole course would take some two months. Now most of them go by bus and it takes about a week. They still dress completely in white. Spring and autumn are the most likely seasons in which to spot pilgrims, or *henro*.

Tokushima itself is a compact city, and easy to explore on foot. Tokushima station is in the northeast of town, and the commercial district lies on the other side of the Shinmachi-gawa River. On the sixth floor of Clement Plaza in Tokugawa station is the **Tokushima Prefecture International Exchange Association (TOPIA)** ((088) 656-3303, a surprisingly useful tourist information center.

There is virtually nothing left of Tokushima-jo Castle, but the castle grounds in **Tokushima Chuo-koen Park** (9:30 AM to 5 PM, closed Mondays), not far east of the station, have a pleasant garden, and there is a museum that features exhibits on the history of Tokushima and its erstwhile castle.

Walk east from the station down Shinmachi-bashi Dori, over the river, and you come to Mount Bi-zan, which has a ropeway to the summit.

Tokushima's best hotel is the **Prince** ((088) 624-1111 FAX (088) 624-2375 WEB SITE www.princehotels.co.jp/tokushima-e/index.html, 3-5-1 Bandai-cho, which has a central location overlooking the river. It has the full complement of restaurants (Chinese, Japanese, Continental) and does a brisk business in mostly Japanese tour groups. Rates are from ¥10,000 per person. Also recommended and conveniently located next to Tokushima station is the new

Takamatsu, the gateway to the island of Shikoku's most famous attraction Ritsurin-koen Park, which features landscaped gardens, tea houses and pagodas. It is the island's best example of a "stroll garden."

Clement Tokushima Hotel ((088) 6563111 FAX (088) 656-3132, 61 Nishi-chome, Terashimahon-cho. It's a 250-room hotel with a swimming pool and great views from its upper floors. Rates are from ¥9,000.

The **Tokushima Youth Hostel** ((088) 663-1505 is a long way out of town, and transportation is inconvenient. If you are looking for budget accommodation, you would be better off heading for Kochi, which has a much better located youth hostel.

If you are just passing through Tokushima, as is the case with most travelers, the station is the best place to grab a bite to eat. If the station selection is unappetizing, try the fifth floor of the adjacent Clement Plaza.

NARUTO

One of the main reasons to visit Tokushima is the Naruto Whirlpools, which surge in the narrow strait between Shikoku and Awaji-shima Island in the Inland Sea. Take a train from Tokushima, and then transfer to a bus for the Naruto-O-hashi Bridge, from where tour boats head out into the whirlpools. It would be wise to check with the tourist information center in Tokushima about weather conditions (which sometimes force the boats to cancel) before heading out to Naruto.

KOCHI

If you are doing a circuit of the island, Kochi is a good city to overnight in. It's a castle town that still has a castle, and there are several attractions around the city that are worth seeing.

The station is in the northeast of town, and running south from it is Harimaya-bashi Dori. The city center is focused on several arcades, which run west of Harimaya-bashi Dori to the south of the Enokuchi-gawa River. The city has a tram network, which runs south along Harimaya-bashi Dori, and west along Dencha Dori, providing access to almost everything of interest within the city.

The **Kochi "i" Information Center** ((088) 882-7777 is in JR Kochi station has English-speaking staff and is a useful source of information.

Kochi's main attraction is **Kochi-jo Castle** (9 AM to 4:30 PM, daily), built in 1603 and rebuilt after a devastating fire around 1750. Some of the castle's interesting exhibits include some wobbly attempts at Roman calligraphy, pre-modern toys (wooden whales on wheels) and impressive photos, blown up to enormous size, of the castle's nineteenth-century samurai proprietors, looking as fierce and noble as American Indians.

From the station, buses run to the **Godaisan-koen Park** (9 AM to 5 PM, daily), a short journey of around 15 minutes. In the garden precincts are **Chikurin-ji Temple**, one of Shikoku's oldest, and the **Makino Botanical Gardens**, both of which are worth a look. **Katsura-hama Beach**, while touted

as a major attraction by city authorities, is really only worth a visit if you have lots of time on your hands. It's 13 km (eight miles) south of the city center; buses run there from Kochi station.

The **New Hankyu Kochi Hotel** ((088) 873-1111 FAX (088) 873-1145, 2-50 4-chome Hon-machi, is a massive luxury hotel, just south of the castle on Dencha Dori. With a swimming pool, fitness center, five restaurants, two bars and 243 rooms, it's actually one of the best hotels on Shikoku.

If you don't mind being outside Kochi proper, the moderately priced, **Hotel Katsurahama-so** ((088) 841-2201 FAX (088) 841-2249, at Katsurahama Beach, 13 km (eight miles) south of Kochi, has Japanese-style rooms, all meals provided, and views of the beach from its hot spring. Rates are from ¥8,500, meals extra.

For something slightly less expensive and closer to town — close to the castle — the **Kochi Green Hotel** ((088) 825-2701 FAX (088) 825-2703,

5-6-11 Hon-machi, is recommended. It's a simple business hotel in a popular chain, but is adequate for an overnight stay, and has rates from ¥7,000.

The **Kochi Eki-mae Youth Hostel** ((088) 883-5086, 3-3-10 Kitahon-machi, is one of the island's best. It has a convenient location around 10 minutes by foot east of the station, and it also has private rooms along with usual dormitory accommodation.

For places to eat, explore the **Otesuji** and **Obiya-machi arcades** in the center of town. Kochi is a lively town by night, with literally dozens of bars and Japanese-style pubs.

Kochi is around two and a half hours by train from Takamatsu on the JR Dosan line.

UWAJIMA

At the western extreme of the island and accessible by rail from the north or south, Uwajima is famous for its bloodless **bullfighting**, in which two of the beasts lock horns and strive to push each other backwards: it's fairly similar to sumo wrestling. The sport takes place only seven days of the year, making it unlikely you will be able to time your trip with a show. Bullfighting dates in Uwajima are as follows: January 2; the first Sunday of March and of April; the third Sunday of May; July 24; August 14; and the third Sunday of November.

Uwajima's other, somewhat quirky, attraction is the fertility shrine **Taga-jinja** (8 AM to 5 PM, daily), which houses a phallic log and a small sex museum, whose exhibits are nothing if not eclectic — not to mention explicit.

Uwajima can be visited en-route between Kochi (three and a half hours) and Matsuyama (one and a half hours), or as a day trip from Matsuyama.

One of Japan's best-preserved castles, Matsuyama-jo Castle with its original keep dating from 1664, is a major tourist attraction in Shikoku.

UCHIKO

Another interesting stopover between Kochi and Matsuyama is the small town of Uchiko, which has a well preserved street of Edo-era (1600-1867) buildings. The attractions are all a good 20-minute trudge, but it is not an unpleasant walk.

Uchiko's old street is **Yoka-ichi**, which means literally "eight-day market." It begins with a sake brewery and the usual tourist shops, before reaching the **Machiya Shiryo-kan Museum**, an interesting restored merchant's house. Farther along the street are numerous other restored houses that can be visited. On the way to Yoka-ichi, or on the way back, look out for the **Uchiko-za Kabuki Theater**, not that performances are held here any more (or only very occasionally). It is open to the public, however, and interesting to poke around in.

Uchiko is just half an hour from Matsuyama by train, or an hour from Uwajima.

MATSUYAMA

It is Shikoku's most populous city (450,000), and in many ways, for anyone who has only time to make a brief excursion into Shikoku, probably the island's most worthwhile excursion. The city came into existence in the early 1600s with the construction of a castle, which despite the usual calamities and repairs is essentially still standing. The city is also famed for its nearby Dogo Onsen, the setting of Soseki Natsume's popular novel *Botchan* — the author's face appears on the ¥1,000 note.

Matsuyama station is in the east of town, but the city center is a short hop away by tram, and once there the city sights are easily explored on foot. In the station you will find the JR **Tourist Information Office** ((089) 931-3914, which can provide maps and English information about the city. But the best place to go for information is the **Ehime Prefectural International Center** ((089)

943-6688, 8 Horinouchi, which is actually inside the castle moat area, to the south of the castle.

The city's number-one attraction is **Matsuyama-jo Castle** (9 AM to 5 PM, daily) with its three-story keep. It commands a central position in the city, and is one of Japan's best-preserved. Set on a hilltop among trees, it provides framed views east to the Inland Sea and west to the Ishizuchi mountains. A ropeway ascends to the castle from the west of the grounds, where you will also find the **Shinonome-jinja Shrine**. Be sure to visit also the **Ninomaru Shiseki Teien Gardens** (closed Mondays), which are in the south of the grounds.

Matsuyama's other outstanding attraction is **Dogo Onsen**, said to be Japan's most ancient hot spring and housed in the Dogo Hon-kan, which dates from the 1890s. A bath here is an obligatory ritual of any visit to Matsuyama, and staff provide an English-language instruction manual to see foreigners through the mysteries of hot-spring bath-

ing. For a little extra (¥1,240) you can bathe in a private room. It is a 15-minute tram ride to the Dogo Onsen stop from Matsuyama station.

Also of interest is **Ishite-ji Temple**, the best-known of the city's eight temples. Located about one kilometer (half a mile) east of Dogo Onsen, its Kamakura-period (1192–1333) gate has been designated a National Treasure.

WHERE TO STAY AND EAT

Matsuyama's top-rated *ryokan* is not surprisingly at Dogo Onsen. The **Funaya Ryokan** ((089) 947-0278, 1-33 Dogo, is the royal *ryokan* experience complete with hot-spring bathing. It is, needless to say, an expensive experience, with rates of over ¥30,000 per person including meals.

Back in town, Matsuyama's best hotel is the **ANA Hotel Matsuyama** ((089) 933-5511 FAX (089) 921-6053 WEB SITE www.ananet.or.jp/anahotels/e/direct/japan/shichu/matsu.html, 3-2-1 Ichiban-cho. It has all the usual luxury amenities, French, Chinese and Japanese restaurants, a shopping arcade, 333 guest rooms, and great views of the nearby castle.

For moderately priced accommodation in the city center, the **Matsuyama Tokyu Hotel** ((089) 941-0109 FAX (089) 934-3725, 3-3-1 Ichiban-cho, is recommended. It's right next to the southeast corner of the castle grounds and the Ichiban-cho tram stop, a perfect location for seeing the city. Rates start at ¥8,000.

The **Matsuyama Youth Hostel** ((089) 933-6366, 22-3 Himezukaotsu, Dogo, is one of Japan's top-rated youth hostels, and with good reason. Along with dormitory accommodation, it has budget double rooms, and the food here is highly rated. With a good location in the Dogo area, it's an excellent place to be based in Matsuyama.

Matsuyama is renowned for its confectionery, of which the *taruto* (derived from the English word "tart") is one of the more famous. You will find many places selling this sweet, sponge-like substance at Dogo. Another famous dish is *somen* noodles, which are multi-colored. Matsuyama's most famous purveyor of this unique dish is **Goshiki Somen** ((089) 933-3838, next to the post office on Sanban-cho Dori, south of the castle.

HOW TO GET THERE

Regular ferries go from the newly expanded Matsuyama Kanko Port to Hiroshima, and take about one hour. To get to the port, take the private Tetsudo line to Takahama, the last stop. The JR Yosan line connects Matsuyama to Takamatsu in a northern route across the island that takes around two and a half hours.

Perhaps Japan's most famous hot-spring resort is Dogo Onsen near Matsuyama. It has been celebrated in literature and has been offering rest in its health-bestowing waters for around four centuries.

Kyushu

HONSHU — JAPAN'S "MAIN ISLAND" — IS THE RECIPIENT of most of Japan's tourist traffic, and rightly so: by virtue of its cultural attractions alone, it is by far the most important of the Japanese islands. When it comes time to jump islands, and you should if you want to experience Japan to the full, the obvious second choice is Kyushu. After all, the most southerly of Japan's four main islands may not have the cultural abundance that Honshu does, but it still manages to pack in a lot to do, and at a less hurried pace than its big northern neighbor.

Kyushu, with its often stunning natural vistas, has a long and rich history and offers some of the most rewarding sightseeing in the country. As the nearest point in Japan to the continent, it was in the early days the jumping-off point for immigrants from China and Korea, and later became a conduit for the foreign ideas that have now permeated modern Japanese society. In the battle to modernize, it was more often than not reformers from Kyushu who were at the avant-garde.

Despite this, oddly enough, Kyushu, especially the south, has been spared the intensity of devel-opment that marks Honshu. The cities are generally compact, friendly places that give way before you know it to unsullied landscapes that in Honshu usually require considerable effort to get to.

Some of Kyushu's highlights include the surprisingly beautiful city of Fukuoka, a modern, increasingly important city that is one of Japan's greenest; Kumamoto, with its castle; the soaring volcanic peak of Mount Aso-san; the tacky and yet fascinating Las Vegas of hot spring resorts, Beppu; the lively port city of Kagoshima, overlooked by the smoking cone of Sakura-jima; Miyazaki, with its beach in a dome; and lastly, but definitely not least, the island's premiere attraction, Nagasaki.

FUKUOKA/HAKATA

Entering Kyushu from the north, the first city trains pass through Kitakyushu (it means "North Kyushu"), the center of a stolid industrial belt, which does not bode well of things to come. It might be easy to think the same is true of Fukuoka, a city of 1.3 million at the southern terminus of the Shinkansen. Nothing could be farther from the truth. Over the last decade Fukuoka has reinvented itself, becoming something of a garden city, a vibrant cultural center, and according to many surveys one of Asia's "most livable cities."

Somewhat confusingly, you will see the names Fukuoka and Hakata used interchangeably. Strictly speaking, the name Fukuoka describes the section of the city west of the Naka-gawa River, while the east side is called Hakata — which is also the name of the railway station, the southwestern terminus of the Tokaido Shinkansen.

Even if you pass on Fukuoka's fairly limited attractions, at least use the city as base to visit nearby shrine and temple town of Dazaifu.

GENERAL INFORMATION

While Fukuoka is a sprawling city, it is not difficult to navigate. The station is in the east (Hakata) section of town, home to the winning Canal City mall development and many of the city's hotels. Meanwhile, west of the Naka-gawa river, which cuts through the center of the city north to south, is the Tenjin commercial district. An island in the river constitutes the famed (at least in Japan) Nakasu entertainment district.

Tourist offices are thick on the ground, and are a good place to collect information, not just on Fukuoka itself but on destinations farther afield in Kyushu. First stop for most visitors is the **Fukuoka City Tourist Information** ((009) 2431-3003 in Hakata station. For more detailed information on Fukuoka the **Fukuoka International Association Rainbow Plaza** ((09) 2733-2220, eighth floor, IMS Building, 1-17-11, Tenjin, Chuo-ku, is an office that is geared mostly to those living or about to settle in Fukuoka, but staff will also gladly help tourists. Also, in the Acros Fukuoka Building in Tenjin is the **Fukuoka Tourist Information Center** ((09) 2725-9100, 1-1-1, Tenjin, Chuo-ku, which is on Showa Dori not far west of the Naka-gawa River.

Walking from one end of town to the other is not a sensible proposition, particularly on a sweaty summer's day, but the city's subway system makes short work of even the most far-flung city destinations. The Kuko line runs from the airport to Hakata and the east-west through central Fukuoka, while the less useful Hakozaki line branches off one stop east of Tenjin station.

WHAT TO SEE AND DO

Fukuoka is an extremely pleasant city to stroll around — vibrant, colorful — and though it's not rich in sights, there are still some worthwhile attractions.

Fifteen minutes on foot north of Hakata station is **Shofukuji**, a temple of the Rinzai Zen sect, which is said to have been founded in 1195 by Eisai

(1141–1215). But apart from its reputed antiquity, it is not a major attraction today, having been badly damaged in World War II.

West of the station look out for **Kushida-jinja**, a shrine with nearly 1,300 years of history, though if it doesn't look that way it's because the shrine is regularly rebuilt, as at Ise. Close by is the **Hakata Machiya Folk Museum** (10 AM to 6 PM, daily), which has exhibits about the city's history with regular dance performances and artisans displaying traditional crafts.

To the west of here, bordering the river, is **Canal City**, a futuristic mall that really does stand out from most of the others around Japan. Its winning feature is its interior courtyard lined with restaurants — a great place to visit early evening and seek out a drink. The **Nakasu** entertainment district to the north of here gets a lot of promotion as one of Japan's largest nightlife areas. But, while a colorful area to explore by night, it's not particularly accessible in terms of nightlife.

Just 30 minutes south of Fukuoka, and virtually a suburb of the city, is the shrine and temple town of **Dazaifu**. The chief attraction is **Temman-gu Shrine** (8:30 AM to 5 PM, daily), which is dedicated to Sugowara no Michizane (AD 845–903), a brilliant scholar exiled to Dazaifu on false charges from Kyoto, which after his death was struck by violent storms and earthquakes. He is now worshipped as a manifestation of Tenjin, and has become the god of scholars. It's a fascinating shrine to explore, and nearby are several temples also worth visiting, notably **Kanzeon-ji Temple**, which has an eighth-century bell.

Dazaifu is easily reached on the Nishitetsu line. Get off at Nishitetsu Fukuoka station in Tenjin, Fukuoka.

WHERE TO STAY AND EAT

Fukuoka's best hotel is far and away the **Grand Hyatt Fukuoka** ((09) 2282-1234 FAX (09) 2282-2817 WEB SITE www.hyatt.com/japan/fukuoka/hotels/hotel_fukgh.html, 1-2-82 Sumiyoshi, Hakata-ku. Apart from anything else, it has a superb location in Canal City, the futuristic mall overlooking the river that is a great place to dine and have fun. As for the hotel itself, it has nine restaurants to choose from. The beautifully appointed rooms come with modems, two telephone lines and personal safes.

Also in Canal City but considerably less expensive is the **Canal City Fukuoka Washington Hotel** ((09) 2282-8900 FAX (09) 2282-0757, 1-2-20 Sumiyoshi, Hakata-ku. With rates from around ¥9,000, it's a smart option that puts you in the thick of things without breaking the budget.

The less expensive accommodation is in the Hakata station area, where you will find the massive **Hakata Green Hotel** ((09) 2451-4111 FAX (09) 2451-4508, 4-4 Hakataeki Chuo-gai, Hakata-ku, where routine business-style rooms start at ¥6,200. There are actually two branches of this hotel, together on the northeast corner of the station, and if one is full they will automatically put you in the other — the contact details above are for the Green Hotel 1.

Fukuoka's nearest youth hostel is in rural town of Dazaifu, just 30 minutes away. The **Dazaifu Youth Hostel** ((09) 2922-8740 is around 10 minutes by foot northwest of the Temman-gu Shrine. Along with dormitory accommodation, it also has a few private rooms.

On the food front, Fukuoka is a surprisingly cosmopolitan city, and it is a good place to take a break from Japanese cuisine. First stop should be

popular bar and a good place to meet people. It's south of Meiji Dori, five minutes walk from the Tenjin subway station; if you're having trouble finding it, stop any wandering *gaijin* and ask for directions.

HOW TO GET THERE

Fukuoka is the main gateway to Kyushu for travelers from Tokyo. Flying to Fukuoka Airport takes one hour from Osaka and one hour 40 minutes from Tokyo. The Tokaido Shinkansen from Tokyo via Kyoto and Osaka terminates at Hakata, Fukuoka's station, and the journey from Tokyo takes about six hours.

Food Live ((09) 2282-1234, the international basement food court in the Grand Hyatt Hotel, Canal City. If "food court" sounds uninspiring, this one may change your mind. The atmosphere is great, and you have a choice of Italian, Chinese, Japanese and Mongolian restaurants (to name a few), all of them top class.

In the Hakata area, try **Ngoi Sao** ((09) 2474-6932, 4-12-27 Hakata-eki-minami, a family run Vietnamese restaurant. For high quality Indian food, look out for branches of the Tokyo chain, **Nanak** ((09) 2713 7900, Second Floor, Ozai Building, 1-1-4 Maizuru, Chuo-ku. There are three branches at last count, but the head branch is in Tenjin, on the corner of Showa Dori and Oyafuku Dori.

For food and drinks, with the option to linger into the wee hours, the **Happy Cock** ((09) 2734 2686, ninth floor, New Palace Building, 51-1 Daimyo 2-chome, Chuo-ku, is Fukuoka's most

BEPPU

Beppu might well classify as Japan's most famous hot-spring resort, and has some startling statistics: more than 12 million visitors a year; more than 3,000 hot springs; and more than 100 million liters (220 million gallons) of hot water bubbling up from underground to the surface daily.

It is without a doubt one of Japan's oddest tourist attractions — at least for foreigners. At Beppu, more than anywhere else in Japan, the hot-spring obsession gets taken to an almost absurd extreme. This is the Las Vegas of hot springs — invariably tacky, overrun with tourists, and immensely popular. In all honesty, it does not deserve a great deal of time. There are several hot-spring sights, but once you are done with them and have had your obligatory soak, there is little else to do but move on.

Beppu station is in the southeast of town, close to Beppu Bay. Call into the station **information desk** ((0977) 23-1119 when you arrive for a free English map and for help with accommodation if you plan to spend the night.

From the east exit of the station, the Kamenoi bus company has buses that head out to Beppu's famous *jigoku*, or "hells." Each of these bubbling, steaming hot-spring hells (the Japanese are fascinated by anything redolent of pain) has its unique character, but you can safely save the price of admission on most of them. The ones worth seeing are **Umi Jigoku** ("sea hell"), with a beautiful expanse of blue water, **Shira-ike Jigoku** ("white pond hell"), which as the name suggests is white —

rather like a pool of milk — and **Chino-ike Jiguku** ("blood pool hell"), which has a pool of … well, you can guess by now.

Not far from Kannawa bus station (close to the hells) is the **Beppu Hino-kan Sex Museum** (9 AM to 11 PM, daily). Sex and hot springs go together like a horse and carriage for the Japanese, and this museum with its titillating displays related to sex in all its permutations (look out for Snow White and the seven dwarves) fits in perfectly with its surroundings.

Also available at Beppu is the famous hot-sand bath, *sunayu*. This is to be found at **Takegawa**, near Beppu station. One of the women at the bath digs a hole in the naturally hot sand for you. Having undressed, and not forgetting your little towel, climb in and she will heap more sand around you, up to the neck if you like. The unearthly feeling of relaxation as the heat penetrates to your bones

has to be experienced to be believed. And it's not expensive — only a few hundred yen.

If you plan to spend a night in Beppu, consider spending it at the luxury **Suginoi Hotel** ((0977) 24-1141 FAX (0977) 21-0010, 1 Kankaiji. It's renowned for its vast baths, housed in glazed structures the size of aircraft hangars (one for each sex) and with the atmosphere of a tropical hot house in a botanical garden. There are dozens of baths of different sizes, shapes and temperatures, and ornaments include a waterfall, a slide, a *torii* gate and a revolving image of a benignly smiling Buddha. Discount rates are available mid-week and off-season.

For somewhere to stay near the station at inexpensive rates, the long-running **Kagetsu Ryokan** ((0977) 24-2355 FAX (0977) 23-7327, 7-22 Tanoyu-cho, is highly recommended. This is not a stand-at-ceremony *ryokan* but a friendly home-stay full of bric-a-brac and tourist information. Rates start from ¥4,500.

Not far south of the Suginoi is **Beppu Youth Hostel** ((0977) 23-4116, 2 Kankaiji. It has private tatami rooms as well as the usual dormitory accommodation, and is one of Japan's better hostels to stay in.

Ferries connect Beppu with Osaka, Hiroshima and Matsuyama (among other places) — they are run by the **Kansai Kisen Ferry Company** ((0977) 22-1311. The JR Nippo line has trains from Fukuoka, which take a little over two hours. The JR Hohi line runs inland from here to Kumamoto via Mount Aso-san.

MOUNT ASO-SAN

The countryside between Beppu on the east and Kumamoto on the west is among the most dramatic on the island. While it can be enjoyed from the train, the trip along Yamanami Highway, which links Beppu with Kumamoto and continues to Nagasaki, is famous for its marvelous views. Whichever way you go, the high point of the trip is Mount Aso-san, one of Japan's most fascinating volcanoes.

The first thing the visitor notices on arriving in the small town of Aso is how extraordinarily flat the tops of the surrounding mountains are; and they are all of uniform height. The reason is that you are standing in the largest volcanic crater of its kind in the world, 24 km (15 miles) long, 19 km (11 miles) wide and 120 km (75 miles) in circumference. Those mountains are the crater's rim. The size of the actual volcano of which in very ancient days this was the active crater boggles the mind. Mount Fuji would have been a mere molehill next to it.

One of Japan's most impressive volcanic calderas can be seen at Mount Aso-san in Kyushu — it is the biggest of its kind in the world, measuring 125 km (75 miles) in circumference.

Buses run from the Sanko bus terminal, next door to Aso station, up the mountain. There's a small **tourist information office** ((0967) 34-0250 in the station, where English is spoken and the staff can help with organizing accommodation.

If you do nothing else, at least take the bus journey up the mountain: Within this huge crater, the countryside is lush and green. Cattle and horses (raw horsemeat, sliced thin and eaten like raw fish, is the local delicacy) graze on the rich grass. There are views of the volcanic peak Komezuka, whose name "rice hill" comes from its indented summit, which looks for all the world like it might have been made by a huge thumb.

Break the journey if you like at the **Aso Volcanic Museum** (9 AM to 5 PM, daily). It has informative displays on seismic and volcanic activity around the world, and best of all video cameras inside the active crater: when an eruption takes place it is possible to watch it on screens at the museum.

The bus terminates at Aso-san Nishi (also West station) from where it's a five-minute ropeway ride or a 15-minute walk to the edge of the crater. As you climb, the landscape grows grim, gray and lifeless. Concrete shelters with massive walls and roofs begin to appear near the road. On the rubble of the most recent eruptions wisps of grass hang tenuously.

Even so, the vast desolation of the crater is an impressive sight. At the bottom is a bright green, steaming lake. This, the largest of the mountain's five craters, is 600 m (1,964 ft) across and 160 m (524 ft) deep. Black, sulphurous clouds bellow from within, and occasionally deep rumblings can be heard.

The volcano is as deadly as it looks. The last major eruption was in 1979, when three died and 16 were injured. Nevertheless, it is closely monitored, and ascents of the mountain are not permitted if it is in a particularly bad mood.

In terms of convenience, the best place to stay is in the Aso station area, where you will find a number of hotels and inns. Providing your visit does not coincide with a major holiday, finding accommodation at the last minute will not be a problem. The **Aso Youth Hostel** ((0967) 34-0804, 922-2 Bochu, Aso-machi, Aso-gun, is around a 20-minute walk from the station (taxis are also available) and is a good place to be based if you want to do longer hikes in the area, as it has maps and information in English. Only dormitory accommodation is available, however.

KUMAMOTO

One hour by train from Aso, Kumamoto might be yet another missable urban agglomeration were it not for a fine reconstructed castle and a splendid stroll garden. As such it makes a good base from which to visit Mount Aso-san, and is interesting enough to merit a morning or an afternoon of sightseeing itself.

GENERAL INFORMATION

Kumamoto can be slightly confusing at first because it is almost like two cities. Kumamoto station is far to the south, with the usual concentration of business hotels, fast-food outlets and shopping centers, while the city center proper is two kilometers (about a mile) north, on the far side of the Shira-kawa River. This is not as problematic as it first appears, however, as a convenient tram system runs from the station into the city, where it splits into two lines: one circling the castle and the other heading into the far east of the town and providing access to the Suizenji-koen Garden.

The Kumamoto City Tourist Information Desk ((096) 352-3743 is inside Kumamoto station. The Kumamoto Airport Information Office ((096) 232-2810 is at the airport, which is around 15 km (nine miles) out of town and linked to Kumamoto by buses that run to the Kumamoto Kotsu Center just south of the castle.

WHAT TO SEE AND DO

Kumamoto's star attraction is **Kumamoto-jo Castle** (8:30 AM to 5:30 PM, daily). It may be a reconstruction, but it is a particularly good one. It is Japan's third largest castle, after Osaka and Nagoya (also reconstructions), and it was first built in 1601. As all the tourist information points out, the walls were built in the *musha gaeshi* style, meaning the concave walls were impossible to scale. The castle was put to the test in 1877 when Saigo Takamori, an important figure in the Meiji restoration who later became disillusioned and raised arms against imperial forces, laid siege to it during the Satsuma Rebellion. The castle held out for 55 days until imperial reinforcements saved the day, but it was nearly destroyed in the process. The best way to approach the castle is from the southwestern entrance next to Kumamotojo-mae tram stop.

Be sure to visit **Suizenji-koen Park** (7:30 AM to 6 PM April to October, 8 AM to 5:30 PM the rest of the year). It was laid out over an 80-year period starting in 1632; it is a depiction of the old Tokaido Road between Kyoto and Tokyo in miniature — the famous scenes are Mount Fuji and Lake Biwa. There is torch-lit *no* theater at the park's Izumi Shrine on the first Saturday evening of August. Get there as early as possible if you want to avoid the crowds. Access is from the Suizenjikoen-mae tram stop.

WHERE TO STAY AND EAT

The **Kumamoto New Otani Hotel** ((096) 326-1111 FAX (096) 326-0800, 1-13-1 Kasuga, is a good luxury choice, even if the location, next to Kumamoto station, is less than ideal. The attractions, however, are easy to reach by tram or taxi, and the hotel offers the reliably high standards maintained by the New Otani group. Rates start at ¥11,000.

The **Kumamoto Hotel Castle** ((096) 326-3311 FAX (096) 326-3324, 4-2 Joto-machi, has an excellent location just south of the castle, and has a range of rooms from standard mid-range at ¥8,500 per person to luxury Japanese and Western suites.

A popular mid-range hotel where English is spoken is the **Hotel Maruko** ((096) 353-1241 FAX (096) 353-1217, 11-10 Kamitori-cho. Rooms are Japanese-style with attached bathrooms and rates are from ¥6,000. It's directly east of the northern part of the castle, though not convenient to any tram stops.

for its *ramen* soup noodles. Its success led to the opening a branch in Tokyo.

HOW TO GET THERE

Kumamoto is well connected with the rest of Kyushu. See under MOUNT ASO-SAN, above, for information on how to get there. The Kagoshima line connects Kumamoto with both Hakata to the north and Kagoshima to the south.

NAGASAKI

If Kyushu has one compelling destination, it is Nagasaki. A port city, like Kobe and Yokohama,

The **Suizenji Youth Hostel** ((096) 9193, 1-2-20 Hakuzan, is out at Suizenji-koen Park. Accommodation is dormitory-style in tatami rooms.

Even if you are just passing through Kumamoto, if you are looking for something decent to eat, the station area is best avoided for the city center, where in the numerous arcade streets clustered between and around Shinshigai and Ginza Doris you will find hundreds of places to eat.

On Ginnan Dori, look for **Ginnan** ((096) 356-7788, Hanabata-cho, one of Kumamoto's most famous outlets for its interesting cuisine. This is the place, should you be game, to try the region's sliced raw horse meat, or *basashi*. There is another branch of this famous restaurant in the Kumamoto Hotel Castle ((096) 326-3311 (see above).

Difficult to find but worth the effort is **Keika Honten** ((096) 325-9609, 11-First Floor, 9KI Building, Hanabata-cho, which is renowned in Kumamoto

it has a vibrant, cosmopolitan atmosphere. Yet, unlike Yokohama and Kobe, it is rich in historical sights, and as Japan's other A-Bomb victim it has another, darker dimension that is superbly underscored in its A-Bomb Hypocenter.

Nagasaki, unlike Hiroshima, was not completely flattened by the world's second A-bomb. In fact, far more than any other Japanese city, Nagasaki is a meeting-place of peoples and cultures, almost a living museum of Japan's interaction with the outside world over the last 400 years.

BACKGROUND

Nagasaki became an important port when it was opened to foreign trade in 1571 at Portuguese request. Commerce and Christianity — which

Oura Catholic Church near Glover Park, built in 1864, is the oldest Gothic-style structure in Japan.

inevitably went hypocritically hand-in-hand during the West's expansion eastwards — flourished.

Not for long. In 1597, 20 Japanese and six Portuguese Christians were crucified. In 1639 the Tokugawa shogunate instituted the National Seclusion policy, which limited foreign trade to the Dutch and the Chinese, isolating them on an artificial island (the beginning of a lasting Japanese obsession, perhaps) in Nagasaki Harbor called Dejima. The National Seclusion policy was to stay in place for 200 years, but it didn't stop Nagasaki becoming a conduit for the percolation of ideas that in their time would change Japan forever.

It's hardly surprising, then, that Puccini's opera *Madam Butterfly* (1904) should have been set in

Board trams at from the rear, and pay the ¥100 flat-fare as you leave the tram from the front. One-day passes for ¥500 are available at Nagasaki hotels and the information desks, and are good value if you are spending a day seeing the sights.

The **Nagasaki City Tourist Information Office** ((095) 823-3631 is just outside Nagasaki station, but a better place to go is across the overhead footbridge to the **Nagasaki Prefectural Tourist Federation** ((095) 826-9407, which is on the second floor of the Kenei bus station, and can suply more detailed information.

Look out for copies of the giveaway English magazine *Nagasaki Beat*, which has information on current events around town.

Nagasaki (though not actually in Thomas Glover's house — see below — as some visitors like to believe). The English writer Rudyard Kipling was here too, in 1888, when he found the city characterized by "perfect cleanliness" and "rare taste." He went on to remark that the landscape was one of delicate pastel shades. The comment is echoed in the title of British novelist Kazuo Ishiguro's novel *A Pale View of the Hills* (1983).

GENERAL INFORMATION

Once you are in the city center, Nagasaki can be explored on foot. Nagasaki station, however, is about a kilometer (half a mile) north of the city center, while the A-Bomb Hypocenter is around two kilometers (a little over a mile) farther north again. As in other Kyushu cities, a tram network saves the day, making it relatively easy to get around.

WHAT TO SEE AND DO

Three days after an atomic bomb was dropped on Hiroshima, at 11:02 AM, August 9, 1945, Nagasaki met the same fate. The temperature at the hypocenter was twice as hot as that needed to melt iron; people three and a half kilometers (over two miles) away suffered skin burns. The Nagasaki bomb, which used plutonium 239, was larger and more powerful than the Hiroshima bomb, but it caused less damage, largely due to the hilly nature of the city and the fact that the bomb was dropped three kilometers (one and a half miles) north of the city center. The death toll in Nagasaki is thought to have been between 60,000 and 70,000 people.

Nagasaki was only chosen as a target when cloud and smoke prevented the bombing of Kokura in Kitakyushu. Matsuyama, which is the hypocenter of the explosion, has several memorials to the event: a black pillar in **Hypocenter Park** marks the exact spot of the explosion; the **Peace Park** with its Peace Statue, and the **Atomic Bomb Museum** (8:30 AM to 5 PM, daily), also known as the **International Culture Hall**.

All deserve visiting, but the Atomic Bomb Museum in particular is a must-see. A spiral walkway takes you past exhibits deeper into scenes of devastation, while other exhibits look at the history of arms proliferation and faltering attempts to impose test-bans. The video library of interviews with survivors is at times heart-breaking. To get there from Nagasaki, take a short tram ride to the Matsuyama stop.

East of Nagasaki station is the **Memorial to the 26 Martyrs**, which remembers Japanese and foreign Christians who were crucified here by the Tokugawa shogunate in 1597 as a warning to the growing Christian community. The turtle-shaped building to the south of here is an eccentric reconstruction of the 1628 **Fukusai-ji Temple**. Inside is a giant Foucault's pendulum. Close by, **Shofuku-ji Temple** survived the bomb, and has pleasant grounds to stroll in. Not far away is **Suwa-jinja Shrine**, which again is notable for its grounds.

From Suwa-jinja, it is recommended to take the pleasant walk along the Nakashima-gawa River, which is crossed by a succession of quaint bridges —most famously **Magane-bashi Bridge**, or "spectacles bridge" on account of its two arches. Cross the bridge and keep walking, and you will reach **Shofuku-ji Temple**, a Chinese Zen (*chan*) temple built by the local Chinese community in 1629. If your legs haven't given out by this point, you can walk south from here through the laid-back **Maruyama** entertainment district (very tame by Japanese standards) to **Chinatown** itself. Like other Japanese Chinatowns, there is not a great deal to see here, but it has more character than its equivalents in Kobe and Yokohama.

The area adjoining here is **Dejima**, which is no longer an island. Once the West's sole point of contact with Japan, and a trading enclave first for the Portuguese and then for the Dutch, there is little to see there now besides the interesting **Nagasaki Museum of History and Foklore** (9 AM to 5 PM, daily), which documents the 200-year history of the former island in scale models and other exhibits.

When Japan's self-imposed isolation ended in the 1850s the foreign community started to look for better lodgings away from Dejima. Many of their old homes survive in **Glover Garden** (8 AM to 6 PM, with some minor seasonal variations, daily) and the **Orando-zaka**, or Dutch Slopes.

Glover Park is something of a memorial to the second great wave of foreign trade that ushered in Japan's modern age. One of the pioneers was a Scottish entrepreneur called Thomas Blake Glover (1838–1911), who settled in the city. His home,

where he lived with his Japanese wife and two children, sports a splendid view of Nagasaki Harbor. Now known as Glover House, it was the first Western-style home in Japan. The park has a number of other interesting foreign homes, notably **Ringer House, Walker House** and **Alt House**. All are worth visiting.

There are more Western buildings at the nearby Dutch Slopes.

HUIS TEN BOSCH

In keeping with Nagasaki's Dutch connection, the nearby Huis ten Bosch (pronounced "house ten bosh") is a miraculous recreation of Holland in

Japan. A Dutch theme park may not sound particularly promising, but this venture is so bold, so technologically breathtaking and so meticulously executed that it is guaranteed to silence even the most dyed-in-the-wool Euro-cynic.

The only complaint that can be leveled at Huis ten Bosch is that it's too big. It would be easy to spend a couple of days exploring it, but given that foreign travelers don't come all the way to Japan to spend days exploring Dutch theme parks, this is clearly not an option. The highlights include a note-perfect replica of the Dutch royal palace, **Palais Huis ten Bosch**, the **Mysterious Escher**, a celebration of the famous graphic artist's work, and the **Voyage Theater**, where you can take to the high seas with Holland's explorers of centuries past.

Huis ten Bosch is actually about far more than Dutch-themed entertainment. It includes an

OPPOSITE: The Dutch presence in Nagasaki dates back a long while. Building on this foreign culture, a resort-cum-theme park, Huis ten Bosch, has been developed along the lines of a seventeenth-century Dutch village. It is an excursion which is probably more interesting to the Japanese or Asian visitor who may never have encountered the Dutch culture, but nevertheless is worth a visit if you are staying in the Goto area. ABOVE: An aged, moss-encrusted statue of Jizo, the patron saint of travelers and children, weathers the elements in a Nagasaki temple.

environmentally controlled community, and there are hotels *in situ* — popular with Japanese and South-East Asian visitors.

It's open 9 AM to 9 PM most of the year, until 7 PM November to February, and entry is in the form of "passports." The standard variety at ¥4,200 is enough for a quick look around, though you will have to pay extra for entry to the attractions inside.

From Nagasaki station, regular trains run to the park, while buses also make the journey from the Kenei bus station opposite the station.

WHERE TO STAY

The best luxury hotel in the station area — indeed in all of Nagasaki — is the **Hotel New Nagasaki** ((095) 826-8000 FAX (095) 823-2000, 14-5 Daikoku-machi. It's an associate of the New Otani group and has nine restaurants and bars, an indoor swimming pool and 149 guest rooms. Rates start at ¥23,000.

Also in the station area and in the luxury category is the **Nagasaki Prince Hotel** ((095) 821-1111 FAX (095) 823-4309 WEB SITE www.princehotels .co.jp/nagasaki-e/, 2-26 Takara-machi. With six restaurants and bars, it has all the amenities you would expect of the Prince group.

Less expensive and in a pleasant part of town, close to the Glover Garden, is the **Nagasaki Tokyu Hotel** ((095) 825-1501 FAX (095) 823-5167 WEB SITE www.tokyu-group.co.jp/eng/guide/165a.html, 1-18 Minamiyamate-machi. If you have stayed in any of the Tokyu hotels before you will know what to expect: a no frills but comfortable upper-end business hotel. Rates start at around ¥10,000.

Slightly cheaper again, and centrally located for Chinatown and downtown dining, shopping and most of the attractions is the **Nagasaki Grand Hotel** ((095) 823-1234 FAX (095) 822-1793, 53 Manzai-machi. Established in 1884, it's Nagasaki's oldest and has both Western and Japanese rooms. The cheaper rooms start at ¥9,000 per person.

The Japanese Inn Group representative in Nagasaki is the **Minshuku Tampopo** ((095) 861-6230 FAX (95) 864-0032, 21-7 Hoei-cho. The rooms are all tatami style and the bathing facilities are shared, but it's a popular place and the English-speaking owners will even pick you up from nearby Urakami station; it's close to Peace Park, in the north of Nagasaki.

Unusually, the **Nagasaki Youth Hostel** ((95) 823-5032, 1-1-16 Tateyama, actually has a convenient location, around a 10-minute walk east of Nagasaki station. The downside is that it only has dormitory accommodation.

WHERE TO EAT

Due to longstanding foreign influences, Nagasaki has some unique contributions to Japanese cuisine, though you won't find any of them in the average Japanese restaurant overseas. The most famous of them is *champon*, a soup/noodle dish packed with vegetables, seafood and meat that is quite unlike usual run-of-the-mill *ramen* dishes, and really quite unlike anything Chinese, the foreign community who brought the dish into being. The place to go to sample *champon* is Chinatown, where you will find **Shikairo**, 4-5 Matsugae-cho, the restaurant that is alleged to have first served the dish. Dozens of other restaurants in Chinatown also serve the dish, and all have window displays for easy ordering.

Nagasaki's other famous dish is *shippoku*, an unusual fusion of European, Chinese and Japanese cuisines served banquet-style in a series of dishes. The famous *shippoku* restaurant (and you need to order in advance and be in a group of at least two people) is **Kagetsu** ((095) 822-0191, 2-1 Maruyama-machi, which has been in business since 1618 and is a wonderfully atmospheric place, to splurge on a meal, with a claassic garden,. Another place serving *shippoku* is **Hamakatsu** ((095) 826-8321, 6-50 Kajiyamachi, where a mini-course can be sampled for ¥3,000. The real thing starts from ¥4,000.

HOW TO GET THERE

The JR Nagasaki line connects Nagasaki with Hakata in a little over two and a half hours. For Kumamoto, you will have to change trains at Tosu station.

MIYAZAKI

There is no compelling reason to stop at Miyazaki, but those who do rarely regret it. It has something to do with the near Mediterranean atmosphere of the place — it has a balmy, laid-back ambiance that is a world away from the bustle of, say, Honshu. But, that said, apart from the modest charms of Heiwadai-koen Park, the ersatz excitement of an artificial beach inside a dome at Seagaia, and a surprisingly good science museum, Miyazaki has only the smallest of claims on the attention of the average traveler to Japan.

The city center fans out to the west of Miyazaki station, which also happens to be one of Japan's most colorful, although there is another center, one stop to the south, at Minami Miyazaki, where you will find the city's long-distance bus center. Most of the city's attractions are in the north of town.

The **Miyazaki City Tourist Information Center** ((0985) 22-6469 is in Miyazaki station, and has English speakers on staff who can dispense the usual English language brochures and help with accommodation reservations.

Even if you only pass through Miyazaki briefly, it is worth popping into the **Science Center** (9 AM to 4:30 PM, closed Mondays) which, apart from what is alleged to be the world's biggest planetarium, has high-tech displays on a number of Kyushu-related subjects. It's on the east side of the station.

Not far north of the station, and with frequent shuttle buses, is **Seagaia** (9:30 AM to 10 PM, daily), Miyazaki's beach inside a dome. It is a peculiarly Japanese experiment, an improvement on nature — no rain, no salt in the "sea water," no nasty jellyfish or sharks. Of course, it is designed to suck as much money out of your wallet as quickly as possible. It costs ¥4,200 per day for basic use of the facilities, but there is the option of a "view pass" for considerably less.

Making a serious time shift, Miyazaki was settled from early times, as evidenced by the archeological finds at nearby Saitobaru, where 311 fifth- and sixth-century tombs have been discovered. Some have been excavated, and a portion of the finds

can be seen in **Heiwadai-koen Park**. About 15 minutes by bus north of the city center, the main attraction is the *haniwa*, clay figures.

Miyazaki has one of Kyushu's top hotels in the **Hotel Ocean 45 (** (0985) 21-1133 FAX (0985) 21-1134, Hamayama, Yamazaki-cho, which is part of the Seagaia complex. At 45 stories, it's Kyushu's tallest hotel too, and features a breathtaking atrium. It's aimed naturally at people who are vacationing in the Seagaia dome, an odd concept but, who knows, perhaps the wave of the future — pardon the pun. The hotel maintains that all 753 rooms have views of the Pacific, a claim that would be time-consuming to verify.

Back in town, and a lot less expensive, is the **Hotel Kensington (** (0985) 20-5500 FAX (0985) 32-7700, 3-4-4 Tachibana-dori Higashi, which urges guests to "enjoy our English atmosphere." It's not particularly "English," but it does have a London

Café and the rooms are reasonable business-style affairs. It's a short walk from the station.

Very close to the station and accustomed to taking foreigners due to recommendations from the station information staff is the **Ryokan Shinshu (** (0985) 23-4008 FAX (0985) 296561, 2-12-24 Hiroshima Dori, a no-frills Japanese inn that can also prepare meals. Rates are from ¥4,500.

A very basic affair with only dormitory style accommodation, is the **Fujin Kai-kan Youth Hostel (** (0985) 24-5785, 1-3-10 Asahi, but if you are looking for budget accommodation, this is the cheapest in town. It's opposite City Hall, around 10 minutes by foot south of the station.

It's possible to get to Miyazaki from almost anywhere in Kyushu in around a half a day or less by train. Kumamoto is a good four and a half hours away. The JR Nippo line connects Beppu and Miyazaki in a little over three hours, before continuing on to Kagoshima which takes two hours. Fukuoka, however, takes much longer — at more than six hours.

KAGOSHIMA

The Japanese like to call it the Naples of Japan, and if you call into this easy-going port city you will soon see why: rising out of Kagoshima Bay is the smoking cone of Sakura-jima, Kagoshima's very own Vesuvius. The city's very active volcano overshadows (literally) Kagoshima's other attractions, but it is worth fitting some of them in, once you have done the obligatory (and fascinating) volcano circuit. Chief among them is Iso-teien Garden, a stroll garden that puts Sakura-jima to good effect in its views.

Originally known as Satsuma, Kagoshima has an interesting historic note, having been dominated by a single family from the twelfth century until the 1868 Meiji restoration. Like Nagasaki, it has long been a conduit for foreign influence, having been a center for China trade and one of the first bases for Christian missionaries.

Sprawling north–south along Kagoshima Bay, Kagoshima is an easy city get around in. Kagoshima is in the north of the city, while the city center lies between here and Nishi Kagoshima station in the south. The two stations are connected by a tram line (one of two) that makes access to the city easy. The **City Tourist Information Service (** (099) 222-2500 at Kagoshima station is a good place to get maps and information and can help with accommodation reservations. There is another equally helpful office at Nishi Kagoshima station **(** (099) 253-2500.

Despite its interesting history, *the* reason to visit Kagoshima is **Sakura-jima**. This is no Fuji-like quiescent cone: Sakura-jima is an unpredictable

Kagoshima's charming Meiji-era street lamps are given a polish by a city worker.

beast, belching fumes and showering the city with ash regularly — locals joke that in Kagoshima you always need an umbrella no matter what the weather. The last big eruption was in 1914, when lava flows formed a bridge from the island to the mainland — it is no longer an island but a peninsula now. But minor eruptions are a common event: in 1999 alone, admittedly a particularly active year, 386 minor eruptions were registered. More than one a day.

The easiest way to see the "island" and its volcano is to take a JR **Red Liner** bus (free if you have a rail pass) from the Sakura-jima pier near Kagoshima station. The buses depart twice a day at 9:30 AM and 1:30 PM, and cost ¥1,700. The only drawback of the tour is the stops at tourist shops along the way.

Next to the pier is the **City Aquarium** (9 AM to 5 PM, daily), which while expensive at ¥1,500 is a good place to take children.

About 10 minutes north of Kagoshima station by bus is **Iso-teien Garden** (8:30 AM to 5 PM, daily), established in 1660 by a Shimazu lord, and after Meiji restoration the home of the Shimazu family. It's not one of Japan's "great" stroll gardens, but it is certainly worth a visit, particularly for its "borrowed views" of Sakura-jima. Entry includes the adjacent museum, the **Shoko Shusei-kan**, which has some interesting exhibits about the Shimazu family, unfortunately though with very little English captioning.

There is little in the way of luxury accommodation in Kagoshima, but the **Shiroyama Kanko Hotel** ((099) 224-2211 FAX (099) 224-2222, 41-1 Shin Shoin-cho, has a superb location on Shiroyama, which overlooks Kagoshima, the bay and Sakura-jima. It has a slew of restaurants, including Japanese, Chinese and Continental. Rates start at ¥10,000 per person.

For a reliable mid-range hotel, try **Kagoshima Tokyu Inn** ((099) 256-0109 FAX (099) 253-3692, 5-1 Chuo-cho. It's just east of then Nishi Kagoshima station, next to the Takami-bashi Bridge, and per-person rates start at ¥8,300.

The most popular budget accommodation in town is the **Nakazano Ryokan** ((099) 226-5125 FAX (099) 226-5126, 1-18 Yasui-cho. A small, family-run place, it has immaculately maintained Japanese-style rooms, and rates from ¥4,500. It's in alley directly east of the Shiyakusho-mae tram stop.

The **Sakurajima Youth Hostel** ((099) 293-2150, Hakama-goshi, Sakurajima-cho, actually sits in the shadow of the volcano, for those who want to live dangerously. Accommodation is dormitory style, and there is *onsen* bathing.

For an excellent sampling of the local cuisine head to **Satsuma-Aji** ((099) 226-0525, 6-29 Higashi-sengoku-cho, a down-home restaurant close to Chuo-koen Park in the center of town. There's no English menu, but the pictures need no explanation.

If you go to Iso-teien Garden, try the **Iso-teien Jumbo-tei** ((099) 247-1551, a restaurant famed for a local specialty called *jambo machi*, or grilled dumplings on a bamboo stick.

If you are flying out of Kagoshima, be aware that the airport is an hour or more (depending on traffic) away from the city center — buses leave from Nishi Kagoshima station.

The JR Kagoshima line connects Kagoshima with Kumamoto (two and a half hours) and Hakata (just under three hours), while the JR Nippo line connects Kagoshima with Kokura in the far north of Kyushu via Beppu.

SATSUMA-HANTO PENINSULA

South of Kagoshima is the boot-shaped Satsuma-hanto Peninsula, which has two attractions that can be visited as a day trip. Chiran is a small town

with an interesting samurai quarter, while Ibusuki is a less famous version of Beppu, a confluence of hot springs and tacky (sometimes seedy) entertainment, that gets the occasional foreign visitor for its bay views and its "sand baths."

Ibusuki, an hour from Kagoshima by train is a compact spa town. Ibusuki station is in the west, while the bayside beaches are close by to the east. There's a **City Tourist Office (** (099) 322-4114 at the station, though not much English is spoken.

It's safe to ignore Ibusuki's expensive hot-spring hotels, and head straight to Suriga-hama Beach, around one kilometer (half a mile) southeast of the station. If you've never been buried up to your neck in piping hot sand, this is your chance. Be warned: it's *hot*. Unless you are Japanese, it is unlikely you will last long before dashing for a cold shower. Trains on the Makurazaki line from Kagoshima take a little over an hour to reach Ibusuki.

From Ibusuki it's possible to continue on by bus to **Chiran**. The town's samurai district lies on a lane that runs parallel to the main street the bus stops at — ask for the *buke yashiki*. Unlike similar districts in other parts of Japan, you can't actually explore the houses (many are still lived in), but some of the beautiful gardens are still open.

Also in Chiran is the **Tokko Heiwa Kai-kan** (9 AM to 5 PM, daily), a museum dedicated to Japan's World War II *kamikaze* pilots. There are exhibits here concerning the more than 1,000 young pilots who, as part of the "Special Attack Force" flew to their deaths in the Battle of Okinawa.

Regular buses run back to Kagoshima from Chiran in around one hour and 20 minutes.

The Japanese call Kagoshima the "Naples of Japan" on account of the smoking cone of Mount Sakura-jima, which frequently sends plumes of dust showering down on the city.

Kyushu

Okinawa

STRAGGLING AROUND 1,000 KM (620 MILES) IN JAPAN'S southwestern wake is a string of islands known as the Ryukyu or sometimes the Southwestern Islands — Nansei Shoto. For the Japanese these subtropical islands, long isolated from the mainstream of Japanese culture, are their Hawaii on the doorstep. Although the islands' unique cultural heritage is an attraction, for the average Japanese visitor the Okinawa islands offer summery weather, beaches and water sports. Few foreign travelers make it to Okinawa, however, and it is easy to see why. While an interesting contrast with the rest of Japan, there are better, and far less expensive, beach destinations around the region, and Okinawa is a long way from anywhere.

signed a treaty with Satsuma that allowed it to retain its independence under the overlordship of the Satsuma domain. But in spite of this agreement, the China-tribute remained in place until 1875, when Japan's new Meiji government asserted control over the islands.

Gaining Japanese citizenship was to have tragic consequences for the Okinawans in World War II. On April 1, 1945, Okinawa became the focus of an Allied onslaught that resulted in some 12,500 American deaths and an amazing quarter of a million Japanese deaths. A vast number of innocent Okinawan civilians were slaughtered in the battles — more than 120,000 lost their lives. The island's towns and villages were reduced to piles of rubble.

Okinawa, the name of the main island of the Okinawa group of islands and the name of the prefecture of which it is the hub, is halfway between Kyushu and Taiwan. The average maximum daily temperature is over 21°C (70°F), and even in January this daily average only goes down to 16.1°C (61°F). Rainfall is so slight it's a problem, though not for the visitor.

BACKGROUND

Until it became Okinawa prefecture in 1879, Okinawa was a kingdom known as Ryukyu. Wedged between the pincer of China to the west and the Satsuma clan in Kyushu to the north, Okinawan kings paid tribute to China, leading to a more marked Chinese influence in these islands than elsewhere in Japan, until Satsuma forces invaded Okinawa island in 1609. In 1611 Okinawa

The bloody final stages of the Battle of Okinawa took place in the extreme south of the main island, and the cliffs here are dotted with various monuments to the fallen. The most moving is the Okinawa Prefectural **Peace Memorial Museum**.

An interlude of de facto American military rule followed World War II, and it was not until 1972 that Okinawa was "reunited" with Japan when it held elections to send seven representatives to the Japanese Diet. American bases in Okinawa remain a source of friction, and foreign men are often assumed to be United States military in Okinawa — they are generally not liked.

Relations with mainland Japan are complicated. Ethnically and linguistically Japan and Okinawa are very close, and it is believed that the islands were originally populated by Japanese drifting south. But through centuries of separation clear differences developed — the Okinawan dialect, for example, as spoken by the older generation, is incomprehensible to mainland Japanese — and when the islands were brought within the Japanese domain, the Japanese decided that the Okinawans were an inferior breed and treated them accordingly.

OKINAWA ISLAND

The main island of the Okinawa island chain is an interesting contrast with the rest of Japan. There is a marked cultural difference with mainland Japan, and at the same time an American influence is more prevalent than elsewhere in Japan. The capital, Naha, has some interesting cultural sights, the legacy of the Ryukyu heritage, while in the south of the island are many moving memorials to the devastating battles of World War II.

NAHA

The capital of Okinawa Prefecture, Naha, on okinawa island, is a largely undistinguished modern city of more than 300,000 people. The focus of the city is Kokusai Dori, a long, broad street lined with restaurants and souvenir shops, lending it, for Japan at least, an unusual sense of a commercial district centered on tourism. Unusual souvenirs available here include army surplus hand grenades and bullets (novelty key rings), extract of snake venom (used medicinally) and *wamori*, the fragrant and fiery local hooch.

General Information
Naha is a compact city, and the airport is conveniently a short three-kilometer (one-and-a-half-mile) bus ride from the city center. Similarly the ferry terminal is a short taxi or bus journey to the north of the city center. For tourist information, look for the Palette Kumoji Department Store at the west end of Kokusai Dori (not far from the Naha bus terminal), where you will find the **Naha "i" Tourist Information Center** ((098) 857-6884. There is also a second tourist information office at the airport.

What to See and Do
Naha's only real attraction is **Shuri-jo Castle** (9 AM to 5:30 PM, daily). Virtually everything here is a reconstruction, due to the destruction caused by the Battle of Okinawa, but the reconstruction work has been tastefully executed, and the castle's surrounding area is the only part of Naha which retains some of its antique, pre-war atmosphere and charm. A narrow stone-paved lane threads between the modest houses and voluptuous gardens of the capital's old ruling class up to the **Shurei-no-mon Gate**. The castle's inner palace, the **Seiden**, commands panoramic views, and was completely restored in 1992.

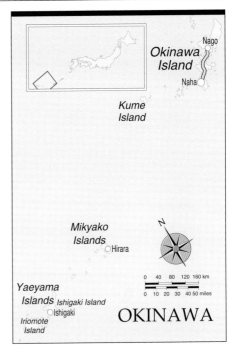

OKINAWA

Also in the vicinity are workshops turning out kimonos and other fabrics dyed glorious colors using the traditional *bingata* techniques. These are among Okinawa's most attractive and distinctive traditional products; the artisans in this area used to supply the needs of the court.

Where to Stay
Naha has a good range of accommodation, though no real luxury hotels of the kind found in major destinations in mainland Japan. A good option is the new **Holiday Inn Express Naha** ((098) 862-7733 FAX (098) 866-0245, 3-11-1 Maejima, close to the harbor, a littleunder a kilometer (half a mile) away from the excitement of Kokusai Dori. It's a modest establishment with 78 guest rooms and one suite, along with three restaurants. There is no swimming pool, but it does have a sauna.

There is excellent mid-range accommodation at the **Hotel Sun Palace** ((098) 863-4181 FAX (098) 863-1313, 2-5-1 Kumoji, which has Japanese and Continental restaurants, and fax machines in its rooms, which come with balconies, a nice, and very unusual touch in Japan. Room rates start at ¥7,000.

The **Naha International Youth Hostel** ((098) 857-0073 FAX (098) 859-3567, 51 Onoyamacho, is south of the western end of Kokusai Dori. It only has dormitory accommodation.

The showcase for Okinawa's Rykyu heritage can be seen at Naha's Shuri-jo Castle, which has been tastefully reconstructed over the last decade. Pictured here is the Shurei-no-mon Gate.

Okinawa

Where to Eat

Kokusai Dori is the place to seek out places to eat. You will find quite a number of American-style steak houses (these are surprisingly popular in Naha), *izakaya* (pubs), and micro-breweries here, alongside restaurants serving cuisine from every corner of Asia and then some, not to mention the occasional sushi bar.

How to Get There

Naha has direct flights from as far away as the United States, though the majority of international flights are from Asian destinations such as Hong Kong and Taiwan. It is also connected by air with almost all major Japanese cities.

Although ferries run between Tokyo, Osaka and Kagoshima, among other places, services are not daily and tend to be slow — it can take up to 40 hours, for example, to get from Osaka to Naha by ferry.

SOUTH OKINAWA

South Okinawa was the focus of much of the fighting in the Battle of Okinawa, and it is here that most of the memorials can be seen.

What to See and Do

Immediately south of Naha are the **Underground Naval Headquarters** (8:30 AM to 5 PM, daily), a warren of tunnels that was a Japanese command center during World War II, and the scene of mass suicides on June 13, 1945, as United States troops closed in.

At the southern tip of the island is **Himeyuri-no-To**, where more than 200 schoolgirls and their teachers committed suicide. They feared they would be raped and mutilated or killed by encroaching United States forces, a not uncommon belief among Japanese at the time. North of this somber monument, a **Peace Memorial Hall** (9 AM to 5 PM, daily) on Mabuni Hill memorializes the heavy casualties of the fighting.

Not far from the Peace Memorial Hall, the **Gyokusen-do Kingdom Village** (9 AM to 5 PM, daily) is a folk village constructed along traditional architectural lines and devoted to Okinawan crafts. The village is built around **Gyokusen-do Cave**, the largest limestone cave in East Asia, which contains almost a million stalactites, stalagmites and connected pillars.

The sights of south Okinawa are not far flung, but getting around them is not at all easy by public transport — the few public bus lines thqat do exist run infrequently. The best way to see get around this part of the island is by joining a tour in Naha. **Naha Kotsu (** (098) 868-3750 has both half-day and full-day tours of the area. For more information check with the Naha tourist office on Kokusai Dori (see above).

CENTRAL AND NORTH OKINAWA

Central and north Okinawa see very few foreign tourists, and in all honesty this is because there is little to see. **Okinawa City**, around 20 km (12 miles) north of Naha, gets a fair amount of Japanese tourism due to its American influence (there's a major United States military base here), but it's of little interest to non-Japanese.

Of more interest is the **Ryukyu Mura Village** (8:30 AM to 5 PM, daily). Somewhat similar to Gyokusen-do Kingdom Village in the south (minus the cave), this fabricated village features interesting examples of traditional Okinawan homes and exhibitions of local crafts.

The small city of **Nago** in the north of the island has virtually nothing to see (it's most frequently touted sight is an old banyan tree) but is a pleasant little place. Buses run directly from the Naha bus

terminal at the western end of Kokusai Dori, taking around one and a half hours. From Nago, it's possible to continue north to the ruins of Nakajin-jo Castle, though bear in mind that "ruins" are the operative word — there's little to see.

SOUTHERN ISLANDS

South of Okinawa main island are two more small groups of islands that are part of the Okinawa group: Miyako Island, around 300 km (186 miles) from Okinawa, and the Yaeyama Islands, around 400 km (249 miles) from Okinawa.

Miyako Island is the transport hub for these two groups of islands. One hour by plane from Naha, it was undamaged in the war and retains more of the look of old Okinawa than Okinawa itself. Many of the old houses survive here, their roofs of brown, semi-circular ceramic tiles so all-embracing that

there is hardly any house to be seen, huddled against the earth to avoid damage from the typhoons that frequently ravage this part of the world.

The main town is **Hirara**, where you will find plentiful accommodation and restaurants, though very few English speakers.

Ishigaki and **Iriomote** are the two principal Yaeyama Islands, and both belong to the area that became a national park in 1972. Ishigaki is accessible by air from Miyako Island; the town has several traditional buildings redolent of the old lifestyle of the island's nobility. Iriomote, one hour from Ishigaki by boat, contains Japan's most unspoiled tropical forest and is popular with serious hikers on that account. Deep in its shade dwell the last of the *yamaneko*, the rare Iriomote Wildcats.

Islands emerging from the mist in a sea of beaten bronze.

Okinawa

Travelers'
Tips

GETTING THERE

With only very few exceptions (ferry services from China, Taiwan, South Korea and, less frequently, from Vladivostok, Russia) the only way to get to Japan is by air. Most visitors touchdown in Honshu, Japan's main island, by one of two international airports: the **New Tokyo International Airport** (Narita) and **Kansai International Airport** (for Osaka and Kyoto). Other Japanese cities have international flights, but usually they service regional destinations.

FROM BRITAIN AND EUROPE

Flights from Britain and Europe go to either Tokyo or Osaka, and the summer months from July through September are the most expensive. It's usually possible, depending on the airline, to find tickets that allow you to fly into one airport (say Tokyo) and out the other, which can save the time and cost of backtracking. Local newspapers are the best place to check for bargains. As always and anywhere, it pays to shop around. Indirect flights, which provide the option of stopovers en-route, are invariably the least expensive way to get to Japan. Only a small number of airlines fly from Britain and Europe non-stop to Tokyo.

FROM THE UNITED STATES AND CANADA

Most flights from the United States and Canada touch down at Tokyo's Narita airport, although alternative destinations are available through **Asiana Airlines**, which flies via Seoul to Fukuoka, Hiroshima, Sendai and Okinawa; **Air Canada**, which flies to Osaka; **Cathay Pacific**, which flies via Hong Kong to a number of Japanese destinations, including Sapporo; and **United**, which flies to both Tokyo and Osaka. Some European airlines, such as **Swissair** and **British Airways**, allow stopovers in Europe en-route.

If you are trying to save money on your flight, avoid traveling in the peak summer months of July and August, and in the Christmas, New Year period. The best deals are usually Apex tickets, which require you book and pay at least three weeks in advance, stay at your destination at least seven days (but no longer than three months), and schedule changes (while sometimes possible) are frowned upon and will sometimes involve further payments, or "penalties."

FROM AUSTRALIA AND NEW ZEALAND

Australia and New Zealand are popular destinations for Japanese tourists, and consequently people "down under" get a relatively good choice of airlines to fly with, many offering the possibility of stopovers in other Asian destinations en-route.

Most flights are to Tokyo or Osaka, but it's also possible to find flights to regional destinations such as Nagoya, Sendai and Sapporo.

The cheapest flights are with Asian carriers such as **Philippine Airlines**, **Korean Air** and **Garuda** (which usually allows a stopover in Bali). These cheaper flights, however, generally have time restrictions and can often involve inconvenient layovers — check the details carefully before making a decision.

BY SEA

Few travelers approach Japan by sea, but for those on extended travels of Asia, it is an interesting option. From Europe, for example, it is possible to travel overland and by sea all the way to Japan by taking the **Trans-Siberian** — which takes eight days to travel from Moscow to Vladivostok, from where a twice-monthly ferry sails to **Niigata** in northern Honshu. Obviously, with so few sailings, timing is of the essence, but should you miss the ferry, Aeroflot has twice-weekly flights to Niigata from Vladivostok.

Another overland possibility is to take the **Trans-Manchurian** via Moscow to Beijing, from where you can travel to **Shanghai**, which has twice-weekly sailings to Kobe and Osaka.

There are also ferry services between **Taiwan** and **Okinawa**. The weekly sailings usually alternate between Keelung in the north of Taiwan and Kaohsiung in the south, and sometimes they stop at Ishigaki en-route.

The most frequent international ferry services are between **Pusan** in South Korea and **Fukuoka** in Kyushu. Sailings are daily, and there are also less-regular ferry services from Pusan to Shimonoseki.

ARRIVING AND LEAVING

VISAS

A tourist visa is not required for the citizens of the following countries, through Reciprocal Visa Exemption arrangements.

For six months or less: Austria, Germany, Ireland, Lichenstein, Mexico, Switzerland, and the United Kingdom (except where the passport was originally issued in a British colonial territory).

For three months or less: Argentina, Bahamas, Barbados, Belgium, Canada, Chile, Colombia, Costa Rica, Croatia, Cyprus, Denmark, Dominica, El Salvador, Finland, France, Greece, Guatemala, Honduras, Iceland, Israel, Italy, Lesotho, Luxembourg, Malta, Mauritius, Netherlands, New Zealand, Norway, Portugal (except where the passport was originally issued in a present or former Portuguese colonial territory), San Marino, Singapore, Slovenia, Spain, Surinam, Sweden, Tunisia, Turkey, Uruguay and the United States.

Note that Australians and South Africans need to apply for a visa before leaving for Japan.

CUSTOMS

You may bring three bottles of alcoholic beverages (up to 760 cc, or 25 fl.oz, each) into Japan with you; also 400 cigarettes or 100 cigars or 500 gm of tobacco, and 56 ml (2 fl.oz) of perfume. In total, goods worth up to ¥200,000 (including watches, jewelry, etc) may be brought in.

Japanese authorities are very strict about drugs, and spot checks are carried out at customs far more regularly than at other Asian destinations. Firearms, too, are strictly controlled.

DEPARTURE TAXES

Departure taxes are levied on international flights at all Japanese airports, though they vary from one airport to the next. The most expensive is Kansai, which costs ¥2,650, making it one of the most expensive in the world. Narita is ¥2,000.

EMBASSIES AND CONSULATES

JAPANESE EMBASSIES ABROAD

For a full run-down on Japanese embassies and consulates overseas, see the Japanese Ministry of Foreign Affairs (MOFA) WEB SITE www.mofa.go.jp/about/emb_cons/over/.

The main embassies are as follows:

Australia ((02) 6273-3244, 112 Empire Circuit, Yarralumla, Canberra ACT 2600.
Austria ((01) 531920, Hessgasse 6, 1010 Wien.
Belgium ((02) 513-2340, Avenue des Arts 58, 1000 Bruxelles.

Three "graces" resplendent in their best kimonos and fine makeup.

Canada ((613) 241-854, 255 Sussex Drive, Ottawa, Ontario K1N 9E6.
Denmark ((45) 3311-3344, Pilestraede 61, 1112, Copenhagen K.
France ((01) 4888-6200, 7 Avenue Hoche, 75008 Paris.
Germany ((030) 210940, Kleiststrasse. 23-26, 10787 Berlin.
Ireland ((01) 269-4244, Nutley Building, Merrion Centre, Nutley Lane, Dublin 4.
Italy ((06) 487991, Via Quintino Sella, 60 00187 Roma.
Netherlands ((070) 3469544, Tobias Asserlaan 2, 2517 KC, The Hague.
New Zealand ((04) 473-1540, Level 18, Majestic Centre, 100 Willis Street, Wellington 1.
Spain ((91) 590-7600, Calle Serrano 109, 28006-Madrid.
Sweden ((08) 663-0440, Gärdesgatan 10, 115 27 Stockholm.
Switzerland ((031) 300-2222, Engestrasse 53, 3012 Berne.
United Kingdom ((020) 465-6500, 101-104 Piccadilly, London, W1V 9FN.
United States ((202) 238-6700, 2520 Massachusetts Avenue, NW, Washington DC, 20008-2869.

FOREIGN EMBASSIES IN JAPAN

The following embassies are located in Tokyo:
Australia ((03) 5232-4111, 2-1-14 Mita, Minato-ku.
Austria ((03) 3451-8281, 1-1-20 Moto-Azabu, Minato-ku.
Canada ((03) 3408-2101/8, 7-3-38 Akasaka, Minato-ku.
Denmark ((03) 3496-3001, 9-12 Nanpeidai-cho, Shibuya-ku.
France ((03) 3448-9540, 4-11-44 Minami-Azabu, Minato-ku.
Germany ((03) 3473-0151/7, 4-5-10 Minami-Azabu, Minato-ku.
Greece ((03) 3403-0871/2, 3-16-30 Nishi-Azabu, Minato-ku.
Ireland ((03) 3264-0911, 3 Niban-cho, Chiyoda-ku.
Italy ((03) 3453-5291/6, 2-5-4 Mita, Minato-ku.
New Zealand ((03) 3467-2271/5, 20-40 Kamiyama-cho, Shibuya-ku.
Spain ((03) 3583-8531/2, 1-3-29 Roppongi, Minato-ku.
Sweden ((03) 5562-5050, 1-10-3-100 Roppongi, Minato-ku.
Switzerland ((03) 3473-0121, 5-9-12 Minami-Azabu, Minato-ku.
United Kingdom ((03) 3265-5511, 1 Ichiban-cho, Chiyoda-ku.
United States ((03) 3224-5000, 1-10-5 Akasaka, Minato-ku.
Osaka has a number of foreign consulates. They can be contacted on the following numbers:
Australia ((06) 6941-9271

Austria ((06) 6241-3011
Belgium ((06) 6361-9432
Canada ((06) 6212-4910
Denmark ((06) 6346-1285
France ((06) 4790-1500
Germany ((06) 6440-5070
Netherlands ((06) 6944-7272
New Zealand ((06) 6942-9016
Sweden ((78) 331-4518
Switzerland ((06) 6344-7671
United Kingdom ((06) 6281-1616
United States ((06) 6315-5900

TOURIST INFORMATION

Japan's tourist services do an admirable job of dispensing tourist information and helping foreign visitors make the most of their stay in Japan. The **Japan National Tourist Organization** (JNTO) maintains offices overseas (see below) and a select number of **Tourist Information Centers** (TICs) in Japan. These are the best places to go for comprehensive Japan-wide information, though offices will also have destination-specific information too if they can find it. Elsewhere around Japan is a network of local **"i" information centers**, more than 90 in total and growing. Most of these centers are situated in JR train stations.

JNTO OFFICES OVERSEAS

JNTO maintains a limited number of offices overseas. Their contact details are as follows:
Australia ((02) 9232 4522, Level 33, The Chifley Tower, 2 Chifley Square, Sydney, NSW 2000.
Canada ((416) 366-7140, 165 University Avenue, Toronto, Ontario M5H 3B8.
France ((01) 42962029, 4 Rue de Ventadour, 75001 Paris.
Germany ((069) 20353, Kaiserstrasse 11, 60311 Frankfurt am Main.
Hong Kong (852) 2968-5688, Suite 3704-05, 37/F, Dorset House, Taikoo Place, Quarry Bay.
United Kingdom ((020) 7734-9638, Heathcoat House, 20 Saville Row, London, W1X 1AE.
United States ((212) 757-5640, One Rockefeller Plaza, Suite 1250, New York, New York 10020; ((312) 222-0874, 401 North Michigan Avenue, Suite 770, Chicago, Illinois 60611; ((415) 989-7140, 360 Post Street, Suite 601, San Francisco, California 94108; ((213) 623-1952, 515 South Figueroa Street, Suite 1470, Los Angeles, California 90071.

TIC OFFICES IN JAPAN

JNTO's local offices are located in Tokyo, Narita Airport, Kyoto and Kansai Airport. Together these offices represent the best places to gather up-to-date tourist information about Japan in English and other languages.

Travelers' Tips

The Tokyo and Kyoto offices are open from 9 AM to 5 PM Monday to Friday and 9 AM to noon on Saturdays, closed on Sundays and national holidays. The office at Narita Airport is open every day of the year from 9 AM to 8 PM, the one at Kansai Airport every day of the year from 9 AM to 9 PM.

The TIC's staff are well aware that there are not nearly enough branches to deal with the large numbers of foreign tourists coming to Japan these days, but they work hard to make up for it and go to a lot of trouble to be helpful. They will give you maps, leaflets, guides and help you with travel schedules. One of the only drawbacks of these offices is the sheer volume of people clamoring for assistance.

If you need travel advice in English and you can't get to a TIC office, call them. Outside Tokyo and Kyoto you can take advantage of the free **Japan Travel-Phone** service. For queries TOLL-FREE (0120) 44-4800 or (0088) 22-4800. The same service is available in Tokyo and Kyoto, but you have to pay the usual local phone charges. The numbers to dial are: in Tokyo ((03) 3201-3331, in Kyoto ((075) 371-5649. The TIC will help you in any way they can, but they make the point that they are not a travel agency. So don't expect them, for example, to make hotel reservations for you.

"I" INFORMATION CENTERS

The "i" information network has over 90 offices in 60 cities around Japan. Don't expect staff in every one of them to speak English, but it is spoken to varying degrees in a surprisingly large number of the offices. Quite often these offices can help with last-minute accommodation requests should you find yourself in a fix. At the very least they will be able to recommend local accommodation. Most of the offices are located in JR train stations.

GETTING AROUND

Trains rule supreme in Japan, which has one of the world's best rail networks. This is not to say that you won't use other forms of transportation: some destinations can only be reached by bus; you will probably take the occasional ferry; and from time to time it's expedient to hang the expense and jump into a taxi. But overall it's the trains that are the most useful mode of transportation, making a Rail Pass (see below) a very worthwhile investment before you go.

BY AIR

The three major operators of domestic air services are **Japan Airlines** (JAL) TOLL-FREE (0120) 25-5971, **All Nippon Airways** (ANA) TOLL-FREE (0120) 02-9222, and **Japan Air System** (JAS) TOLL-FREE (0120) 51-1283. Since deregulation in 1996, domestic routes have seen the emergence of new carriers, but their impact has yet to be felt in a major way, and most routes are dominated by the big three. An exception is in the Okinawa region, where **South West Airlines** (SWAL) have a reasonably good selection of routes.

It's often worth checking the price of domestic flights against train travel, as there is often little difference. Flights also become much cheaper if you are able to book well in advance — up to 50 percent cheaper if you can book two months ahead. Such discounts are not available in the peak periods noted above.

BY TRAIN

The Japanese railway network is one of the best and most comprehensive in the world. The privatized national system, known simply as JR, is expensive to use, but the trains are fast, clean and very punctual. As the land area of Japan is not very large, and as roads are frequently clogged with cars, rail travel is the most attractive way for most visitors to see Japan.

Japan Rail (JR) Services

Even if you do it only once, a trip on one of Japan's legendary **Shinkansen**, or "bullet trains," is an obligatory part of the Japan experience. Running at maximum speeds of 300 km/h (186 mph), they are the fastest trains in the world.

Watering the pigeons in central Yokohama.

There are six Shinkansen lines in total. The **Tokaido line** runs southwest through Honshu from Tokyo to Kyoto and Osaka before terminating in Hakata (Fukuoka), Kyushu. The remaining lines all service northern Honshu: the **Tohoku line** runs from Tokyo to Morioka via Sendai; the **Akita line** splits off from Morioka for Akita, while the **Yamagata line** does the same for Yamagata; the **Joetsu line** runs from Tokyo to Niigata; lastly the new Hokuriku line, built for the 1998 Winter Olympics, branches off from the Joetsu line at Takasaki for Nagano.

The Shinkansen is rather like being on a plane. Attendants circulate the train with drinks and food, and announcements are made in English as well as Japanese.

Other JR rail services include *tokkyu* trains (limited express), which are the fastest trains after the Shinkansen; *kyuko* trains (ordinary express), which stop at less important destinations; and *futsu* trains (ordinary), which stop everywhere.

Fares are calculated according to distance, with express surcharges added according to the service you use. All services faster than *futsu* incur extra charges; extra is also charged for reserved seats. The Green Window (*Midori-no-mado guchi*) and Travel Service Centers at JR stations sell these surcharge tickets, as well as berth tickets for sleeping cars.

The surcharge for *tokkyu* trains is cheaper than for the Shinkansen, but the trip of course takes longer, and on lines that run parallel with Shinkansen services there are not many trains. A few *kyuko* and *futsu* trains cover long distances overnight with no sleeping cars. It may be hard to sleep but these, along with JR's bus service from Tokyo to Kyoto, are the cheapest ways of crossing the country.

Japan Rail Pass

Buying a **Japan Rail Pass** before you get to Japan is highly recommended — they can't be bought inside Japan. They come in two classes, Green or Ordinary. Green Passes entitle the holder to travel in Green Cars, a euphemism for First Class. (As Japan's Ordinary Class is equal in comfort to most other countries' First Class, there would seem to be little point in paying the extra). The passes run for 7, 14 or 21 days, and constitute an immense saving if you plan to travel a lot. A seven-day ordinary pass currently costs ¥28,300; a 14-day ordinary costs ¥45,100; and a 21-day ordinary, ¥57,000. Children are half-price. These prices are for Ordinary Class; Green Car passes are some 35 percent more. Payment is in your local currency at that day's official exchange rate.

The procedure for obtaining a JR Pass is as follows. Before leaving home, go to one of the agents appointed to sell you an Exchange Order. Japan Travel Bureau, Nippon Travel Agency, Kinki Nippon Tourist, Tokyu Tourist Corporation, and Japan Airlines should all be able to do this; the nearest office of the Japan National Tourist Organization will advise you in case of difficulty.

On arrival in Japan you hand in the Exchange Order at any JR station that has a Japan Rail Pass exchange office and in return receive your pass. There are two such offices at Narita (Tokyo's main international airport), one for Terminal One, the other for Terminals Two and Three. They are open from 7 AM to 11 PM. In Tokyo itself there are offices at Tokyo, Ueno, Shinjuku, Ikebukuro and Shibuya JR stations. Most other major JR stations around the country will have an office where you can validate your exchange order.

One small point — you must arrive in Japan on a "temporary visitor" status. Almost every tourist is given this category. But if you are, for instance, coming in on "trainee" entry status, then you will, unfortunately, not be eligible for a Rail Pass.

The only JR trains you cannot use your pass on without paying a surcharge are the super-fast Nozomi Shinkansen services. For trips on all other long-distance Shinkansen, or any other trains, go to the ticket office, present your pass, and you will be given a reserved seat ticket free of charge, unless of course the train you choose is fully booked. Departures are frequent enough that it is usually possible (holidays apart) to get a seat a few minutes before departure.

How much do you save with a Japan Rail Pass? Take the example of a round trip fare from Tokyo's Shinjuku Station to Matsumoto, gateway to the Japan Alps: at ¥14,600, it's over half the seven-day rate for a rail pass. The trip takes on average two and three quarter hours in each direction.

Excursion Tickets

Excursion tickets, called *shuyuken*, can be economical if you plan to travel from Tokyo to a particular area, for example Kyushu, and travel around in that area for some days. The details of such tickets, however, tend to be complicated and subject to frequent change; ask the TIC to help, or take a Japanese-speaking friend to the station with you.

Timetables

The TIC can provide a *Condensed Railway Timetable* in English, which gives details of all Shinkansen and some other main-line services. It also gives a good run-down on fares and other details. It's not unusual to see Japanese travelers on trains leafing through the *Jikokuhyo*, the "book of timetables," the size of the average telephone directory, it's a monthly guide to all trains, buses, planes and ferries in the country. You will need to have spent at least a year learning *kanji* to make any sense of its contents.

Moving away from tradition, street theater has become more popular in the urban centers of Japan.

BY BUS

Buses are the least foreigner-friendly mode of Japanese transportation, in that English is rarely used for destinations, either at bus stations or on the buses themselves. The system of payment for local buses varies from place to place, so that you might pay on boarding, or on disembarking, or you might need a pre-paid ticket. Generally, however, there will be someone on hand to help out.

Buses are useful if you are traveling on the cheap and you don't have a Rail Pass. Long distance bus services run between all Japan's major cities and are often the cheapest way to get from one place to another. For those who are really economizing, the night bus services that run between major destinations such as Tokyo and Kyoto offer the double advantage of an economical journey and a saving on a night's accommodation.

BY CAR

If you have a valid international driver's permit you can rent a car from **Nippon Rent-a-Car**, **Toyota Rent-a-Car**, **Mazda Rent-a-Car**, and **Japaren**, among others. Offices for these companies can be found at train stations and airports countrywide. **Eki Rent-a-Car** is run by Japan Railways, and offices can be found at all major JR stations and some of the minor ones.

Representative price ranges for rented vehicles are officially quoted as follows: 1000–1300 cc. — ¥9,000 to ¥14,000 a day; 1500–1800 cc. — ¥13,000 to ¥20,000 a day; 2000 cc. — ¥21,000 to ¥35,000 a day; 3000 cc. — ¥27,000 to ¥38,000 a day.

Driving around Japan won't be all plain sailing. Romanization of road signs can be patchy, and will inevitably let you down when you need it most. It's a good idea to travel with two maps, one romanized and one in Japanese for comparison. Better still, buy a copy of the *Japan Road Atlas* published by Shobunsha, which is fully bilingual. Another useful publication is the *Japan Rules of the Road*, published by **Japan Auto Federation** ((03) 3436-2811.

Worth noting before you actually rent a car is that your travel costs will not be limited to the cost of the vehicle and road-stops at gas stations. Japan has a toll system that operates on all major highways (and trying to avoid them is about as feasible as dodging raindrops in a shower), and can get extremely expensive over long distances. In fact, on a long haul, say Tokyo to Kyoto, the sum of the various tolls en-route can amass to nearly the cost of a single Shinkansen fare — tolerable perhaps if there are four of you in the car, less viable if you are a solitary traveler.

Another caveat worth noting is that off the beaten track, roads narrow to the point that they

can become quite dangerous. In rural areas, you will note mirrors mounted on sharp bends that show on-coming traffic. They're there with reason: the oncoming traffic is practically in the same lane you are.

TAXIS

A taxi with a red light in the window is cruising for a fare. The door at the back on the left-hand side will open and close automatically (it is operated by the driver). Minimum fares vary from place to place in Japan, from around ¥500 to ¥700. This flag-fall fare is marked on the nearside rear seat window. If you are stuck in traffic you pay for the time you spend there too. The fare that registers on the meter is the total charge. Fares are higher between 11 PM and 5 AM. Before using an expressway in Tokyo the driver will normally ask your

permission, as the toll, ¥600, will go on your bill. Tipping is neither necessary nor expected.

ACCOMMODATION

Japan has a wider range of accommodation than anywhere else in Asia, if not the world. The range is less a function of rates (though on this front too the extremes can be staggering) than in the kinds of accommodation available. Broadly, it makes sense to divide these into Japanese-style and Western-style. Odds are, if you are in Japan for any length of time, you will end up staying in different varieties of both.

TICs in Tokyo and Kyoto can help with reservations for two hotel groups that they have close relations with. The **Japanese Inn Group** brings together 70 budget *ryokan* around the country that are accustomed to the ways of foreigners, and usually offer simple Japanese-style rooms with no meals and shared bathing for around ¥4,000 per person. Invariably friendly and clean, and often good sources of information, they are excellent places to stay in while traveling around the country.

The **Welcome Inns Group** is similar, except that its members also include business hotels (see below).

JAPANESE STYLE

The most famous Japanese style of accommodation is the *ryokan*, or the Japanese inn. It by no means exhausts the Japanese accommodation experience, however. Other forms of Japanese-style accommodation include *minshuku*, or family lodges, and *kokuminshukusha*, or people's lodges.

True to its name, Thunder Falls drops with a deafening roar into Matsukawa Gorge, part of the beautiful Japanese Alps.

At some point or another nearly everybody who visits Japan ends up spending a night in a *ryokan*. It's almost a rite of passage. Some love it; some are happy to have done it but spend the rest of their trip staying in Western-style digs. But, however, you feel about the experience, there is no denying that is quintessentially Japanese. The rooms are invariably simple affairs — no matter how much the *ryokan* costs — the floor made of straw matting, or tatami, and the furnishings often limited to a picture on the wall and a knee-high table for dining. The bedding is usually rolled up in a closet, and won't make an appearance until after dinner and bathing. With the exception of budget *ryokan* that are accustomed to *gaijin* guests, breakfast and dinner (never lunch) are served in your room, and rates will often include meals. Rates (always per person) for inexpensive *ryokan* listed in this book range from ¥4,000; for mid-range from ¥10,000; and for luxury between ¥20,000 and ¥30,000.

In parts of rural Japan, the most economical places to stay are *minshuku*. Usually family run, *minshuku* are homier than *ryokan*, and the rates (which usually hover around ¥6,500 per person) always include breakfast and dinner.

Kokuminshukusha are family-style accommodation, and are usually found in national parks and scenic areas. Aimed at Japanese families minding their yen while on vacation, some (but not all) are happy to accept foreign guests too. As with *minshuku*, rates include two meals and usually come out at around ¥6,500 per person.

Other less common forms of accommodation include *shukubo*, or temple (sometimes shrine) lodgings. The most famous place for *shukubo* is **Mount Koya-san** (see page 160 in the KAISAN section). In hot-spring resorts you will come across *onsen* hotels, which almost belong in a category of their own — often a mixture of Japanese and Western styles, the focus of these hotels is the hot spring water piped into both communal and private (in the rooms) baths.

WESTERN STYLE

Japan wouldn't be Japan if it didn't take the hotel and put its own unique spin on it. Three spins to be precise: business hotels, capsule hotels and love hotels. While few travelers have occasion to stay in the latter (though they are rarely seedy, and are actually quite a fun experience), and only the most adventurous stay a night in a capsule, most travelers end up spending a night or two in the ubiquitous business hotel, or *bijinesu hoteru*.

Of course, in all major cities, you will find international-class Western-style hotels with no unique Japanese surprises. These are usually listed in the luxury bracket of accommodation in this book. Rates usually range from around ¥15,000 for a single room, and from around ¥22,000 for a double, though in the case of Japan's best it may well be much more than that.

Japan's best luxury hotels are to be found, as you might expect, in the major cities and premiere tourist destinations. Tokyo and Kyoto are home to the majority of them. Start getting farther afield and they become scarcer. Get off the beaten track, and the closest you will come to international-class luxury is the business hotel.

Business hotels are what they say they are: functional places to stay aimed at businesspeople (almost always men) on the move. Almost every train station in Japan has a cluster of them, and rates typically range from ¥6,000 to ¥9,000 for a

single, ¥10,000 to ¥15,000 for a double, or often a twin. The rooms are small and compact, and a special feature is the tiny molded fiberglass bathroom unit.

Capsule hotels can also sometimes be found in station areas, but only in big cities. They are aimed at businessmen (the whole of Japan has less than a handful of capsule hotels for women) who have missed the last train home — usually due to a night out with the boys — and need somewhere to sleep.

Love hotels are the domain of couples — more often than not married — who are looking for intimacy they can't enjoy in their tiny homes. Rates are quoted in two-hour installments, but after 10 PM they are usually available for the night from around ¥8,000. In a squeeze, they are a perfectly acceptable accommodation option, and with their opulent theme decor can make for an interesting stay.

Lastly, in rural Japan you may come across pensions. Usually family-run and decked out with European trimmings, these are economical places to stay, though English is rarely spoken. Usually found in mountainous regions, they are inspired by the chalet, and provide Japanese with the possibility to imagine themselves in the Swiss Alps. Rates usually range from around ¥7,000, more with meals.

YOUTH HOSTELS

Japanese youth hostels are like youth hostels in many other countries: cheap, rough-and-ready, over-organized and segregated by sex. There are two types: Japan Youth Hostels, Inc. hostels and public hostels run by local authorities. The latter have no membership requirement, and even with the ones where membership is required you can pay ¥600 at reception for a Welcome Stamp, and six stamps within a year entitle you to an International Card without further payment. As there are over 500 hostels nationwide, many located in remote and picturesque spots, and some occupying the spare rooms of old temples, they are one of the best bets for the intrepid. If that means you, don't leave Tokyo without copies of *Youth Hostels Map of Japan* and *Public Youth Hostels*. Together they contain the addresses and phone numbers of all the country's youth hostels and are available at the TICs. Remember to book well in advance for holiday periods.

EATING OUT

No matter how conservative you are when it comes to food, you need not find Japan a frightening proposition. To be sure the Japanese enjoy *sushi* and *sashimi*, two variations on the raw fish concept, not to mention many other much odder things, but they are also fanatical about everything from hamburgers to pizza. In other words, no matter where you go in Japan you will find a good range of restaurants, from Japanese haute cuisine and regional specialties to the fast-food barns you thought you'd left behind when you headed East.

The hardest part about dining out in Japan is ordering. Menus are usually in Japanese, even if you are in a steak restaurant. Fortunately, another unique Japanese innovation comes to the rescue. The majority of Japanese restaurants — at least the less expensive variety — sport window displays with extremely realistic plastic models of their dishes on display. At a pinch, you can always drag a staff member outside and point to your dinner. Also common is the picture menu, which saves you having to take anyone outside.

For food on the run, the best places to look are the many department stores (which invariably have a *resutoran-gai*, or "restaurant street") and train stations, both inside and outside. It won't take long before you get used to the standard array of restaurants that occupy these public spaces: the *sushi* shop; the *tonkatsu* (breaded pork chop) restaurant; the *ramen* (noodle soup) restaurant; the *karii raisu* (curry rice) restaurant; the coffee shop (usually with inexpensive *setto*, or set meals); the pizza restaurant; and of course familiar fast food chains, and some less familiar such as Mos Burger and Lotteria, two home-grown hamburger franchises. In any of these styles of restaurants, which can be found the length and breadth of the land, you can take lunch or dinner for around ¥800.

The recommendations in this book generally fall into a more expensive category, usually ¥2,000

per person and upwards. The rationale is that the restaurants found in train stations, commercial districts and department stores are of such uniform standard and so plentiful that recommendations should be reserved for special meals.

BASICS

BUSINESS AND BANKING HOURS

Business hours in Japan are much the same as those in the West — at least when it comes to banks and government offices. Banks are open weekdays from 9 AM to 3 PM. The hours for post offices vary according to place, but the core hours are

OPPOSITE: A country full of paradoxes, Japan adheres to many of its traditions yet is able to embrace some totally different Western values. ABOVE: The finishing touches on a festival dress.

usually 9 AM to 5 PM. Department stores open later and close later than is usual in the West, usually 10 AM to 8 PM, sometimes later. They are almost always open weekends, and usually the major department stores rotate their weekly day off so that if, say, Mitsukoshi is closed Tuesday, then Seibu is closed Wednesday. Most museums in Japan are closed Mondays.

TIME

Japan is nine hours ahead of GMT, which means it is 17 hours ahead of Los Angeles, 14 hours ahead of New York, eight hours ahead of Paris, Frankfurt, Rome and Amsterdam, six hours ahead of Moscow, one hour ahead of Beijing and Hong Kong, one hour behind Sydney, and three hours behind Auckland.

NATIONAL HOLIDAYS

Japan's public holidays are as follows:

January 1   **Ganjitsu** (New Year)
January 15   **Adult's Day**
February 11   **National Foundation Day**
March 21 (or 22)   **Spring Equinox**
April 29   **Green Day**
May 3   **Constitution Day**
May 5   **Children's Day**
September 15   **Respect for the Elderly Day**
September 23 (or 24)   **Autumn Equinox**
October 10   **Sports Day**
November 3   **Culture Day**
November 23   **Labor Thanksgiving Day**
December 23   the **Emperor's Birthday**

ELECTRICITY

The electric current in Japan is mostly 100 volts AC, but two different cycles are used: 50 in Eastern Japan (including Tokyo) and 60 in Western Japan (including Nagoya, Kyoto and Osaka). At major hotels there will be two outlets for both 110 volts and 220 volts installed for, electric razors, hair driers, portable computers etc.

WEIGHTS AND MEASURES

Japan uses the metric system: centigrade, liters, kilometers and meters. A few old measures — *i-sho*, about half a gallon, used for sake, and *tsubo*, the area of two tatami mats, used for measuring the area of land — add some spice.

CURRENCY

The Japanese currency is the yen. Exchange rates have been known to fluctuate with little warning, so check for the latest before you leave and while you are travelling.

US$1 = ¥122
1 euro = ¥1085
£1 = ¥170
Can$ = ¥77
Aus$1 = ¥63
NZ$ = 51

Yen come in 1-yen, 5-yen, 10-yen, 50-yen, 100-yen and 500-yen coins, and 1,000-yen, 5,000-yen and 10,000-yen notes.

Credit cards are becoming increasingly prevalent, though this is a very recent phenomenon compared to other wealthy countries, and it is still not a good idea to rely on your credit card: in Japan cash reigns supreme. As a basic rule of thumb, the more international the shop/hotel/restaurant, the more likely you are to be able to use an international credit card — go local, and if credit cards are accepted at all they are likely to be only locally issued cards.

TIPPING

Tipping is not expected in Japan, and consequently it shouldn't be given. Many Japanese, if offered a tip, will simply be confused and will try to give the money back.

COMMUNICATION AND MEDIA

POST

Japan has an efficient postal system, and post offices (*yubinkyoku*) can be found wherever you go across the country. Postal rates are very reasonable, providing you are only sending postcards (¥70 to any destination), aerogrammes (¥90 to any destination) and letters under 25 grams, for which the price varies from ¥90 to ¥130 depending on where it's going.

Poste restante is only understood and practiced in the central post offices of major cities, and mail will only be held for 30 days before it is sent back.

TELEPHONES

Public telephones, like vending machines, are thick on the ground in Japan, and it's rare to come across one that does not work. They come in a variety of colors, but they are all much of a muchness when it comes to using them: almost all take both ¥10 and ¥100 coins, and most take prepaid telephone cards (*telefon kado*), which can be bought at any convenience store in ¥500 and ¥1,000 varieties. If you are feeding coins into a telephone, stick to ¥10 coins, as they will not return unused fractions of ¥100 coins.

The phone numbers listed in this book include the local area code. When dialing from outside of Japan, drop the zero from the beginning of the area code.

International Calls

To make an international direct-dial call, you can use any of three prefixes — 001, 0041, or 0061 — followed by the country code of the country you are calling. If you use the prefix 002, a call-back service quotes the cost of the call. To speak to an international operator dial 0051.

There is little to choose between Japan's three international operators — they are all expensive. Calls are charged in six-second units, at one rate during the first minute you are connected, and then at another during all subsequent minutes. Cheaper international rates apply from 7 PM to 8 AM, and all day on weekends.

Directory Enquiries

For Directory Enquiries (in English) ((03) 3277-1010 in Tokyo ((045) 322-1010 in Yokohama, and ((0476) 28-1010 at Narita Airport.

Some hotels have copies of the English telephone directory, *Town Page*. It contains ordinary and classified (yellow page) listings, and comes in two volumes, one for East Japan and another for West Japan.

For reverse-charge (collect) international calls, the Home Country Direct service puts you in touch with an operator in your home country: **Australia** (0039-611, **Canada** (0039-161, **New Zealand** (0039-641; **United Kingdom** (0039-441; **United States** (0031-111.

Emergencies

In an emergency, dial (110 for **police**, and (119 for **fire** or **ambulance** services. From a public call box you will not need a coin for these calls, but you must press the red button before dialing the number.

If no one speaks English, **Japan Helpline** TOLL-FREE (0120) 46-1997 is available 24 hours.

FAX AND E-MAIL

Most hotels can send and receive faxes for you in Japan, and most convenience stores also have fax machines that you can use nowadays. E-mail is a little more problematic. While luxury hotels (but not luxury *ryokan*) have Internet access, most mid-range and budget hotels have been slow to adapt to the digital revolution. The best way to find out where you can log on is to check the following web site, **www.netcafeguide.com/japan.htm**. which is frequently updated and carries a list of Internet cafés (they can come and go amazingly quickly) throughout Japan.

NEWSPAPERS AND MAGAZINES

Japan's most widely available English-language newspaper is the *Japan Times* (¥160). Nobody could accuse it of being racy or sensationalizing its coverage, but it does provide a solid round-up of news

from Japan and around the world. It's available in major cities throughout Japan.

The *Times* main rival is the *Daily Yomiuri* (¥120), which has a loyal following among foreign residents of Japan for its weekly round-up from the *Los Angeles Times* on Saturdays and Britain's *Independent* on Sundays. Unfortunately, it is hard to come by outside of Tokyo.

The two other English-language dailies are the *Mainichi Daily News* (¥120) and the *Asahi Evening News* (¥120), both offshoots of Japanese-language papers. In Tokyo, Kyoto and Osaka, it is possible to find copies of the *Asian Wall Street Journal*, the *International Herald Tribune* and the *Financial Times*.

The monthly *Tokyo Journal*, ¥600, is the best source of information in English about what's on in town, including concerts and out-of-the-way cinemas and theaters. *Kansai Time Out* (¥300) does the same for the Kansai region.

International magazines and papers are available in some bookshops and in major hotels, but again, outside Tokyo, Kyoto and Osaka, it's slim pickings.

TELEVISION AND RADIO

Make a point of watching some Japanese television while you are in Japan. Not because it's any good — it isn't — but because, if what you've seen out on the streets hasn't already done so, it will remind you that you are truly in another country.

The distinctive carp banners flying to celebrate Boy's Day Festival in early May.

You may have heard of Japan's wacky game shows; what you probably didn't realize is that there is little else screening on Japanese television.

The exception is the educational NHK, which is Japan's answer to Britain's BBC or the United State's PBS. If your hotel has a bilingual television, NHK has nightly English news broadcasts at 7 PM. Bilingual televisions also allow you to watch foreign movies in their original languages — almost all foreign television broadcasts are dubbed into Japanese.

Major hotels have cable and satellite television that show CNN and BBC World Service, along with movie channels and the usual Discovery repeats about sharks.

Japanese radio can be hard to approach for foreign listeners. J-Wave (81.3MHz) and Inter FM (76.1MHz) in Tokyo play MOR pop and rock, and are bilingual, while FM-CO CO LO (76.5MHz) does the same in the Kansai area. For straight musical entertainment — Western classical, Japanese pop and traditional, and much else, NHK-FM broadcasts on 82.5MHz in Tokyo, 88.1MHz in Osaka, 82.5MHz in Nagoya, 84.8MHz in Fukuoka and 85.2MHz in Sapporo.

ETIQUETTE

Much is made of Japanese etiquette, and to be sure it can be exacting. It's easy for foreigners to start feeling clumsy and ignorant in the company of their bowing and scraping Japanese hosts, never sure which slippers they should be wearing, where to put the chopsticks, or whether it's okay to stretch their deadened legs out from beneath them after 15 minutes on the tatami. The best advice is to relax. Japanese daily life is highly rule-bound, and people are very polite to each other, but allowances are made for foreigners, especially those who have just arrived. If in doubt, smile and bob your head in an approximation of a bow — you will find yourself doing it habitually in no time anyway.

The rules, as outlined in countless guidebooks and scholarly tomes dedicated to the "mysterious Japanese" might be summed up in brief:
• Japanese, when they meet, bow rather than shake hands (though many young people and professionals shake hands); strictly speaking status dictates the depth of the bow, but as a newly arrived foreigner you are exempt.
• Accept and give name-cards (if you don't have any, get some) with both hands and examine them respectfully before filing them away into a pocket or a wallet.
• Never stick your chopsticks into a bowl of rice (it has associations with Buddhist funerary rites).
• If eating in a group Japanese-style, try to sit with your legs beneath you; if you stretch them out, try not to point your feet at anyone.
• Lastly, try not to be too direct or argumentative

in conversations with Japanese; if in doubt, smile and agree no matter what nonsense you are listening too; harmony is the key word in Japanese social intercourse, as it is throughout Asia.

HEALTH

Along with Singapore and Hong Kong, Japan has the highest health standards in Asia. You need no immunizations, the food and water are safe and, apart from the usual bugs like colds and flus, it's unlikely that you will come down with anything while traveling in Japan.

That said, if you *do* get sick, medical treatment in Japan, while of a high standard, is expensive. Take out a travel insurance policy before you arrive. In the event of a medical emergency, call the 24-hour **Japan Helpline** TOLL-FREE (0120) 46-1997.

If you are using prescription drugs, bring them with you, along with the prescription (which will help if you are questioned by customs and if you need to replace them). Japan has very few international pharmacies, and if you need a foreign-prescribed drug it is a good idea to have the generic name and not just the brand name — the brand you are using may not be available.

SAFETY

Japan is one of the safest countries in the world. The nationwide network of neighborhood police boxes (*koban*) helps to keep it that way, and if you should have any problems remember that there is usually one close by.

Women travelers can move around safely in Japan, but as is the case in many other countries it is a good idea to travel with a companion. An ongoing problem for women is the groping that goes on in crowded trains and buses. The only way to be sure that you do not become a victim is to avoid crowded trains and buses, though this is not always possible. The standard advice given should a male begin to make inappropriate movements towards you in a crowded public place is to grab his hand and hold it up, and embarrass him as much as possible.

The emergency number for **police** is (110. **Japan Helpline** TOLL-FREE (0120) 46-1997 can also provide assistance in the event of an emergency.

WHEN TO GO

The best times to be in Japan are spring and autumn. Spring (March to May) coincides with the beautiful cherry-blossom season (April), and usually has a large number of clear, blue-sky days, while autumn (September to November) is the season of falling leaves, when rural Japan is at its best. Summer and winter, while not to be avoided, are less than ideal times to tour the country. Summer

(June to August) is hot and humid, and typhoons can bring everything to a standstill with gale-force winds and torrential rains. In winter, much of northern Japan gets snowed in and travel becomes difficult, though rural areas like Nikko are particularly beautiful under a blanket of snow.

Regional variations of climate are worth factoring in, however. When Tokyo and Kyoto are sweltering in the height of the summer, Hokkaido can be quite be pleasant. Similarly, Kyushu and Okinawa are much more temperate in the cold winter months than the rest of Japan.

One thing to be aware of is the congestion that occurs at Japan's three big holidays. The week either side of **New Year** can be very busy, though not as busy as **Golden Week**, which falls in late April and early May. **O-bon**, when Japanese return to their home towns to honor ancestors in mid-August, is another busy period. At these times of the year, getting around and finding accommodation is no fun — avoid them if at all possible.

WHAT TO TAKE

Japan is an advanced country, and almost anything you forget to bring with you can be bought once you arrive. If you are traveling in summer but intend to do some hiking in the mountains, it is a good idea to bring warm clothes. Casual wear is acceptable in all but the most expensive restaurants and night clubs.

A fold-up umbrella is useful at any time of the year, though they can be bought inexpensively once you arrive. If you have large feet, it's probably not a good idea to plan to buy shoes in Japan — large sizes can be hard to find. It's also a good idea to bring or buy a towel, as those provided in many mid-range hotels and *ryokan* are little larger than a handkerchief.

PHOTOGRAPHY

Japan is a nation in the grip of photography fever. Buying film and camera gear is no problem, and there are no restrictions on what you photograph. It's polite to ask before taking somebody's picture, but nobody is likely to object. At festivals, feel free to snap away to your heart's content — everybody else will.

LANGUAGE BASICS

Picking up Japanese is not like picking up French or German (or English as the case may be). Grammatically it is very different from the Indo-European Germanic and Romance languages. The difficulty levels are compounded by *keigo*, or politeness embedded in the language, and a writing system that employs nearly 2,000 Chinese characters (*kanji*) on an everyday level, and two separate syllabaries (a system of characters representing syllables serving the purpose of an alphabet): *hiragana* (for native Japanese words) and *katakana* (mostly for foreign loan words).

But don't despair. Japanese is at least an easy language to pronounce (unlike Chinese, Thai and Vietnamese, to name a few phonetically challenging Asian tongues). It is not tonal, and it employs a limited number of vowels and consonants, almost all of which are present in English ("r" and "f" are the exceptions). In fact, within a couple of weeks, if you make an effort, you should have a basic inventory of phrases that can help you get around, shop and dine out. You might even tackle the syllabaries, if you are really keen. *Katakana* is

useful for menus, while *hiragana* is useful in rural Japan for recognizing station names. Both can be learned in around two weeks with daily study.

For the most part, pronounce romanizations (*romaji*) the way they look. The "tt" is pronounced as in "hat trick." The "e" is always pronounced as is the "e" in terrible, even when it appears as a final letter. "O" is always pronounced as in "hot," British-style.

Consonants are easy too, roughly the same as English except for "g" which is always hard, and "r" which is somewhere between "r" and "l." The Japanese cannot in fact distinguish between the two sounds, which causes endless problems with words like "pray," "clap" and — the source of some amusing stories — "election."

Less easy is distinguishing among the vast number of homonyms in Japanese. Romanization often uses a bar (or macron) over vowels to distinguish a short or long vowel pronunciation. A bar over a vowel lengthens it: "kyu" (abrupt) becomes "kyuuu", for example; "hot" becomes "ho-o-ot" (not "hoot").

Most Japanese words end with a vowel. This is why borrowed words sound strange. "Beer" becomes *"beer-u,"* "baseball" becomes *"beisuboor-u,"* "hot" becomes *"hot-to"* and so on.

A young couple feeding the birds in Ueno Park.

A few basic phrases will delight the Japanese because it means you are trying hard. Soon you will hear that great word "*jozu!*" ("skillful!") ringing in your ears.

Good morning   *O-ha-yo go-za-i-mas.*
Good afternoon   *Kon-ni-chi-wa.*
Good evening   *Kon-ban-wa.*
Good night   *O-ya-su-mi-na-sai.*
Goodbye   *Sayonara.*
Yes   *Hai.*
No   *Ie.*
Beer, please   *Beeru ku-da-sai.*
Coffee, please   *Kohi ku-da-sai.*
Menu, please   *Menu ku-da-sai.*
Thanks   *A-ri-ga-to* or *domo*
Thank you very much   *Do-mo a-ri-ga-to.*
That's all right   *Do i-ta-shi-ma-sh'te.*
No (as in, "that's incorrect")   *Chi-ga-i-ma-su.*
That's right   *So des'.*
I don't understand   *Wa-ka-ri-ma-sen.*
I understand   *Wa-ka-ri-ma-shi-ta.*
Please wait a minute   *Chot-to-mat-te ku-da-sai.*
I'm sorry   *Su-mi-ma-sen.*
Please (offering something)   *Do-zoh*
Please take me to Tokyo station   *To-kyo eki ma-de o-ne-gai-shi-mas*
Where is...?…   *wa do-ko des ka?*
How much?   *I-ku-ra-des ka?*
Please show me a cheaper one.   *Mo yasui-no-wo-mi-se-te ku-da-sai.*
Where is the restroom?   *O-te-a-rai wa do-ko des'ka?*

The most important point to bear in mind is that you should enunciate each syllable separately and distinctly, without slurring. We don't do this in English so it takes some practice.

WEB SITES

There is a lot of information about Japan on the Internet, but much of it is scattered, and even more of it is in Japanese. The best overall English web site is the Japan National Tourist Organization's **www.jnto.go.jp**, which covers every aspect of travel in Japan, from the latest news on sights to accommodation and dining.

Another good overall site is Stockton's Links to Japan **ww2.lafayette.edu/~stocktoj/home/japanl.html**. Broken down into categories such as Government and Travel & Regional, this site has valuable links to other sites covering almost everything imaginable that is Japan-related.

For information on Tokyo, a good place to start is *Tokyo Journal*, the monthly listings magazine, though only a fraction of its material appears in the online edition, **www.tokyo.to**. Another online Tokyo listings magazine is the giveaway *Tokyo Classifieds*, which has a wide selection of features and reviews on Tokyo at **www.tokyoclassified.com**.

For Kyoto information, try Digital City Kyoto **www.digitalcity.gr.jp/kfg** which has a map and reviews of restaurants, bars and the sights of Kyoto. It's updated frequently. KansaiNow.com (**www.kansainow.com**) is less comprehensive and more of a community bulletin board, but it's worth a look if you are going to be spending any length of time in the Kansai area.

For coverage of destinations elsewhere around Japan, you will have to search hard. Most of the sites about Japanese regional destinations are short on practical information and have a homemade look about them.

For news, the best place to look for local English coverage is the *Japan Times* **www.japantimes.co.jp**.

Recommended Reading

ABE, KOBO. *The Woman in the Dunes*. 1962; Vintage, 1991. This is a classic by the surrealist author who spent his life struggling with place and identity.

BASHO, MATSUO. *The Narrow Road to the Deep North and Other Travel Sketches*. Vintage, 1967. Translated by Yuasa Nobuyuki. The classic journey of discovery by Japan's seventeenth-century literary master.

BENEDICT, RUTH. *The Chrysanthemum and the Sword*. 1946; Houghton Mifflin Co., 1989. The classic pioneering study of Japanese social relationships that spawned a genre; as fascinating as ever.

BOOTH, ALLAN. *The Roads to Sata*. Weatherhill, 1996. One of the classics of modern travel writing about Japan, Englishman Booth walks from the northern tip of Hokkaido to the southern tip of Kyushu without once generalizing about Japan.

BORNOFF, NICHOLAS. *Pink Samurai*. Trafalgar Square, 1994. Everything you wanted to know about sex in Japan but were afraid to ask.

BROWN, JAN. *Exploring Tohoku*. Tokyo, Weatherhill, 1983. A detailed guide to Japan's deep north by a long-time resident.

BURUMA, IAN. *The Wages of Guilt*. Farrar, Strauss & Giroux, 1994. The two defeated nations of World War II responded very differently; Buruma wonders why.

CLAVELL, JAMES. *Shogun*. London, Hodder & Stoughton, 1975. Potboiler about Englishman Will Adams in Tokugawa Japan.

GOLDEN, ARTHUR. *Memoirs of a Geisha*. Vintage, 1997. Best-selling and entirely fictional life of a geisha written by a foreign male; superbly done and very authentic.

GUEST, HARRY (Ed.). *Travellers' Literary Companion: Japan*. Lincolnwood, Passport Books, 1995. Snippets from Japanese literature and foreign writings on Japan that make for good bedtime reading in your *ryokan*.

HERSEY, JOHN. *Hiroshima*. Knopf, 1985. Classic first-hand account of the aftermath of Hiroshima's devastation by an atomic bomb.

ISHIGURO, KAZUO. *A Pale View of the Hills*. Vintage, 1990. A haunting tale set in Nagasaki by British-raised Japanese writer.

IYER, PICO. *The Lady and the Monk*. Vintage, 1992. The author of the best-selling *Video Night in*

Kathmandu falls in love with Kyoto; a little cloying for some, but interesting all the same.

KAPLAN, DAVID and ANDREW MARSHALL. *The Cult at the End of the World*. Crown, 1996. How the Aum cult amassed the means to gas the subways of Tokyo, and how it could have been much worse.

KERR, ALEX. *Lost Japan*. Lonely Planet, 1996. A good alternative to Iyer's impassioned *Lady and the Monk*: Kerr, a long-time Japanese resident and enthusiast of Japanese culture muses, on how things aren't what they used to be.

MASUJI, IBUSE. *Black Rain*. Tokyo, 1969; Kodansha International, 1999. A classic and moving fictional account of life in the aftermath of the atomic bombing of Hiroshima.

sometimes claimed to be the first novel ever written, a dubious claim for a nevertheless fascinating, if slow, book.

OE, KENZABURO. *Nip the Buds, Shoot the Kids*. 1958; Grove Press, 1996. A Nobel Prize has shot Oe onto the world stage; *Nip the Buds* was his first novel.

SEIDENSTICKER, EDWARD. *Low City, High City*, Harvard University Press, 1991; and *Tokyo Rising: The City Since the Great Earthquake*, Harvard University Press, 1990. The classic accounts of the vicissitudes of Tokyo's history, complete with fascinating anecdotal background information; a must for anyone spending any time in Tokyo.

TASKER, PETER. *Inside Japan*. Penguin, 1987. It's out of date, but this study of Japan written by a financial

MISHIMA, YUKIO. *The Sea of Fertility*. 1970; Vintage, 1999. The culmination of his career before ritually disemboweling himself, this tetralogy is Mishima's most important work, though anything by Japan's most controversial twentieth-century writer is worth reading.

MURAKAMI, HARUKI. *Dance, Dance, Dance*. Vintage, 1995. The *wunderkind* of contemporary Japanese fiction spins a surreal post-modern tale about a man in search of something in the Dolphin Hotel, Sapporo. Also look out for *A Wild Sheep Chase* (1990).

MURAKAMI RYU. *Coin Locker Babies*. Kodansha International, 1998. A dark tail of revenge worked around two babies dumped in Tokyo coin lockers, written by one of the more adventurous of Japan's younger novelists.

MURASAKI, SHIIKUBU. *The Tale of Genji*. Random House, 1983. Translated by Edward G. Seidensticker. Written *circa* AD 1000, this courtly melodrama is

analyst remains one of the best overall introductions to Japan and what makes it tick.

VAN WOLFEREN, KAREL. *The Enigma of Japanese Power*. Knopf, 1989. Written at the height of United States anxiety about unfair Japanese business practices, this remains a fascinating insight into the confluence of politics, bureaucracy and money in modern Japan.

A band plays at a Shinto street festival in Osaka.

Quick Reference A–Z Guide
to Places and Topics of Interest with Listed Accommodation, Restaurants and Useful Telephone Numbers

The symbols ⓣ TOLL-FREE, ⓕ FAX, ⓔ E-MAIL, ⓦ WEB-SITE refer to additional contact information found in the chapter listings.

Photo credits

All photos in this book are by **Nik Wheeler** except those listed below:

Derek Davies: pages 4, 18, 30, 42, 44, 45, 54, 62, 64, 66 *top and bottom*, 67, 81, 85, 87 *bottom*, 88, 95, 96, 97, 102, 103, 104, 146, 159.
Robert Holmes: pages 40, 55, 56, 59, 71, 72, 120, 121, 145, 155, 182, 223, 227, 228, 235.

Chris Taylor: pages 13, 47, 208.

Adina Tovy: pages 7 *left*, 8 *right*, 12, 27, 39, 156, 171.

Bradley Winterton: pages 16, 17, 24, 35, 57, 139.

Japan Photo Archiv: front cover, pages 5 *left and right*, 7 *right*, 8 *left*, 9 *left and right*, 28, 68, 87 *top*, 91, 108-110, 115, 122, 130, 132, 138, 173, 174, 184, 185, 188-190, 192-194, 196, 198, 200, 201, 204, 209, 211, 213-216.